MEDEA

MEDEA

ESSAYS ON MEDEA IN MYTH, LITERATURE, PHILOSOPHY, AND ART

James J. Clauss and
Sarah Iles Johnston,
Editors

PRINCETON UNIVERSITY PRESS

PRINCETON, NEW JERSEY

COPYRIGHT © 1997 BY PRINCETON UNIVERSITY PRESS

PUBLISHED BY PRINCETON UNIVERSITY PRESS, 41 WILLIAM STREET,

PRINCETON, NEW JERSEY 08540

IN THE UNITED KINGDOM: PRINCETON UNIVERSITY PRESS,

CHICHESTER, WEST SUSSEX

The cover shows Frederick Sandys' *Medea*, painted between 1866 and 1868. The painting was accepted for the Royal Academy in 1868 but was not exhibited, which brought storms of protest from the art world of the time. The model for the painting was probably Sandys' mistress, a gypsy named Keomi. The painting is reproduced here with the kind permission of the Birmingham Museum and Art Gallery, Birmingham, England.

LIBRARY OF CONGRESS CATALOGUING-IN-PUBLICATION DATA

Medea: essays on Medea in myth, literature, philosophy, and art / James J. Clauss and Sarah Iles Johnston, editors.

p.   cm.

Includes bibliographical references and index.

ISBN 0-691-04377-9 (alk. paper). — ISBN 0-691-04376-0 (pbk.: alk. paper)

1. Medea (Greek mythology).   2. Medea (Greek mythology) in literature.

3. Medea (Greek mythology) in art.   4. Philosophy, Ancient.

I. Clauss, James Joseph.   II. Johnston, Sarah Iles, 1957–.

BL820.M37M43   1997   292.2'13—dc20   96–8537

This book has been composed in Palatino

PRINTED IN THE UNITED STATES OF AMERICA

3 5 7 9 10 8 6 4 2

3 5 7 9 10 8 6 4 2

(PBK)

http://pup.princeton.edu

For Louise, Gerard, Michael, and Elizabeth Clauss
LeRoy, Tristan, and Pelham Johnston

CONTENTS

PREFACE

THE PRESENT COLLECTION of papers began as a panel organized by Sarah Iles Johnston for the 1991 meeting of the American Philological Association in Chicago, entitled "Maiden and Murderess: Medea's Portrayal in Greek and Roman Literature." The original participants were Dolores M. O'Higgins, Deborah Boedeker, Carole E. Newlands, Sarah Iles Johnston, and myself. Gordon M. Kirkwood closed the panel with his helpful and insightful responses to each of the papers. Because of the success of the program, I suggested that we publish the papers in a collection, especially since it seemed that together the essays provided an interesting picture of this fascinating and influential mythological figure. Professor Johnston and I agreed to be co-editors. Πάθει μάθος!

After the participants agreed to the idea of a joint publication, Professor Johnston and I were fortunate in eliciting seven other contributions from Jan N. Bremmer, John M. Dillon, Fritz Graf, Nita Krevans, Marianne McDonald, Martha C. Nussbaum, and Christiane Sourvinou-Inwood. These additions, we believed, gave our study the breadth and depth that a *persona* as complex as Medea requires. In arranging the essays, four clear sections emerged. In the first, "Mythic Representations," Graf, Johnston, Krevans, and Bremmer provide insights into the evolution of Medea's mythological career. Balancing these four papers are the four essays on Medea's literary roles—"Literary Portraits"—by O'Higgins, Boedeker, Clauss, and Newlands, which look at four of the most important ancient treatments of Medea by Pindar, Euripides, Apollonius, and Ovid. The third section, "Under Philosophical Investigation," comprises two contributions by Dillon and Nussbaum and reveals the influence that Medea's mythic and literary representations had on ancient philosophers who tried to come to terms with the effects of passion on the human psyche. In the fourth and final section, "Beyond the Euripidean Stage," Sourvinou-Inwood and McDonald trace influences of Euripides' *Medea* in two very different areas: ancient vase painting and the modern stage.

The bibliography includes all books and articles referred to among the papers that deal with Medea, directly and indirectly. Only a very few (mostly encyclopedic) items that were deemed tangential were left fully cited in the notes. The result is a fairly complete collection of works on Medea that, we hope, will be as useful as the papers themselves. For the reader's information and convenience, at the end of each reference the names of the persons citing the work have been included in square brackets. In any lengthy bibliography, particularly one assembled from different formats and different word processing programs, errors are inevitable; we apologize in advance for any mistakes that were not able to be caught before publication.

There are a number of people and institutions whom we are pleased to thank for their help in bringing this project through to completion. First of all, we thank Professor Gordon M. Kirkwood for his participation on the panel. We also express our gratitude to the editors and their assistants at Princeton University Press who were supportive of the project at all stages in its evolution: Lauren Osborne, Brigitta von Rheinberg, Colin C. Barr, Licia Wise, and Molan Chun Goldstein. To Ann Michelini and the other anonymous readers selected by the press we offer our gratitude for their sensitive readings and excellent comments both on the collection as a whole and on the individual papers. We would like to acknowledge the meticulous work of our copy editor, Alice Falk. We are also indebted to Princeton University Press for agreeing to allow us to publish a version of Martha Nussbaum's "Serpents in the Soul," abbreviated from the larger study in which it originally appeared, *The Therapy of Desire: Theory and Practice in Hellenistic Ethics* (Princeton 1994). The Cleveland Museum of Art and British Museum kindly granted their permission to publish photographs of the vases discussed by Christiane Sourvinou-Inwood (figures 1–5), and permission to reproduce Frederick Sandys' Medea for the cover was granted by the Birmingham Museums and Art Gallery. Thanks also to Stephen Thielke, Priscilla Rogers, and Bartley Brown, who saved us from many inconsistencies and errors among the references, and to Ethan Adams, who worked on the Index Locorum. Others who have assisted or in any way helped the individual contributors will be acknowledged in the essays.

Organizing and editing collections of essays are notoriously difficult tasks, from approaching busy scholars, actually getting their papers, negotiating different scholarly methodologies and word processing programs, rephrasing referees' comments, all the way to the final stages of production. While this has been a demanding project, Sarah and I have been fortunate in having such excellent—and cooperative—contributors to work with. Throughout, our respective families were most supportive, and it is to them that we dedicate this book.

James J. Clauss

ABBREVIATIONS

ABBREVIATIONS of Greek and Roman authors and their works, journals, lexica, and encyclopedias are those found in Liddell, Scott, and Jones's *Greek-English Lexicon;* P. G. W. Glare (ed.), *Oxford Latin Dictionary;* and *L'Année Philologique.* In addition to these we make special note of the following abbreviations employed in this volume:

ABV	J. D. Beazley, *Attic Black-Figure Vase-Painters* (Oxford 1956)
ARV	J. D. Beazley, *Attic Red-Figure Vase-Painters* (Oxford 1942)
CAF	T. Kock (ed.), *Comicorum Atticorum Fragmenta*, 3 vols. (Leipzig 1880–88)
Campbell	D. A. Campbell (trans.), *Greek Lyric*, 5 vols. (Cambridge, Mass./London 1982–94)
CEG	P. A. Hansen (ed.), *Carmina Epigraphica Graeca* (Berlin 1983–)
CIG	A. Boeckh (ed.), *Corpus Inscriptionum Graecarum*, 4 vols. (Berlin 1828–77)
Cramer	J. A. Cramer (ed.), *Anecdota Graeca*, 4 vols. (Oxford 1835–37; rpt. Hildesheim 1967)
CVA	*Corpus Vasorum Antiquorum*
Davies	M. Davies (ed.), *Epicorum Graecorum Fragmenta* (Göttingen 1988)
De Lacy	P. H. De Lacy (ed.), *Galen, De Placitis Hippocratis et Platonis*, 2 vols. (Berlin 1978–80)
Dindorf	W. Dindorf, *Aristides* (Leipzig 1829; rpt. Hildesheim 1964)
Drachmann	A. B. Drachmann, *Scholia Vetera in Pindari Carmina* (Leipzig 1910)
Dübner	F. Dübner, *Theophrasti Characteres; Marci Antonini Commentarii; Epicteti Dissertationes ab Arriano Literis Mandatae Fragmenta et Enchiridion cum Commentario Simplicii* (Paris 1840)
Edmonds	J. M. Edmonds (ed.), *The Fragments of Attic Comedy*, 3 vols. (Leiden 1957–61)
Elmsley	P. Elmsley (ed.), *Euripidis Medea in unum studiosae juventutis* (Leipzig 1822)
EM	T. Gaisford (ed.), *Etymologicum Magnum* (Amsterdam 1967)
FGrHist	F. Jacoby, *Die Fragmente der griechischen Historiker* (Berlin 1923–)
FHG	C. Müller (ed.), *Fragmenta Historicorum Graecorum*, 5 vols. (Paris 1841–70)

Gow-Page	A. S. F. Gow and D. L. Page (eds.), *Hellenistic Epigrams*, 2 vols. (Cambridge 1965)
Hense	C. Wachsmuth and O. Hense (eds.), *Anthologium* (Berlin 1958)
Hermann	K. F. Hermann (ed.), *Platonis dialogi secundum Thrasylli tetralogias*, vol. 6 (Leipzig 1853)
Kalbfleisch	K. Kalbfleisch (ed.), *Simplicii in Aristotelis Categorias Commentarium* (Berlin 1907)
Keil	B. Keil, *Aelii Aristidis Smyrnaei quae supersunt omnia* (Berlin 1898; rpt. 1958)
Kinkel	G. Kinkel (ed.), *Epicorum Graecorum Fragmenta* (Leipzig 1877)
Köhler	F. W. Köhler (ed.), *Hieroclis in Aureum Pythagoreorum Carmen Commentarius* (Stuttgart 1974)
L.-P.	E. Lobel and D. Page, *Poetarum Lesbiorum Fragmenta* (Oxford 1955)
LIMC	John Boardman et al. (eds.), *Lexicon Iconographicum Mythologiae Classicae* (Zurich 1981–)
LSJ	H. G. Liddell, R. Scott, and H. S. Jones (eds.), *A Greek-English Lexicon*, 9th ed. with suppl. (Oxford 1968)
M.-W.	R. Merkelbach and M. L. West (eds.), *Fragmenta Hesiodea* (Oxford 1967)
Nauck	A. Nauck (ed.), *Tragicorum Graecorum Fragmenta* (Leipzig 1856; rpt. Hildesheim 1964)
Pf.	R. Pfeiffer (ed.), *Callimachus*, 2 vols. (Oxford 1949–53)
PMG	D. L. Page (ed.), *Poeti Melici Graeci* (Oxford 1962; rpt. 1967)
Powell	J. U. Powell, *Collectanea Alexandrina* (Oxford 1925)
Radt	S. Radt et al. (eds.), *Tragicorum Graecorum Fragmenta* (*TrGF*), vols. 3 (Aeschylus) and 4 (Sophocles) (Göttingen 1985, 1977)
RE	G. Wissowa et al. (eds.), *Pauly's Realencyclopädie der classischen Altertumswissenschaft* (Stuttgart 1894–)
RL	R. H. Roscher, *Ausführliches Lexicon der griechischen und römischen Mythologie*, 6 vols. (Leipzig 1884–1937)
SH	H. Lloyd-Jones and P. Parsons (eds.), *Supplementum Hellenisticum* (Berlin 1983)
Slater	W. J. Slater (ed.), *Aristophanis Byzantii Fragmenta* (New York 1986)
Snell-Maehler	B. Snell and H. Maehler (eds.), *Pindari Epinicia*, 8th ed. (Leipzig 1987)
Spiro	F. Spiro (ed.), *Pausaniae Graeciae Descriptio*, 3 vols. (Leipzig 1903; rpt. Stuttgart 1967)

SVF	H. von Arnim (ed.), *Stoicorum Veterum Fragmenta*, 4 vols. (Leipzig 1924)
Terzaghi	N. Terzaghi (ed.), *Hymni et Opuscula*, 2 vols. (Rome 1944–49)
Thalheim	T. Thalheim (ed.), *Lysiae Orationes* (Leipzig 1901)
Waszink	J. H. Waszink (ed.), *Timaeus a Calcidio Translatus* (London 1962)
West	M. L. West (ed.), *Iambi et Elegi Graeci Ante Alexandrum Cantati*, 2 vols. (Oxford 1971–72)
Westerink	L. G. Westerink, *Anonymous Prolegomena to Platonic Philosophy* (Amsterdam 1962)

MEDEA

INTRODUCTION

Sarah Iles Johnston

L IKE THE ARGO on which she sailed, Medea has been "of interest
to everyone" (*Od.* 12.70) from the dawn of European literature.
Although the earliest works in which she appeared are no longer
intact,[1] their fragments suggest that her story was an old and popular
one by at least the eighth century B.C. The number and the richness of
those works that have survived from antiquity attest to her continuing
fascination among the Greeks and Romans. From the fifth century B.C.
we have both Pindar's fourth *Pythian* and Euripides' *Medea.* The third
century offers us Apollonius of Rhodes' epic treatment of her tale. The
first century A.D. seems to have found Medea particularly compelling:
Ovid explored her myth in three different works, Seneca wrote his
tragedy *Medea,* and Valerius Flaccus undertook an extensive treatment
of Medea and Jason's story. In addition to these well-known, lengthy
treatments of Medea's myth, there are references to her tale in the
works of countless other ancient poets, philosophers, and rhetoricians.
Ancient artists were mesmerized by her as well: we meet her image
in Greek vase paintings, engraved Roman gemstones, Italian terra-
cottas, and Pompeian wall murals. Most surprisingly, perhaps, we
find her murdering her children on Roman sarcophagi and funerary
monuments.[2]

But Medea's popularity has far outlasted antiquity and found expression in a variety of forms, as just a few of many possible examples
will demonstrate.[3] Pierre Corneille dramatized her story in 1635; using
Corneille's play as a libretto, Gustave Charpentier composed the first
of numerous operas about Medea in 1693. The ballet *Médée et Jason*
(1763), which was considered the crowning achievement of the French
choreographer Jean Georges Noverre's career, helped to earn him the

---

[1] E.g., the *Corinthiaca* of Naupactus, as well as the *Building of the Argo* and the *Journey
of Jason to the Colchians* by Epimenides of Crete. Braswell 1988:6–23 provides a useful
summary of the early history of the Argonautic saga.

[2] See M. Schmidt 1992.

[3] Some portions of the résumé that follows were drawn from Reid 1993:2.643–50, in
which the interested reader can find many further examples of Medea's appearances in
postclassical art.

title "Father of Modern Ballet." The pathos that underlies Medea's myth was poignantly expressed in Austrian playwright Franz Grillparzer's trilogy *Das goldene Vlies* (1822), written after his mother's suicide.

Our own century has been particularly captivated by Medea. There have been yet further operatic treatments of her story, among which that of Darius Milhaud (1938) stands out.[4] Robinson Jeffers's 1937 translation of Euripides' *Medea* newly interpreted the classical image of the heroine; its production in 1947 provided Dame Judith Anderson with what was to become one of her most famous roles, and its revival in 1982 brought Zoe Caldwell a Tony award. Audiences in 1946 saw the composition of both Samuel Barber's ballet music *Cave of the Heart* (later retitled *Medea's Meditation and Dance of Vengeance*), which was created specifically for the dynamic talents of Martha Graham, and Jean Anouilh's drama *Médée*, in which the tortured mother killed herself as well as her children. Pier Paolo Pasolini directed Maria Callas in a powerful cinematic version of Medea's myth (1970) and in Jules Dassin's 1978 film, "A Dream of Passion," an actress playing Euripides' Medea (Melina Mercouri) confronted a woman serving time for having murdered her children (Ellen Burstyn). Most recently, Diana Rigg won critical acclaim in the title role of a revival of Euripides' *Medea* on the London stage. Perhaps what is most interesting about the twentieth century's reaction to Medea, however, is the way in which her struggle and sufferings have been used to express the problems of many different cultures and groups. The black actress Agnes Straub revived Grillparzer's trilogy in 1933 and used it to make a statement about Nazi racist policies. Maxwell Anderson set her story in the South Seas (*The Wingless Victory*, 1936), Güngör Dilmen in Turkey (*Kurban*, 1967) and Willy Kyrklund in Africa (*Medea från Mbongo*, 1967). Brendan Kennelly's *Medea* (1988) uses her story to explore the conflict between the English and the Irish.[5] Nor is the role of Medea restricted to women alone: two years ago, in Seattle, a gay theatrical group staged a version in which Medea was played by a man and Jason by a woman. The conflict between genders that has always been a theme in Medea's myth can work both ways. Often, these modern versions of the myth show considerable sympathy for Medea. Jacqueline Crossland's 1992 *Collateral Damage* takes this idea

[4] Reid 1993 lists a total of twenty-eight operas about Medea, ten of them from the twentieth century. We can add to this list the 1991 opera of Theodorakis and 1995 opera of Liebermann (see McDonald's article in the present volume).

[5] See further McDonald's contribution to this volume.

even further, portraying an innocent Medea who has been framed by the Corinthian princess.

In the visual arts, too, Medea has continued to make appearances. Painters as diverse as the German academician Anselm Feuerbach, the French Romantic Eugéne Delacroix, and the Pre-Raphaelite F. A. Sandys have illustrated her myth. Particularly compelling among recent treatments is British pop artist Eduardo Paolozzi's 1964 sculpture *Medea*, constructed of angular machine parts resting atop writhing bronze tubes. Simultaneously, Paolozzi presents us with the cold, inhuman precision of an automaton and earthy, female passion.

What kind of woman casts such an enduring spell? Answering this question is a bit tricky. Narratively, Medea first appears as a lovely and lovelorn princess who enables Jason to steal the Golden Fleece. In this role she fits the paradigm of the "helper-maiden," which is found in the fairy tales or myths of virtually all cultures. Later in her story, however, Medea appears as a wrathful woman whose lust for vengeance drives her to slaughter her own children. In this role, of course, she is the utter opposite of the "good" or "helpful" woman. Indeed, when we look closely at the variant versions of this story, we realize that infanticidal Medea resembles a type of female demon, feared in traditional cultures throughout the ancient and modern world, who specializes in killing children.

What could possibly unite these conflicting figures? Further details only make the problem more difficult. We hear of Medea tricking the Athenian king Aegeus into nearly murdering his son Theseus, yet we also hear of her founding cities, which the Greeks and Romans regarded as a strongly positive act. Sophocles and Seneca portray Medea as a famous witch, adept in herbal poisons and surrounded by snakes, yet Ibycus and Simonides tell of her marrying the hero Achilles after her death, in the blessed Elysian Plain, where only privileged souls find rest.[6]

In the form that we have received it from antiquity, Medea's mythic history seems to have made some attempts to harmonize these and other disparate elements. For example, as Medea leaves Colchis, where she played the role of helpful princess, she brutally kills and dismembers her brother Apsyrtus, an act that can be understood to foreshadow her infanticide in Corinth. Even in her role as helper-

---

[6] Soph. frs. 534–36 (Radt) with comments; Seneca, see Nussbaum's contribution to this volume; Ibycus fr. 291 (Campbell) = Simon. fr. 558 (Campbell); Apollonius tells this story as well (4.805ff.).

maiden, Medea uses magic, which for the Greeks was always a frightening and disreputable art in the hands of women. These episodes seem to suggest that the wicked woman always lurked within the helper-maiden. But it is difficult to determine whether such darker elements as fratricide and magic were really always part of the story of Medea and Jason's early life. It is possible that they were introduced by ancient authors who wanted to smooth over the dissonances between the different "Medeas" whom they had inherited from tradition.

For present purposes, the resolution of this issue is relatively unimportant; what I wish to emphasize is that from at least the early fifth century B.C., Medea was represented by the Greeks as a complex figure, fraught with conflicting desires and exhibiting an extraordinary range of behavior. In this regard, she differs from most of the other figures we meet in Greek myth, who present far simpler *personae*. In some cases, the mythic *persona* is simpler because the character is connected with only one famous act or story (e.g., Tithonus, Callisto). Frequently, such figures represent a "type" (mortal man disabled after sleeping with goddess, virgin who meets with danger during her transition into motherhood), which finds expression in other mythic figures as well (Endymion, Io). In other cases, the character is associated with more than one story, but his or her personality and behavior change little from one to the next. Odysseus, for instance, has many different adventures, both during the Trojan War and afterward, but throughout them he is marked by his cleverness and endurance. Although some such characters probably had fuller personalities once, they apparently served both mythic and literary purposes well in their comparatively circumscribed forms.

Notably, however, many of the mythological figures who have fascinated us most deeply throughout the centuries are, like Medea, figures who defy simple description. Heracles, who is probably the best known of all Greek mythic figures, is a perfect example: he was a glutton, a rapist, and a maddened infanticide, and yet also a civilizing hero, a protophilosopher, and a model for the Roman emperors. It is always possible to propose reasons that such complex characters developed as they did, but what I wish to emphasize at the moment is the fact that once they had become complex, they were allowed to remain that way. This implies that it is their complexity itself that appeals to the artist, the author, and their audiences. In seeking to understand the powerful hold that Medea has had upon our imaginations for almost three millennia, therefore, we must embrace her complexity and look within it for the secret of her longevity.

The essays in this volume set out to do just that. One of the results of asking twelve different scholars to write about Medea is that each of them, of course, sees something different. Remarkably, however, many of the essays share a particular observation, through which, perhaps, we can begin to understand the appeal of Medea's complexity. This figure who contained within herself mutually contradictory traits was an ideal vehicle through whom authors and artists could explore what modern scholarship has called the problem of "self" and "other." Let me briefly review what is usually meant by this phrase. Typically, it is employed with reference to the ways in which an individual or group seeks to define what it is and, equally important, what it is not. Quite often, the two definitions go hand in hand: for every rule or custom that is embraced by the individual or group, there can be found a polar opposite, which is rejected. Frequently, the opposing rules and customs are ascribed (correctly or incorrectly) to another person or group that has been chosen to fill the role of "other." A well-known example of this from ancient Greece is Herodotus' ascription to the Egyptians of personal and social habits that are inversions of what he understands to be the norm (i.e., what occurred in his own country): other societies cut their hair to show mourning, but Egyptians allow their hair to grow; everywhere else weavers work the weft upward, but Egyptian weavers work it downward; and so on. Ascribing behavior that is the opposite of that within one's own society can sometimes be used to censure the other culture or persons and their behavior. Thus, the Cyclopes of *Odyssey* 9 are described as holding no counsels, having no laws, practicing no agriculture, and possessing no knowledge of wine. In other words, Homer takes some pains to portray them as being completely unacquainted with customs that defined civilization for the Greeks, and thus as being "other" in all respects. Cumulatively, Homer's portrayal can be understood to further censure cannibalism, the antisocial, abnormal behavior of the Cyclopes par excellence, on which *Odyssey* 9 focuses (cf. the remarks of Graf in this volume). When self is opposed to other, and particularly when that other is meant to be censured, there usually are no "in-betweens." Such absolute divisions can have a reassuring effect, both because they impose firm rules and boundaries upon the world and because they imply that other is safely and permanently separated from self. The whole system can have a strong normative value, for by describing what is unacceptable or atypical and assigning it to the other, one implicitly describes the acceptable or typical and demands it from anyone who wishes to belong to the group marked self. Thus, the dichotomizing of self and other serves as an important means both of organizing the world and of enforcing behavioral desiderata.

Myths frequently express this dichotomy by means of opposing characters. Hero myths, for example, often set a human defender of civilized life against a monster who threatens to destroy it, perhaps by scourging the crops and herds that allow the stable, settled life of the city to continue; it is for this reason that Saint George kills the dragon and Bellerephon the chimaera. It is somewhat unusual, however, to find the dichotomy encapsulated within a *single* mythic figure, which brings us back to Medea. Not only does her checkered career allow authors and artists to explore the opposing concepts of self and other, as she veers between desirable and undesirable behavior, between Greek and foreigner; it also allows them to raise the disturbing possibility of *otherness lurking within self*—the possibility that the "normal" carry within themselves the potential for abnormal behavior, that the boundaries expected to keep our world safe are not impermeable. Initially, Medea adhered to the womanly duties expected of her by helping Jason achieve his goals; later, however, she committed the absolutely unwomanly act of killing her children. Initially, Medea seemed to have been tamed by Jason and incorporated into Greek life; later, however, her barbarian blood proved true.

In the late fifth century, shortly after the production of Euripides' *Medea* (431 B.C.), artists began to emphasize Medea's role as a foreigner within Greek society by portraying her in oriental clothing rather than the dress of the normal Greek woman: visually, she became the paradigmatic outsider. In "Medea at a Shifting Distance: Images and Euripidean Tragedy," Christiane Sourvinou-Inwood reconstructs both the origin of this iconographic trend and Euripides' use of visual signals. Her detailed analyses of the separate elements of the oriental dress, and of the specific scenes from Medea's story with which those elements are associated in the vase paintings, lead to the conclusion that Euripides' play probably presented Medea in traditional Greek apparel—that is, as a more-or-less normal woman—until the final scene. It was only then, when she loomed above the stage in her dragon chariot, holding the corpses of her slaughtered sons, that she appeared (perhaps for the first time anywhere) in an oriental costume, which signaled her utter abandonment of Greek mores and her complete alignment with

the world of the foreign, the abnormal. Sourvinou-Inwood's rea
of the *Medea* itself supports this analysis. She notes that through
most of the play, Euripides moves his heroine back and forth between
opposing categories such as "good" and "bad," or "mortal" and "divine," encouraging us alternately to sympathize with her and then to be
shocked by her. By doing this, he repeatedly challenges established categories, thereby forcing his audience to reexamine their presumptions
about what the "norm" really is. In such scenes, Medea's Greek dress
would have been an asset, as it would have subtly suggested her representation of the world in which the audience lived. Only in the final
scene, in which Euripides wishes to present the victorious infanticide
as a creature completely detached from normalcy, would "abnormal"
oriental dress have been both an appropriate and a powerful iconographic signal. The tragic theater, which often reflected societal values,
can challenge their integrity as well, presenting an other that can appear
uncomfortably similar to the self and can eventually work from within
to topple it.

On an individual level, in ancient Greece and other cultures, the invasion of self by other could be understood as the cause of bad behavior; it
was not unusual for an individual's madness to be traced to demons
or divine forces, for example.[7] Ancient Greek and Roman philosophers
generally rejected such explanations, yet the possibility of a chaotic force
overwhelming the virtue within an individual nonetheless entered into
their debates on the nature of the soul. Platonists, on the one hand,
argued that bad behavior occurred when the virtuous, rational portion
of the tripartite soul was conquered by the irrational portion. Stoics,
on the other hand, rejected the idea of a battle within the soul; rather,
they understood the soul to be unified and thus to make every decision, good or bad, as a whole. Notably, as John M. Dillon discusses in
"Medea among the Philosophers," both Platonists and Stoics adduced
Medea's infanticide—particularly as presented by Euripides—in support of their views. Especially important to the debate was the passage
in which Medea announces, "I understand the evils I am going to do,
but anger prevails over my counsels" (lines 1078–79). Platonists such as
Galen saw in this passage a clear proof for the divided soul, but Stoics

---

[7] One of the earliest European variations of this theme is Agamemnon's apology to
Achilles (*Il.* 19.86–89), in which he states that when he stole the concubine Briseis, he
was acting under the compulsion of the goddess Ate ("Folly"). The classic discussion
is "Agamemnon's Apology," in Dodds 1951:1–27. For more recent examinations of the
concept of external forces causing madness or bad behavior, see Padel 1992, 1994.

rgued that although Medea may have tried to
r anger, they were nonetheless her own actions.
sophers chose to make an "argument from the
m they focused was Euripidean Medea. By
gies that every soul underwent, this most foreign
u be used to represent us all.

urse, in challenging the assumption that other could be kept
completely separate from self, Medea also compelled people to consider
what drove the human soul to inhuman behavior, and whether any soul
was truly immune. Behind Medea's story lurked the possibility that
other Greek women might do what she had done, if pressed far enough.
The question of whether there might be justifiable reasons for doing
wrong was open to reconsideration as well. Euripides in particular,
although not condoning Medea's infanticide, forces us to empathize
with her situation. Euripides and several other authors also said that
Medea's passion for Jason—which led her to betray her father, kill her
brother, and commit many other heinous deeds—was inflicted by the
gods. Did this exculpate her? Even if the gods were not responsible
for her passion, could love itself excuse all? Or is falling in love itself
a culpable mistake?

The Stoic philosopher and dramatist Seneca used his *Medea* to provide an answer to just this question, as Martha C. Nussbaum shows
in her essay "Serpents in the Soul: A Reading of Seneca's *Medea*." The
Stoic view of the human condition claimed that no soul, once love had
entered it, could safely guarantee that hostility, rage, and murder would
not follow. The play provides an exemplum of this belief that was intended to engage the heart of each audience member in a scrutiny of
its own commitments. Most frightening of all is the realization, forced
upon us by Seneca as the play progresses, that it is the one who really
loves properly and loyally who will be the most upset by a loss of
love and thus most liable to wreak havoc. The love, grief, and anger
among which Medea veers are inextricably connected with one another
in the Stoic view because they all arise when one mistakenly allows
one's soul to become passionately engaged with another. How can the
experience of a life in which the most important things are affected by
external agents be anything but excruciating to one who values her selfhood? Love leads almost inevitably to wounds and thus to retaliation.
And yet the Stoic ideal—the rejection of passion and of inappropriate
attachment to others—is perhaps not completely embraced by Seneca;
we sense in reading his play an admiration for the heroic Medea and

her pursuit of love. By the end, the audience is forced to realize that love is a great good, but one that cannot always be forced into safe domestication and completely moral bounds.

Deborah Boedeker also examines the question of what drove Medea's actions. In "Becoming Medea: Assimilation in Euripides," Boedeker begins by observing that there were always alternative Medeas available to ancient authors. Even within a single episode, such as the story of the death of Medea's children, an author had to make choices. Would the Corinthians kill the children? Would Medea? If Medea killed them, would she do so intentionally or accidentally? Each author who took up Medea's story was responsible not only for choosing an ending but for motivating it. Euripides' version became canonical, Boedeker suggests, because of the brilliance with which he simultaneously tied motivation to personality and showed how that personality developed—how Medea became Medea. Throughout the play, Euripides assimilates Medea to the people and things that surround her, which has the cumulative effect of suggesting that the seemingly proud and independent Medea was actually no more than the sum of those with whom she interacted. This includes, most importantly, her own enemies (Jason and his bride) and the goddess who stands at the back of all her problems (Aphrodite). At the same time as these assimilations take place, Euripidean Medea becomes *dissociated* from the very things that should most obviously describe her: the words "woman" and "mother" are used of Medea in this play only ironically. In its fight for survival, Boedeker suggests, Medea's self has been consumed by the other. Victim turned victimizer, Euripidean Medea is truly a woman whom we can both pity and fear.

Sometimes, alongside the danger that the other represents, there exist traits or abilities that the self desires. Dolores M. O'Higgins shows how Medea's myth can be used to explore this dilemma in "Medea as Muse: Pindar's *Pythian* 4." Opening with the observation that Medea "appears both exceptional and typical of all females, as they were generally perceived," O'Higgins suggests that Medea is emblematic of all ancient women, who, like her, were "outsiders," viewed with distrust even within the families that relied on their services as wives and child bearers. The Muses and other oracular females were similarly regarded; without the Muses, the poet could not create, yet they were a potentially deceptive force, as Hesiod tells us, liable to lie when the poet relied on them to tell the truth. As in the case of Zeus' swallowing of Metis ("Wisdom"), foreign female intelligence had to be skillfully appropriated and subordinated before it could safely be used in the male world. In *Pythian* 4, as O'Higgins shows, Pindar plays on these ideas by presenting Medea both as an oracular power who aids the Argonauts in their journey home and as a muselike creature who helps the epinician poet tell his story. Whereas Pindar manages to keep Medea under control, however, and make of her voice a serviceable tool, the audience knows that Jason's control is only tenuous and will eventually give way to his own destruction. Pindar himself is at some pains to make this clear: the epinician poet prides himself on succeeding where the traditional hero had not.

In "The Metamorphosis of Ovid's Medea," Carole E. Newlands takes up both the question of what drives a person to heinous acts, as do Boedeker and Nussbaum, and the question of whether the other can ever really be incorporated into the self, as does O'Higgins. Newlands begins by noting that in the *Metamorphoses,* far from smoothing over the inconsistencies in Medea's myth as he had in his earlier *Heroides,* Ovid allows them to jar us. Medea appears both as a lovelorn maiden and as an accomplished, manipulative witch, without any exploration of the psychological forces that compelled this change. Newlands then considers the problem of how a woman is to make the transition from being her father's daughter to her husband's wife. She observes that Ovid weaves Medea's tale in and out of others that tell of mythic loves, each of which explores the alienation that women suffer through their alliances with men, particularly men who are outside of—or even inimical to—their family groups. Through the stories of Procne, Scylla, and Procris, whose relationships end disastrously in familial betrayal and murder, and that of Orythia, whose marriage ends happily, Ovid compels us to reconsider the social and moral ambiguities of love, marriage, and filial duty and seems to suggest that women are "the prisoners of social conventions that fail to protect them" (p. 203). The stories of the other women offer fuller psychological portraits than Ovid's treatment of Medea had and thereby help explain how such "good" women became "bad." By implicitly comparing Medea to them, Ovid suggests that even this most dissonant of mythic figures—whom he has carefully allowed to remain dissonant by refusing to address the contradictions in her *persona*—can be understood as a victim of flawed social conventions as well as of her passions. In seeking conformance from its members, perhaps, society drives them to rebellion.

In his analysis of Medea's role in book 3 of Apollonius' *Argonautica* ("Conquest of the Mephistophelian Nausicaa: Medea's Role in

Apollonius' Redefinition of the Epic Hero"), James J. Clauss reveals yet another way in which ancient authors played on Medea's "otherness." Contrary to recent scholarly attempts to see Medea as the hero of this epic, Clauss argues that she fulfills there her traditional role of "helper-maiden." Because she is conjoined to a hero who falls short of his epic precedents, however, the level of help required from Medea turns out to be much higher than that required of other, traditional helper-maidens such as Ariadne. In particular, as Clauss demonstrates, Apollonius uses allusions and references to implicitly compare Medea and Jason to Nausicaa and Odysseus as they appear in book 5 of the *Odyssey*, one of the earliest and most famous tales of a hero and helper-maiden. There are several ironies in this comparison. Jason's cluelessness provides a striking contrast to Odysseus' resourcefulness, and similarly, Nausicaa's meekness and concern for family and social decorum—the concerns that any "normal" Greek woman should have—are the utter opposites of Medea's uncontrollable passions and eventual betrayal of her family. The systematic imitation of Nausicaa's words and experiences sets Medea's foreignness in relief by placing in the background the icon not merely of a Hellenic woman, but of one who was best known for her virtue and restraint. Moreover, Medea's means of helping Jason calls into question the whole notion of heroism in a postmythic world. By emphasizing her magical powers, Apollonius suggests that only magic and drugs can enable a man of his times to perform the feats of an Odysseus or Heracles.

Of course, it would be impossible to explore the ways in which authors and artists used Medea's story to express themselves without understanding the elements that make up that story. The four essays that open this volume examine the various episodes within Medea's life, tracing their possible origins and developments and suggesting reasons that they captured the mythic imagination. In the first essay, "Medea, the Enchantress from Afar: Remarks on a Well-Known Myth," Fritz Graf gives an overview of Medea's myth, concentrating on its five major episodes (Medea's sojourns in Colchis, Iolcus, Corinth, Athens, and Persia). He begins by noting that for this mythic figure and others, there is what he calls the "vertical tradition"—different versions of the same mythic episode, developed over the course of centuries—and the "horizontal tradition"—a running biography composed of the individual episodes. To understand a complex mythic figure fully, we must first examine the themes and variations within both of these traditions, noting the consistencies and tensions between them. Following detailed

analyses of the individual episodes, Graf is able to offer a broader interpretation of Medea's myth, arguing that two unifying ideas repeatedly
occur. One of them, in which we can find some of the roots of Medea's
representation of the other, is her foreignness. It is well known that
Medea comes from a far-away land where strange rites such as ritual
murder are practiced; this makes her a geographic and cultural stranger
in the land of Greece. But she is also a stranger in the sense that she
is repeatedly exiled *within* Greece. As she enters city after city, bringing
violence and grief to each, she implicitly demonstrates how the outsider,
the other, is a threat to the inside, to the self. The other unifying theme is
that of initiation. In Athens, the myth of Medea's attack on Theseus was
connected with rituals in the Delphinion practiced by young men. In
Corinth, the myth of her children's death was connected with a cult
in which both boys and girls participated. In each case, we could understand Medea to be a mythic reflection of the ritualistic dangers that
initiates often face. Possibly, she originally had an active role in such
cults themselves. Her original role in the story of Jason's quest was
initiatory, too, Graf argues, which aligns with the generally initiatory
tone of the Argonautica.

In my own essay ("Corinthian Medea and the Cult of Hera Akraia"),
I use information regarding the Corinthian cult of Hera and Medea's
children to argue that no single ancient author "invented" the figure of
infanticidal Medea; rather, the figure evolved out of a paradigm found
in the folk beliefs of Greece and many other Mediterranean cultures—
the reproductive demon, who persecuted pregnant women and young
children. Through analysis of votive offerings and cultic *aitia*, I begin
by suggesting that Hera's Corinthian cult focused on mothers' concerns
about bearing and rearing healthy children. I then note that, according to Pausanias, when the Corinthians asked an oracle how to stop
the wholesale death of their own infants, which followed the death of
Medea's children, they had been told not only to found this cult but
also to erect a statue of a frightening, ugly woman. Because apotropaic
statues in the ancient Mediterranean often worked on the principle of
"like averts like," I suggest that the Corinthian statue was intended
to represent and thus protect against reproductive demons, who were
regularly imagined in the ancient Mediterranean to take the form of
frightening, ugly women. Analysis of early myths describing Medea's
loss of her children indicates that before she became identified with the
Colchian figure of epic, Corinthian Medea was known as a local woman
whose children had died because Hera failed to protect them. In this

respect, Medea's story aligns with those of other reproductive demons: typically, such demons are thought to be the souls of women who have lost their own children, sometimes through the perfidy of a divinity. Frequently, an alternative version of the demon's story develops, however, according to which the reproductive demon's first victims are her own children. I conclude that the story of Corinthian Medea began as a mythic reflex of the local cult of Hera, meant to demonstrate the effects of Hera's neglect or hatred; subsequently developed so as to make the bereft Medea into a reproductive demon; and eventually blamed the death of Medea's children on Medea herself. Here, then, is yet another root of Medea's otherness: like other reproductive demons, she is a mother who commits the most unmaternal of crimes.

Myths concerning the foundation of cities were fairly common in antiquity. Because every populace wanted to be able to trace itself back to an important ancestor, these myths typically ascribed foundation to a god or hero. In "Medea as Foundation-Heroine," Nita Krevans explores what is a perplexing and often overlooked tradition connected with Medea: her role as a founder of cities. Typically, the key players in foundation stories are male. Females appear, if at all, as kidnapped and raped virgins who give their names and their sons to the new city, or whose brothers, in seeking a kidnapped sister, found cities themselves. Although some foundation stories involving Medea place her in these traditional roles, in other foundation myths she once again proves to be a defiant anomaly by inverting them. Rather than the kidnapped virgin sought by a brother, for example, she is the kidnapping sister whose murdered brother gives his name to the place of his death, either directly (the "Apsyrtides" Islands) or indirectly (the name of the city "Tomi," meaning "cut," is explained with reference to Medea's dismemberment of Apsyrtus' body). Rather than receiving prophecies from a male god concerning future cities, as other virgins do, Medea is a prophetic divinity, who foretells the foundation of Cyrene. Sometimes Medea's connection with foundation presents her in a positive light, fulfilling a desirable role, as I noted earlier in this introduction. More often, however, cities commemorate her brutality or foreignness. In either case, she is once again a character who challenges a boundary— here the boundary between male and female—by acting in ways that are contrary to the norm.

Jan N. Bremmer, in "Why Did Medea Kill Her Brother Apsyrtus?" investigates the significance of one of Medea's earliest crimes, the murder of her brother as she escaped with Jason from Colchis. Bremmer begins by surveying our versions of this story, concluding that authors were at some pains to make this murder appear as abominable as possible through such devices as situating it at an altar. Building on this, Bremmer goes on to consider the question of why myth made Medea's first victim her *brother*, rather than her father, mother, sister, or some other member of the natal family from whom she was fleeing. Using *comparanda* from Mediterranean and other cultures to reinforce the ancient Greek evidence, Bremmer examines the significance of the brother-sister relationship in detail, first preparing the ground by examining brother-brother and sister-sister relationships. He notes that in reality and in myth, brother-brother relationships were frequently fraught with competitiveness and strife. Our evidence concerning sister-sister relationships suggests that they were somewhat closer, yet also marked by rivalry and envy. In contrast to these, the relationship between brother and sister was, under normal circumstances, a very close one. Especially important was the brother's role as his sister's protector, most notably (although not exclusively) in the absence of his father. Her sexual honor, in particular, fell under his protection. In killing Apsyrtus, then, Medea severs her ties to her natal family and also demonstrates that she will be the mistress of her own affairs. This not only underlines her desire to align herself with her new husband at any expense but also prepares the ground for what is emphasized by several classical authors: once having left Colchis under such circumstances, Medea can never return; she is an exile with no other resource than Jason.

The final essay in our volume, Marianne McDonald's "Medea as Politician and Diva: Riding the Dragon into the Future," shows that even now, "Medea's name is on people's lips and she haunts their dreams" (p. 299). Her myth is used especially to express the desperation of the oppressed and the destruction that their rebellion—however justified it may be—brings with it. In particular, McDonald shows that Medea has become an idol for the sexually, politically, and racially oppressed, who, like her, are exploited and then discarded by their exploiters. Just as Sophocles' Antigone has become an inspiring symbol of "civil disobedience" for modern audiences, McDonald argues, Euripides' Medea has come to symbolize the freedom fighter, celebrating the right of the oppressed to fight back with whatever weapons they have. McDonald begins by briefly reviewing the numerous dramatizations of Medea's story that have been offered in recent years, and she then goes on to explore two contemporary versions of Medea's story in detail. Brendan Kennelly's *Medea* (1988) both examines the rage of women betrayed by the men who "colonize" their bodies through sex and also explores the problematic relationship between the Irish ("Medea") and the English ("Jason") by setting the play in contemporary Dublin. A Cromwellian Jason argues that Medea should be grateful for the Protestant virtue and discipline that England has brought to her "barbarian," Catholic land. Mikis Theodorakis' opera *Medea* (unpublished; performed in Bilbao, Spain, in 1991), like many of his other works based on ancient dramas, presents human beings as responsible for their own choices, and as groping with the self-knowledge that accompanies those choices. Theodorakis' work offers us the "rarefied and clarified essence of human emotion" (p. 313) through which we can learn to appreciate what it means to be brutally oppressed and to fight back.

It is this facet of Medea that has moved to the forefront in the twentieth century—her role as the other whose allegedly "barbarian" actions force us to reevaluate the depths of our *own* souls. Appropriately so, for we no longer live in a world where the other can be embellished with the elaborate fantasies of a Herodotus or Homer and, thus, be banished to a convenient and reassuring distance. The other confronts us day and night in our newspapers and on our television screens, forcing the realization that it is in most ways just like us, whatever we may imagine "us" to be. It is no longer possible to sanction rules that once divided men from women, "civilized" nations from "uncivilized," blacks from whites, or any other group from another, as previous societies did. Nor is it any longer possible to pretend that terrible crimes such as infanticide do not take place in average towns, among seemingly normal people. For better and for worse, we live in a world where there seem to be no limits. Perhaps this is why Medea continues to challenge our imaginations: like our neighbors, our colleagues, and the more distant people whom the news media bring to our attention each day, she evokes both our pity and our fear, our admiration and our horror. In confronting Medea, we confront our deepest feelings and realize that behind the delicate order we have sought to impose upon our world lurks chaos.[8]

---

[8] It should be noted that the work of Moreau 1994 appeared too late to be taken into consideration by most of the contributors to this volume, although several cite his earlier work on Medea.

PART I

MYTHIC REPRESENTATIONS

1

MEDEA, THE ENCHANTRESS FROM AFAR

REMARKS ON A WELL-KNOWN MYTH

Fritz Graf

TO THOSE OF US who have grown up with it, Greek myth seems to consist of stories about individual, noninterchangeable figures—Odysseus, Orestes, or indeed Medea—each of whom seems to have been shaped by a single, authoritative literary work: Homer's *Odyssey*, Aeschylus' *Oresteia*, Euripides' *Medea*. We tend to forget that, in reality, each of these works is just a single link in a chain of narrative transmission: on either side of the version that is authoritative for us, there stands a long line of other versions. Moreover, many of these versions not only refer to the episode treated in the authoritative literary work but also include other details, which help to round out a mythic biography. The first phenomenon—the fact that there exist different versions of the same mythic episode—might be called the *vertical* tradition. The other phenomenon—the fact that the different versions yield a running biography of the mythic figure—might be called the *horizontal* tradition. (I am aware that the boundaries between the two phenomena are far from precise.) Tensions exist between individual narratives of the same episode, as well as between each of these existing narratives and what might be called the imaginary core narrative, although whether there really ever was such a thing is one question that must be considered. How severe the tensions and differences are between this "core" narrative and existing narratives is another important question: how great is the plasticity of myth?[1]

One character who presents herself as the subject of such questions is Medea. Her mythic biography was elaborated enthusiastically by

I thank Bruno Gentili and his Istituto in Urbino for affording me the opportunity to present a first version of this paper to a stimulating and critical audience and Sarah Iles Johnston for discussing my ideas and translating my German.
[1] Halm-Tisserant 1993 bases her work on a comparable model of myth, and Bremmer 1988 investigates the "plasticité" of the Meleager myth.

ancient authors. Already in the fifth century, she was portrayed fully by Pindar and Euripides. Five individual episodes, each of which is tied closely to a specific locale, construct the horizontal tradition:[2]

a. The Colchian story: Medea helps Jason, who has arrived with the Argonauts, obtain the Golden Fleece; she then must flee with him.
b. The Iolcan story: Medea helps Jason to avenge himself on Pelias; they then must flee from the Peliades, who seek revenge.
c. The Corinthian story: Medea avenges herself on Jason, who has abandoned her, by killing the Corinthian king, his daughter, and the children whom Medea has borne to Jason; she then must flee.
d. The Athenian story: Medea becomes the companion of King Aegeus and almost kills his son Theseus; she then must flee.
e. The Median story: after fleeing from Athens, Medea settles among the Arioi in the Iranian highlands, who since that time have been called "Medes" (Hdt. 7.62).[3]

Not all of these episodes are documented in equal detail by ancient sources. In the next section of this paper, I will turn my attention to the one for which we have the greatest number of narratives from different time periods—the episode in Colchis—and examine their diversity. In the sections that follow, I will examine the remaining episodes individually and offer some suggestions as to what links all these stories about Medea—about all of Medea's *personae*—together.

Medea in Colchis: The Course of the Narrative

"Would that the Argo had never reached the land of Colchis, sailing through the dark Symplegades, and that the spruce had never fallen in the glades of Pelion." With this famous example of *hysteron proteron*— reformulated in ordinary word order by Ennius as recorded by Cicero (*Tusc.* 3.63), and exploited by Cicero against the femme fatale Clodia, the

---

[2] Of particular importance to my discussion are the following works: Friedländer 1914; Séchan 1927; von Fritz 1959; Mimoso-Ruiz 1982; Archellaschi 1990; Dräger 1993. See also Gordon 1987a, and the relevant articles in *RE, RL,* and *LIMC.* Moreau 1994 unfortunately arrived too late to be fully received into my arguments; since, however, the book thoroughly reworks and expands on a topic published in an earlier series of articles, "Introduction à la mythologie X–XIX: Les mille et une facettes de Médée," in the not very accessible periodical *Connaissance hellénique* 24–33 (1985–87), I refer to Moreau 1994 where, in an earlier version, I would have referred to these papers.

[3] See discussion of the date below, p. 37.

sister of Clodius Pulcher (*Cael.* 18)[4]—begins Euripides' *Medea*. It was the Argo that fetched Medea to Greece, and it is during the narration of that first sea voyage that she makes her debut in Greek myth. Our detailed accounts of the story are all from later sources; with them we will begin.

Apollonius of Rhodes

Central to a working history of the Argonautica theme is the *Argonautica* of Apollonius Rhodius, a learned (and, in its literary surroundings, somewhat idiosyncratic) epic of the third century B.C.[5] This work not only defined the story of the Argonautica for later authors,[6] but it also left its stamp on the *Aeneid.* The relevant episodes of the well-known plot might be summarized as follows. Even before Jason arrived in Colchis, the goddesses Hera and Athena had prepared the ground by securing the help of Aphrodite on his behalf. Later, when Jason asked for the Golden Fleece during an audience with King Aeëtes, Eros was present as well; by means of a well-aimed shot, he ensured that the king's daughter, Medea, would fall in love with the newly arrived stranger. Aeëtes demanded that Jason win the fleece by completing a series of tasks that Jason rightly feared would kill him: he was to yoke fire-breathing bulls and use them to plow a field; following this, he was to sow the field with dragon's teeth. After a long inner battle, and at the urging of her sister Chalciope (the widow of Phrixus and thereby a woman well disposed toward the Greeks), Medea yielded to her love for Jason and betrayed her father and homeland: she gave Jason a magical salve that would protect him against the steers' breath and she taught him a trick by which he could deflect the soldiers that sprang up when the dragon's teeth were sown. Later, she gave him a sleeping potion that would render harmless the dragon who guarded the fleece (which, of course, Aeëtes would not hand over to Jason even after the tasks had been successfully completed).

Apollonius builds the tale of Jason, Medea, and her father upon a story type that was already familiar in Hellenistic literature: the "Tarpeia-type," named after a well-known Roman myth.[7] This type

---

[4] But see Skinner 1983.

[5] See Clauss in this volume.

[6] Foremost among them Valerius Flaccus and his *Argonautica*. See Salemme 1991, which includes a considerable bibliography.

[7] For this story type, which is found in many different cultures, see Krappe 1929 (with a diffusionist explanation); for the Roman myth and its background Dumézil 1947 (a

centers on a triangle comprising a father, who usually is the king of a city, his daughter, and a foreign enemy. The enemy attacks the city but cannot conquer it because the father protects it, sometimes by supernatural means. The daughter, however, who has fallen in love with the foreigner, betrays her father, in hopes that her treachery will be rewarded by the fulfillment of her love. Usually, she finds she has deceived herself in this expectation. In itself, this story type is pre-Hellenistic; we first find it in Aeschylus' reference to the fate of Scylla of Megara, who betrayed her father for the sake of vile gold (*Cho.* 612). Later narrators (including Prop. 4.4 and Ovid in *Met.* 8.6–151) changed both the girl's motivation and the narrator's point of view: Tarpeia is driven by love, not gold,[8] and her feelings are focused upon by the narrator. Apollonius' portrayal of Medea aligns with both tendencies, which are, of course, overtly Hellenistic: his Medea acts out of love, and we are asked to see the situation through her eyes.

In three respects, however, Apollonius' story differs from most other examples of this type. First, it is the only one to take place at the limits of the known world; all others take place in a Greek state or in Rome, never in foreign parts. Second, Jason does not go to Colchis with the same intentions as his homologues: he does not want to conquer Colchis, he wants merely to take home the fleece. Apollonius emphasizes this point by making Jason first ask for the fleece and then offer to perform some service in return for it (3.177–93, 351–53, 393–95). Third, Medea's character as a priestess of Hecate and an enchantress is unusual: typically, the maiden in this story type is young, beautiful, and somewhat dumb (consider, for example, Ovid's Scylla). If supernatural powers are brought into the story, they usually belong to the maiden's father, the king of the city: Scylla's father, Nisus, has a purple lock of hair, for example, on which Megara's fate depends.

Closer to Apollonius' version of the story of Jason, Aeëtes, and Medea is the tale of Theseus, Minos, and Ariadne. It also plays upon the father-daughter-stranger triangle, but, like Apollonius' Medea-story, it does not align fully with the Tarpeia-type: Theseus arrives not as a conqueror and enemy of Crete, but rather as a rescuer of his countrymen.

comparatist's view), Devoto 1967 (earlier views); for the myth of Tarpeia, see Bremmer and Horsfall 1987:68–73.

[8] Krappe 1929 shows that this later motivation is more common by far, both in Greece and Rome and in cultures throughout the world. For the use Ovid makes of some myths of this type—Medea and Scylla—see Newlands in this volume.

Moreover, Ariadne's love finds fulfillment (at least at first), for Theseus takes her with him and rescues her from the fury of her father. In later versions, the story is told so as to put Ariadne at the center (e.g., Catullus 64; Ovid *Met.* 8.169–82).

The tensions between Apollonius' version of Medea's story and more-or-less contemporary narrations of the Tarpeia-type suggest that Medea's story originally ran somewhat differently: Medea was not always a little maiden of the Tarpeia-type. Apollonius had to take pains to ease the tensions between the maidenly—and impossibly infatuated—Medea that he wanted to present and another Medea, already familiar to his readers, who was skilled in magic and a priestess of Hecate.

Dionysius Scytobrachion

At about the same time as Apollonius was writing, the mythographer Dionysius Scytobrachion wrote his prose version of the Argonautica; we know it through the rather detailed adaptation by Diodorus Siculus (4.40–48).[9] It differs from Apollonius' version in two significant ways—one that occurs at the beginning of the story and another that occurs at the end. According to Dionysius, Aeëtes once was warned by an oracle that a stranger would kill him and steal the Golden Fleece. Apollonius, in contrast, tells us that Helios used an oracle to warn Aeëtes about the deceit of a relative, which Aeëtes took to mean not Medea but rather the son of his other daughter, Chalciope (3.597–600). In order to protect himself, Dionysius tells us, Aeëtes decreed that all foreigners were to be sacrificed to Artemis and installed Medea as the priestess of this cult. This was a rash action, as becomes clear: Medea opposed the barbarian human sacrifices and secretly used her position to rescue as many Greeks as she could. She was found out, of course, and, because of her father's anger, had to seek asylum in the temple of Helios, her ancestor and her familial god. Here she was found by the Argonauts, who had landed without being noticed; she threw her lot in with theirs. At the end of the story, according to Dionysius, there was a battle between the Colchians and the Argonauts, in which Aeëtes was killed.

This version, which aligns with the euhemeristic rationalism of Dionysius Scytobrachion in excluding divine intervention, initially seems to be closer to the Tarpeia-type than Apollonius' version. The

---

[9] See Moreau 1994:224–32. On Dionysius Scytobrachion, see esp. Rusten 1982.

Golden Fleece is the talisman of the king and his reign, as was the purple hair of Nisus.[10] Jason is denounced as an enemy of the country, and in the end he kills the king. However, Dionysius introduces another motif, which is otherwise not associated with this story type: ξενοκτονία (the sacrifice of foreigners). This motif stresses the strangeness of Aeëtes' barbarian land; the Greeks, of course, do not sacrifice ξένοι—indeed, for the Greeks, strangers enjoy the special protection of Zeus Xenios. Medea rejects ξενοκτονία and is persecuted for her choice: this action explains why she chooses to align herself with Jason, a Greek. The Colchians' ξενοκτονία also helps make Aeëtes' death at Jason's hands morally acceptable—he is truly a barbarian, unlike his more sensitive daughter.

The ξενοκτονία motif also appears in another version, albeit in a less moralistic form: as a priestess of Artemis, Medea willingly performed the human offerings until the arrival of Jason. Just as she was to sacrifice Jason, a god—either Aphrodite or Eros—intervened to prevent the murder. This version first is narrated fully by Dracontius, a Latin poet of the sixth century A.D., but as W.-H. Friedrich has shown, Dracontius must have drawn on a tragedy of the fourth, or at latest the third, century B.C.[11] Whether this tragedy preceded or followed Dionysius Scytobrachion's version is open to debate. In my opinion, the tragedy probably was earlier: aside from certain euhemeristic rationalizations that are typical to Dionysius, his version offers nothing new, compared with Dracontius' quite dramatic account.

A whole series of Greek myths discusses the sacrifice of foreigners, the most familiar of which is that of Taurian Iphigenia, made famous by Euripides' play. We also have the myth of King Busiris of Egypt, who killed all travelers to his land until he suffered death at Heracles' hands. Euripides draws on Busiris' myth in his *Helen*, in which Teucer and Menelaus await the same fate until Helen rescues them; there, it was the Egyptian King Theoclymenus who contrived the sacrifice.[12] Ovid relates another, less familiar myth: that of the Cyprian Κεράσται (those with horns), who sacrificed all foreigners to "Jupiter Hospes," that is, "Zeus Xenios" (*Met.* 10.219–37). (In reality, behind the Κεράσται we

---

[10] This is made clear at Hyg. *Fab.* 22, according to which the oracle said that Aeëtes would be in power as long as the fleece was kept in the sanctuary of Mars (*regnum habiturum quamdiu ea pellis ... in fano Martis esset*). Hyginus' source is unknown; Rose 1958:25 hides behind "*satis antiqua.*"

[11] Friedrich 1966.

[12] Eur. *Hel.* 154ff.; for the Euripidean invention, see Kannicht 1969:1.50ff.

can glimpse archaic, uncanny Cypriote rites that used steer ᵢ.
scarcely human sacrifice.)[13] The myth of Taurian Iphigenia is un̄
stood by Euripides to be the *aition* for a strange rite performed in the
sanctuary of Artemis Tauropolos in the Attic deme of Halai Araphenides
(although any real historical link to a Taurian cult is quite impossible):[14]
a young man's neck was scratched, or rather cut, with a knife until his
blood ran. Later myths about ξενοκτονία appear to have lacked cultic associations; they seem to have been merely later narrations based
on earlier models. The motif, particularly as found in Medea's myth,
perhaps was adopted from Euripides' *Helen* and *Iphigenia* and then
expanded.

All of the stories that involve ξενοκτονία can be understood as pro-
jections of an intrinsically Greek problem, as mythic considerations of
ξενία (hospitality), a value central to Greek society. The stories assert
that at the edges of the world, among those peoples who were radically
different from the Greeks, this central value was not honored. Once
we appreciate this point, the relative age of any single narrative that
uses the theme of ξενοκτονία becomes less important. Already in the
Odyssey, the cannibalistic Cyclopes, whose society is absolutely opposite to that of the Greeks who visit them, exemplify the same issue.
Whether the real Colchians or Taurians were radically different from
the Greeks was not all that important to the authors who made use
of the motif: we recall that Herodotus similarly developed the concept of "otherness" for the Egyptians (see especially 2.35–37).[15] The use
of the ξενοκτονία-motif in connection with Cyprus and the Κεράσται
remains somewhat puzzling; perhaps the answer lies in the fact that
we find it associated with Amathontian Aphrodite, who, as an oriental
goddess, displayed other characteristics of marginality and foreignness
as well.[16]

Except in Apollonius' work, the theme of the Colchians as foreigners
was retained in early versions of the story. Indeed it was sharpened:
the Colchians stood side by side with the Egyptians, the Taurians, and
the Cyclopes of other stories. Even Apollonius did not suppress the
foreign character of the Colchians completely; rather, he restricted it to

---

[13] Graf 1985:415ff.

[14] Graf 1979b; Hughes 1991:89ff.

[15] Cf. Hartog 1980.

[16] See, e.g., the remarks on Adonis' grave at Paus. 9.41.2; on Aphrodite's grave (!)
at Clemens Romanus *Hom.* 5.23 (i.e., Ariadne's grave, which also is referred to in Plut.
Thes. 20); strange sacrifices to Aphrodite are described at Hesychius, s.v. "χάρπωσις."

a few details. Some of these are ethnographically precise:[17] when they had landed, for example, the Argonauts came upon corpses wrapped in animal skins and hanging from trees (3.200–206), a well-attested north Eurasian funerary practice.[18] Other details in Apollonius' work drew on familiar mythical topoi: in Aeëtes' palace, the Greeks found springs of milk, wine, and oil, which other myths had associated with the Isles of the Blessed (3.222ff.).[19] Otherwise, however, and especially in the actions, thoughts, and feelings of the protagonists, Apollonius chose not to emphasize Colchis' foreignness. What mattered to him before all else were the impulses within Medea's soul—and they, of course, could not be allowed to seem exotic. The historians Dionysius and Diodorus stand in contrast to both Apollonius and the earlier authors: their concern was to make history out of myth: that is, to relate the tale in the most realistic and historical form they possibly could.[20]

The Fifth Century: Herodotus, Euripides, and Pindar

The only complete pre-Hellenistic version of the Argonautica that we possess is found in Pindar's fourth Pythian ode, composed to celebrate Arcesilas of Cyrene's victory in the chariot race of 462.[21] Jason's Colchian deeds are narrated concisely (lines 211–50). In a quick voyage, with only one stop midway, he sailed the Argo to Colchis and to a fight with Aeëtes and the dark-skinned Colchians (κελαινώπεσσι Κόλχοισιν, 212). Aphrodite teaches Jason how to use the *iynx*, a love charm with which he can take away Medea's respect for her parents (Μηδείας τοκέων ἀφέλοιτ' αἰδῶ, 218),[22] and, thus enchanted, the "foreign woman who knows all healing arts" (παμφάρμακος ξεῖνα, 233) procures for him protection against the fire-breathing bulls. His success at plowing

---

[17] Though we cannot of course establish whether they would be correct for the inhabitants of ancient Colchis—but this does not matter anyway.

[18] The ethnographical information is found in the schol. to 3.302, following "Nymphodorus of Amphipolis." Modern references are collected in Meuli 1975, esp. 1088–91, 1103–5.

[19] Cf. Graf 1980.

[20] The method is spelled out by Plutarch in the introduction to his *Life of Theseus;* see Graf 1993:124ff.

[21] In the past decade, two lengthy discussions of the ode have appeared: Segal 1986 and Braswell 1988 (on pp. 6–23, Braswell gives an account of the story of the Argonauts as it existed before Pindar).

[22] This passage, which gives an etiological myth for erotic magic, has lately attracted considerable scholarly interest, see Graf 1994:110ff. and the bibliography 282 n. 16. See also Johnston 1995b and O'Higgins in this volume.

MEDEA, THE ENCHANTRESS FROM AFAR 29

allows him access to the fleece, but he is surprised to find it guarded by the snake that is "as long and wide as a fifty-oared ship" (ὃς πάχει μάκει τε πεντηκόντερον ναῦν κράτει, 245), about which Aeëtes prudently had remained silent. Jason kills the snake by means of certain skills (τέχναις). One would love to know more about these skills—extant information offers only two traditions. According to Apollonius, Medea provided Jason with a sleeping potion, which he administered to the snake before killing it. A vase painting suggests an alternative version in which the snake first swallowed Jason, and then Jason somehow freed himself again.[23] I would guess that Pindar considered Jason's interaction with the snake—in whatever version he knew it—to be less than heroic, and therefore inappropriate to epinician poetry. Thus, the poet passed over it quickly.

Having killed the snake, Jason successfully abducts the fleece—and also Medea—"with her consent" (κλέψεν τε Μήδειαν σὺν αὐτᾶι, 250). With this phrase, Pindar built tension into the character of Medea by refusing to give a simple answer to an important question: does Medea herself make the decision to flee with Jason or is she influenced by Aphrodite? (Note, incidentally, that here it is not the *arrow* of a Hellenistic Eros that affects Medea but rather Aphrodite's *iynx*—an ironic situation: the παμφάρμακος ξείνα, the woman with knowledge of magical plants, is not safe from divine love magic.) This ambivalence of motivation is exploited by Euripides in his *Medea* in the first great dialogue between the two quarreling spouses (475–544). There, Medea argues that her help was freely given in order to emphasize Jason's obligations to her. Jason, however, cites the intervention of Cypris, whose power overcame Medea. What in the mythic tradition was ambivalence in drama became two personal readings of the past.

Euripides' drama paints the rest of the Colchian story with only the broadest of strokes. Medea refers briefly to the help that she provided in yoking the bulls and battling the warriors born from the dragon's teeth (476–79); she says that she killed the snake herself (480–82). Throughout this passage, she gives a favorable cast to the story by avoiding any mention of drugs, φάρμακα. Not that Euripides has completely repressed her knowledge of such things, as Bernard Knox tried to maintain:[24] Creon exiles her because she is σοφὴ ... καὶ κακῶν

---

[23] The pictorial evidence (three Greek vases and three Etruscan images) is collected in *LIMC* 5 (1990) 62 nos. 30–35.

[24] Knox 1977. Knox overstates his case in reacting to the interpretation of Medea as a sorceress, made known especially by Page 1938.

πολλῶν ἴδρις (clever ... and knowledgeable in many evil things, 285), which must refer to her magical arts, and she herself boasts that with her knowledge of φάρμακα she will be able, among other things, to help Aegeus overcome his childlessness.[25] Nonetheless, in Euripides' play Medea is in no way the witch that Ovid and Seneca later make her out to be.

The Archaic Period

In the lyric and epic treatments of Medea's story that preceded Pindar, the fluctuating stories of Jason's encounter with Medea are only found in fragmentary forms. The significance of the Argonautica within the epic repertoire is suggested by a phrase at Odyssey 12.70: "The Argo, which is of interest to everyone," Ἀργὼ πᾶσι μέλουσα; Karl Meuli demonstrated how individual apologues of the Odyssey were inspired by tales of the Argonautica.[26] It is scarcely proper, however, to think of that much-cited, imaginary "old Argonautica" as a model, if one seeks a defined narration of the theme; during the oral phase of Greek epic narration, from which the Odyssey emerged, it was the revision of the formulaic theme of the Argonautica—indeed, the myth itself—that was of interest to poets and their audiences. The fact that we have received no epic version of the Argonautica from the archaic period proves how much less authoritative the *individual versions* of the myth must have been than the *myth itself,* and how free in its details the tradition was. The important thing for us to do, therefore, is to note what remains constant in the archaic tradition and, more particularly, what varies.

One of the constants appears to have been the role of Aphrodite; it was always the goddess of love who obtained Medea's help on Jason's behalf. The pseudo-Hesiodic end of the *Theogony,* which belongs in the sixth rather than in the seventh century, portrays Medea as fleeing with Jason and marrying him.[27] On the late archaic Cypselus-chest, the two were shown being married in the presence of Aphrodite;[28] and in the

---

[25] Eur. *Med.* 718. Cf. 385 (she will take revenge by means of her σοφία [wisdom] and her φάρμακα [drugs]); 789 (she prepares the presents); 806 (her gifts will cause death); 1126 (the effect of the presents); 1201 (the effect of the presents). See McDermott 1989, esp. chap. 3.

[26] Meuli 1921 and again in Meuli 1975:593–676.

[27] Hes. *Th.* 992–1002; the date derives from the fact that their son, Medeus, the ancestor of the Medoi, cannot be earlier than the sixth century B.C.; see West 1966 *ad loc.*

[28] Paus. 5.18.3. For the date of the chest, see (with earlier bibliography) Shapiro 1993:22ff.

anonymous, also late archaic *Carmen Naupacticum,* Jason laid an ambush for the maiden while Aphrodite diverted her parents (fr. 7 Davies = 4.7.9 Kinkel). Herodotus also knew of this abduction (7.62); it is possible that Pindar's mention of Medea's consent is an attempt to change this story. Certainly an analogous situation exists for Paris and Helen: we possess both versions in which Helen went freely and versions in which she did not. But let us not forget, in any case, that the deciding factor in archaic society was not the consent of the maiden but rather the consent of her father.

The other constant in archaic lyric and epic versions of the story is Medea's power as a φαρμακεύτρια (expert in drugs). This is already revealed by her genealogy: as early as the *Theogony,* Medea is called the niece of Circe and the daughter of Idyia ("the Knowledgeable One"),[29] a name that well fits a woman who has magical powers (and a name that perhaps rings out in Creon's description of Medea as κακῶν πολλῶν ἴδρις, "knowing many evils"). The Hesiodic genealogy, which makes Medea the granddaughter of Helios through Aeëtes, remains canonical. It is Diodorus (probably after Dionysius Scytobrachion) who first makes her the sister of Circe and the daughter of Hecate: this further underlines her connection with magic and ghosts at a time when Medea has gone from being a simple παμφάρμακος ξείνα to a powerful witch (4.45, cf. Hes. *Th.* 956–62).

Hesiod emphasizes Medea's powers in a different way: he explicitly describes her as a goddess.[30] Her relationship with Jason, from which their son Medeus was born, is included in the catalog of relationships between goddesses and mortal men that produced mortal children; there, she stands side by side with Demeter, Harmonia, Eos, the Oceanids, the Nereids, Aphrodite, and, finally, Circe and Calypso. The canonical genealogy of Medea, according to which her grandfather was none other than Helios, always awards her this status at least implicitly, even if later authors would prefer to forget it by transforming Medea into a (near-)mortal woman or into a very young, somewhat shy virgin.[31]

Finally, the tradition of an oracle that warned Aeëtes of Jason is also very old. When Apollonius, in contrast, mentions only a vague warning about Medea, which promptly is misunderstood by Aeëtes, he is transferring to Medea what traditionally had been associated with

---

[29] See Wilamowitz 1924:2.234 ("die Wissende also die Zauberkundige").
[30] See Krevans' essay in this volume.
[31] Moreau 1994:191–94 insists much too much on Medea the (divine) sorceress.

Jason. This is typical of Apollonius' narrative, which, as a whole, centers upon Medea.

The details that remain constant stand in contrast to a fundamental change made in the story during the archaic period. According to Pindar, the goal of Jason's journey was Phasis, a Milesian colony of perhaps the late sixth century. This localizing of the land of the Colchians in the southeastern corner of the Black Sea cannot be very old;[32] one and a half centuries before, Mimnermus of Colophon had described Aia, the goal of Jason's journey, thus: "the city of Aeëtes, where swift Helios shines in golden strength, lies at the edge of the Ocean" (Mimnermus fr. 11 West). Aeëtes is the man from Aia and the son of Helios. As Albin Lesky showed, although Helios' dwelling place logically could be at either one of two points where the Sun meets the Ocean, it is always assumed to be at the eastern point, the point from which Helios began his journey day after day.[33] In short, the place to which Jason sails initially was imagined to exist at the eastern limit of human geography. The archaic age was, in general, a time when epic was becoming Panhellenic and systematized, when every myth became situated in the human geography of the Greek world, and when, moreover, the mythic places that had been exiled from the real world became localized at the border of ever more distant geographical horizons. Certainly, at the time of the *Odyssey*'s composition, this process had scarcely begun; by the time of Pindar, however, it was nearly completed. The black complexions of the Colchians that Pindar mentions commemorate their old geographical location, for it is the peoples of the far East and the far West who usually are thought of as black, as "burned" by the Sun as he rises or sinks. Pindar retains this idea, despite the fact that the fair skins of the Scythian and the Georgian races prove it false.[34]

We have traced Medea's story back, at last, to a time when Jason journeyed to the eastern rim of the world in order to obtain the fleece and was aided by Aphrodite in that endeavor: she made the daughter of the Sun-god fall in love with him, and that daughter, in turn, aided Jason by means of magical herbs that enabled him to overcome all dangers. Together, Jason and the Sun-god's daughter traveled back to his homeland, the homeland of heroes.

The idea that such a folktale lies at the core of the Argonautica is not new; Ludwig Radermacher long ago suggested that a "Journey to

[32] See Boardman 1980:252.
[33] Lesky 1948.
[34] Two Ethiopias are mentioned already by Homer at *Od.* 1.23.

the Land of the Sun" folktale was the basis of an imagined *Iasonis*.[35] In the neoanalytical reaction of Meuli, in contrast, the Argonautic tales were connected with the folktale type usually called the "hero's helpers–type," in which a hero sets out to perform a difficult task in the company of a group of friendly animals.[36] Nowadays, few would maintain that myth and epic developed from folktales: it is a theory based on the wrong but romantic conception of the originality of popular narrative, and the differentiation between myth and folktale has become only a matter of terminology, not of evolution.[37] What is more important is to note that Jason's quest for the fleece actually aligns with a widely dispersed narrative type that has been analyzed well by Vladimir Propp, the "Quest-type."[38] Medea's later biography, however, has no place in this folktale type. The questions, then, are how did this later biography arise, and from where did it obtain its coherency?

Medea's Mythic Biography

Let us begin with an overview of the other episodes in Medea's life.

Iolcus

When, in the high archaic version of the tale, Jason's journey leaves the realm of real geography, the point from which he departs becomes central to the story. The story of Medea belongs not to Colchis, in other words, but to Iolcus, the city from which Jason sets out and to which he returns with Medea. In Iolcus, the second episode of Medea's mythic biography is played out: to their ruin, she teaches the daughters of Pelias fruitless rejuvenation techniques that result in their father's death. Τὰν Πελίαο φονόν, "murderer of Pelias," is what Pindar calls Medea (*Pyth.* 4.250).

This ritual of rejuvenation takes virtually the same form in all versions: Medea chops up a ram and cooks him in a big pot, after having added the correct herbs to the water. Sophocles, in his *Rhizotomoi*, describes Medea as gathering herbs,[39] and many vase paintings, dating

---

[35] Radermacher 1943. See also Moreau 1994:253–57.

[36] Meuli 1921:1–24 = Meuli 1975:593–610.

[37] Graf 1993:6ff.

[38] Propp 1968; see Moreau 257 1994:257–66, who analyzes the myth along the themes of Propp. See also the developments in Burkert 1979, esp. 14–18.

[39] Macrobius *Sat.* 5.19.9: *in qua Medeam describit maleficas herbas secantem* ([the play] in which Sophocles describes Medea cutting maleficent herbs) = Soph. fr. 492 Radt.

from the late sixth century onward, portray the decisive scene: lively and young, the ram springs from the kettle, to the astonishment of the Peliades, who are standing near by.[40] The Peliades then try to do the same thing for their father, but because Medea has withheld the correct herbs, they fail. The hypothesis of Euripides' *Medea* gives a list of those she rejuvenated successfully: Aeson, Jason's elderly father (this is mentioned already in the *Nostoi* and so is a story dating to the high archaic period; see fr. 6 Kinkel/Davies); Dionysus' nurses and their husbands (perhaps an invention of Aeschylus for his satyr play, *The Nurses of Dionysus*); and finally, Jason himself (so says Simonides in the late sixth century and Pherecydes in the late fifth century: Simon. fr. 548 *PMG*; Pherec. *FGrHist* 3 F 113a). Jason's inclusion in this list surprises us—after all, he is a young man when he journeys to Colchis and scarcely would need rejuvenation upon return to Iolcus.[41]

Corinth

After killing Pelias in vengeance, Medea flees to Corinth with Jason. The tradition that binds her to this city is well attested—thanks, not least, to Euripides' *Medea*. Already in antiquity, the scholia debated about what Euripides' innovations to the Corinthian story were; modern scholars have followed suit.[42]

Medea's connection to Corinth is attested as early as the *Corinthiaca* of the Corinthian poet Eumelus. This was an epic made up of local stories, composed perhaps in the seventh century; the relevant portions are set forth by Pausanias in a prose version (2.3.10–11 = *Corinthiaca* fr. 3a Davies); one must, therefore, contend with the possibility that Pausanias modernized the original tale. According to the story, Aeëtes, the son of Helios, was the king of Ephyra, the old name for Corinth. For some unspecified reason, Aeëtes left Corinth for Colchis, appointing a deputy to rule in his place. After four generations of such deputies, the Corinthians called Medea home from Iolcus, where she was dwelling with Jason, and asked her to rule her ancestral kingdom. By accepting their offer, she made Jason king of Corinth. Eumelus must have been trying to combine two king-lists, which were not completely compatible: between Aeëtes and Medea—father and daughter—he had to insert

---

[40] Meyer 1980 and Vojatzi 1982:94–100; Halm-Tisserant 1993:38–43.

[41] But corrections of the text are excluded by the iconography, Neils 1990:637; see also Sourvinou-Inwood in this volume.

[42] Moreau 1994:101–13 and Johnston in this volume.

four generations of deputies.[43] He then attached the whole myth of the *Argonautica* to this Corinthian story: it was because of the *Argonautica* that Medea was in Iolcus; it was also because of the *Argonautica*, during the course of which Jason met Medea, that Jason eventually became the king of Corinth. The story takes a bad turn: every time that Medea had a child, she hid it (καταχρύπτειν) in the temenos of Hera, in order to make it immortal; all of these children died, however. Jason became angry over this and returned to Iolcus; Medea, too, left Corinth and her throne.

A little light is shed on Medea's puzzling relationship with her children by a story found in the scholia to Pindar (ad *Ol.* 13.74), according to which Zeus fell in love with Medea in Corinth but was refused by her. Grateful for this, Hera promised to make Medea's children immortal, if she brought them into Hera's sanctuary. Medea did as Hera directed, but the children died and Medea had to flee from Corinth.[44]

There are other versions of this story. They differ in details (e.g., sometimes there are two children, sometimes there are two times seven children), but all of them insist that the children died and that Medea was innocent of the deaths. Moreover, all of the versions are etiological in character: they are intended to explain why the Corinthians annually send seven boys and seven girls from noble families into the sanctuary of Hera Akraia to serve the goddess and why, at the same time, the Corinthians offer sacrifices to the children of Medea during a major civic festival. The institution of this festival is predicted by Euripides' *Medea* before she leaves the city, goddesslike, in her dragon chariot.[45] Later scholiasts give the details.[46]

The Corinthian Medea had little to do with the Medea whom epic located in Colchis and Iolcus. Herbal magic was not her concern—and far less magic of any other kind. Just the opposite: whereas the Medea we meet in Iolcus could rejuvenate Aeson, the Corinthian Medea failed to immortalize her own children. The Corinthian story reminds us of those of Thetis, who wanted to immortalize the young Achilles, and

---

[43] I do not think that Eumelus presented Medea and her father as being divine and thus beyond human genealogies; rather, they seem to have been presented as a heroic king and queen among other heroic figures. Medea's failure to have her children immortalized, discussed below, would seem to support this.

[44] This could be another instance of Hera's usual mythic malevolence or could have more specific reasons, as Johnston persuasively argues in this volume.

[45] 1378–83; see now Worthington 1990.

[46] Collected and discussed by Nilsson 1906:57–61 and esp. Brelich 1959:213–54 (whose findings are accepted by Hughes 1991:181) and Johnston in this volume.

of Demeter, who wanted to immortalize the son of the king of Eleusis; both attempts failed because of the interference of the mortal parents (Peleus and the Eleusinian queen). Medea, in contrast, was unable to perform such a miraculous rite for herself. This Medea was no goddess; indeed, she required the assistance of one, who, in the end, failed her for reasons unknown to us.[47]

Athens

Euripides allows Medea to flee to King Aegeus of Athens. Later we learn more from a detailed account given by Plutarch in his *Life of Theseus* (12.3–7). When the young Theseus arrived in Athens from Troizen, Medea recognized him for what he was and convinced Aegeus that he should poison the dangerous stranger. Aegeus' anxiety concerning the arriving stranger was narrated already by Bacchylides (fr. 18 Campbell). Theseus was received and entertained in the Delphinion, but before he could drink the beaker of poison that Medea had arranged, Aegeus recognized his son and knocked the beaker from Theseus' hand. Medea, the author of the attempted murder, fled. A sacred enclosure in the Delphinion commemorated, as late as Plutarch's day, the spot where the poison had been spilled.

Scholars have long agreed that this story draws upon a lost tragedy; its similarity to the plot of Euripides' *Ion* is obvious, and there is not much doubt that Euripides told the story of Theseus and Medea themselves in his lost *Aegeus*, probably before production of his *Medea* in 431.[48] What is still contested, however, is whether the story of Medea's attack on Theseus first was invented by Euripides. It may be older, for Herodotus tells us at 7.62 that Medea fled out of Athens to the land of the Medes and gave her name to them. Herodotus' story is too vague to allow us to assume that Euripides' version was derived from it. Moreover, for Euripides, Medus, the son of Medea and Aegeus, must have been important, for he would have provided Medea's motive for killing Theseus, Aegeus' firstborn son. Later, this Medus, and not his mother, becomes the eponym of the Medes (Strabo 11.526). In any case, whatever we make of Herodotus' comments, we cannot take the Athenian story much further back than to the *Theseis*

---

[47] *Pace* Radermacher 1943.

[48] At least according to the *communis opinio*, which goes back to Wilamowitz 1880; see Lesky 1972:305. Knox 1977:316 n. 5 argued against it (but cf. Page 1938:xxix). At any rate, the resolution of this issue does not much matter to my argument.

of the late sixth century, whose existence has been conjectured on other grounds.[49]

In this tale Medea once more has assumed new roles—she is the fairy-tale stepmother and the poisoner without moral scruples. Here, she did not need any knowledge of specific drugs, as she did in Colchis, where she covered Jason with drugs to protect him against fire and used drugs to send the snake to sleep, or as she did in Iolcus, where she created the drug mixture necessary for rejuvenation. Her plot against Theseus required only a gardener's knowledge of poisonous plants, like that which Creusa has in the *Ion*. We lack the text of Euripides' *Aegeus*, of course; it is difficult, however, to see how the Medea that he probably presented there could have developed into the looming, fascinating figure of danger that she is in his *Medea*.

Afterward: Medea and the Medes

The connection between Medea and the Medes is found in surprisingly early sources. The pseudo-Hesiodic ending of the *Theogony* says that Medea had a son named Medeus, who was the eponymous hero of the Medes (*Th.* 1001). Later, this son was called Medus and Aegeus became his father. Martin West has explained that this myth need not be older than the change from Μᾶδοι to Μῆδοι in Ionic-Attic.[50] Historical arguments place the etiology nearer to the sixth century. The pseudo-Hesiodic source is as lacking in details as Herodotus is. In the classical period, however, the theme must have been treated in a tragedy, as Hyginus' résumé says. In that tragedy, Medea appeared as a supposed priestess of Artemis and an unscrupulous foreigner, who tried to deceive the king of the Medes but who, in the end, was thwarted.

The Unity of the Narrative

Narrativity as a Common Denominator

Our survey of the individual episodes within Medea's life, although brief, has shown how disparate they are. At the core of the biography lies Medea's help to Jason in Aia; all the other episodes appear to

---

[49] It is difficult to decide whether the vases collected by Sourvinou-Inwood 1979, which are dated to the early fifth century, already presuppose our myth. As to the *Theseis*, see the discussion in Calame 1990.

[50] See M. West 1966:430.

be chance additions, accrued during centuries of storytelling. Many scholars have suspected that our composite story originated from the conflation of two homonyms—a Thessalian and a Corinthian Medea.[51] This is a solution born of despair, however, especially as "Medea" is a name that is very specific and one not easily etymologized. The motivation for connecting Medea to the Medes is self-evident: the Greek way of looking at the world demanded that the Medes have an eponymous hero, and that this eponymous hero, in turn, have a genealogy. Because of her name, Medea was an obvious candidate for the role; for the Greeks, the fact that she was a barbarian and came from roughly the same part of the world as the Medes would have clinched the idea.[52]

So, wherein lies the unifying theme that ties together all of our stories about Medea?

Let us begin by excluding some possibilities. First, the character of Medea itself could have in no way sufficed to unify such disparate episodes. Our brief overview of the development of the Colchian story already has demonstrated how widely her character varied with individual authors' narrative intentions. Our overview of the individual local narratives only made this point clearer. Even within the corpus of Athenian tragedy—a body of literature born within a relatively short time span—we find no unity. There seems to be no way to leap from the herb-gathering witch of Sophocles' *Rhizotomoi* (fr. 492 Radt) to the heroine of Euripides' *Medea*, who is deeply concerned with her personal honor. Even within an author we find little unity: the heroine of Euripides' *Aegeus* seems to have born little resemblence to that of his *Medea*. Our attempts to compare the stories in a vertical line also fail: within the Colchian tale we move from a narrative of the Quest-type to that of the Tarpeia-type; local traditions, again, are quite different from one another.

There are, nonetheless, some unifying elements. To begin with, the basic theme of Medea's *persona* remains constant: she is a foreigner, who lives outside of the known world or comes to a city from outside; each time she enters a city where she dwells, she comes from a distant place, and when she leaves that city, she again goes to a distant place. This sense of Medea's "foreignness" is expressed and articulated differently by each author who portrays her, but it is always there. Characteristic of this element is the goddess with whom she is

---

[51] See Lesky 1931:48–50.
[52] Note that at Hyg. *Fab.* 50, Perses and Aeëtes are called brothers.

connected: in Euripides she calls on (besides her ancestor Helios and Themis as the protector of rights) the goddess Artemis (line 160) and the goddess Hecate. Hecate, indeed, is called her personal goddess, "the mistress whom I worship above all others and name as my helper" (τὴν δέσποιναν ἣν ἐγώ / σέβω μάλιστα πάντων καὶ ξυνεργὸν εἱλόμην, 395ff.). Perhaps—although I doubt it—Hecate is already a goddess of magic by the time of Euripides; but in any case, she is certainly a strange, Carian, and non-Olympian goddess for the Greeks.[53] Medea is Hecate's priestess in Apollonius (3.251ff.), she is even her daughter in Dionysius Scytobrachion (Diod. Sic. 4.45.3). Although this idea undoubtedly was adopted from the myth of Taurian Iphigenia, it is not without significance, as further examples make clear: according to two myths handed down by Hyginus, it is as the priestess of Diana (i.e., Artemis), that Medea presents herself to the Peliades and to Perses, the ancestor of the Persians (Hyg. *Fab.* 24, 27).[54] For Hellenistic authors Medea had affinities not only to Hecate, the goddess of crossroads and ghosts, but also to Artemis, an only slightly less threatening goddess of the wild outdoors.

Medea and Ritual

There is a second unifying element, which brings us back to Medea's connections with cult and ritual. In Athens, and even more so in Corinth, the myth of Medea's residence in the city had etiological importance: in the Athenian Delphinion her name was connected with a monument that commemorated her failed attempt to murder Theseus. In Corinth, she was connected to the annual ritual involving seven boys and seven girls. Both *aitia* are grounded in the same idea: Henri Jeanmaire argued over fifty years ago that the Corinthian ritual could be explained as an initiation ritual,[55] and the same can be argued for the Athenian ritual at the Delphinion and its accompanying myth.[56] It is Medea's nearly successful attempt to kill Theseus in the Delphinion that enables Aegeus to recognize him, and thus, in the long run, it is Medea who brings about his initiation into the role of crown prince. The Medea who "hides" (ἀποκρύπτει) her children in the sanctuary of

[53] Kraus 1960; Graf 1985:257ff., 42 n. 112 (she receives sacrifices of sacrificial dogs, which marks her as marginal); Johnston 1990:chap. 2.

[54] In Athens, on the contrary, she had provoked the anger of the priestess of Artemis: Hyg. *Fab.* 26.

[55] Jeanmaire 1939:300; see also Brelich 1959.

[56] Graf 1979a.

Hera Akraia, and so provides the model for the annual dedication of Corinthian children, is an initiator too: the ritual follows the pattern of rites developed from an initiatory background, like the ones of the Athenian Arrhephoroi, the Brauronian "bears,"[57] or the Locrian Maidens,[58] and the term ἀποκρύπτειν recalls the κρυπτεία, a term at home in the context of the initiation of Spartan youths. When Sarah Iles Johnston in her admirable essay (in this volume) understands the ritual as a rite to appease Hera's wrath, which would have been dangerous to small children, this seems indeed to be the meaning the Corinthians gave it—but this reading does not explain the ritual form of confining a group of black-clad children for a certain period inside a sacred precinct, details that all find an explanation in the initiatory pattern, as explained by Jeanmaire and Brelich. As in many an instance, actual Greek ritual, though formally belonging to the archaic initiatory pattern, developed new functions; in the indigenous explanations of Brauron or Locri, or even in Sparta with the Orthia ritual, every one of these rites is understood as intended to avert the wrath of a powerful and potentially dangerous goddess.

Incidentally, these initiatory roles that Medea plays at Corinth and Athens would be appropriate as well to Artemis, who is the goddess who protects youths in countless rites that have initiatory backgrounds. The connection between Artemis and Medea, after all, may be grounded in common ritual functions.

Medea's role in the Argonautica undoubtedly can be explained similarly: the prince, who goes out in order to prove his worth and so win the kingship, the prince who must come back not only as a future king but with a queen whom he has conquered, must undergo a change of status similar to that which adolescents undergo in initiation rituals. Angelo Brelich has shown that the story that precedes Jason's travels on the Argo—the story of Jason *monosandalos*—also has an initiatory background; Vladimir Propp has tied the Quest-tale motif to initiation, as well; most recently, Alain Moreau reassembled the arguments for an initiatory background to Jason and the Argonauts; and Charles Segal has shown how significant the initiation motif already was in Pindar's fourth Pythian.[59] In all of these narrations, Medea can be understood as initiatrix; such a role, moreover, would align well with her divine

---

[57] Brulé 1987:179–262.

[58] Graf 1978; cf. Hughes 1991:166–84.

[59] Brelich 1955–57; Propp 1946; Moreau 1994:117–38; Segal 1986:chap. 3 (see also Braswell 1988:ad *Pyth.* 4.83–85).

character.[60] But in our extant narrations (as opposed to possible earlier narrations) she neither is a goddess nor performs initiations; rather, she seems to be a human albeit powerful helper. Once her myths had been inserted into the polytheistic system, Panhellenic cult goddesses (namely Hera and Aphrodite) took over her former initiatory roles. In the Corinthian ritual it was Hera who guarded the young girls and boys who were about to enter into the *polis* (just as she did in Tiryns for girls and in Argos for boys).[61] Aphrodite was at home in many initiatory rituals and myths, for certainly the experience of sexuality was an integral part of the entry into adulthood.[62] Medea, who existed not in cult but rather in myth, became subordinated to the cult goddesses; in the last analysis, "Medea as initiatrix" was no more than a persona who may have belonged to the prehistory of our extant myths, if anything.

The same thing happened to a myth which is analogous to that of Medea and Jason: the myth of Ariadne and Theseus. Theseus' journey to Crete has the same initiatory background as Jason's. Ariadne, who like Medea was probably a goddess before she became a heroine, was, like Medea, replaced by Aphrodite, whose image Ariadne carried out of Crete and set up on Delos in thanks for her help. In Cypriot Amathus, there was a cult of "Ariadne Aphrodite" (Plut. *Thes.* 20 = Paion of Amathus, *FGrHist* 757 F 2).

We still must consider the ritual of rejuvenation that took place in Iolcus. Here, associations must remain tentative. Rejuvenation, obviously, means a change of status: from an old man one becomes a man, if not, indeed, a child or an adolescent. Such changes would have been particularly significant in ancient society. The ritual that Medea used to accomplish these changes is also significant: she cut up and cooked human meat in a great kettle. These are elements found in other myths and rituals connected with initiation, such as the Arcadian ritual of the *Männerbünde* on Mount Lycaeus, and the myth of Pelops, who was cut up, cooked, and finally revived. In the far distance stand shamanistic rites of initiatory character that also involve the cutting of flesh.[63] It is tempting to see the same background in the story of Jason's

---

[60] I would, however, resist Moreau 1994:112, who characterizes early Medea as "une déesse-mère, proche de Cybèle, Rhéa ou Gaia, … déesse chthonienne et agraire"; this presupposes a much too uniform function of a (prehistoric) Great Goddess—though the development he then describes agrees with my view.

[61] See Burkert 1983:162–68 (Argos), 168–71 (Tiryns); Dowden 1989:117–45.

[62] Pirenne-Delforge 1994:520, s.v. "initiation."

[63] Uhsadel-Gülke 1972.

rejuvenation—that is, in the initiation of King Jason by Medea—but this idea must remain tentative.

Myth and Ritual: The Connection

Thus, Medea appears to be connected with a whole line of narratives that clearly are associated with initiation rites. At this point, however, the issue becomes trickier than has been previously recognized: the myth cannot have come simply from the ritual, Medea cannot be simply an initiatrix, and her myth cannot simply have originated in initiation rituals.

On the one hand, the rites are generally analogous to one another, but differ in specifics. So far as Jason is concerned, we are dealing with the changing of a prince into a king, as in the case of Theseus; in Corinth we are dealing with the maturation of παῖδες and παρθένοι (young boys and girls). Although we cannot simply equate them or try to construct a historical connection, the initiation of young people and that of the king may belong together structurally.

On the other hand, we encounter a surprising paradox. In Corinth and Athens, Medea already was associated by ancient authors with rituals, but not in Colchis and Iolcus. This fact is perplexing, because, if our previous analysis is correct, the myth of Jason's travels and Medea's help were truly at home in Iolcus, whereas the connection between myth and ritual, as shown, was late and secondary in both Corinth and Athens. In Athens the connection seems first to have been made between the time of the epic *Theseis* and Euripides' *Aegeus* (therefore between 525 and 430); in Corinth the myth first is found in Eumelus (and may well have been his own invention) and thus cannot be traced back any further than perhaps the eighth century. The situation is tangled: where the etiology is clearly young and secondary (in the Corinthian and Attic rituals), we can find a rite to connect it to; in Iolcus, where the myth really began, in contrast, there seems to have been no ritual to which the myth could have been connected.

The paradox can be resolved by a moment's further thought, however. The resolution lies in the fact that the narratives of Jason's journey to the court of Aeëtes, as well as the connected story of Medea's revenge against Pelias—as we know them—long ago moved away from any possible ritual context in order to become the stuff of Panhellenic epic. Indeed, as early as the *Odyssey*, (12.70) Ἀργὼ πᾶσι μέλουσα (the

Argo that is of interest to all) refuses to be tied to any locale; there is no ground for the hypothesis that during the archaic period, the story of the Argonautica was told strictly in connection with a ritual performed in Iolcus.

This conclusion leads to further thoughts about the relationship between myth and ritual. If Medea can be plucked out of Panhellenic myth and used in ritual etiologies—rituals to which she might have had some original affinity, but from which, in general, she had distanced herself long ago—then this can only mean one thing: the mythmakers of the Greek archaic and classical periods were able to see (or rather sense) such affinities and to make them useful in new etiological narratives. When a pure story without any previous connection to a ritual lay before them, the general structure of the tale could suffice to hint at a ritual. We, who belong to another, later culture, a culture far more distant from the world of myths, have lost this capability; we can recapture it only through laborious (and controversial) analyses.

2

CORINTHIAN MEDEA AND THE CULT

OF HERA AKRAIA

Sarah Iles Johnston

Colchida respersam puerorum sanguine culpant
(Ovid *Amores* 2.14.29)

O F ALL THE IMAGES of Medea, the one that has most fascinated authors and artists throughout the centuries is that of
the murderous mother. This fascination owes much to the
fact that a mother's deliberate slaughter of her children undermines
one of the basic assumptions upon which society—indeed humanity—
is constructed: mothers nurture their children. Once this assumption breaks down, all others are open to reconsideration—is anything
that we assumed about the world or the human soul really unassail-
able? Of course, anyone who knows the tragedies of Euripides and
Seneca realizes that even the most destructive of mothers can, indeed,
love her children even as she destroys them, but this is of little comfort. The final image of a bloody-handed Medea overwhelms anything that we see or hear earlier in these plays. The children's horrible cries and their pitiful corpses are scarcely mitigated by her soul's
debate.

The Greek of the most important ancient passages that are referred to but not quoted
in the body of the paper can be found in the appendix at the end. All translations,
unless otherwise noted, are my own. All references to Graf and Bremmer, unless otherwise specified, are to their papers in this collection. I am grateful for the comments
of audiences at Cornell University, Indiana University (particularly Matthew Christ and
Timothy Long), and the 1991 APA, who heard earlier versions of the arguments presented here. I also benefited from the advice of James J. Clauss, Fritz Graf, and David
Leitao at later stages of the article's development. Inez Cardozo-Freeman, David Frank-
furter, Lindsay Jones, and Michael Swartz helped me with some of the evidence from
cultures other than the Greek that is discussed in "Hera as Mother" and "The Infanticide
Motif."

For more than a century, scholars have argued about whether this infanticidal Medea was the product of a single, brilliant mind—that of Euripides—or, rather, was a figure whom Euripides inherited and then developed in his own way.[1] Recently, several scholars have re-examined the possibility that Euripides followed the poet Neophron in making Medea an infanticide,[2] but this premise, be it true or false, has little to do with the question that really interests me: can the infanticidal Medea whom we know so well be the product of *any* single mind, however brilliant, or was she, rather, a preexisting mythic construct?

In this essay, I will argue that our information concerning the Corinthian cult of Hera Akraia (with which the mythic figure of Medea was closely connected) supports the idea that fifth-century authors inherited an infanticidal Medea from myth. Specifically, I will suggest that the Medea whom we meet in Euripides' play developed out of a folkloric paradigm that was widespread both in ancient Greece and in other ancient Mediterranean countries—the paradigm of the reproductive demon—and that this paradigm is likely to have been associated with the Corinthian cult of Hera Akraia.

A word about names before we begin. For convenience, I will continue to call the Corinthian heroine I discuss in this essay "Medea," although the question of whether this name belonged originally to the Colchian figure who helped the Argonauts in their exploits, or to the Corinthian figure whose children died, is as far from settled as is the question of how these two quite different figures came to merge into a single individual during the archaic age. (As Graf notes in the preceding essay, the name is very specific; this lessens the probability that we are dealing with two homonyms whose myths were combined by virtue of the name alone.) At the end of this essay I will suggest one reason that the two Medeas may have become identified; for the moment, however, let us concentrate on Medea as she was best known in Corinth.

---

[1] Wilamowitz 1880:486 argued that the portrait of Medea as intentional infanticide was completely Euripides' invention. Among the many subsequent treatments of the question, some of the most recent and/or important are McDermott 1989; Michelini 1989 (see also her review of McDermott's book in *AJP* 112 [1991] 401–3); Manuwald 1983; Knox 1977, esp. 193–94; Thompson 1944:10–14; Séchan 1925:Appendix 6, 1927; Roussel 1920. Dunn 1994, which was not published until the spring of 1995, appeared too late to be taken into account in my analysis.

[2] Michelini 1987, 1989, who does a thorough job of citing earlier scholars' arguments regarding this question.

The Cult of Hera Akraia

Ancient sources call Medea the founder of the cult of Hera Akraia and of its annual festival, the Akraia, which was dedicated both to the goddess and to Medea's dead children.[3] This has led scholars to suggest that Medea was an earlier goddess of the Corinthians whom Hera displaced. Therefore, it is assumed that the original Corinthian Medea shared interests with Hera Akraia.[4] The assumption is reasonable, but really only leads to another series of questions, for to know more about Corinthian Medea, we will need to know more about Hera Akraia and her cult. I will begin with a review of evidence that will establish with which sanctuary the cult and the festival were connected, and then move on to evidence from both the sanctuary itself and from ancient literary sources that will help clarify the cult's concerns. Once these tasks are finished, I will be able to return to Medea's story, which, as we will see, expresses the same concerns that the cult tried to address. This observation, finally, will help us understand better the nature of Corinthian Medea.

Location of the Cult

In the early 1930s, the British School began excavating Perachora, a small site on the tip of the peninsula just across the bay from the city of Corinth. The archaeologists turned up a large sanctuary identified by inscriptions as that of Hera Akraia, which dates back at least to the early eighth century.[5]

Previously, scholars had assumed that the Akraia festival in honor of Hera and of Medea's children was celebrated at some undiscovered temple of Hera Akraia within the city of Corinth itself.[6] This assumption seemed to be supported by Pausanias' statement that there was a μνῆμα (monument) to Medea's children in the Corinthian agora near the

[3] Eur. *Med.* 1378–83, Zenobius 1.27; and see Nilsson 1906:58.

[4] E.g., Nilsson 1906:59, Will 1955:103–118; Farnell 1896–1909:1.401–4.

[5] Two of the most recent discussions of the Perachoran Heraion, which include references to earlier work on questions of date, succession of temples, inscriptions, etc., are Tomlinson 1977:197–202 and Salmon 1972:159–204. I will not review here the question of whether the title "Limenia," found on spits dedicated to Hera at Perachora, indicates that there were two separate cults at Perachora (one to Hera Akraia and one to Hera Limenia). Regarding this issue, I am convinced by the arguments of Tomlinson and Salmon, who understand "Limenia" as a secondary epithet for Hera Akraia and thus consider the Perachoran Heraion to be the site of a single cult—to Hera Akraia.

[6] Notably Nilsson 1906:57–61 and Roussel 1920.

Odeion, which was itself located near the fountain of Glauce—the fountain into which the Corinthian princess was said to have thrown herself when set ablaze by Medea's poisonous robe and crown (Paus. 2.3.6). Scholars further assumed that an εἰκών (statue) to which Pausanias refers at 2.3.7, describing it as a δεῖμα (terror), also was located near the Odeion and the fountain of Glauce. When the Corinthians had asked the gods how to stop the wholesale death of Corinthian infants that had followed their murder of Medea's children, they had been told to set up this statue, as well as to institute a cult to Medea's children.

Following the discovery of the Perachoran temple, Picard argued that the cult connected with Medea's children focused on two separate centers: one in Corinth, at the monument that Picard still assumed to have been located in the agora, and one in Perachora. Picard suggested that it was to the latter site that fourteen Corinthian children annually were sent, to live for a year in the sanctuary of the goddess, as Pausanias had described. The rituals at the monument would have been chthonic in character, Picard hypothesized; the rituals at the Perachoran temple would have been appropriate for an Olympian goddess.[7]

Brelich rightly criticized Picard's arguments as largely *ex silentio*: the single literary source that Picard adduced to support the division of the cult between the city of Corinth and Perachora (Eur. *Med.* 1379–83) must be strained to derive such a conclusion. Will, additionally, opposed Picard's theory by following Scranton's hypothesis[8] that a temple built during the Roman period near the fountain of Glauce in the Corinthian agora (and thus, Will assumed, near the monument of the children that Pausanias mentions) was to be identified as a temple to Hera Akraia.[9] Scranton suggested that an earlier temple to Hera Akraia may have been built on the roof of the rock-cut fountain house, where there are traces of some sort of structure. Because no inscriptions or other evidence have been found that identify either of these buildings, however, and because neither Pausanias nor any other ancient author explicitly mentions a sanctuary of Hera Akraia within Corinth proper, Scranton's theory is just as much an *argumentum ex silentio* as is Picard's theory of two separate cultic centers.[10]

---

[7] Picard 1932:218–29.

[8] Scranton 1941:1.2, 131–65. The temple referred to in the records is designated "Temple C."

[9] Brelich 1959, esp. 217 and n. 4; Will 1955:89 and n. 2.

[10] Scranton 1941 himself admits the weakness of his conjecture at several points (particularly 149, 164). I would add that some of his assumptions concerning the cult and its myth, on which he builds his hypothesis, seem to me unsupportable or even

Given that we have absolutely no indications, archaeological or otherwise, that a temple of Hera Akraia ever existed within the city of Corinth, it is dangerous to build arguments on the assumption that one was there. The Perachoran sanctuary to Hera Akraia had existed since at least the eighth century, was within Corinthian territory, and was "one of the richest minor sanctuaries in Greece."[11] It seems sensible to assume that it is to this temple that Euripides and all the other ancient sources refer when describing the place at which Medea established a cult to Hera and her own children.

This does not contradict the idea that the children's burial place was within Hera's sanctuary, as ancient sources say.[12] For the monument to Medea's children that Pausanias saw near the fountain of Glauce in the agora need not have been understood as a tomb. In Pausanias and elsewhere, μνῆμα can refer to a monument erected in memory of a dead person or people, rather than an actual grave. In three passages in Pausanias, in fact, a μνῆμα explicitly is called κενόν (empty), implying that no body is within.[13]

---

incorrect. For example: (1) He states that "according to most of the stories [about Medea's children] [Glauce] was the cause of a series of tragic incidents from which ultimately grew an elaborate cult" (158). Glauce, however, does not appear until Euripides' version of the story and is not mentioned by Creophylus or Parmeniscus (both *ap.* schol. Eur. *Med.* 264). Thus, Scranton's argument that the cult of Hera Akraia must be near the fountain of Glauce is baseless (see also Will 1955:90–97, who thinks that Glauce's myth was originally separate from that of Medea and Jason). (2) He assumes that any ritual for the children must have included a "mimetic dance, in which would be represented some of the more important incidents in their lives" (160), and from this builds the idea that the cult must have included a representation of Glauce's leap into the fountain, necessitating the cult's location near the fountain. Although mimetic dances certainly were part of some cults, there is no reason to assume that they were part of the cult of Medea's children. See also Williams and Zervos 1984:97–104, who offer some additional arguments against Scranton's theory—most significantly, that no fountain house (indeed, perhaps no source of water at all) existed on the site before early Roman times.

Brelich 1959 does not overtly suggest any specific location within Corinth for the cult of Hera Akraia but seems to assume that some temple of Hera Akraia was there, near which were the monument of the children and the statue. An assumption that there was a temple to Hera Akraia in Corinth, where the cult of Medea's children was carried out, is also made by Payne 1940:1.19ff., and Salmon 1972:203 n. 8.

[11] Stroud 1976:688.

[12] Diod. Sic. 4.54–55.1; Eur. *Med.* 1378–79.

[13] Μνήματα κενά: Paus. 4.32.3.1, 6.23.3.6, 9.18.4.1. Will 1955:92 also suggested that the monument to Medea's children was not believed to be their tomb. He went on to presume, however, that the real burial place was within the hypothetical temple of Hera Akraia = "Temple C." Scranton 1941:160 admits the possibility that the μνῆμα was only a monument, not a tomb.

The statue described as a "terror" probably was in the Perachoran sanctuary as well. At 2.3.6, Pausanias begins to describe the monuments and buildings located on the road to Sikyon that leads out of the Corinthian agora, but he soon embarks on an excursus regarding the legend of Medea's children and the cult that commemorated them, which continues into 2.3.8. He does not return to a discussion of the Corinthian agora until 2.4.1, after an extended narration of Medea's early myths and her travels after leaving Corinth. It is in the midst of his excursus on the cult, rather than during his description of the agora itself, that Pausanias describes the statue. He clearly indicates that it was believed to have been connected with the institution of the children's cult when he says that the Corinthians were required to erect it, as well as to institute a cult to Medea's children, in order to stop the deaths of their own infants, which followed on those of Medea's children. Moreover, Pausanias sets the fact that this statue still remains standing against the fact that the Corinthians no longer offer sacrifices to Medea's children and that the Corinthian children no longer cut their hair in their honor and wear black clothing:

τοῦτο μὲν δὴ καὶ ἐς ἡμᾶς ἔτι λείπεται, γυναικὸς ἐς τὸ φοβερώτερον εἰκὼν πεποιημένη· Κορίνθου δὲ ἀναστάτου γενομένης ὑπὸ ῾Ρωμαίων καὶ Κορινθίων τῶν ἀρχαίων ἀπολομένων, οὐκέτι ἐκεῖναι καθεστήκασιν αὐτοῖς αἱ θυσίαι παρὰ τῶν ἐποίκων οὐδὲ ἀποχείρονταί σφισιν οἱ παῖδες οὐδὲ μέλαιναν φοροῦσιν ἐσθῆτα.

This [terror] still exists in our time, a most frightful statue made in the form of a woman; but after Corinth was laid to waste by the Romans and the old Corinthians were destroyed, no longer were sacrifices offered to [Medea's children] by the inhabitants, nor do their children cut their hair for them, nor do they wear black clothing.

The contrast is between the survival of a cultic artifact (a statue) and the dying out of the cultic practices themselves.

In sum, the literary and archaeological evidence can be kept intact and *argumenta ex silentio* can be avoided if we assume that when literary sources for the cult of Medea's children refer to the temple of Hera Akraia, they mean the temple on Perachora, and if we further assume that the burial place of the children (as opposed to a secondary monument) and the terrifying statue were within that Perachoran temenos.

Function of the Cult

Our literary evidence for the cult of Medea's children has led scholars to conclude that it centered on rites of atonement.[14] Each year, seven boys and seven girls from noble Corinthian families were dressed in black and sent to live for a year in the sanctuary of Hera Akraia. These fourteen children cut their hair and dedicated it to Medea's children, an act that served to identify them with their mythic counterparts. Θρῆνοι (funeral songs) were sung by someone to propitiate Medea's children—perhaps by the fourteen consecrated youths, as fourteen would be a suitable number for a choir.[15] Yearly ἐναγίσματα (chthonic sacrifices) also were used to propitiate Medea's children.[16]

Ancient versions of the cultic myth vary in details, which will be examined later, but the basic story accords with the pattern usually found in myths associated with cults of atonement.[17] A catastrophe occurs—in this case, Medea's children die. The community suffers punishment (in this case, widespread infant deaths) and consults an oracle for help.[18] The oracle tells the town to institute a cult to atone for the catastrophe and avert the anger of the injured god or hero (in this case, Hera, Medea's children, or both).

Brelich suggested that the cult also served as an adolescent initiation cult:[19] the fourteen Corinthian children cut their hair, like initiates; they were secluded from their society, like initiates; they wore unusual clothes, like initiates. The myth, like that for many adolescent initiation cults, tells of individuals who died or were buried in the same place that the real individuals must perform their service. Brelich's argument as it stands is inconclusive, however, because these traits that he cites are shared by other cults or rites that have nothing to do with adolescent initiation. Any time that individuals leave the everyday world and enter into the service of a god or into a marginal period such as mourning, they symbolically enter into a different way of life for the duration of that

[14] First stated explicitly by Nilsson 1906:57. The Akraia festival explicitly was called a πένθιμος ἑορτή (schol. Eur. Med. 1379); to what degree this festival involved Medea's children or the fourteen Corinthian dedicatees, however, is unclear.

[15] Suggested already by Nilsson 1906:60 and Jeanmaire 1939:300.

[16] Literary evidence for these cultic practices at Parmeniscus ap. schol. Eur. Med. 264; Paus. 2.3.7; Aelian VH 5.21; Philostr. Her. 53, 4; schol. Eur. Med. 1382.

[17] Cf. the discussion by Nilsson 1906:57–61.

[18] Parmeniscus ap schol. Eur. Med. 264; Paus. 2.3.6–7; schol. Eur. Med. 1382.

[19] Brelich 1959:n. 11; he follows a suggestion of Jeanmaire 1939:298–301. The idea is taken up again by Graf, although developed with reference to Medea's mythic (and in Athens perhaps cultic) role as initiatrix.

service. To signify this, they frequently do things that set them apart and mark their special status, such as cutting hair, wearing unusual clothes, or living apart from their family or society. Many other, noninitiatory cults or rituals, too, involve a hero's grave, such as the rites of the skirophoria that are associated with the grave of Erechtheus in Athens.

Brelich's adolescent initiation theory also must be reconsidered in light of the fact that both boys and girls were sent to the sanctuary each year. Adolescent initiation cults, as at Brauron or Orthia, for example, typically involve one gender only. We also should note that Medea's children, in several versions of the myth, including the earliest one, die as infants—not really an appropriate mythic precedent for adolescent initiation.[20] Finally, the myths talk not so much about the *children*, and their ordeal, as they do about *Medea* and hers; the children as individuals are so relatively unimportant that their names, number, ages, and even genders vary from account to account. If this myth really served as the *aition* of a cult whose primary focus was adolescent initiation, it would have been natural for one or more of the children to have developed into a figure along the lines of Iphigenia or Leucippus, on whose sufferings the myth could focus.

Because the figure who remains constant in the myths is Medea herself,[21] and because votive offerings found at Perachora suggest that the sanctuary of Hera Akraia particularly attracted women,[22] it is worth considering whether the cult focused primarily on mothers and their concerns, rather than on adolescents and theirs. This is not to say that the yearlong service of the fourteen Corinthian children did not mark a transitional point in their lives; indeed, over time, the ritual may have taken on initiatory functions. Rather, it is to suggest that, in order to understand the cult and its accompanying myth fully, we must shift

---

[20] This was noted as well by Will 1955:97 and n. 2, from a somewhat different standpoint.

[21] *Pace* Nilsson 1906:59: "Die Hauptpersonen sind die Kinder Medeas und Hera Akraia; Medea spielt keine Rolle in dem Kult, soviel wir wissen."

[22] An unusually large number of spindle whorls (more than sixty) were found, some of which are as early as the first half of the sixth century; bobbins and loom weights were found as well (Payne and Dunbabin 1962:99–124, 130–31, 330–31). Also noteworthy is that numerous pyxides, dating from as early as the first half of the sixth century, were excavated (99–125, 158–87, 226, 304, 307); although it is impossible to be sure that pyxides were "female" dedications, their usual function as containers of cosmetics or small trinkets makes this likely. Sixty ivory "spectacle"-type fibulae also were excavated—the largest number at any site—as well as some fibulae of other types (433–39). E. Simon 1987:161 notes that fibulae and other small, personal items are typical votive offerings at kourotrophic sanctuaries; she cites as evidence the work of Pingiatoglou 1981:55ff., which I have not been able to obtain. On the votive offerings at Perachora, see also p. 55, below.

our point of view away from the children—both mythic and real—and toward the mothers who bore them and set out to rear them to adulthood.[23] In the next section, I will offer an overview of Hera's mythic and cultic relationship to mothers and their children.

Hera as Mother

Although modern scholarly discussions tend to emphasize Hera's cultic associations with brides,[24] she was closely associated with parturient women and mothers as well,[25] especially in the Argolid or areas colonized by Argolid peoples.[26] Kourotrophic figurines from all artistic epochs and terra-cottas have been excavated at the Argive Heraion;[27] Hesychius says that the Argives celebrated a festival in honor of

[23] This same general theory was put forth by Will 1955, although he developed it in a different way than I will (97–118, especially 114–18). In the children's deaths in Hera's temple, Will saw a pattern of dying and rebirth linked to the agricultural year, and therefore in Medea/Hera he saw versions of the "Great Goddess" who served as both *kourotrophos* and *karpotrophos* for her worshipers. Regarding the agrarian interpretation, we must remain skeptical. There is no evidence in the cult remains at Perachora and only faint remains in the myth of Medea that would encourage such a theory. Medea stops a Corinthian famine by praying to Demeter and the Lemnian nymphs, according to Eumelus *ap.* schol. Pindar *Ol.* 13.74; the result of her children's deaths, according to the scholiast on Eur. *Med.* 1382, was a Corinthian famine (other versions make the Corinthian punishment a plague; λοιμός and λιμός are scarcely to be distinguished, anyway—see Delcourt 1938:chap. 1). Elsewhere in Greece, Hera's agricultural interests are scant (Hera is called "Antheia" at Argos [Paus. 2.22.1] ὅτι ἀνίησι τοὺς καρπούς, "because she makes the fruits grow" [*EM*, s.v. "Ἄνθεια"]). The small amount of additional evidence for Hera's agricultural interests (which I find debatable) is assembled by Picard 1946:460–62.

Will's kourotrophic ideas, however, are worth pursuing. Cf. also Jeanmaire 1939:298–300, who sees kourotrophic traits behind Medea, and Graf, who understands Corinthian Hera, under whose patronage the fourteen Corinthian children were initiated, as a goddess who protects "the young girls and boys who are about to enter into the life of the *polis*" (p. 42).

[24] On Hera's role as bride, see discussions with ancient citations at Burkert 1985: 132ff.; Nilsson 1906:51ff., 1967:27–33. Burkert goes too far, I think, in suggesting that her role as bride excluded any role as mother. See also Barrera 1989, who suggests that Hera's primary role is that of the sexually active woman.

[25] Picard 1946:460–62 collected the evidence for Hera's presentation as a mother in cult that was available at his time. T. Price's work is the only recent treatment of Hera's cultic role as a goddess of mothers, to my knowledge (1978:*passim*; see index, s.v. "Hera"). See Jeanmaire 1939; E. Simon 1987:161–62 (a more conservative evaluation of Hera's kourotrophic powers than Price's); and further individual examples in the notes immediately below.

[26] T. Price 1978:*passim*, but explicitly discussed at 138–41, 145–46.

[27] T. Price 1978:19–21, 43, 144–46; cf. the figure of a little girl holding a doll described on 57.

"Hera Lecherna," "Hera of the Childbed."[28] Much evidence for Hera's kourotrophic functions—including statuettes of nursing goddesses, of babies, and of uteri—has been found at the sanctuary of Hera Argeia in Lucania, an area colonized by Peloponnesians in the seventh century.[29] There is also evidence for Hera's kourotrophic interests in Croton, Selinus, and throughout Apulia.[30] Hera's Samian cult, too, probably had kourotrophic functions;[31] most recently, Fridh-Haneson has argued that a seventh-century Samian relief, which traditionally has been understood to show Zeus grasping Hera's breast as part of a "sacred marriage," actually shows Hera preparing to suckle a youth.[32] Fridh-Haneson adduces Near Eastern parallels for this scene and concludes that Hera here represents a goddess whose milk gives immortality or surpassing strength to the youth who receives it and that, therefore, Hera's cultic roles on Samos included nurture and protection of the young.[33] Several tales make Hera the nurse of famous individuals, for better or for worse. In Thebes, she was tricked into nursing her stepson Heracles briefly, thus giving him superior strength.[34] The *Iliad* made her the nurse of Thetis (24.59–60), which, Hera argued, conferred great honor on both Thetis and her son Achilles. According to Hesiod, Hera nursed the Nemean Lion and Lernaean Hydra, the two first monsters to challenge Heracles (*Th.* 313–14, 327–28). Clearly, Hera's milk endowed her nurslings with exceptional characteristics. Hera's association in myth with Eileithyia, who usually is said to be her daughter, also bespeaks her concern with childbirth and nurture; sometimes the name is used as an epithet of Hera herself.

Myth often portrays a deity as withholding the very blessings that are sought in cult, or even as inflicting the opposite of those blessings upon an unfortunate mortal. Hera's myths are no exception: her effect on

[28] Hesychius, s.v. "λεχέρνα"; T. Price 1978:206.

[29] T. Price 1978:21–22, 43, 146, 170, 179–81.

[30] Apulia: T. Price 1978:39, 176, 178; Selinus: 22; Croton: 1978:179–80.

[31] T. Price 1978:58, 153.

[32] Fridh-Haneson 1988:205–13; cf. in the same collection Kyrieleis 1988:215–21, who finds evidence for Hera's role as a goddess of human fertility in the pinecones and representations of pinecones excavated at the Samian Heraion (dated to the archaic period). He argues that these are votive offerings whose many seeds symbolized fecundity, like those of the poppy heads and pomegranates that also are found at Samos and that sometimes are represented in Hera's cults elsewhere.

[33] Cf. T. Price's analysis of such nursing scenes, 1978:7.

[34] Paus. 9.25.2. The story is illustrated on Etruscan mirrors from the fourth and third centuries B.C., some of which are illustrated in Fridh-Haneson 1988. Fridh-Haneson would, in fact, identify the youth preparing to suckle on the Samian relief mentioned immediately above as Heracles. On Hera as *kourotrophos* in Thebes, see also *AP* 9.589.

mothers and children is potentially fatal or disfiguring. She attacks the
young child (Heracles, Dionysus), attacks the mother either while she
is pregnant or during parturition (Alcmene, Leto), or attacks both the
mother and the infant simultaneously, sometimes before birth in such
a way as to put the child at risk (Semele, Aphrodite)[35] and sometimes
afterward, driving the mother to kill the child (Ino, Aëdon, Lamia).[36]
Indeed, this pattern comes forth even in the way in which myth attached
Hera to Hephaestus. Early versions tell of Hephaestus' parthenogenic
birth by Hera; the result of Hera's efforts, however, was so disappointing
that she tossed her crippled child from Olympus in disgust. This story
simultaneously represents Hera herself as a mother who has failed
to produce a healthy child and exemplifies Hera's tendency to attack
children, as seen in some of the other myths I have just reviewed. In
real terms, I suggest, all of these myths represent Hera's power either to
let loose or to hold back the disease and death that frequently brought
pregnancy and childhood to unhappy ends in antiquity;[37] this would
accord with her cultic role as aider of parturient women and mothers.

The combined picture, built from cultic as well as mythic material,
suggests that when we find Hera associated with children in a cult,
we should look for further signs that the cult is one concerned with
a mother's bearing and rearing of healthy children. This is especially
important when the cult in question is of Argive derivation, as the
Perachoran cult was,[38] because, as I noted above, Hera's kourotrophic

[35] Hera touches Aphrodite's pregnant belly maliciously; the result is the deformed
Priapus: schol. Ap. Rhod. 1.932; Suidas, s.v. "Πρίαπος" III; EM, s.v. "Ἀβαρνίδα"; Tzetzes
ad. Lyc. 831. R. Lullies, "Priapos," RE 22.2 col. 1917, thinks the story was known at least as
early as the second-century B.C. elegist Artemidorus of Ephesus.

[36] In the version of Aëdon's story given by Antoninus Liberalis (Met. 11, following
Boios), it is Aëdon's insulting of Hera that leads to her husband's infidelity and thus,
eventually, to Aëdon's vengeful murder of her own child. Here, the mother's destruction
of her own child is one element among several that represents Hera's capacity to destroy a
woman's marriage and family life. On Hera's mythic antagonism toward Lamia: Duris
FGrHist 76 F 17; Diod. Sic. 20.41; schol. on Aristides p. 41 Dindorf.

[37] This comes out particularly clearly in some myths connected with Heracles' birth.
According to Paus. 9.11.3, Hera delays Heracles' birth by sending to Alcmene's labor
room certain demonic figures called φαρμακίδες ("those who are experts in charms")
who "stand in the way of" (ἐμπόδια εἶναι) the birth. Elsewhere (Antoninus Liberalis Met.
29, following Nicander) Hera sends Eileithyia and the Moirai to obstruct Alcmene's labor
(κατεῖχον ἐν ταῖς ὠδῖσι τὴν Ἀλκμήνην) or else sends Eileithyia (Lucina) alone (Ovid
Met. 9.295ff.) to obstruct the birth. Cf. the remarks of E. Simon 1987:161.

[38] On the Argive basis of the Perachoran cult, see most recently Salmon 1972:160, 179,
195. Notably, the other myth that strongly connects Hera with a mother and her children in
a cultic context—the myth of Cleobis and Biton—also is Argive (Hdt. 1.31; Cic. Tusc. 1.47).
Here we find several of the elements present in the story of Medea's children, although

interests were particularly strong in the Argolid and its colonies. Only one kourotrophic representation has been found at Perachora (a terracotta of a seated woman with child, dated to the mid-sixth century). However, a very large number of ceramic representations of *koulouria* (twisted or circular cakes) have been found as well; these frequently have been found at other sites of known kourotrophic cults elsewhere in Greece.[39] Also found were thirteen figurines or partial figurines of Bes, the Egyptian god who protected pregnant women and young children. Some of these date to the protogeometric and archaic periods; others are unstratified. Egyptian statuettes of Isis nursing Horus (unstratified) and of Sekhmet, an Egyptian goddess concerned with warding off illnesses (in a deposit of protocorinthian and Corinthian pottery), also were excavated at the Perachoran Heraion.[40] These figurines strengthen the likelihood that the Perachoran cult had kourotrophic concerns. An examination of Pausanias' information about the cult will support this idea and take us closer to understanding Corinthian Medea's association with Hera.

Further Analysis of the Cult at Corinth: Pausanias' "Terror"

Pausanias describes what the Corinthians had to do to end the wholesale infant deaths that followed the murder of Medea's children (2.3.6–7; the text is Spiro's):

καταλιθωθῆναι δὲ ὑπὸ Κορινθίων λέγονται τῶν δώρων ἕνεκα ὧν τῇ Γλαύκῃ κομίσαι φασὶν [παῖδας Μηδείας]· ἅτε δὲ τοῦ θανάτου βιαίου καὶ οὐ σὺν τῷ δικαίῳ γενομένου, τὰ τέκνα Κορινθίων τὰ νήπια ὑπ᾽ αὐτῶν ἐφθείρετο,

they emerge in a slightly different pattern: (1) a priestess of Hera asks the goddess to grant her children a great boon (unspecified by Herodotus and Cicero, but we might assume it was health and successful maturation, which would be the natural request for a mother to make); (2) Hera instead kills the children, in her temple; and (3) the children receive heroic honors. Herodotus' narrator, Solon, emphasizes the fact that their death conferred great honor and benefit upon Cleobis and Biton—after all, this is his point in telling the story to Croesus—yet behind the tale seems to lurk a darker cultic *aition* much like that of Medea's children: Hera fails to give a mother what she seeks for her children and they die.

[39] T. Price 1978:146; cf. Salmon 1972:180–82 and Payne 1940:7ff.; Payne and Dunbabin 1962:328–30. Cf. T. Price 135, 152–53, 208; Salmon further notes that such votive *koulouria* also have been found at the Argive and Corcyrean sanctuaries of Hera.

[40] For the figurines, see Payne and Dunbabin 1962:512. The only other Egyptian divinity represented at the site is Amen-Re, the main god of the pantheon (fragments of two figurines, found in the protocorinthian deposit).

πρὶν ἢ χρήσαντος τοῦ θεοῦ θυσίαι τε αὐτοῖς ἐπέτειοι κατέστησαν καὶ δεῖμα ἐπεστάθη. τοῦτο μὲν δὴ καὶ ἐς ἡμᾶς ἔτι λείπεται, γυναικὸς ἐς τὸ φοβερώτερον εἰκὼν πεποιημένη.

[The children of Medea] are said to have been stoned to death by the Corinthians on account of the gifts that legend says they took to Glauce. But because their deaths were violent and unjust, the babies of the Corinthians were killed by [the children's ghosts] until, at the command of a god, yearly sacrifices were established in honor of [Medea's children] and a "terror" was set up. This [terror] still exists in our time, a most frightful statue made in the form of a woman.

Who or what was this "terror" (δεῖμα)? Will suggested, contrary to all other translators and commentators, that we understand the word δεῖμα as a common noun rather than as the name of a deity. The statue was not *of* Δεῖμα—some goddess named "Terror"—but rather it was *a* δεῖμα—a terrifying object. Its function, Will suggested, was to serve as an *apotropaion*, to prevent another spate of infant deaths.[41] This idea, ignored for so many years, deserves reconsideration; I will begin by making two points about Greek apotropaic statues that will be important to my discussion. First, although apotropaic statues could be used to avert all kinds of evil—including plagues of grasshoppers—one of their uses in Greece and elsewhere throughout the Mediterranean was to control the restless, potentially harmful souls of the unhappy dead. Picard and Faraone have noted that this use was particularly at home in the Peloponnesus and areas colonized by Peloponnesians.

Second, apotropaic statues often worked by the logic of *similia similibus*, or "like averts like." The statue represented the evil it was intended to ward off. The decoration of ancient buildings with *gorgoneia* worked similarly: the horrifically grinning face averted evil influences. Similar, too, is the age-old use, familiar to any traveler in Mediterranean lands, of eyelike charms to avert the "Evil Eye."[42]

---

[41] Will 1955:94.

[42] Greek apotropaic statues have most recently been treated by Faraone 1992, esp. chaps. 3, 4, 5. On the aversion of ghosts, see esp. 79–84 and cf. 38; this is an abbreviated version of his discussion in Faraone 1991; see there esp. 180–89. Earlier treatments are Picard 1933 and, for discussion of *kolossoi* in Greek aversion rituals, Vernant 1979:105–37.

Two familiar examples of *similia similibus*, are the statue of a locust that Peisistratus set up to keep a plague of locusts away from Athens (Hesychius s.v. "καταχήνη"; discussed by Faraone 1992:41, Lobeck 1829:2.970–74, and Jahn 1855:36–37) and statues of Apollo the archer erected to prevent the plague, seemingly on the argument that the sender of plagues can also avert them (see Faraone 1992: 57–66; Parke 1985:150–59; M. West 1967; Weinreich 1913; Buresch 1889:81–86). Scholarship on Mediterranean beliefs in the Evil Eye and its aversion is vast; the interested reader might start with Stewart 1991:232–37. The

What sort of evil looks like an ugly or frightening woman? As a matter of fact, a whole class of such evils existed in ancient Greece and throughout the ancient Mediterranean. Scholars of classical religion have taken relatively little notice of them, however, and thus we would do well to begin with a survey of these creatures, which I will call "reproductive demons."[43]

The Paradigm of the Reproductive Demon

Wherever they are found in ancient or modern cultures, reproductive demons consistently display two traits. (1) They kill or weaken infants and young children and they sometimes kill pregnant, parturient, or newly delivered women, as well. In other words, reproductive demons are explanations of such hard-to-explain illnesses as crib death, neonatal sepsis, puerperal fever, and eclampsia. (2) Reproductive demons are believed to be the souls of women who died as virgins, died in childbirth, or died shortly after the deaths of their own children.[44] These women

---

classic discussion, with many examples of eyelike amulets from throughout the world, is Jahn 1855.

[43] On the Greek reproductive demon, see Johnston 1994, 1995a; D. West 1991:361–68; Burkert 1992:82–87; Halm-Tisserant 1989; Vermeule 1977 plus plates (on the possible identification of a lion-woman in vase paintings as a *lamia*); Herter 1950, esp. 118–20; Rohde 1925:app. 6. See also the relevant *RE* articles by Maas (s.v. "Gello"), Tambornino (s.v. "Mormo"), and Schwenn (s.v. "Lamia").

Scholarship on reproductive demons in other cultures (also called "child-killing demons" or "child-stealing witches") is vast; here I can give only a few titles. Bibliographies in these sources can lead the interested reader further. Stewart 1991; Scurlock 1991; T. Gaster 1942 (on Near Eastern types; Burkert includes further citations for work on the phenomenon in the ancient Near East in his notes); M. Gaster 1900; Lawson 1910:174–84 (still a good place to find the evidence collected); Perdrizet 1922:11–27 (on the Byzantine Greek reproductive demon and her aversion); Allatius 1645:chaps. 1–9 (the source from which we derive much of knowledge concerning Byzantine Greek beliefs in reproductive demons). See also the photograph in *Life*, Oct. 1991, p. 78: a young Rumanian woman lies in her coffin, dressed in her wedding gown and with a small baby-doll at her side. Killed before her time, she is receiving the traditional *nunta mortului* (wedding of the dead) in order that her soul might not return to earth as a *strigoi* (child-killing demon).

[44] In some cultures, male reproductive demons also occur; like the females, they are individuals who have failed to reproduce successfully before dying. For example, Mesopotamian *lilu*—demons that attack infants and children—are created when either a male or female dies without marrying. However, in most cultures, the female reproductive demon is by the far the norm, undoubtedly because the woman's role in life is more explicitly reproductive, and thus her "success" in life rests more heavily on the issue of whether she bears and nurtures children. Compare also the Mesopotamian demon called "Kubu": this demonic attacker of infants was said to have been a stillborn infant him(her?)self (on *lilu* and Kubu, see Scurlock 1991:23–5, 27–30).

fail to complete the reproductive cycle, in other words, and, becoming
demons after death as a result of this incompleteness, they inflict the
same fate they suffered upon other women.

There exist quite a few Greek and Roman magical texts that describe amulets and spells to avert female demons from young children and parturient women, which indicates that such creatures were
sincerely feared in antiquity.[45] More familiar Greek and Roman literary sources also refer to reproductive demons. For example, this
is surely the implication behind lines 227–30 of the *Homeric Hymn to
Demeter*, where Demeter—the kourotrophic goddess par excellence—
promises to protect the infant Demophon from demonic attack.[46] As
in most cultures, there developed out of the general Greek belief in
reproductive demons certain individual demons, complete with names
and etiological myths. The two that I will focus on here as examples
are Lamia and Mormo.[47] Their transparently adjectival names, which
mean "Devourer" and "Frightful," undoubtedly began as appellatives
for such creatures in general. Their myths express in story form the
same fears that the demons described in the magical texts personify:
both Lamia and Mormo are said to kill children. Their myths also show
that the Greek reproductive demon—like her sisters around the world—
was believed to have suffered the same fate as she inflicted upon other
women. Lamia bore many children to Zeus but lost each baby soon
after its birth, because Hera killed them. Mormo killed and ate her own
children in a maddened fit.[48]

Like reproductive demons in most cultures, Greek reproductive
demons are imagined to be physically repulsive and frightening; indeed, Lamia's hideousness and Mormo's frightfulness were proverbial

[45] I have discussed these in Johnston 1994, 1995a.

[46] Another well-known example is Ovid's description of protecting Roman doors with
buckthorn to keep the *striges* (demons thought to suck infant blood) away after a child
is born (*Fasti* 6.101ff.) For further examples and discussion see Johnston, 1995a.

[47] I will not be examining here the third Greek reproductive demon who developed an
individual *persona*: Gello. The *aition* for this demon's existence was that she died a virgin;
thus, although she fits the general pattern of having died without nurturing children,
she does not fit the subpattern I am discussing here, of the woman who reproduces but
subsequently loses or kills her children. I have discussed Gello and virginal reproductive
demons elsewhere in more depth; see Johnston 1994, 1995a.

[48] For Lamia's myth, see Diod. Sic. 20.41; Dion. Hal. *Thuc.* 6; Duris *FGrHist* 76 F 17;
schol. on Aristides p. 41 Dindorf; schol. on Theoc. *Id.* 15.40; Strabo 1.2.19. For Mormo's
myth, see schol. Theoc. *Id.* 15.40; schol. Aristides p. 41 Dindorf. Additional references
to them attacking and eating children at Hor. *Ars* 340; Heraclitus *Incred.* 34. The demon
described by Philostratus as an *empousa*, *mormolukeia*, and *lamia* at *VA* 4.25 also will devour
her victim (see n. 64, below).

in antiquity.[49] Even allowing for comic exaggeration, descriptions of Lamia as "farting in the agora" or "having filthy testicles" suggest a loathsome creature. Erinna describes Mormo as running around on all fours and as having big ears and a face that changes constantly; Theocritus likens her to a frightening horse. Byzantine and contemporary Greek descriptions of *lamiai* and *mormones* continue to emphasize their frightful, ugly, or bizarre appearances.[50]

A Corinthian Reproductive Demon

Pausanias' description of the Corinthian δεῖμα is just what we would expect a statue of a reproductive demon to look like—female and frightful. Although we have no explicit evidence that large *apotropaia* such as this δεῖμα were erected against reproductive demons in Greece, it would not be surprising. After all, reproductive demons were just the sort of restless, ghostly souls that other Argive *apotropaia* attempted to avert. Faraone has noted that demons who were averted from the individual person by charms worn on the body or hung in the house frequently were also averted from the city at large by a statue.[51] The amulets against reproductive demons that I mentioned above would be the individual charms; Pausanias' δεῖμα would be the citywide *apotropaion*.

A demonic figure associated with a deity represents the evils against which the deity is expected to protect the worshipers. The converse way of looking at this, of course, is that the demon represents the way in which the deity may harm the worshipers, either directly or

---

[49] On Lamia's proverbial hideousness, see Ps.-Diogenianus *ap.* Choerob. in Cramer 2.293 and further at Schwenn, "Lamia" *RE* 12:545. On Mormo as the essence of fearsomeness or *mormō* as a synonym for *phobos*: Ar. *Eq.* 693; Xen. *Hell.* 4.4.17; schol. Ar. *Ach.* 582; schol. Ar. *Pax* 474 and often elsewhere; Hesychius and Photius explain cognates of *mormō* by cognates of *phobos*.

[50] Lamia as farting: Ar. *Vesp.* 1177; Crates *ap.* schol. Ar. *Eccl.* 77 = fr. 18 of *CAF* 1.136; Lamia's filthy testicles: Ar. *Pax* 758 = *Vesp.* 1035. Also Erinna, *Distaff* 24–27; Theoc. *Id.* 15.40. Other descriptions of Lamia and/or Mormo as frightening and ugly: Duris *FGrHist* 76 F 17 (Lamia becomes ugly after her death); Antoninus Liberalis *Met.* 8 (Lamia called a beast); Stesich. fr. 220 Campbell (Lamia is Scylla's mother). Apul. *Met.* 1.17 and Lucian *Tox.* 24 use *lamia* and *mormolukeia* to refer to frightening, ugly women. On the ugliness of Byzantine Greek reproductive demons, see, for example, B. Schmidt 1871:134 (hideously huge breasts); Lawson 1910:174–76. On the strange appearance of contemporary Greek reproductive demons, see Stewart 1991:180–83 (they often have reversed feet or hands, or have animal legs or feet). Ancient Near Eastern reproductive demons were hideous, too: see Scurlock 1991.

[51] See Faraone 1991.

by withholding aid. The possibility that the Corinthians erected an *apotropaion* against reproductive demons in connection with the cult of Hera Akraia fits in well with Hera's cultic protection of motherhood and with her mythic portrait as a goddess who attacked mothers and children. Cultically, she helped to protect against the forces that brought pregnancy and childhood to unhappy ends; mythically, she was represented as one of them herself. Her mythic association with Lamia is particularly telling in this respect.

When we find a dangerous force being averted, we often find it being appeased in some way, as well; frequently, the aversion occurs on the level of what often is called magic (e.g., by means of erecting *apotropaia* and using amulets) and the complementary appeasement on the level of more formal, cultic religion. This brings us back to the annual dedication of the fourteen Corinthian children at the sanctuary of Hera Akraia. The children's black clothing suggests that during their year of service, they were temporarily "dead," having been "sacrificed" to Hera to appease her and thus dissuade her from seizing the children of the Corinthians more widely and permanently.[52] The two techniques— averting *apotropaion* and appeasing dedication of children—worked toward the same end.

There is one more element within the Akraian cult that must be considered. Several ancient sources indicate that the ghosts of Medea's children had to be appeased, as well as the goddess (Paus. 2.3.7; schol. Eur. *Med.* 264, 1382; Aelian *VH* 5.21; Philostr. *Her.* 53.4). Will suggested that the cult as we know it was an assimilation of what were once two cults with different focuses. In one cult, originally, child heroes were worshiped, who—like many heroes who received cult[53]—were said to have been murdered by the local inhabitants, perhaps in the sanctuary where they subsequently were worshiped. The other cult, according to Will, centered on a goddess or heroine known as Hera or

---

[52] A somewhat similar function may be conjectured, perhaps, for the Eleusinian παῖς ἀφ' ἑστίας μυηθείς (child initiated from the hearth) who ἀντὶ πάντων τῶν μυουμένων ἀπομειλίσσεται τὸ θεῖον (propitiates the divinity on behalf of all the initiates; Porphyry *Abst.* 4.5. My suggestion regarding the Corinthian children accords generally with that of Burkert 1966:117–19, who argues that the dedication of black-clad children symbolizes a child sacrifice. Burkert goes on to argue, adducing the statements of Marcellus in Eusebius *Adv. Marc.* 1.3, that the black she-goat sacrificed to Hera during the Akraia festival was a substitute for the fourteen Corinthian children and that its death freed them from their yearlong obligations. (*Contra* Nilsson 1906:60–62, who argues that the Corinthian children were never more than a choir and that their black clothing was necessitated only by the fact that they were singing in honor of the dead.)

[53] On this, see Visser 1982.

Medea and on her children. Eventually, the two sets of children became one and the same. The site at which the child heroes were murdered and buried was conflated with the place at which Medea's children underwent an attempted immortalization; Medea, who in the original myth was the mother of the children who died due to Hera's neglect (more on this below), became identified as the mother of the children murdered by the Corinthians. It was the conflation of these two cults, Will further suggests, that eventually led to the mythic variant whereby the *Corinthians* killed Medea's children.[54]

I agree with Will's idea, but I further distinguish between the two original cults as follows. The ἐναγίσματα (chthonic sacrifices) and θρῆνοι (funeral songs) that our sources say were directed to "Medea's children" probably were directed originally to the murdered child heroes of the other cult, but the annual dedication of the fourteen Corinthian children must have been directed toward Hera/Medea along the lines that I have suggested above, and not to the murdered child heroes. Individuals usually are dedicated not to the service of a heroic figure, but rather to the god with whom that heroic figure is connected; the dedicatees often are understood to *represent* or *stand in for* the heroic figures associated with the god, and they play out, in some way, the mythic relationship between the deity and the heroic figure. The Athenian Arrhephoroi, to take a parallel example, are dedicated to Athena's service, and are understood to represent the mythic Cecropides who were once under Athena's care; the she-bears at Brauron similarly are dedicated to Artemis and represent Artemis' former companion, Iphigenia. The Corinthian dedicatees' cutting of their hair for Medea's children (Paus. 2.3.7) further identifies them with the mythic children of Medea whom they replace.

The Myth of Corinthian Medea

I began this article by noting that most scholars agree that Corinthian Medea was originally a goddess, whose cult was displaced by that of

---

[54] Will 1955:94. On the myth, see also Séchan 1925:app. 1, 1927:266–70. See also Arist. *Poet.* 1453b18–30, who urges poets to dramatize old "traditional" stories in which relatives kill one another and includes Euripides' *Medea* as an example. Notably, even in the versions whereby the Corinthians kill the children, Medea often is not exculpated: it is by her neglect that the children are left in dangerous situations: Creophylus *ap.* schol. Eur. *Med.* 264; Apollod. 1.145–46. This suggests that the version whereby Medea herself killed the children was strong enough to resist complete subordination.

Hera and whose interests and character were similar to those of Hera. Frequently, the myths surrounding such figures set them in opposition to the deities who displace them; specifically, the mythic hero or heroine often is persecuted in a way that reflects the sphere over which the deity has control, along the lines that I sketched above in "Hera as Mother." With this in mind, we can use what has been suggested about the nature of Argive Hera and specifically about the cult of Hera Akraia to reevaluate the myth of Corinthian Medea.

The Infanticide Motif

If we eliminate from our consideration the variation of the myth in which the Corinthians killed the children, setting it aside as a secondary development of the original myth as Will and others have proposed (although a version that may well have been in circulation by Euripides' time),[55] then we are left with two variations that possibly reflect Medea's original character. In the first and earliest attested variant, which I will call the immortalization variant, Eumelus portrays Medea as seeking Hera's help in protecting her children from mortality—that is, I suggest, in protecting them from the manifold diseases to which young children were prey in antiquity. Hera breaks her promise and the children die. This reflects what has been suggested already about Hera: she was an appropriate goddess to ask for such help, but also one who, at least in myth, might refuse to protect a child.

It is important to note that neither of the sources for Eumelus' immortalization variant state that Medea *killed* the children, even accidentally.[56] Pausanias says only that Medea realized that her hopes of immortalizing the children were empty. Her act of "hiding" them—whatever "hiding" implies—is not said to be the cause of their eventual death, any more than Demeter's hiding of Demophon in the fire is said to be the cause of his failure to escape his mortality or, similarly, Thetis' hiding of Achilles in a fire is said to be the cause of *his* eventual death (Ap. Rhod. 4.869ff.; Apollod. 3.13.6; cf. Isis' actions at Plut. *Is. et Os.* 16). Some scholars have assumed that the reason Jason "would not forgive" Medea was that he saw her killing the child, but a safer inference to make from the passage is that he saw her performing some ceremony of

---

[55] Michelini 1989 suggests that throughout his work, Euripides plays on the audience's knowledge of this variant of the myth; until the infanticide actually occurs, the audience cannot be sure by which means the childrens' deaths will be brought about.

[56] See the first two passages in the appendix.

hiding the children and misinterpreted it as injurious, just as Metaneira saw and misinterpreted Demeter's actions, and Peleus misinterpreted those of Thetis. In the scholiast's résumé of Eumelus' story, the only reason given for the children's death is Hera's perfidy. Hera did not immortalize them as she had promised, and—as must have been the case for many children in antiquity—without her protection, they subsequently died before reaching maturity. Medea is not implicated in any way in this version of the story, either.

The immortalization variant of the myth, then, expresses Hera's failure to deliver the protection that Medea, as a mother, sought for her children. In the other early variant, for which Euripides is our oldest extant source, Medea killed the children. We see here the same split as is found in the myths of Lamia and Mormo and in the myths of reproductive demons elsewhere throughout the world: sometimes the mother's child dies at another's hands (Hera kills Lamia's children), sometimes the mother kills the child herself (Mormo). The first set of circumstances suffices perfectly well to explain the existence of a reproductive demon. For, according to the "rules" of this folk belief, all that is required for a woman to become a demon after her death is that she be left childless. The development of the second variant arises from the tendency of myth and folk belief to present polarized versions of archetypal figures. A demon who kills children certainly represents an archetypally "bad" female, but a demon who kills her *own* children is infinitely worse. Thus, the dreadful child-killing "Strangler" demon of Aramaic and Syriac beliefs is referred to as "the mother who strangles her own children" in incantations found in texts of the first six centuries A.D. (scholars agree that the incantations themselves are much older). By at least the early medieval period, the Jewish reproductive demon Lilith is said to turn on her own children when she finds no others to attack. Sometimes, as in the case of Mormo, killing her own children becomes the reproductive demon's first act—the act that "creates" her demonic identity. According to Southwestern American and Mexican folklore, La Llorona ("The Weeping Woman") is the spirit of a mother who, having murdered her own children, spends eternity wandering the earth looking for others to kill.[57]

---

[57] On the Aramaic and Syriac sources, see T. Gaster 1942:51–52. On Lilith, see Scholem 1972:247, who cites *Bar-Midbar Rabbah* 16.

On La Llorona, see the brief survey, with references to other scholarship, in Dorson 1964:436–38. Scholars agree that La Llorona as we know her today draws on both Aztec myths and European stories brought in by Spanish colonizers. According to one version,

I suggest that Medea's mythic personality developed along just these lines. As a heroine associated with Hera Akraia's cult, Corinthian Medea originally emblematized the results of Hera's neglect or anger— Medea was a mother who lost her children due to Hera's refusal to protect them and help nurture them to maturity. By the rules of folk belief, this loss would have caused Medea to become, like Lamia, a demon that killed other mothers' children—one of the reproductive demons against whom Hera's help was sought during pregnancy, parturition, and early childhood.[58] As with Mormo, Lilith, the Syriac "Strangler," and La Llorona, myth eventually would have moved Medea yet further away from the archetype of the "good" woman, negatively polarizing her as the killer of her *own* children, as well.

It is to be noted, of course, that extant myth says nothing about Medea killing other children after the death of her own children, as a reproductive demon would. This part of the reproductive demon's paradigm inevitably would have been softened under the influence of "Colchian Medea"—the "Medea" of epic with whom Corinthian Medea became identified during the early archaic period.[59] It would have been difficult for Greek authors to portray the wife of an epic hero and the granddaughter of the Sun-god becoming a full-fledged demon along

indeed, La Llorona is a peasant girl who kills her children when her noble husband abandons her to marry a woman of his own class; this version surely shows the influence of European stories about Medea. Nonetheless, it is telling that European "Medea" stories and the local reproductive demon attracted one another so easily. Note too that La Llorona was linked to the Aztec goddess Cihuacoatl or Chihuacohuatl, who, in addition to more bloodthirsty pursuits, was concerned with midwifery and motherhood. Sometimes, Cihuacoatl herself was said to wander among the people carrying a cradle or papoose pack, which she eventually abandoned. When the people looked into the cradle, they found an arrowhead shaped like an Aztec sacrificial knife (Dorson 436–37). It is tempting to see in this relationship a connection such as the one that I am proposing for Hera and Lamia and Hera and Medea. However, the complex *personae* of the Aztec gods and the transmission of Aztec myth through European witnesses make it difficult to be certain of anything. Brundage 1979:168–70 offers an interpretation of the knife-in-the-cradle story that connects it closely with Cihuacoatl's bloodthirstiness rather than with motherhood.

[58] T. Price 1978:144 briefly suggests during her discussion of Corinthian *kourotrophoi* that Medea may have begun as something similar to the demonic φαρμακίδες (enchantresses) who obstructed Heracles' birth (see above, n. 37), and that Medea was a minor goddess who had to be propitiated to avoid bad labor. However, Price bases this idea primarily on Medea's general reputation as a πολυφάρμακος (expert in enchantments) woman, rather than on an evaluation of the Corinthian cult and myth itself. (She develops an idea presented by Rzach, s.v. "Thebai," *RE* 5.A.2 col. 1542–43.)

[59] On the question of "Colchian" Medea's and "Corinthian" Medea's identification during the early archaic age, see Graf, pp. 37–38; Lesky 1931:cols. 49–53; Will 1955:88, 118–21; and Wilamowitz 1906:3.173ff., 1924.2.240, 1931–32.2.10.

the lines of Mormo and Lamia. The concept is not altogether absent from Medea's mythic history, however: Medea murders her brother Apsyrtus, who in some versions of the story is just a child at the time (see Bremmer's contribution to this volume), and she attempts to murder Theseus on the brink of his passage from childhood to adulthood (see Graf's contribution to this volume). The latter story, in the form that we have it, has been interpreted as expressing the danger that the adolescent must face at the time of his "initiation,"[60] but it is surely significant that myth insists on making that danger Medea, a mythic character already associated with children's deaths. The other part of the reproductive demon's paradigm—the part that narrates her own children's deaths—could be retained by classical authors even in the extreme version that presented Medea herself as their murderer, for infanticide was well within the limits of heroic behavior—remember, for example, Heracles, Agamemnon, Procne, and Ino. Of course, the shocking nature of infanticide would have made this variation all the more attractive to the dramatists, who were particularly fond of presenting familial crimes on stage.

Colchian Medea, Corinthian Medea

One question yet remains, but before we move on to its consideration, it might be helpful to summarize the hypothesis that I have presented in this essay. I have suggested that the Corinthian cult of Hera Akraia focused on nurturing children, which included protecting them from the manifold diseases and disasters that might befall them before they reached maturity. Building on the idea that Corinthian Medea was originally a goddess of similar interests, displaced by Hera, I have further suggested that she became the mythic elaboration of a demonic force against which Akraian Hera was expected to protect her worshipers— she was a mother who had lost her children and who thus became, after her death, a "reproductive demon." Like other reproductive demons in ancient Greece and elsewhere, this Medea also became known as the killer of her own children in some versions of her myth.

If my reconstruction of Corinthian Medea's early *persona* is correct, there is no need to assume that any single classical author "invented" the infanticidal Medea whom we know from Euripides and elsewhere;

---

[60] See Graf, pp. 39–43.

rather, she evolved out of one variant of the original myth. We are left, however, with the final question of why this Corinthian child-killer became identified with the "Enchantress from Afar" whom Graf has discussed in the preceding essay. Broadly, we can respond by noting that the desire of cities, during the archaic period, to link themselves to the figures of Panhellenic epic would have encouraged the identification of some local Corinthian hero or heroine with a character from one of the great sagas. If the voyage of the Argo was already "of interest to everyone" by the time of the *Odyssey*'s composition (*Od.* 12.70), then certainly its characters would be good candidates for such identifications.

More specific reasons for the Corinthians' equation of their local heroine with the Colchian princess can only be guessed at. Certainly, the paradigm of the initiatrix (which Graf identifies as an important part of Colchian Medea's personality) and that of the potentially destructive mother (which I have discussed here) share an important feature: both represent the risks faced by the child during the period between birth and maturity. In some cultures, mothers or other female relatives threaten the adolescent as part of the initiation ritual.[61] This is another expression of a larger idea that lurks behind the paradigm of the reproductive demon: she who gives life is also understood to have the power to truncate it before it comes to fruition. Although mothers never actually threaten initiates in Greek ritual, we can glimpse the idea, perhaps, behind mythic figures such as Clytemnestra, Eriphyle, or Althaea, who kill or try to kill their adolescent sons.

Bremmer notes (in this volume) that Medea's murder of her brother Apsyrtus can be traced with certainty only so far as the early fifth century, a period by which Colchian and Corinthian Medea were already inextricably linked, but he suggests that its origins are older. Apsyrtus' name, "unshorn," alluding as it does to his preadolescent status, suggests that he originally was understood to be a *child* at the time that Medea murdered him. If Apsyrtus' murder was part of the Argonauts' story from early times, it would certainly have encouraged the identification of Colchian and Corinthian Medea. If it was not, however,

---

[61] For a discussion of these ideas in connection with Greek initiation cult, and with references to their expression in other cultures, see Leitao 1993, esp. 8–23. Leitao 1995 discusses how the son's attachment to his mother's feminine sphere presents an obstacle to his maturation in some Greek initiatory rites and myths. In these cases, the mother does not threaten the child by inverting her role as nurturer; rather, it is in the very fulfillment of that role that she potentially impedes her child's maturation.

perhaps it expresses the influence that Corinthian Medea's *persona* had begun to have on that of Colchian Medea.

The specific reasons that the Colchian and Corinthian heroines were joined together are beyond our secure recovery. But whatever they may have been, as audience members, readers, and scholars we cannot agree with the famous words of Medea's nurse, who wished that the Argo had never brought her from Colchis to the land of Greece (Eur. *Med.* 1–11). The combination of helper maiden and infanticide wrought by that legendary voyage makes for an intriguing figure, who continues to haunt us even now, more than twenty-five hundred years after her birth.

Afterword: Corinthian Mormo

The scholiast to Aristides' *Panathenaikos* (p. 42 Dindorf) gives us the core of Mormo's story: φασὶ [Μορμὼ] γυναῖκα εἶναι Κορινθίαν, ἥτις ἐν ἑσπέρᾳ τὰ παιδία αὐτῆς καταφαγοῦσα ἀνέπτη, κατά τινα πρόνοιαν (they say that [Mormo] is a Corinthian woman who knowingly devoured her own children one night and then flew away).

Lenz has argued that the author of the scholion was the rhetor Sopater.[62] If so, then we know that in the fourth century A.D. Mormo's association with Corinth was proverbial even in Athens, for the remark occurs in a group of scholia intended to remind us of which particular lands are inhabited by which particular remarkable creatures. We are also told, for example, that gold-carrying ants are from India, that lions are from Africa, that the best horses come from Thessaly, that Lamia was born in Libya (a point with which other myths about Lamia agree), and, finally, that Mormo is from Corinth. All of the other geographical attachments are well known and quite old, which suggests that the attachment of Mormo to Corinth was, too. It is most likely to have arisen from Mormo's association with one of Corinth's myths. The details of Mormo's story as told by the scholiast match those found in various versions of Medea's story[63]—save for the fact that Mormo not only kills her children but goes on to consume them.

[62] Lenz 1964:31–33.

[63] The "flying away" from Corinth reminds us particularly of of Euripides' dragon chariot; the setting of the deed at night reminds us particularly of the story that Diodorus tells.

I would suggest that when Corinthian Medea became identified with Colchian Medea and, thus, took on a mythic personality that no longer allowed her to be identified fully with the reproductive demon associated with Hera Akraia's cult, the reproductive demon associated with the cult did not completely disappear; rather, it came to be referred to, like other reproductive demons, simply as "the frightening one"— the *mormō*. The Akraian reproductive demon and the new Medea continued to share some mythic features, but whereas literature now portrayed Medea as flying off to Athens or Thebes after her children's deaths, never to be seen by the Corinthians again, Mormo, as before, flew off just a little way, leaving open the possibility that, like all reproductive demons, she might return some evening to seek her prey in Corinthian cradles.[64]

---

[64] Also interesting with respect to Corinth and reproductive demons is the story told by Philostratus (*VA* 4.25), which was later retold by Keats in his poem "Lamia" and which probably was also the inspiration, in combination with a tale from Phlegon's *Mirabilia*, for Goethe's *Die Braut von Corinth*. On the road from Corinth to Cenchreae, a young philosopher encounters a beautiful woman who claims to live in a Corinthian suburb, and falls in love with her. Eventually, through the perspicuity of Apollonius, this woman is revealed to be "an *empousa*, a *lamia*, a *mormolukeia*," waiting to devour the young man's flesh as soon as she has enjoyed his sexual favors. This was, according to Philostratus, "the best-known story about Apollonius.... [M]any people have heard of how he had caught the *lamia* in Corinth." This story illustrates a development of the reproductive demon's *persona* that I will be discussing in depth elsewhere—that is, a development whereby the Greek reproductive demon, like those of other lands, eventually comes to be associated with the sort of demon who preys not only upon children but also upon young men, both sexually and with the intent to devour them. We also see here another tendency that increases with time: all mythic reproductive demons, who once may have had separate characteristics to some degree and may have originated in separate places, become conflated and *lamiai* becomes the generic term for all of them. Underneath the popularity of the story that Philostratus recounts there lies a tacit assumption that Corinth was just the place to encounter such a creature—perhaps because, as the scholiast on Aristides tells us, a famous one once dwelt there.

Appendix: Selected Ancient Sources in Greek
(in chronological order)

Paus. 2.3.11 (after Eumelus)

[Eumelus says that] Μηδείᾳ δὲ παῖδας μὲν γίνεσθαι, τὸ δὲ ἀεὶ τικτόμενον κατακρύπτειν αὐτὸ ἐς τὸ ἱερὸν φέρουσαν τῆς Ἥρας, κατακρύπτειν δὲ ἀθανάτους ἔσεσθαι νομίζουσαν· τέλος δὲ αὐτήν τε μαθεῖν ὡς ἡμαρτήκοι τῆς ἐλπίδος καὶ ἅμα ὑπὸ τοῦ Ἰάσονος φωραθεῖσαν—οὐ γὰρ αὐτὸν ἔχειν δεομένῃ συγγνώμην, ἀποπλέοντα δὲ ἐς Ἰωλκὸν οἴχεσθαι—τούτων δὲ ἕνεκα ἀπελθεῖν καὶ Μήδειαν παραδοῦσαν Σισύφῳ τὴν ἀρχήν.

Schol. Pindar *Ol.* 13.74 (after Eumelus)

[Μήδεια] ἐν Κορίνθῳ κατῴκει καὶ ἔπαυσε Κορινθίους λιμῷ κατεχομένους θύσασα Δήμητρι καὶ Νύμφαις Λημνίαις. ἐκεῖ δὲ αὐτῆς ὁ Ζεὺς ἠράσθη. οὐκ ἐπείθετο δὲ ἡ Μήδεια τὸν τῆς Ἥρας ἐκκλίνουσα χόλον· διὸ καὶ Ἥρα ὑπέσχετο αὐτῇ ἀθανάτους ποιῆσαι τοὺς παῖδας· ἀποθανόντας δὲ τούτους τιμῶσι Κορίνθιοι, καλοῦντες μιξοβαρβάρους.

Eur. *Med.* 1378–83

> σφας τῇδ' ἐγὼ θάψω χερί,
> φέρουσ' ἐς Ἥρας τέμενος Ἀκραίας θεοῦ,
> ὡς μή τις αὐτοὺς πολεμίων καθυβρίσῃ,
> τύμβους ἀνασπῶν· γῇ δὲ τῇδε Σισύφου
> σεμνὴν ἑορτὴν καὶ τέλη προσάψομεν
> τὸ λοιπὸν ἀντὶ τοῦδε δυσσεβοῦς φόνου.

Schol. Eur. *Med.* 264 = Didymus quoting the historian Creophylus (= *FGrH* 417 F 3) (fourth or fifth century B.C.?)

Δίδυμος δὲ ἐναντιοῦται τούτῳ καὶ παρατίθεται τὰ Κρεωφύλου ἔχοντα οὕτως· "τὴν γὰρ Μήδειαν λέγεται διατρίβουσαν ἐν Κορίνθῳ τὸν ἄρχοντα τότε τῆς πόλεως Κρέοντα ἀποκτεῖναι φαρμάκοις. δείσασαν δὲ τοὺς φίλους καὶ τοὺς συγγενεῖς αὐτοῦ φυγεῖν εἰς Ἀθήνας, τοὺς δὲ υἱούς, ἐπεὶ νεώτεροι ὄντες οὐκ ἠδύναντο ἀκολουθεῖν, ἐπὶ τὸν βωμὸν τῆς Ἀκραίας Ἥρας καθίσαι νομίσασαν τὸν πατέρα αὐτῶν φροντιεῖν τῆς σωτηρίας αὐτῶν. τοὺς δὲ Κρέοντος οἰκείους ἀποκτείναντας αὐτοὺς διαδοῦναι λόγον ὅτι ἡ Μήδεια οὐ μόνον τὸν Κρέοντα, ἀλλὰ καὶ τοὺς ἑαυτῆς παῖδας ἀπέκτεινε."

Schol. Eur. *Med*. 264 = Parmeniscus (first–second century B.C.)

Παρμενίσκος γράφει κατὰ λέξιν οὕτως· "ταῖς δὲ Κορινθίαις οὐ βουλομέναις ὑπὸ βαρβάρου καὶ φαρμακίδος γυναικὸς ἄρχεσθαι αὐτῇ τε ἐπιβουλεῦσαι καὶ τὰ τέκνα αὐτῆς ἀνελεῖν ἑπτὰ μὲν ἄρσενα ἑπτὰ δὲ θήλεα. [Εὐριπίδης δὲ δυσὶ μόνοις φησὶν αὐτὴν κεχρῆσθαι.] Ταῦτα δὲ διωκόμενα καταφυγεῖν εἰς τὸ τῆς Ἀκραίας Ἥρας ἱερὸν καὶ ἐπὶ τὸ ἱερὸν καθίσαι. Κορινθίους δὲ αὐτῶν οὐδὲ οὕτως ἀπέχεσθαι, ἀλλ' ἐπὶ τοῦ βωμοῦ πάντα ταῦτα ἀποσφάξαι. Λοιμοῦ δὲ γενομένου εἰς τὴν πόλιν, πολλὰ σώματα ὑπὸ τῆς νόσου διαφθείρεσθαι· μαντευομένοις δὲ αὐτοῖς χρησμῳδῆσαι τὸν θεὸν ἱλάσκεσθαι τὸ τῶν Μηδείας τέκνων ἄγος, ὅθεν Κορινθίοις μέχρι τῶν καιρῶν τῶν καθ' ἡμᾶς καθ' ἕκαστον ἐνιαυτὸν ἑπτὰ κούρους καὶ ἑπτὰ κούρας τῶν ἐπισημοτάτων ἀνδρῶν ἐναπενιαυτίζειν ἐν τῷ τῆς θεᾶς τεμένει καὶ μετὰ θυσιῶν ἱλάσκεσθαι τὴν ἐκείνων μῆνιν καὶ τὴν δί ἐκείνους γενομένην τῆς θεᾶς ὀργήν."

Diod. Sic. 4.54.7

[They say that] ... πλὴν γὰρ ἑνὸς τοῦ διαφυγόντος τοὺς ἄλλους υἱοὺς ἀποσφάξαι [Μήδειαν] καὶ τὰ σώματα τούτων ἐν τῷ τῆς Ἥρας τεμένει θάψαι καὶ μετὰ τῶν πιστοτάτων θεραπαινίδων ἔτι νυκτὸς μέσης φυγεῖν ἐκ τῆς Κορίνθου, καὶ διεκπεσεῖν εἰς Θήβας πρὸς Ἡρακλέα.

Apollod. *Bibl*. 1.145–46

... [Μήδεια] τοὺς παῖδας ... ἀπέκτεινε.... (Or another version Apollodorus knows is that) ... [Μήδεια] φεύγουσα, τοὺς παῖδας ἔτι νηπίους ὄντας κατέλιπεν, ἱκέτας καθίσασα ἐπὶ τὸν βωμὸν τῆς Ἥρας τῆς Ἀκραίας· Κορίνθιοι δὲ αὐτοὺς ἀναστήσαντες κατετραυμάτισαν.

Aelian *VH* 5.21

ὑπὲρ δὲ τοῦ τολμήματός (the Corinthians' murder of the children) φασι μέχρι τοῦ νῦν ἐναγίζουσι τοῖς παισὶ Κορίνθιοι, οἱονεὶ δασμὸν τούτοις ἀποδίδοντες.

Philostr. *Her*. 53.4

[the Corinthians honor Medea's children] ... θρήνῳ εἴκασται τελεστικῷ τε καὶ ἐνθέῳ· τοὺς μὲν γὰρ μειλίσσονται....

Schol. Eur. *Med*. 1382

λιμωξάντων Κορινθίων ἔχρησεν ὁ θεὸς τιμῆσαι τοὺς τῆς Μηδείας παῖδας.

3

MEDEA AS FOUNDATION-HEROINE

Nita Krevans

O my America! my new-found-land . . .
How blest am I in this discovering thee!
(Donne, "To His Mistris Going to Bed")

THE EQUATION of the female body with landscape is an old and
persistent metaphor, and one with particular resonance for tales
of exploration and foundation. Embedded in common phrases
such as "virgin territory" we find a cluster of assumptions about the
process of claiming unoccupied regions for the human society about
to settle there: that the landscape is potentially fertile but currently
barren, that it is empty and immature, that political development and
reproduction must both await the arrival of the male founder.[1] Greek
foundation stories (*ktisis*-sagas), which take this metaphor as the basis
for their narratives, provide a set of tales in which traditional notions of
male and female are emphatically presented—the wandering hero, torn
from his family, leader of his people; the faceless nymph, fixed in the
earth she personifies, mother of kings.

How does Medea fit into this picture? We do not normally associate her with etiological tales of the origin of cities and states.
Yet most of the surviving Greek texts that discuss Medea link her
in some way with *ktiseis*: Pindar shows her prophesying the foundation of Cyrene; Herodotus makes her the eponymous legendary ruler
of the Medes; Callimachus and Apollonius describe colonies founded
by Colchians originally sent out in pursuit of her. An examination of
the varying stories involving Medea and foundation legends is an instructive glimpse into a different heroine, often completely removed
from the better-known witch and child murderer, but still hovering

I would like to thank Jim Clauss, Sarah Iles Johnston, and Alison Keith for many
valuable comments and suggestions.
[1] Dougherty 1993:63–76.

ambiguously between divine and human in the same manner as her darker, Corinthian incarnation. Most striking is the contrast between Medea and other female figures in *ktisis*-sagas, and I will focus my discussion on the persistent reversals of male and female types in the Medean examples.

It must be conceded at the outset that legendary tales associated with foundations in antiquity center primarily on male founders. Homer's tale of Tlepolemus (*Il.* 2.653–70), one of the oldest surviving examples, already exhibits in condensed form the typical narrative pattern of many later stories: the hero is introduced (son of Astyocheia and Heracles); a cause for seeking new land is given (accidental kin-murder); he prepares ships and assembles colonists, arrives at the site of the colony (Rhodes), and establishes his rule.[2] In this scheme, all the key players are male. The minor status of Tlepolemus' mother is signaled by the slippage in her name; in Homer she is Astyocheia, and elsewhere Astyoche, Astydameia, or Antigone.[3]

There are, however, several traditional roles for heroines in these tales. The most important female role is that of the eponymous nymph, who brings to life the metaphor of woman-as-landscape. These are divine maidens who are ravished by male deities, uprooted, and settled in a new location that thereafter bears their name. Cyrene and Rhodes are perhaps the best-known examples, since their stories are featured in Pindar, and the two present an interesting contrast. Rhodes is spotted and claimed by Helios while still a subterranean island (*Ol.* 7.54–63); she is referred to as γαῖαν (land, 63) and νᾶσος (island, 70) and is never identified as a maiden even when the god weds her and begets children (71–73).[4]

Cyrene, on the other hand, is unmistakably a maiden (*Pyth.* 9). She has a father (Hypseus, line 13), a homeland (Thessaly, 5), and a distinct personality: a daddy's girl who scorns weaving and parties in favor of big-game hunting (17–25). The land she will name is already extant as part of Libya (55–58), also here personified (πότνια Λιβύα, "Lady Libya"; 55). Yet Cyrene, upon her marriage, is immediately associated with the territory newly carved out of Libya (ἵνα οἱ χθονὸς αἶσαν / αὐτίκα συντελέθειν ἔννομον δωρήσεται "where she [Libya] shall at once grant her a portion of land rightly her own"; 56–57). Only after this topographical

---

[2] Schmid 1947:5–6.

[3] Apollod. 2.7.6, Pindar *Ol.* 7.23 and schol. *ad loc.*

[4] As Segal 1986:177 points out, it is Helios rather than Rhodes who gives birth! See also Dougherty 1993:70–72.

definition is the birth of her divine child Aristaeus mentioned. Like Rhodes, she is the natural, spatial component of the colony, a place marker waiting for the male hero to arrive as founder.[5]

Many sources thus offer two foundation myths for a single state: the territorial foundation myth (female) and the civic foundation myth (male). Both myths about Rhodes, for example, are told in *Olympian 7*, both myths of Cyrene in Callimachus' *Hymn to Apollo*. It is worth emphasizing the distinction between eponymous heroines and eponymous heroes, which continues the motif of woman as earth: females usually give their names to land, males to nations or cities.[6] Thus Rhodes is the island, but her progeny by Helios produce the eponymous heroes of the Rhodian cities (*Ol.* 7.71–76):

ἔνθα ʻΡόδῳ ποτὲ μιχθεὶς τέκεν
ἑπτὰ σοφώτατα νοήματ' ἐπὶ προτέρων
ἀνδρῶν παραδεξαμένους
παῖδας, ὧν εἷς μὲν Κάμιρον
πρεσβύτατόν τε ᾿Ιάλυ-
σον ἔτεκεν Λίνδον τ'· ἀπάτερθε δ' ἔχον
διὰ γαῖαν τρίχα δασσάμενοι πατρωΐαν
ἀστέων μοίρας, κέκληνται δέ σφιν ἕδραι.

There long ago mingling with Rhodes he sired
seven sons, who had minds wiser
than men of old; of these one bore Cameirus,
and Ialysus as eldest, and Lindus.
These had for their cities separate shares
of their father's land, dividing it in three, and
each one's seat was named in his honor.

The second possible female role in foundation tales is that of the dynastic heroine, mother of a founder or of a line of local rulers. The two are not exclusive: Rhodes, in the passage above, plays both parts. Although this role is often little more than a footnote, as in the case of Astyocheia, there are tales that center on the dynastic heroine rather than on her offspring. These involve stories similar to those of the eponymous nymphs, in which a maiden attracts the attention of a god and leaves her original home. In these cases, however, the mother is

[5] See further Diod. Sic. 4.72 and Dougherty 1993:65–67, 141–52. An interesting rationalization appears in Apollonius, where the clod of earth that is to become Thera appears as a maiden who lies with the hero Euphamus—but only in a dream (4.1731ff.).

[6] Schmid 1947:138–41 calls the territorial type of foundation the "Urktisis," but he does not distinguish female eponyms from male.

normally a mortal, her displacement is usually traumatic—involving
exile, imprisonment, or abduction—and she does not give her name to
her new land; foundations are instead associated with her heroic child.[7]

A good example is the elaborate tale of Antiope, who is ravished
by Zeus, driven into exile, and eventually rescued from mistreatment
by her semidivine sons Amphion and Zethus, the builders of Thebes.[8]
Callisto, another victim of Zeus, is also driven from home (changed into
a bear); she becomes the mother of Arcas, hero of Arcadia.[9] Boeotus
and Aeolus, eponymous heroes of the Boeotians and Aeolians, are
the children of Poseidon and Melanippe; the heroine is blinded and
imprisoned when the pregnancy is discovered.[10] Europa, kidnapped
by Zeus, is carried across the sea and gives birth to a line of Cretan
kings;[11] Io, forced into bovine exile, settles at last in Egypt and bears
Epaphus, fulfilling her colonizing destiny as prophesied by Prometheus
(Aes. *PV* 813–15):

> οὗτός σ᾿ ὁδώσει τὴν τρίγωνον ἐς χθόνα
> Νειλῶτιν, οὗ δὴ τὴν μακρὰν ἀποικίαν,
> Ἰοῖ, πέπρωται σοί τε καὶ τέκνοις κτίσαι.

> [the river] will guide you to the triangular land
> of the Nile, where it is fated for you and your
> children, Io, to found your distant colony.

In cases such as those of Io and Europa, in which the heroine is kidnapped rather than exiled, she can play the last of the traditional roles
for heroines in foundation legend: the missing girl is sought by a male
kinsman (or kinsmen), who found new cities rather than return to the
angry father to report that their quest has failed. Europa, of course, is

[7] Burkert 1979:6–7 calls these tales "the girl's tragedy," corrected by Bremmer 1987b:
28–29 to "the mother's tragedy"; for further examples and discussion, see Burkert;
Bremmer; and Rose 1958:289.

[8] Reflecting a different version of Thebes' founding, which was later integrated with
the Cadmean and Labdacid tales; see Buck 1979:45–52, 57; see also Schmid 1947:176 on
wall building as an essential ingredient of the *ktisis*-saga. It is noteworthy that in one
version, Apollodorus 3.5.6, Zethus marries Thebe, who gives the city her name.

[9] Ovid *Met.* 2.401–530; Hes. fr. 163 M.-W.; Apollod. 3.8.2 with Frazer 1921: *ad loc.*

[10] Hyg. *Fab.* 186; Eur. frs. 480–514 Nauck.

[11] It may be objected that Europa is indeed an eponymous nymph, but the identification
of the maiden with the land area is very problematic. A few ancient etymologies connect
the two, but the majority of the evidence points to two distinct entities. The situation is
complicated by the presence of additional, more obscure female figures named Europa
who appear in the tradition alongside the territorial name. See Dombrowski 1984; M. West
1966:ad 357; Callimachus fr. 622 Pf.

sought by Cadmus, who then founds Thebes; Io by Cyrnus, supposedly the eponymous founder of a city in Caria.[12]

I have gone into some detail about the patterns of male and female roles in foundation mythology because Medea's appearances in foundation stories form a striking exception when seen against this backdrop. True, there are tales that portray her as a typical dynastic heroine or as the kidnapped maiden. Yet, for every version in which she seems to follow the normal scheme, there is a variant that portrays her as a defiant anomaly.

The simplest foundation tale connected with Medea is an etymologizing myth that connects her with the Medes.[13] In a sixth-century section of Hesiod's *Theogony*[14] we are told that Jason returns with Medea after his adventures and makes her his wife; thereupon she bears him Medeus, who is raised by the centaur Chiron (1000–2):

> καί ῥ' ἥ γε δμηθεῖσ' ὑπ' Ἰήσονι ποιμένι λαῶν
> Μήδειον τέκε παῖδα, τὸν οὔρεσιν ἔτρεφε Χείρων
> Φιλλυρίδης· μεγάλου δὲ Διὸς νόος ἐξετελεῖτο.

> And she, tamed by Jason, shepherd of the people,
> bore a child Medeus, whom Chiron son of Philyra
> raised in the mountains; the plan of great Zeus was fulfilled.

There is no hint here of sorcery or child murder; Medea is a princess who leaves her own land and bears a heroic child who gives his name to a nation.[15] Medeus is the equivalent of Arcas, or Boeotus, or Aeolus, and Medea takes her place as a dynastic heroine like Callisto. The one

---

[12] Cadmus and Europa: e.g., Eur. *Phoen.* 638–75, Ap. Rhod. 3.1178–87; in some versions additional brothers appear, as Apollod. 3.1.1. Cyrnus: Diod. Sic. 5.60.4–5; the name is uncertain (see Parthenius 1.1). Compare the quest of Otys and Ephialtes for their kidnapped mother and sister, Diod. Sic. 5.51, and see further Krevans 1993:264.

[13] The etymological connection of Medea with the Medes is maintained in some authors by a variant spelling Μήδειοι for the Medes (e.g., Pindar *Pyth.* 1.78; Ibycus fr. 39 *PMG*; Callimachus fr. 110.46 Pf.), or conversely Μήδη instead of Medea (e.g., Euphorion fr. 14.3 Powell). Her name also, of course, is linked to the Greek word for "plan, counsel"; see O'Higgins in this volume, p. 114.

[14] On the date of this section of the *Theogony*, see M. West 1966:ad 881, 947, 1001, 1016. The archaic epic poet Cinaethon also seems to have known Jason and Medea's male child Medeus (Paus. 2.3.9), so the story is early.

[15] The presence of Chiron marks Medeus' heroic status; the centaur tutors Achilles (*Il.* 11.832), Asclepius (*Il.* 4.219; Pindar *Pyth.* 3.45) and Jason himself (Pindar *Pyth.* 4.102) among others; Medeus' dynastic future is then implied not only by the mention of the "will of Zeus" but also by his association with Latinus and Phocus, who appear in the following verses. See M. West 1966:ad 1001.

slightly unusual feature is that the father is not a divinity; the divine
parent seems instead to be Medea.[16]

Herodotus, however, gives another version of the connection between Medea and the Medes. In his account, the Medes were initially
called Arians, but changed their name when Medea arrived among them
after fleeing Athens (Hdt. 7.62). Pausanias (2.3.8) follows Herodotus but
adds a son, Medus, by Aegeus; Apollodorus (1.9.28) also has Medus
as a son of Medea and Aegeus but credits the son rather than the
mother with the conquest and naming (1.9.28): ἀλλ' οὗτος μὲν πολλῶν
κρατήσας βαρβάρων τὴν ὑφ' ἑαυτὸν χώραν ἅπασαν Μηδίαν ἐκάλεσε, καὶ
στρατευόμενος ἐπὶ 'Ινδοὺς ἀπέθανε[17] (But he, after conquering many
barbarian peoples, called the whole place Media after himself. Then,
leading his army against the Indians, he perished.) The variation in
the stories is revealing, because we find the slippage now on the male
side: it is the name of the father and not the mother that varies (another
signal of Medea's divine nature), and next to conventional representations of Medeus or Medus as an eponymous hero we find the early
Herodotean version, which ignores him and in essence grants the status
of eponymous hero to Medea.[18]

The second set of ktisis-tales involve foundations by the unsuccessful
Colchian pursuers of Medea. Callimachus recounts in the Aetia how the
Colchians become "weary with wandering" (fr. 10 Pf.), and one band
founds a city (Pola) in Illyria (fr. 11.3–5 Pf.):

> οἱ μὲν ἐπ' 'Ιλλυρικοῖο πόρου σχάσσαντες ἐρετμά
>   λᾶα πάρα ξανθῆς 'Αρμονίης ὄφιος
> ἄστυρον ἐκτίσσαντο ...

> Some, letting fall their oars by the Illyrian strait,
>   founded a small city by the stone of the tawny serpent (?)
> Harmonia ...

Another group settles on Corcyra and then eventually founds Aman-
tine, by Oricus (fr. 12 Pf.).[19] Apollonius, too, tells of a Colchian

---

[16] On Medea's divinity see M. West 1966:ad 992; compare Hesiod fr. 376 M.-W. =
Alcman fr. 163 PMG, where see Page ad loc.

[17] There is a suspicious resemblance to the biography of Alexander here.

[18] There is similar variation in late versions of the myth of Cyrene; see, e.g., the schol.
ad Ap. Rhod. 2.498 and further citations in Dougherty-Glenn 1988:200. For Medea as
ruler, compare the story of her rule of Corinth (Paus. 2.3.10); see also Diod. Sic. 4.55–56 on
these tales.

[19] On this second foundation see Pfeiffer 1949–53:ad loc.

foundation in Illyria "by the tomb of Harmonia" (4.517) and of one near Oricus, in the Thundering Mountains (4.518–21).[20]

In these foundation stories, Medea plays the part of the kidnapped maiden, and we find further indications that she can be seen as another Europa or Io. Herodotus certainly views her in this way; he begins his work by discussing the abductions of Io, Europa, Medea, and Helen as pretexts for Greco-Persian enmity (1.1–4). On a more subtle level we find within the various treatments of Medea's story links to Europa and Thebes: the sowing of the dragon's teeth, the mention of Harmonia and Cadmus in connection with the founding of Pola, the theme of the father's wrath preventing the return of the searchers.[21] Io is less prominent, but also appears: Medea's dream in book 3 of the *Argonautica* (3.616–32) has connections to the dream of Io in the *Prometheus* (Aes. 645–49), and Valerius Flaccus compares Medea explicitly to Io in his poem (7.111–13).[22]

There are, however, other foundations connected with the pursuit of Medea that cast her in quite a different light. Apollonius not only mentions the Illyrian and Corcyran *ktiseis* but also tells us that some Colchians settled the islands the Argonauts had held during the negotiations with Apsyrtus, whose murder makes him the eponymous hero of the new territories (4.514–15):[23] οἱ μὲν ἐπ' αὐτάων νήσων ἔβαν ᾗσιν ἐπέσχον / ἥρωες, ναίουσι δ' ἐπώνυμοι Ἀψύρτοιο (Some went onto the very islands the heroes had occupied, and they live there, taking their name from Apsyrtos.) Although Medea herself does not actually kill her brother in the *Argonautica*, she is sprinkled with his blood and must be cleansed by Circe (4.471–76, 4.557–61). The resulting web of pollution, wandering, and purification belongs not to tales of foundation heroines but to tales of foundation heroes.

In the lives of *ktisis*-heroes, the theme of exile stemming from family pollution appears frequently. Caunus flees Miletus to avoid the incestuous love of his sister Byblis and founds the Carian city that bears his name; Althaemenes leaves Crete to thwart an oracle predicting he will kill his father and founds the temple of Zeus by Cameirus; brothers

---

[20] On Apollonius' correction of Callimachus' geography, see Vian and Delage 1981:34–35.

[21] On Aeëtes' wrath (Callimachus fr. 7.27–34 Pf.; Ap. Rhod. 4.512) see Vian and Delage 1981:168 *ad* 512.

[22] On the dreams of Io, Europa, Medea, and Ilia and their connection to foundation lore, see Krevans 1993.

[23] See also Apollod. 1.9.25; Strabo 7.5.5.

Sarpedon and Minos quarrel over a lover and Sarpedon departs for Lycia.[24]

By far the most common story is that the hero is responsible for the death of a kinsman. So Tlepolemus leaves Tiryns and founds Rhodes after killing his uncle (*Il.* 2. 662–63; Pindar *Ol.* 7.27–30); the sons of Helios leave Rhodes after killing their brother (Diodorus Siculus 5.57) and found several different cities. The hero does not necessarily physically murder the victim himself: Teucer leaves Salamis when his father blames him for the death of Ajax and eventually founds a city on Cyprus (Eur. *Hel.* 89–150).[25] Settlements associated with the murdered Apsyrtus, then, inevitably move Medea away from her original status as kidnapped maiden and present her as someone who looks remarkably like a male founder. This aggressive Medea is more in accord with most versions of Medea's and Jason's story, where her voluntary departure with Jason undercuts the comparison with Europa and Io.[26]

An even grislier tale lies behind the second foundation associated with Apsyrtus—the foundation of Tomi. In this legend, Apsyrtus is not a grown man who pursues the errant Medea; rather, he is a younger brother who is taken by Medea as she flees and dismembered to slow Aeëtes' pursuit (Apollod. 1.23–24; Ovid *Tr.* 3.9). The site of the murder takes its name from the "cutting" of the body.[27] With this story we arrive at a complete inversion of the "kidnapped heroine" motif. The maiden is the kidnapper, not the victim; the male pursuer is now the helpless sacrifice whose death is commemorated in the new territory.

The final foundation tale to be considered treats Medea as a prophet who instructs future settlers about the location and destiny of the colony. This is the story of the miraculous clod of earth recounted in Pindar's fourth Pythian ode.[28] The god Triton had given the clod to the Argonaut Euphamus, but it was washed overboard (*Pyth.* 4.19–40); when the Argo reaches Thera, Medea utters an ἔπος (oracular statement) predicting the

---

[24] Caunus: Ovid *Met.* 9.450–655, cf. Parthenius 11.1–3. Althaemenes: Diod. Sic. 5.59, Apollod. 3.2. Sarpedon: Apollod. 3.1.2; but cf. Diod. Sic. 5.79.3 and Hdt. 1.173.

[25] Further examples and discussion, Dougherty 1993:38–41; Schmid 1947:170; on the Teucer story see Prinz 1979:56–77.

[26] So already in Pindar (*Ol.* 13.53) Medea "decides on her own marriage, in opposition to her father"; compare *Pyth.* 4.250, discussed below.

[27] This version seems to go back to Pherecydes (schol. *ad* Ap. Rhod. 4.223). On the divergent accounts of Apsyrtus and his death see Vian and Delage 1981:20–23 and Bremmer in this volume.

[28] Other foundation tales also feature clods of earth; see Braswell 1988:ad *Pyth.* 4.21; Jackson 1987:26–27; Dougherty-Glenn 1988:179–80.

future dominion of Euphamus' descendants on Thera and the eventual colonization of Cyrene by the Theran Battus (9–58).

Here Medea is a powerful oracular figure who not only correctly predicts the establishment of Thera but also sees far beyond the fate of the clod to the later foundation of Cyrene. She is even able to predict hypothetical alternatives (43–49, what would have happened had the clod not been lost). Her words emerge from "an immortal mouth" (ἀθανάτου στόματος, 11) and they immobilize and silence the male heroes (ibid. 57–58):[29] ἔπταξαν δ' ἀκίνητοι σιωπᾷ / ἥροες ἀντίθεοι πυκινὰν μῆτιν κλύοντες (the godlike heroes cowered in silence, unmoving, listening to her deep thinking).

It is not only the heroes who are overpowered, however. The Delphic oracle itself is virtually subordinated to her, its command to Battus presented as a frame for her speech, a later and derivative confirmation of her original utterance (τὸ Μηδείας ἔπος ἀγκομίσαι, "to fulfil the word of Medea," 9; ἐν τούτῳ λόγῳ, "in accordance with this speech [of Medea]," 59–60).[30] While by this point we may no longer be surprised to find Medea portrayed as a divinity, heroines in foundation tales normally receive prophecies rather than utter them. Io, for example, is consoled for her suffering by Prometheus' prediction of the fame of her children (Aes. PV 846–74); Tyro hears a similar oracle from her seducer Poseidon (Od. 11.248–50). It is particularly telling that the portrait of an oracular and authoritative Medea in Pythian 4 is at the expense of the normal guide of colonists, the male Olympian Apollo.[31]

Pythian 4 reveals the unconventional nature of Medea in a more disquieting fashion just before it concludes. Breaking off his detailed, expansive narrative as Jason approaches the fleece, Pindar suddenly compresses the remainder of the tale into fourteen lines (249–62). Jason kills the monster, carries off the princess, and sails off with his heroic crew to a foreign land, where the seed of future kings is

[29] See Braswell 1988:ad loc. and O'Higgins in this volume, pp. 113–14. Segal 1986:139–40 sees a sinister tone to Pindar's description of her powers.

[30] On the reference to Medea in 59–60 see Braswell 1988:ad loc.; more generally on the connection between Medea's oracle and the Delphic oracle see Segal 1986:74–76, 139–45, 182–83. Segal 142 believes Pindar is "counteracting" Medea's darker speech with "Apolline wisdom"; I agree that the two are contrasted but see Medea's as the stronger voice in the poem.

[31] On the role of the Delphic oracle in foundation lore, see Dougherty 1993:18–21, 32–35, 45–47; Schmid 1947:148–67; Fontenrose 1978:137ff. Pindar also toys with Apollo's role in Pythian 9, where Chiron delivers a foundation oracle to the god as he contemplates abducting the nymph Cyrene; he is given the same epithet (ζαμενής, "spirited," Pyth. 9.38, 4.10, on which see Braswell 1988:ad loc.).

planted.[32] With this outline, and a different heroine, we would expect the future kings to be the offspring of hero and maiden, whose marriage is clearly anticipated by the structure of the story.[33] In fact, the marriage of Jason and Medea is suppressed; the seed is the seed of Euphamus, planted in the ominous locale of the "husband-murdering" Lemnian women (252).[34]

The Lemnian women thus replace Medea as brides and mothers of future founders, a substitution that cannot help but underscore her persistent unwillingness to play a proper heroine's role in the story. When Jason abducts her, even in the newly compressed narrative, Pindar is compelled to add: "with her help" (250). In that same line, he grants her the epithet "slayer of Pelias" (Πελίαο φονόν). This not only links her to the Lemnian women who substitute for her but is based on the Homeric epithet "man-slaying," traditionally used of war heroes.[35] Both Pindaric allusions to the Thera/Cyrene foundation, then, present Medea in powerful, masculine roles incompatible with female fertility.[36]

In Apollonius' version of this episode, the dominant role of Medea disappears. It is Orpheus who commands the Argonauts to set out the tripod that brings the epiphany of Triton and the gift of the clod (4.1547–49); it is Jason who interprets Euphamus' mysterious dream, foretelling the growth of Thera from the clod (4.1731–54).[37] Yet, as I have argued elsewhere, Euphamus' dream, in which the clod turns into a maiden, is in fact a version of heroines' dreams found in many instances of the "girl's tragedy."[38] Medea herself, as noted earlier, has a similar dream in book 3 (3.616–32). Apollonius transfers the prophecy from Medea to Jason, emphasizing Jason's rapport with Apollo,[39] but he retains

---

[32] On this metaphor see Dougherty 1993:63; Braswell 1988:*ad loc.*; duBois 1988: 67.

[33] Segal 1986:70–71.

[34] The return of Pindar's Argonauts via Lemnos creates both geographical and narrative difficulties; Braswell 1988:*ad loc.* shows the necessity of concluding with Lemnos to authenticate the Cyrenean foundation oracle uttered by Medea earlier in the poem.

[35] ἀνδροφόνος, the epithet of Hector; see Braswell 1988:*ad loc.* on the formation of the epithet. Some editors prefer to read the adjective as two separate words, but textual evidence does not support this.

[36] On Medea's masculinity more generally see Foley 1989:61ff.

[37] On the more general significance of the changes made by Apollonius here, see Jackson 1987; Braswell 1988:ad *Pyth.* 4.42.

[38] Krevans 1993:262–65.

[39] So Jackson 1987:28. The importance of Apollo for Jason in the poem is described by Clauss 1993:76–79.

a subtle link with the masculinized Medea of Pindar by feminizing Euphamus.

There are traces of Pindar's prophetic Medea elsewhere. Asclepiades the mythographer is quoted as saying οὐδὲν τῶν ῥηθέντων ὑπ' αὐτῆς ἀτελὲς γεγένηται οὐδὲ ἐφθάρη (none of her utterances went unfulfilled, nor did any perish; schol. ad Pindar Pyth. 4.18). For the most part, however, later authors do not depict Medea as clairvoyant. In Euripides' Medea, Aegeus consults her about Delphi's puzzling response to his inquiry about how to sire children (674–81). Medea's response to Aegeus' request is not an interpretation of the oracle but a promise of magical drugs to end childlessness (717–18).[40] The witch and the prophet seem to a certain extent mutually exclusive: Pindar reduces Medea's sorcery in Pythian 4 to scattered one-word hints,[41] while the remodeled, Medea-less Euphamus episode in Apollonius follows closely upon a spectacular and chilling display of her magic power against the bronze giant Talus (4.1638–88).

The inconsistency in the Euphamus story, as with the other tales examined here, does resolve itself when viewed more abstractly. Both versions emphasize abnormal forces in Medea. Apollonius underscores her sorcery in the grim final vignette of her attack on the monster Talus, and that portrait remains unrelieved by the positive powers she might have displayed had he not removed her from the Theran foundation myth. Pindar depicts her as less than female and more than human as he stamps her mantic skill with a retroactive seal of approval from Delphi. The focus on her prophetic powers is sharpened by the suppression of witchcraft. Her effect on observers in each case is the same: the awed silence of the Argonauts after Medea's prophecy is echoed by Apollonius' response to the Talus episode: ἦ μέγα δή μοι ἐνὶ φρεσὶ θάμβος ἄηται (truly great wonder is wafted into my mind, 4.1673).

As we have seen, these hints of divinity and gender inversion are found in most of the stories about Medea and foundations. Her ambiguous status appears everywhere: Is Medea the mother of the eponym, or is she herself the eponym? Is Medea the kidnapped heroine or is she herself a kidnapper? Is she in fact a heroine—or is she a hero? The tales considered here often play on that ambiguity in a positive way, giving her divine attributes, a heroic child, and even oracular powers. Most

---

[40] This promise has sinister overtones, foreshadowing the attempt to poison Theseus already shown by Euripides in his earlier Aegeus. On this play see most recently Sutton 1987.

[41] Πελίαο φονόν, discussed above; παμφαρμάκου (skilled in drugs, Pyth. 4.233).

legends about Medea, however, find in that same indeterminate nature an extraordinary capacity for destruction. From Colchis to Thessaly to Corinth to Athens to Persia she flees, eternally unable to take root in the Greek mythic landscape—a heroine not of foundation but of annihilation.

4

WHY DID MEDEA KILL HER

BROTHER APSYRTUS?

Jan N. Bremmer

S URPRISINGLY, THE DEATH of Medea's brother has received
little attention from classical scholars, a neglect that I shall attempt
to redress in this essay. My discussion falls into two parts. First, I
will examine the specifics of the murder as it was described in the ancient
sources in order to clarify the ways in which ancient authors presented
it. Second, I will elucidate the murder's significance by examining the
value placed on the bond between brother and sister in ancient Greece
and, for comparative purposes, in other traditional cultures.

The Murder

To orient ourselves, let us begin with our most detailed account of the
murder from Greek sources, that of Apollonius of Rhodes (4.452–76).[1]
His description is brief but realistic:

After Jason had managed to steal the Golden Fleece with the help
of Medea, the couple escaped from Colchis with the Argonauts. Under the command of Medea's brother Apsyrtus, the angry Colchians
immediately began to pursue them down the river Ister and blocked
off virtually every exit to the sea, except for two islands, which were
sacred to Artemis. Here the Argonauts sought refuge. Negotiations
were initiated, and it was agreed that Jason could keep the fleece, but
that Medea should stay behind in the temple of Artemis on one of the
islands. Unhappy with this decision, Medea convinced Jason to take her
home with him. Jason proposed to accomplish this by luring Apsyrtus
into the temple and murdering him. Medea supported the scheme by

For advice and observations I thank Annette Harder, Margot Schmidt, and Sarah Iles
Johnston, who also skillfully revised my English.
[1] Cf. Wilamowitz 1924:191–96.

sending false messages to Apsyrtus, promising to steal the fleece and hand it back to him. Tempted by her treacherous offer, Apsyrtus came to the sanctuary of Artemis at night and was jumped upon by Jason as he spoke with his sister. Medea quickly covered her eyes with her veil to avoid seeing Jason hit her brother "as an ox-slayer strikes a big, powerful bull" (4.468).[2] Jason cut off Apsyrtus' extremities and "three times he licked up some blood and three times he spat out the pollution, as killers are wont to do in order to expiate treacherous murders" (477–79). Deprived of their commander, the Colchians became easy prey for the Argonauts, who successfully defeated them.

Apollonius emphasizes the brutality and treachery of the murder. Judging from his comparison of Jason to an ox striker, who was employed at sacrifices to stun the largest victims by hitting them on the back of the head before their throats were slit,[3] Apollonius pictured Jason as leaping upon Apsyrtus from behind. Although the Greeks had few objections to killing enemies in whatever way they could during the archaic period, in later times they rejected the idea of killing "by stealth" and fiercely condemned such murders.[4] The killers themselves also felt this social disapproval, which was reflected in the serious *miasma* attached to the act. To prevent the ghost of such a victim from returning and seeking vengeance, they mutilated the corpse by cutting off its extremities, just as Jason did to Apsyrtus, tying the severed parts around his neck and under his armpits (*maschalismos*).[5] It also was common for Greek murderers to lick up and then spit out the blood of their victims, as Jason did, in hopes they thus would rid themselves of the *miasma* they had incurred.[6] It is typical, furthermore, of the Greek mentality of the postarchaic period that these actions were to no avail: Zeus decreed that not only Jason but Medea, as well, would suffer countless pains despite their efforts at self-purification (4.557–61).

---

[2] However, Apollonius still implicates her strongly in the killing, as Apsyrtus' blood paints his sister's silvery veil and dress red (4.474); similarly, in Aeschylus' *Agamemnon* (1389f.) the blood of her husband strikes Clytemnestra, although Aegisthus is the actual murderer. This detail has to be added to other echoes of Agamemnon's death in Apollonius' epic; cf. Hunter 1993:61 n. 69.

[3] Berthiaume 1982:18ff.

[4] On stealth, see Parker 1983:132ff.

[5] On this ritual, see most recently Teufel 1939:91–104; M. Schmidt 1979:242 f.; Parker 1984:138 (commenting on *SEG* 35.113). All literary sources on the ritual go back to the third-century B.C. grammarian Aristophanes of Byzantium fr. 142 Slater.

[6] For spitting out pollution, see Parker 1983:108, 133 n. 11; Oudemans and Lardinois 1987:183.

Apollonius made the murder more abominable by situating it in a temple. For the Greeks, death of any kind within a sanctuary amounted to sacrilege. Indeed, in 426/5 B.C., it was decided that all existing graves, except for the tombs of heroes, had to be removed from Apollo's sacred island, Delos. The scholiast on Euripides' *Medea* 1334, who seems to have only vaguely remembered the passage of the *Argonautica* that describes the murder, specifies that Apollonius situated the murder at an altar. If indeed that really had been the case, the murder would have been even more horrible. Greek suppliants sometimes took refuge at altars to avoid death; murder at the altar was therefore sacrilege in the extreme, and it was expected that the gods would severely punish the offenders. In history, such murders and their consequences were long remembered.[7]

The Euripidean passage on which the scholiast was commenting actually says that Medea killed her brother "near the hearth." The scholiast's mistake is understandable, however, because in essence the two locations—altar and hearth—amount to the same thing, religiously. Like altars, the hearths of either private houses or cities were sacred centers that symbolized the solidarity of the family and the community. They were also both places where suppliants could expect protection.[8] Euripides probably pictured Apsyrtus at his ancestral hearth, judging from the fact that Sophocles (fr. 343 Radt) and Callimachus (fr. 8 Pf.) state that his murder took place at home. Like Apollonius, then, Euripides took some trouble to represent the murder as particularly sacrilegious. Both poets drew on a long tradition of such murders, as already in the *Odyssey* Aegisthus and Clytemnestra are portrayed as killing Agamemnon at his ancestral hearth (3.324).

The mythographer Pherecydes (a perhaps older contemporary of Sophocles and Euripides) presents a rather different version of Apsyrtus' death. According to him, Medea took the young Apsyrtus with her when the Argonauts fled from Colchis by ship. As her father Aeëtes pursued them, she killed her brother and cut him into pieces, which she then threw into the river in order to delay her father's pursuit.[9] Roman authors, including Ovid, combined the various versions of the murder in innovative ways, describing how Apsyrtus was killed in a battle at the mouth of the Danube and had his limbs scattered over the

---

[7] See Parker 1983:33 (death in temple), 182–85 (murder at an altar); add Bremmer 1991:25 and Pomari 1992.

[8] See Bremmer 1991:25.

[9] Pherec. *FGrHist* 32 F 3; Cic. *Leg. Man.* 22; Apollod. 1.9.24.

neighboring fields.[10] It is notable, however, that in the oldest sources (Pherecydes, Euripides), it was Medea herself who killed and dismembered her brother and that this tradition resurfaced in later sources.[11] As bad as it was for Medea to have conspired in the death of her brother, it was far worse for her to have struck the blows herself. Like situating the murder at an altar or hearth, making Medea the actual murderer increased the horror of the story.

Medea's active role in the murder may go back even further than Pherecydes. Wilamowitz, the greatest classical scholar of this century, suggested that the name Apsyrtus already was included in the *Corinthiaca*, an epic credited to the early archaic Corinthian poet Eumelus. He based this supposition on the considerable role that Medea played in Eumelus' epic and the frequent linking of Apsyrtus' name with the Apsyrtides Islands, which were near the Illyrian coast and within the Corinthian sphere of influence.[12] This etymology was so popular that in early imperial times the grave of Apsyrtus could be shown to tourists passing the islands (Arrian *Periplus* 6.3); and the sixth-century historian Procopius (*Goth.* 2.11f., 14) mentions that in his time the inhabitants of Apsaros, a city that once was called Apsyrtus, still claimed that the murder had taken place on the islands. Even if Wilamowitz's suggestion is correct, however, can we safely conclude that Medea's fratricide belongs to the oldest strata of the myth of the Argonauts?[13]

In his contribution to this volume, Fritz Graf convincingly argues that originally Medea was a divine character who functioned as an initiatrix for Jason. In support of his thesis we may perhaps compare the experiences of Odysseus, whose voyage also displays unmistakably initiatory elements.[14] During his wanderings Odysseus stays for a while with Circe, who strongly resembles Medea as a loving goddess and "witch," and who is explicitly identified as the sister of Medea's

[10] Ovid *Tr.* 3.9.21–34, *Her.* 6.129f., 12.131f.; Valerius Flaccus 8.261–467.

[11] Later sources: Callimachus fr. 8 Pf. (probably); Strabo 7.5.5; Hermogenes 2.28, 31, 35; *Argonautica Orphica* 1033f.; Stephanus Byzantius, s.v. "Apsyrtides." In the earliest sources Apsyrtus is still a (very) young child: Moreau 1994:71ff.

[12] Eumelus frs. 2ab, 3ab Davies. Apsyrtus and the Apsyrtides Islands: Wilamowitz 1924:1.193ff. and Krevans in this volume. For an (unlikely) Abchasian etymology of Apsyrtus, see Charachidzé 1986:335 n. 3.

[13] Unfortunately, virtually all archaic Argonautic poetry has been lost. A small fragment, though, has recently been published: *POxy.* 53.3698, which mentions Orpheus, Mopsus, and Aeëtes.

[14] See Bremmer 1978 and the differing reactions of Graf 1991:358–60 (sympathetic) and Versnel 1993:68–74 (critical).

father Aeëtes (*Od.* 10.137).[15] Did the poet of the *Odyssey* want us to see a connection here? This does not seem impossible, as he also supplies another clear initiatory pointer. Before Odysseus arrives in Phaeacia, he is saved by Ino-Leucothea, who gives him a veil. In his recent commentary on books 5–8 of the *Odyssey*, J. B. Hainsworth has persuasively compared her to the "divine helper" who assists the hero at a critical moment, as analyzed by Vladimir Propp in his classic study of the morphology of the folktale.[16] But the helper and the object given by her are put by Propp in an explicit initiatory context in his later study of the historical roots of the folktale.[17] And indeed, Ino-Leucothea still functioned as an initiatory goddess in historical times.[18] As the poet of the *Odyssey* clearly knew the myth of the Argonauts,[19] the parallel between Circe and Medea is a further argument for Graf's view of Medea as an originally initiatory goddess.[20] Apparently, Homer still realized the initiatory nature of Medea, just as did other mythmakers of early Greece.[21]

But if Medea was a goddess in the oldest strata of the myth of the Argonauts, she will hardly have been the murderess of Apsyrtus from the very beginning. Where, then, did the motif of the dismembering fratricide originate? We could point to other archaic and classical stories about murder and dismemberment, hypothesizing that Medea's was based on these. A *maschalismos* is also found in Sophocles' drama about Achilles' murder of the Trojan prince Troilus (fr. 623 Radt), which took place in the sanctuary of Apollo Thymbraios before the walls of Troy. Curiously, in the same sanctuary another *maschalismos* took place: here snakes tore to pieces the priest Laokoön and his sons, literally so, as a late-fifth-century South Italian krater illustrates. The motif, then, is at home at this sanctuary and may have been inspired by a kind of abnormal sacrifice.[22] We also know that on an early Etruscan vase

[15] For the resemblance between Medea and Circe, see Crane 1988:142.

[16] Cf. Heubeck 1988:282 (ad *Od.* 5.333–34). "Divine helper": Propp 1968:39–50.

[17] I have used the Italian edition (Propp 1972) of this seminal work, which originally appeared in Russia in 1946.

[18] See the discussion by Graf 1985:405ff.; Bremmer 1992:193ff.

[19] On this much discussed problem, see most recently Kullmann 1991:449–52.

[20] Note also that the encounter between Circe and Odysseus was the most popular theme on the vases of the Theban Kabirion, a sanctuary in which initiations took place; see Moret 1991.

[21] See the important conclusion of Graf in this volume.

[22] For this suggestion and the connection of the two murders, see M. Schmidt 1979; E. Simon, s.v. "Laokoön," *LIMC* 6.1 (1992) no. 1; A. Kossatz-Deissmann, *LIMC* 1.1 (1981) 72–95 (Achilles and Troilus).

Achilles is shown cutting off the head of Troilus and so making his own flight possible.[23] Can it be that an archaic poem about the Argonauts borrowed a motif from the myths surrounding the Trojan War, just as Homer had borrowed from the Argonauts' myth?

Whatever the mythic antecedents may have been for Medea committing a treacherous, sacrilegious, and brutal murder, we are left with the question of its resonance within her larger mythic history and within the history of the Argonautica. It has been suggested by Versnel that the dismemberment of Apsyrtus served as a sacrifice to avert extreme danger at sea,[24] but because in the oldest tradition Apsyrtus was killed at home, it is clear that this interpretation can be valid at most only for the later versions of the story. Later sources also say that Medea used her brother's dismembered corpse to delay the Colchian "posse"; this logical explanation for the act may have been offered in earlier versions of the story as well. Neither of these "realistic" readings, however, explains why Greek myth chose to associate such a dreadful murder with Medea or why it was a brother—rather than a sister, for example—whom she killed. Our understanding of the murder, therefore, will be enriched by an examination of Greek attitudes toward fratricide and consideration of the importance that the Greeks placed on brother-sister relationships, as opposed to brother-brother or sister-sister relationships.

Greek Sibling Relationships

Let us start with the relationship between brothers.[25] What did the Greeks consider to be the ideal? As so often, our fullest evidence comes from Athens, but this city is unlikely to have been markedly atypical in this respect. We are particularly fortunate that fourth-century forensic speeches supply various examples of what Athenian males, who constituted the juries, expected of such relationships. One man claimed that he would not conceal even his mother's mistreatment of his brother (Dem. 36.20) and another man claimed that he and his half-brother never quarreled (Isaeus 9.30). Such unanimity and

---

[23] This is the suggestion of A. Lesky, s.v. "Troilus," *RE* 7.A.1 (1948) cols. 603ff.

[24] See Versnel 1973, considered "not very persuasive" by Ginzburg 1990:286. For other equally not very persuasive explanations, see Moreau 1994:125–28.

[25] For my discussion of the mythological brother-brother relationship I have greatly profited from the approach adopted by Buxton 1994:142–44, which he kindly showed me in advance of publication. For the "historical" examples I am especially indebted to Humphreys 1986:73–75; Cox 1988:380ff.; Golden 1990:115–21.

closeness between brothers were evidently the general expectation, as one brother might be sued as the heir of another ([Dem.] 35.3) or be asked to provide information regarding his dead brother's financial affairs (Lysias 32.26ff.). Opponents could dismiss testimony by arguing that it came from a brother ([Dem.] 47.11, 46), or they could state that damning testimony had to be true because it came from a brother (Dem. 29.15, 23). This expectation regarding the brother's role was so strong that when his brother Pasicles did not join him in prosecuting Phormion, Apollodorus insisted that he was not really his father's son (Dem. 45.83f.). The fourth-century playwright Menander (fr. 809 Edmonds) even spoke of a "passion (ἔρος) for concord" among brothers.

This feeling that brothers should be very close and supportive of one another also is reflected in the proverb "let a brother help a man," which is quoted by Plato (*Rep.* 362d).[26] It is hardly surprising that we find this sentiment also in older, non-Athenian literature. Hesiod (*Op.* 707) already exhorts: "Do not treat a friend as (closely as) if he were your brother," and the same sentiment recurs in Theognis (97–99). This solidarity extended even toward matricide. According to one version of the story, Alcmaeon killed his mother Eriphyle with the cooperation of his brother, thus avenging the betrayal of their father Amphiaraus (Apollod. 3.7.5). Homer mentions many brothers and repeatedly stresses their solidarity, shared command, and, sometimes, shared death.[27] We find this close relationship reflected in names of Homeric heroes: the names of Agamemnon and Menelaus both stress the ideal of steadfastness in battles, and those of Castor and Polydeuces, the Dioscuri, both reflect the ideal of "excellence, brilliance."[28]

This stress on fraternal solidarity is hardly surprising, as it was the keystone of the family structure. In the prestate and protostate society that was early Greece, men had to be able to depend unreservedly on their brothers. We find this feeling reflected in the fact that closed groups of males and warriors called themselves φράτερες, the inherited Indo-European term for "brothers"; the normal Greek word for "brother," ἀδελφός, was an innovation.[29]

[26] The proverb also is cited by Diogenianus 3.29; Apostolius 1.36; Macarius 1.29 (a slight variant).

[27] See, e.g., *Il.* 9.82; 11.59–60, 329–34, 709–10; 14.484–85; 15.545–46; 20.460–62; S. Saïd 1993:301–7.

[28] For the etymologies, see García-Ramón 1988–90:53. For the ideal of steadfastness, see Bremmer 1991:23–25. Note also the archaic Homeric dual *Aiante* for Aias and his half-brother Teukros; cf. Wackernagel 1955:538–46.

[29] For these terms, see Benveniste 1969:212–15.

A comparable view of the brother-brother relationship can be found in modern Greece, where the Sarakatsani attach great value to the solidarity of brothers and promote it in two ways. First, they treat brothers as absolutely equal. Brothers must take an equal role in avenging the family honor and they receive an exactly equal share of the patrimony. Moreover, the Sarakatsani try to discourage rivalry between brothers by encouraging them to pursue different vocations— one a muleteer, the other a cheesemaker, for example.[30] We may wonder whether the same custom existed in early Greece, for in myth brothers sometimes are clearly distinguished by activity. This is particularly the case with twins, brothers who are especially likely to quarrel (see further on this point below). The Dioscuri are described as "Castor, tamer of horses, and Polydeuces, good with his fists" (*Il.* 3.279 = *Od.* 11.300); Hector and Poulydamas are "a man of the spear and a man of speech" (*Il.* 18.252), and Thebes was founded by the twins Amphion and Zetus, one of whom was a musician and the other an athlete.[31] Yet at the same time, these efforts to distinguish brothers show that rivalry was always a possible threat to fraternal harmony.

In Athens, two factors played an important role in creating rivalry between brothers. First, there was the competition between the older and younger brother(s).[32] The older had certain advantages. Like the eldest sister (see below), he could marry first and register his name on a stone immediately after the name of his father (Thuc. 6.55). Moreover, his younger brother was expected to treat him with respect, as Polyneices insisted that Eteocles do in Sophocles' *Oedipus at Colonus* (1422ff.) and Smicrines did in Menander's *Aspis* (172, 255). And in Athenian mythology, Sophocles (fr. 24.2 Radt) portrayed Aegeus' father as giving him the best part of Attica because he was the eldest son. This inequality of privileges must also have occurred outside of Athens, since in his *Politics* (5.1305b10) Aristotle mentions that certain states forbid an elder and a younger brother from holding office simultaneously. Around the end of the first century A.D., Plutarch, who wrote an essay entitled *On Brotherly Love* (*Mor.* 478a–492d), still noted that the disparity between an older and a younger brother's rights and roles could be a source of rivalry.

---

[30] Sarakatsani: J. Campbell 1964:174–76. The encouragement of specialization among brothers is also noted by Bourdieu 1977:63 (on Algerian Kabylia).

[31] F. Heger, s.v. "Amphion," *LIMC* 1.1 (1981); add now M. Schmidt 1990.

[32] On the differences between elder and younger brothers, see S. Saïd 1993b.

A more significant source of trouble will have been the division of the inheritance.[33] Small plots of land must have caused many worries. It is understandable that Hesiod in his *Works and Days* (376–79) advised men to have only one son, as he himself had had a quarrel with his brother Perses over their inheritance. Among the Kabylian Berbers, this problem is solved by leaving the land undivided; the same thing sometimes happened among the Athenians.[34] Another way of minimizing conflict, which also is found in modern Greece, was to divide up the patrimony into shares agreed to be equal and then allocate them by lot; in this way Cronus' sons divided the universe.[35] A third possibility was to let one brother divide up the property and the other choose his portion first ([Dem.] 48.12). Sometimes, one brother even agreed to accept a smaller portion (Lysias 16.10). We may perhaps add in this respect the agreement struck by the sons of Oedipus, as described in Euripides' *Phoenissae*, whereby Polyneices and Eteocles would rule during alternate years.[36] Complete prevention of rivalry was impossible, however, and in speeches from the Athenian law courts we hear of one brother depriving the other of his patrimony (Lysias 10.5) and even of a fatal assault over the division of property (Isaeus 9.17).[37] These examples will hardly have been exceptions to the rule, as in his *Laws* (868c, 869c–d, 873a–b) Plato proposed detailed legislation on the subject, and "Brothers"—that is to say, "Quarreling Brothers"—was a favorite title for New Comedy plays.[38]

Yet the example of comedy, in particular, reminds us to be careful in our application of literary topoi to real life: comedy usually presupposes a pair of brothers (or sisters), whereas in reality, of course, there must have been many cases of families with more than two sons. Mythology is sometimes more "realistic" in this respect. For example, myth tells of how Archelaus of Macedonia was banished by his brothers, despite the fact that he was the eldest.[39] Moreover, comedy usually ends on a happy note, whereas myth treats the theme of brotherly rivalry in a

---

[33] The royal epithet *Philadelphos* of Hellenistic kings perhaps proclaims this lack of rivalry in cases of inheritance in a more positive way; see Muccioli 1994.

[34] Berbers: Bourdieu 1977:64. Athenians: Harrison 1968:239–44; Fox 1985:211–14.

[35] *Il.* 15.184–99 (cf. Burkert 1992:88–93 for a possible dependence of this passage on the Akkadian epic *Atrahasis*); *Od.* 14.208f.; Stesich. 222 (b) 220ff. Davies (cf. Bremer 1987:167ff.); Apollod. 2.8.4; Friedl 1962:60–64.

[36] This is a relatively late version of the myth, although cf. Moreau 1988.

[37] For more examples, see Cox 1988:384–86.

[38] See the enumeration by Kassel and Austin 1983–:*ad* Diphilus F 3; note also their commentary on Alexis F 113.

[39] Hyg. *Fab.* 219; cf. Harder 1985:170.

much more sombre way.[40] Tydeus killed his brother Olenias (Pherec. FGrHist 3 F 122a) or Melanippus, during a hunt (Hyg. Fab. 69), just as Bellerophon accidentally killed his brother Deliades (Apollod. 2.3.1). The fatal feuds between Eteocles and Polyneices or between Atreus and Thyestes display fratricide at its worst, leading to the extinction of a whole family. It is hard not to feel that these myths sounded a warning note to competing successors to a throne, a situation that must have been far from unusual during the time that Greece was still ruled by kings.

The rivalry between brothers is virtually inevitable between twins, who immediately have to compete for their mother's milk and later in life must compete for succession to their father's position.[41] In many societies, therefore, twins are a symbol of rivalry and some communities expelled them altogether.[42] It is this symbolic significance that explains their prominence in the mythology of various cultures, such as Rome (Romulus and Remus) and ancient Israel (Jacob and Esau).[43] It is not surprising that Greek mythology had its sets of warring twins as well, such as Pelias and Neleus (Apollod. 1.9.9) or Danaus and Aegyptus (Apollod. 2.1.4). Like Jacob and Esau (Gen. 25), the twins Proetus and Acrisius (Apollod. 2.2.1) and Panopeus and Crisus (Lycophron 939f.) were already quarreling in the womb.

As one might expect, we are far less informed about the relationship between sisters.[44] It is clear, however, that fathers tried to promote solidarity among their daughters as well as their sons, as we hear regularly of fathers giving their daughters equal dowries.[45] The fact that according to ancient scholars a special pet name, appha, was used among sisters in Athens also suggests a close relationship.[46] Outside Athens, information is virtually nonexistent, but it is significant that in the Odyssey, it is Penelope's sister Iphthime whom the gods send to comfort her in a dream (4.795–841); Apollonius of Rhodes pictures

[40] Unfortunately, the entry on fratricides in Hyginus (Fab. 236: qui fratres suos occiderunt) has been lost.

[41] Unfortunately, we cannot reconstruct the plots of the various comedies entitled "Twins." Cf. Kassel and Austin 1983–:ad Xenarchus' Didymoi.

[42] For a full bibliography, see Schoffeleers 1991.

[43] Romulus and Remus: Bremmer and Horsfall 1987:25–48. Jacob and Esau: Westermann 1974:428–30.

[44] But see Golden 1990:135ff. For comedies entitled "Sisters," see Kassel and Austin 1983– on Alcaeus F 1. There were also comedies about twin sisters, but as is the case with those about twin brothers, the content of these plays cannot be reconstructed satisfactorily. Cf. Kassel and Austin 1983– on Aristophanes' Didymai.

[45] Lysias 6.10; Dem. 41.26; Isaeus 2.5, 5.6; IG 2².5673.

[46] Eustathius ad Il. 5.408; Theodoridis 1975.

a close relationship between Medea and her older sister Chalciope (3.611ff.).

Yet despite the seemingly good relationships between sisters, conflicts may have existed. In modern Greece, differences in wealth can harm the relationship between sisters, as well as the custom that the eldest sister had to marry before the younger.[47] Similarly, in the *Iliad*, the married daughter who is mentioned is always the eldest daughter; lack of data prevents us knowing whether in poorer families this custom led to problems.[48] Sophocles could represent sisters in contrasting pairs: Antigone and Ismene in the *Antigone*, and Electra and Chrysothemis in the *Electra*, although the duplication of the motif perhaps suggests that the dramatist was using a literary motif in these cases rather than drawing on his own experiences.

Did sisters keep up a regular contact after marriage? Such contact is presupposed by the myth of Philomela, who, on her way to visit her married sister Procne, was raped and robbed of her tongue by her sister's husband, Tereus. Philomela managed to send a plea for help to Procne by means of a cloth into which she had woven the story of her sufferings.[49] We cannot, however, generalize from this one example. Among the Sarakatsani, where sisters are particularly close, they keep up a frequent visiting pattern if they live in the same neighborhood, but elsewhere in contemporary Greece contacts can be much rarer, even if sisters are living in the same village.[50]

Having examined the relationships between brother and brother and, lacking sufficient data, more briefly those between sister and sister, we now can turn to the relationship between sister and brother.[51] Brothers and sisters erected gravestones for one another, and Athenian grave reliefs regularly display a brother and sister standing together.[52] As is so often the case with gravestones, the reliefs should not necessarily be taken as a reflection of real life but as a statement of the ideal relationship: the parents probably wanted to stress the closeness of their children. We may then assume that, as was the case in the relationships

---

[47] Wealth: Kennedy 1986:131. Eldest sister: several postwar Greek films picture the frustration of the younger sister as she waits for the wedding of her older sister (oral communication of Stella Karageorgiou).

[48] *Il.* 11.740, 13.429, 21.143; cf. Janko 1992:100ff.

[49] Cf. Burkert 1983:180–82.

[50] Sarakatsani: J. Campbell 1964:104, 178 (close contact). Elsewhere: Du Boulay 1974:136ff.

[51] See Bachofen 1966:157–86; Cox 1988:380–82; Golden 1990:121–35; Davidoff 1992.

[52] Hansen 1983, index, s.v. "*adelphos (ē)*"; Golden 1990:125–29.

among brothers and among sisters, parents also endeavored to promote solidarity between brothers and sisters. And as far as we can see, they generally succeeded in their attempts, as we regularly hear of close contacts between brother and sister. In the tragic history of Periander (ca. 625–585), as related by Herodotus (3.53, and in this form possibly not his own invention),[53] the Corinthian tyrant, having failed to mend the rift between himself and his son Lycophron, finally sent Lycophron's sister to persuade him, hoping that she would succeed where he had continually failed. Around 500 B.C., Simachus, the tyrant of Sicilian Centuripi, was so impressed by Pythagoras' teachings that he abdicated and divided his goods between his sister and his fellow citizens.[54] In the fifth century, we may perhaps see as examples of the close bond between brother and sister the joy of recognition manifested by Electra and Orestes in Sophocles' *Electra* and the close cooperation between the same pair in Euripides' *Electra*, although in these cases the joy and the initiative seem to be more on Electra's part than on Orestes'. In the fourth century, Onetor's sister helped him to defraud Demosthenes (Dem. 31.11f.) and Dionysodorus asked his sister to visit him in prison before his execution (Lysias 13.41). A sister even committed suicide in grief at her brother's death (Lysias fr. 22 Thalheim). Such suicides may not have been as unusual in ancient Greece as one might expect; Callimachus dedicated an epigram to a girl from Cyrene who committed suicide on the very same day as her brother had died (*Ep.* 20 Pf. = 32 Gow-Page).

The mourning sister is also a familiar figure in Greek mythology. In Xenocles' *Likymnius* (*TGF* 33 F 2), Alcmene mourned her brother. The sisters of Meleager (discussed below) mourned their brother until Artemis changed them into birds called *meleagrides*. And of course, the sisters of Phaethon mourned him eternally, having been transformed into weeping poplars.[55] Greek myth also knew of other examples of close contact between sister and brother(s). Alcmene refused to marry Amphitryon until after he had avenged her brothers' deaths (Apollod. 2.4.6), just as in Euripides' *Trojan Women* (359–60), Cassandra vowed to murder Agamemnon in vengeance for the deaths of her father and brothers. Hyginus (*Fab.* 109) relates the strange story of Priam's daughter Iliona, who raised her brother Polydorus as her own son and her real son by the Thracian king Polymestor as her brother. When, after

---

[53] On this story, see the fine analysis of Sourvinou-Inwood 1991:244–84.

[54] Porphyry *Life of Pythagoras* 21.

[55] Meleager: Soph. fr. 830a Radt; Antoninus Liberalis 2.6; Ovid *Met.* 8.542–46; Hyg. *Fab.* 174. Phaethon: *SH Adesp.* 988; Ovid *Met.* 2.340–66.

the fall of Troy, the king gave in to the Greeks' requests to do away with the Trojan prince, Polymestor unknowingly killed his own son instead.

In Greece, this close contact between sisters and brothers must have continued even after the sister's marriage, for from Homeric times until the end of the classical age there was a close relationship between a man and his sister's son; the uncle often served as a role model for the nephew.[56] The interaction between brother and sister must sometimes have been so close that political opponents could successfully insinuate that they enjoyed an incestuous relationship, as in the case of Cimon and his sister Elpinice; similarly, young Alcibiades was accused of having entered his sister's house "not as her brother but as her husband."[57]

In fact, brothers were supposed to guard the honor, and in particular the sexual honor, of their sisters. When the Athenian tyrant Hipparchus slighted Harmodius' sister by refusing, at the last minute, to let her act as basket carrier in the Great Panathenaic procession, Harmodius was sufficiently angered to murder Hipparchus.[58] We also find this concern for the sister's honor in myths. When Alcmaeon, who first had married Arsinoe, tried to regain his wedding present to Arsinoe in order that he might give it to his second wife, Callirhoe, Arsinoe's brothers killed him (Apollod. 3.7.5f.). Events could turn out just as seriously when the sexual honor of the sister was at stake. Among the various versions of the death of Alcibiades that Plutarch relates in his biography (39.5) is one that says he was killed by the brothers of a girl whom he had "corrupted"; according to legend, the poet Hesiod was murdered for the same reasons.[59] We find this concern expressed in myths also. When Achilles sacked Tenedos, he pursued the beautiful sister of Tenes, who tried to defend her. The sister escaped, but Tenes was killed by Achilles (Plut. *Mor.* 297e–f). The Greek poetess Myrtis told the sad story of the chaste hero Eunostus, who resisted the advances of his cousin Ochna. She subsequently denounced him to her brothers, who became incensed and killed the innocent boy in an ambush (*ap.* Plut. *Mor.* 300–301). Equally tragic was the end of Apemosyne. When Hermes fell in love with her, she first eluded the god by outrunning him. To catch her, he spread fresh hides on the path she took home from the

---

[56] For many examples, see Bremmer 1983b.

[57] Cimon and Elpinice: Andocides 4.33; Plut. *Cimon* 4.5–7; Mattingly 1971. Alcibiades: Lysias 14.28.

[58] Cf. Lavelle 1986.

[59] See most recently Mandilaras 1992.

spring;[60] when she slipped on the hides, the god grabbed his opportunity. When Apemosyne told her brother about the rape, he, failing to believe her, kicked her to death (Apollod. 3.2.2).

In fourth-century sources we hear of brothers who fail their sisters. Diocles refused to find a husband for his widowed sister so that he could continue to exploit her services (Isaeus 8.36), and Olympiodorus let his sister live in poverty ([Dem.] 48.54ff.). In the latter case, the orator adds that she was "a sister of the same father and the same mother" to make the horror of the story greater. Timocrates was reproached for having "sold his sister into export"—that is to say, for marrying her off to an inhabitant of Corcyra (Dem. 24.202ff.). Is this story a sign of its times, an indication that the character of the family was changing and friendship was becoming more important than in earlier periods? Or is it simply a matter of our sources of information changing? In either case, it should be emphasized that a brother's mistreatment of his sister was regarded as heinous. It is also notable that brother-sister conflicts are very rare in Greek myth.[61] When Phalces murders his sister Hyrnetho, he does so unintentionally (Paus. 2.28.3) and when, in Euripides' *Helen*, the priestess Theonoe opposes her brother, she is reconciled with him by the end of the play.

The close relationship between sister and brother is equally attested in contemporary Greece. Among the Sarakatsani, as elsewhere, a brother is expected to guard his sister against rape and insults. He also watches over his sister after his father's death and she, in turn, provides him with new social and political connections by marrying. Maniote folk laments even suggest that sisters will avenge their brothers when no male relative is available, or else bring up their own sons to fulfill this duty upon reaching adulthood.[62]

Did the close relationship between brother and sister lead to conflicts of interest after marriage? There are two cases in particular that reveal some of the tensions often suffered by a married Greek woman. Already in the *Iliad* we hear of Meleager, who killed his maternal uncles during that most famous of all mythical hunts, the Calydonian boar hunt. Meleager's mother, Althaea, was so enraged by the deaths of her

[60] In Greek and Roman myths, girls are particularly vulnerable to attack while they are fetching water. Cf. Bremmer and Horsfall 1987:52 (with earlier bibliography); Manfrini 1992.

[61] As observed by Humphreys 1983:71.

[62] Sarakatsani: J. Campbell 1964:178ff. Elsewhere: Du Boulay 1974:157. Mani: Holst-Warhaft 1992:84–86.

brothers that she cursed her son and, at least in later versions of the story, committed suicide.[63] A different conflict is narrated by Herodotus, who tells of how the wife of Intaphernes, after the arrest of her husband, children, and near relatives, posted herself at the royal door and kept up a lament. Finally, the king allowed her to choose one prisoner to be saved. She chose her brother. When asked why by the surprised king, she explained: "I can always have another husband ... but in no way can I ever have another brother" (3.119).

The motif of the sister who privileges her brother's life over those of her husband and children is not unique to Greece; already at the end of the nineteenth century, scholars began to find parallels in the literature of India and Persia.[64] The oldest is found in the *Jataka* (1.7 [67]), a collection of stories about the former births of the Buddha, which might date to the last centuries B.C.[65] A woman whose son, husband, and brother are arrested is allowed by the king to choose one of them to be saved and chooses her brother because "[another] son, O Lord, [I may find] in my womb; a husband by searching the street; but I do not see the place from which I could recover a brother."[66] The fact that these words are a verse within a story told in prose leaves open the possibility that the verse originally belonged to an earlier tradition and was only later incorporated into the *Jakata*. Such an incorporation clearly has taken place in some versions of the Sanskrit *Ramayana*, which seems to quote the second half of this Pali verse. When Rama gets into a fight during the quest for his wife Sita, he believes that his younger brother Laksama has fallen in battle and he exclaims, "A wife could be [found] anywhere, even a son and other relatives, but nowhere do I see the place where is [another] brother born from the same womb."[67] In their present form, the Indian examples are at least a few centuries later than Herodotus,

---

[63] For a full analysis, see Bremmer 1988; see also Seaford 1990:166ff.; S. Woodford et al., s.v. "Meleagros," *LIMC* 6.1 (1992).

[64] India: Slezák 1981:124 n. 27 has overlooked that the first to notice the resemblance between the Indian and the Greek examples was Tawney 1881, not Pischel 1893. Persia: the parallel first was noted by Nöldeke 1894.

[65] Previous discussions of the Indian material have not taken into sufficient account matters of chronology and textual criticism. If I have made progress in this respect, this is due to the advice of Hans Bakker and Harunaga Isaacson.

[66] Cf. Fausbøll 1877:306–8, Cowell 1895:102–4.

[67] The fact that this verse calls Rama's brother a "brother of the same womb," although he is only a half-brother, seems to support the decision of the recent critical edition of the *Ramayana* to relegate it to the critical apparatus. Cf. the *Valmiki-Ramayana* critical edition, 7 vols. (London, 1960–75) *ad* 6.39.5. For the close relationship between the two brothers see Goldman 1980. The reading accepted by the critical edition is indeed somewhat less pointed: "Of what use to me is the recovery of Sita, of what use is even my life to me,

although the possibility that the *Jataka* incorporated older material into
its text cannot be wholly excluded. In any case, there is no proof
whatsoever that the Herodotean motif is to be derived from India.[68]

It is interesting to see that the motif recurs in the Near East during
the medieval period. In the Persian *Marzuban-nama*, a collection of
fables and anecdotes written between 1210 and 1225, we find the tale
of a king named Zahhak, who has to feed with human flesh two
serpents that grow out of his shoulders. One day, the husband, son,
and brother of a certain woman named Hanbuiy are seized for this
purpose. Pitying the lamenting woman, Zahhak allows her a choice of
one of the three. After various considerations, she chooses her brother
because, she says, she can marry again and have another son, but as
her parents are separated she can never have another brother. When
the king hears her story, he orders that her husband and son should
be released as well.[69] Curiously, we find a close parallel in the story of
the notorious Umayyadic governor al-Hajjâj (died A.D. 714) in a roughly
contemporaneous Arabic anthology. After the governor had arrested
the husband, son, and brother of a certain woman, she was allowed to
choose one of them to be spared. She answered, "My husband? I shall
find another. My son? I shall again be a mother. But I never shall find
again my brother." Because of her eloquent answer in rhyming prose,
the governor releases all three prisoners.[70] Being so close in time and
space, these two stories must be connected, but, unfortunately, we can
no longer trace the paths along which these stories traveled. It seems
more than likely, however, that they were linked in an oral tradition.

Before we conjecture a connection between the Herodotean passage
and the Indian, Persian, and Arabic parallels, we should note that the
motif is also popular elsewhere. In West Africa, the following problem
has been recorded: "During a crossing of a river, a proa capsized. On it
was a man with his sister, his wife and mother-in-law, none of the latter
being able to swim. Whom did he save?" The following comments are
made in response: "If you save your sister and let your wife drown, you
have to pay a new dowry. If you save your wife and abandon your
sister, your parents will strongly reproach you, But if you choose to

---

when I see my brother lying down fallen in battle? By searching it is possible to find a
woman equal to Sita, but not a brother like Laksama, an associate, a comrade" (6.39.5–6).

[68] *Contra* Beekes 1986:231–33.

[69] Varavini 1909; Levy 1959:16ff.

[70] The Arabic has *al-zawj mawjûd, wa-l-ibn mawlûd, wa-l-akh mafqûd*. I owe this parallel
to my colleague Geert Jan van Gelder, who refers me to the following edition: al-Isfahâni
1870:225.

save your mother-in-law, you are an idiot!"[71] Just as conflicts between natal and conjugal families must have been widespread in traditional cultures, problems such as the one illustrated by Herodotus' story must have arisen independently in many cultures' myths.[72]

To return to ancient Greece, there is widespread agreement that the Herodotean anecdote was echoed by Sophocles in his *Antigone* (909–12),[73] where Antigone bursts out, "The husband lost, another might have been found, and child from another, to replace the first-born; but, father and mother hidden in Hades, no brother's life could ever bloom for me again" (trans. Jebb). There is, of course, something incredibly poignant to her claim, as her brother is already dead. Moreover, the Athenian audience would perhaps not have approved of a girl who preferred her brother over her husband.[74] Yet would they have strongly disapproved of her choice?[75] The loyalty of Athenian males was first to their parents and kinsmen, only after that to their wife and children.[76] Would Athenian men really have expected their own sisters to behave differently? Real life must have posed great problems for Athenian wives more than once.

Medea and Apsyrtus

Our discussion of sibling relationships has made it clear why Medea's murder of a *brother* had greater impact than the murder of, say, a sister or cousin would have. Sisters would be friends with one another, but as equals; neither sister could significantly affect the life of the other. Brothers would be friends but also possible rivals, openly vying for superiority within the family and the *polis*. The relationship between a sister and brother was something altogether different from these.

---

[71] Paulme 1976:51–54.

[72] Note also the following altercation in Seneca's *De remediis fortuitorum* (the text was published in the *Revue de Philologie*, n.s., 12 [1888] 118–27: "S. Amisi uxorem bonam. – R. Soror reparari bona non potest: uxor adventicum est; non est inter illa quae semel unicuique contingunt" (127).

[73] Cf. the detailed discussion by Slezák 1981:112f. The passage at lines 904–20 has often been suspected, but its authenticity has recently been stressed by Oudemans and Lardinois 1987:186f., 192, and Lloyd-Jones and Wilson 1990:138.

[74] As is forcefully argued by Sourvinou-Inwood 1987–88, 1990a.

[75] Holst-Warhaft 1992:163 unequivocally states that the women would have followed the ties of blood.

[76] Cf. Dover 1974:272, 302ff.; Visser 1986:149–65, with many perceptive observations on the myth of Medea.

Brother and sister were imagined to be especially close, as Antigone's words attest, but their closeness arose in part from the fact that the brother was *responsible* for the sister, and she was *dependent* upon him. He was expected to defend and yet also discipline his sister, particularly after the death of her father; she was expected to conduct herself in a way that would bring no shame upon him. By killing her brother, Medea not only committed the heinous act of spilling familial blood, she also permanently severed all ties to her natal home and the role that it would normally play in her adult life. Through Apsyrtus' murder, she simultaneously declared her independence from her family and forfeited her right to any protection from it. This aspect of the act seems to have been underlined already in the oldest versions of the myth, which deliberately polarized reality by representing Medea as having only one brother (the modern ideal of a two-child family did not exist in ancient Greece). Once Apsyrtus was gone, Medea was brotherless. There was only one way for Medea to go, then: she had to follow Jason and never look back.

Of course, we should not overlook the fact that whatever social conventions may have led to the special closeness between brother and sister, the closeness was genuine and important in and of itself. We may assume that Medea's fratricide elicited great feelings of horror on the part of the Greek audience. And indeed, just as the Greeks considered parricide such an appalling crime that the murder of Laius by Oedipus was virtually never represented on Greek vases, so we hardly find any artistic representations of Apsyrtus' murder.[77] Moreover, Sophocles (fr. 546 Radt) explicitly states that Apsyrtus was only a half-brother of Medea, being the son of a Nereid; and Apollonius makes Apsyrtus the son of a Caucasian concubine, Asterodeia, and Medea the daughter of Aeëtes' later, official wife, Eiduia: apparently, both mythmakers wanted to "soften" the crime of fratricide.

Our discussion of Apsyrtus' murder has, I hope, illuminated the reason that Medea murdered her *brother*. This is not to say that the meaning of the murder is altogether crystal clear even now. Why did Greek myth represent Medea as the kin killer par excellence? Is there a connection with the initiatory background of the expedition of the Argonauts?[78] The myth of Medea still poses many problems.

---

[77] Parricide: Bremmer 1987a:49. Apsyrtus: C. Clairmont, s.v. "Apsyrtus," *LIMC* 1.1 (1981); Blome 1983; M. Schmidt 1992.

[78] For this background, see Graf 1987:95–99 and in this volume.

PART II

LITERARY PORTRAITS

5

MEDEA AS MUSE

PINDAR'S *PYTHIAN* 4

Dolores M. O'Higgins

ONE OF THE PARADOXES surrounding the Medea of the famous fifth-century texts—Euripides' play and the great *Pythian* 4 of Pindar (first performed thirty-one years earlier)—is that she appears both exceptional and typical of all females, as they were generally perceived.[1] Indeed much of Medea's extraordinariness lies in the degree to which she displays traits regarded as characteristically feminine. Let me begin by touching on some of these traits, so as to indicate the framework of my analysis of her role in *Pythian* 4, particularly her relationship to Pindar's epinician Muse.

As Bergren has shown, human and divine females were considered to be a source both of truth and of lies in archaic Greece; Hesiod's Muses, who know how to "speak things *like* the truth" and, when they wish, "speak true things," are the most famous examples.[2] Pindar's Medea embodies this ambiguous power, since at the start of *Pythian* 4 she speaks with oracular authority while her final appearance in the poem as the "Death-of-Pelias" (Πελιαοφόνον, 250) hints at her infamous duplicity;

I first presented this article as a paper in a symposium in October 1991 at Cornell, organized by P. Mitsis and P. Pucci. A shorter version appeared in the 1991 APA Medea panel organized by S. I. Johnston. As far as my work on the Muses is concerned, I am particularly indebted to Pucci 1977 and 1979. Two book-length studies of the fourth Pythian were helpful to me at many points: Segal 1986 and Braswell 1988. I have also consulted Kirkwood 1982:161–200. J. S. Clay, C. Dufner, S. I. Johnston, and G. M. Kirkwood have helped me with comments and suggestions as the paper developed. All references to the text are in accordance with the 1987 Snell-Maehler edition and the translations are my own.

[1] *Pythian* 4 was written for a Pythian chariot victory in 462 B.C., and Euripides' *Medea* was performed in the spring of 431.

[2] *Th.* 26–28. Bergren 1983 discusses (*inter alia*) the female as a simultaneous source of truth and lies, as an unstable "sign" in the (marital) communication between men, and as a possessor of *mētis*. Other general studies include Arthur 1973, Loraux 1978, and Humphreys 1983.

the epithet refers to her murderous tricking of Pelias' daughters and Pelias himself.[3]

The female's power over truth and lies was in part connected with her reproductive powers, and particularly with her unique ability to know her children's paternity and so their legitimacy. This knowledge was critical in a patriarchal society, and it gave women a potential weapon; they could supplant the real heir with a counterfeit just as Rhea cheated Cronus with a stone; they could deny legitimacy to, as well as confer legitimacy on, a man's heirs: in other words, they could take away the critical benefit of legitimate succession. The Athenian dramatists Neophron and Euripides developed a Medea who stole Jason's heirs in the most violent manner imaginable, but in a sense this murder was but the most extreme expression of a universal subversive power in women's hands.[4]

This perceived subversiveness extended to the very moment of a wife's arrival in her husband's house. She was necessary to provide a man's heirs, but she was introduced into his home from outside, and her requisite shift of loyalty from her paternal household to that of her husband inspired anxiety as to her trustworthiness. Medea—as both Pindar and Euripides show—was *the* outsider par excellence, a foreign woman who (in Euripides) brutally exposes the risks of all such "imports," and in Pindar also represents geographical remoteness and racial and cultural "difference." All women were outsiders, but none more conspicuously than Medea. Pindar's Medea does not carry out the filicidal program of the Euripidean heroine, but with her pharmaceutical skills and murderous powers she evokes familiar fears of a subtle, alien

[3] In a fine article that draws on (post)modern theories of the text's openness, Farenga 1977 argues that *Pythian* 4 subverts traditional epinician motifs and language. The poem simultaneously employs the authoritative *logos* of traditional song and the politically subversive language of fifth-century rhetoric. As I shall argue, the character of Medea also can be "read" as potentially subversive of the poem's orderly message of flattery and hope.

[4] Pericles' legislation of 451–450 B.C., requiring Athenian citizens to demonstrate native Athenian descent on both the father's and the mother's side, focused a new attention—and anxiety—on the married woman and mother, and on her power to affect the status and livelihood of citizens. Such legislation—which undoubtedly influenced Athenian literature, including these Medea plays—seems *not* to have applied in Cyrene, the poem's destination, during the Hellenistic or classical periods. Kwapong 1969 discusses a fourth-century inscription commissioned by Ptolemy I (Soter) and addressed to the citizens of Cyrene following his conquest. It begins by defining Cyrenean citizens as the children of Greek parents on both sides or of Greek fathers and Libyan mothers. In the latter case the individuals must be resident within Cyrenean territory. See below for the archaic constitution of Demonax, which defined Cyrenean citizenship during an earlier period.

menace at the very heart of a man's life. As I shall show, Medea's potential dangerousness, as evoked by Pindar, plays a central part in his encomiastic program for *Pythian* 4.

Pindar writes as a Greek for a fellow Greek, although *Pythian* 4's recipient and honoree, Arcesilas, was in fact a colonist of North Africa, a member of a long-established dynasty, the Battiads.[5] In the poem, Pindar describes the founding of the colony by Battus, although it is Herodotus to whom we must turn for the details of what happened subsequently. Following the original foundation of the city by a small group from Thera, further waves of immigrants from Greece followed; eventually tensions between different members of the royal family— some of whom exploited the growing dissatisfaction of the Libyans with the exploding immigrant population—erupted into civil war, which was resolved by a Delphic arbitrator, Demonax of Mantinea. He developed a new constitution, reducing the power of the king and handing it over to the people—who were divided into three tribes, the first of which contained a mixture of περίοικοι (local people) and Theraeans; the second, Peloponnesians; and the third, Cretans (Hdt. 4.161). The constitution of Demonax of Mantinea apparently divided the population into three tribes, as noted above. Under Battus IV, the father of the victor, Arcesilas, the kingly powers were restored by means of the help of the Persian satrap in Egypt, who had been enlisted by Pheretima, a formidable dowager queen of Cyrene.[6] As Chamoux observes, the diminution of Persian overseas influence following the defeats of Salamis and Plataea—welcomed at the time as freeing Cyrene—ultimately spelled the downfall of the monarchy, which was an anachronism in the Greek world.[7]

That some of the colonists wished to maintain their ties with the "mother" country is obvious from the extensive building programs of the sixth and early fifth centuries, from Cyrenean willingness to

---

[5] Hdt. 4.145–205 is our principal source for the Battiads, whose arrival in Cyrene he dates to 631 B.C. See also Kwapong 1969 and Chamoux 1953 on the archaeological evidence.

[6] Pheretima was the mother of Arcesilas III, who had been overthrown and killed in an oligarchic coup. She sought refuge in Egypt, with the Persian satrap, Aryandes (Egypt had been under Persian dominion since 525 B.C.). Her vengeance on her son's murderers and their wives was worthy of a Medea. Battus IV, Arcesilas' father, seems to have maintained a policy of dependence on Persian power in Egypt, which ended (as did his rule) in 480.

[7] Chamoux 1953:166–68. There is evidence of new Cyrenean coinage dating to ca. 480 B.C. Cyrenean participation in the Panhellenic games in the subsequent period also testifies to the end of Persian dominion.

accept Delphic arbitration and their participation in the major athletic competitions (Arcesilas also won the chariot victory at Olympia in 460 B.C.), and from commissions to Pindar (Telesicrates of Cyrene is celebrated in the ninth Pythian ode of Pindar, datable to 474 B.C.). At the same time, not surprisingly, Libyan beliefs and practices made an impact on the population; for example, Herodotus mentions that in Cyrene and its sister city Barca women honored Isis and refrained from cows' flesh.[8]

Of course, from the point of view of many of the inhabitants of Libya, Arcesilas no doubt remained an outsider. Not long after this poem was commissioned, Arcesilas was killed by the Cyreneans and the line of eight kings was replaced by a democracy.[9] Yet at the same time his ties with his birthplace, Cyrene, were real; most interesting from the point of view of *Pythian* 4 and Medea's role in it is the fact that Arcesilas was—almost certainly—dark-skinned (from a Greek perspective), because of the intermarriage between Greeks and Libyans in his family. Such intermarriage was common in Cyrene and apparently unproblematic in itself; indeed as far as the constitution of Demonax was concerned, the tribe jointly comprising the περίοικοι and the original Theraean settlers apparently constituted the most privileged group within the state.[10] Ironically, although Arcesilas clearly wished to identify himself with Greece, his real claim to legitimacy in Libya might be said to be his Libyan ancestry, witnessed by his dark skin.[11]

It comes as no surprise, however, that Pindar attempts to legitimate Arcesilas within a Panhellenic context by means of Greek culture and institutions, including the Oracle at Delphi and Arcesilas' victory at the games there. There is a particular irony in Pindar's treatment

[8] Hdt. 4.86. The powerful role that many of the queens of Cyrene played in politics also may reflect African rather than Greek traditions.

[9] This may have been a period of about twenty years—possibly less. A scholiast to Pindar (Drachmann 2.93) mentions that the monarchy lasted for two hundred years. Since its beginning was thought to be ca. 640 B.C., the rough date for its end will be 440. See Chamoux 1953:201–10 on this question.

[10] See Kwapong 1969 on the race of the Cyreneans. The mid-fifth-century writer Stratonicus the flute player (in Ath. 8.351–52) describes the citizens of Cyrene as dark skinned. Herodotus notes that the original colonists were all men; intermarriage was thus a necessity if they were to survive. A ruler of Barce was called Alazir (a Libyan name), and his daughter married Arcesilas III (Hdt. 4.164; *CIG* 5147).

[11] Both the beginning and the end of the Battiad dynasty seem to have been heralded by the appearance of a white crow. All crows were sacred to Apollo, a divinity especially associated with the family and Cyrene; a *white* crow, a proverbial rarity, may also represent and legitimate the paradox of an African ruling family with (partially) Greek origins. See Chamoux 1953:205; *FHG* 2.212; Callimachus *Hymns* 2.65ff.

of Medea within the overall scheme of the poem. As we shall see, she is one of the χελαινώπεσσι Κόλχοισιν or "black-visaged" Egyptian Colchians, implicitly different from Jason and his crew. Her sexual, racial, and cultural "difference" becomes a predominant theme in the poem, providing a foundation for Pindar's constructed parallel between the Hellenizing magic of Jason and the "civilizing" powers of his own poetry and of Arcesilas' rule. Like Pindar himself, Arcesilas comes to represent a powerful mediator of the gulf between the Greek "self" and the potentially dangerous "other." Medea, of course, is the "other" in every sense of the word, defining the Hellenic (male) self by epitomizing its antithesis. She is like a lightning rod, deflecting attention away from Arcesilas' own ambivalent identity and (evidently) unstable political position.

From a Greek perspective, a woman functioned as the currency of marriage, a silent sign in the language of exchange between households; Pindar's Medea bridges a gulf between Greece and the distant cultures of the East—and of Egypt—and she epitomizes the conflicts inherent in the process of exchanging women.[12] Calculated exchange is also central to epinician's own proper function, and Medea serves Pindar's laudatory goal extraordinarily well—both in the poem's more usual aspects and in the particular and unusual situation that apparently lay behind the commissioning of *Pythian* 4.[13]

In her service to Pindar's poetic and ideological requirements also, and her diverse services to Jason within the poem, Medea represents all women. She epitomizes the quality known as μῆτις or cunning intelligence, as it has been interpreted by Detienne and Vernant: a capacity (among other things) to deploy the skills of another—especially an adversary—to one's own advantage.[14] Medea's cunning undermines and defeats that of her father, Aeëtes, and that of Jason's uncle, Pelias. Her trickery responds to theirs and defeats them on their own ground. More significantly, her triumphs illustrate the prior operation of μῆτις on

[12] On the notion of traffic in women see Bergren 1983; Vernant 1983:133–34.

[13] The poem itself and its scholia constitute our principal source for the circumstances of its composition—obviously a risky one. Hdt. 4.153–65 also mentions Damophilus, who apparently had participated in a coup against the king and was exiled. Since the poem ends most unusually—with a request to king Arcesilas to restore Damophilus from exile—some have speculated that Damophilus may have requested and paid for *Pythian* 4 as an expensive bribe or tribute. It seems likely that he had something to do with its commissioning. Farenga 1977:9 discusses the (disguised) subversiveness of the "triangle" of victor, buyer, and seller-poet.

[14] Detienne and Vernant 1978. Segal 1986:165–79, discusses in detail the question of the appropriation of μῆτις in *Pythian* 4.

Medea herself; Jason's native μῆτις (assisted by Aphrodite's technical invention, the *iynx*) already has overcome Medea's and appropriated it, so that she fights his enemies for him. This male appropriation of female intelligence—famously enacted in the primordial swallowing of the goddess Metis by Zeus—is central to the myth of Jason and Medea as Pindar tells it. It also colors Pindar's self-presentation, his relationship to his Muse and to Medea, whose role in the poem parallels and illuminates that of the epinician Muse. Before talking about the poem itself, I will briefly discuss the relationship between poet and Muse as defined in epic to provide a context for my analysis of Pindar's transformed Muse—and of Medea—in *Pythian* 4.

The Bard and Muse

Traditionally the process of song making—including epic and often lyric—was a joint effort, whether it took place on the divine or human level.[15] The human bard requires a song of the Muses; the poem is exchanged between divine and human realms as the goddess communicates with the poet—but we only hear its manifestation on the human level, as the poet sings to his audience, both human and divine. The creative "team" thus consists of a male and female, the female element being immortal and otherworldly, the male a mortal, his limitations and weaknesses sharply defined. The resulting collaboration is strikingly unequal, as a superior female intellect is vented through a humble male instrument. In a society in which young and relatively ignorant girls were married to older and more knowledgeable men, this intellectual bias in favor of the female may have seemed anomalous.[16]

---

[15] See, for example, Hes. *Scut.* 201ff., where Apollo plays in the midst of the immortals; the Muses then begin the song. The Homeric *Hymn to Pythian Apollo* at 189ff. shows Apollo playing in the midst of the immortals, while the Muses begin the song and the gods dance. Pindar *Nem.* 5.22ff. again shows Apollo conducting the song of the Muses with his lyre; at *Pyth.* 1, the lyre is jointly owned by Apollo and the Muses; Paus. 5.18.4 (in the description of Cypselus' coffer) depicts Apollo leading the Muses, who are singing.

[16] See Sealey 1990:42. Ancient advice to marry very young girls includes Hes. *Op.* 695–707; Xen. *Oec.* 7.4. On the other hand, Arist. *Pol.* 7.1335a6–35 argues that girls should not marry before eighteen (their husbands being about thirty-seven). Whichever the case, the preference clearly was for wives to be much younger than husbands. Xenophon tell us that Ischomachus' wife was not yet fifteen and had spent the previous part of her life under the strictest restraint, so that she might see as little, hear as little, and ask as few questions as possible. The youthfulness of a wife relative to her husband is implied also in Plutarch's *Advice to the Bride and Groom* (*Mor.* 138.d–e), where he recommends that

The human epic poet seems the very antithesis of the divinities who inspire him. Often portrayed as old and blind, human bards differ dramatically from young, all-seeing Apollo.[17] In fact ancient hexameter and lyric primarily focus on and dramatize the relationship between the *Muses* and poet, inviting us to contemplate that gulf, and momentary contact, between female divinity and male mortal.[18] Their incongruous alliance has a tragic fruitfulness best illustrated by the *Iliad*'s first line: Μῆνιν ἄειδε, θεά, Πηλειάδεω Ἀχιλῆος (Sing, goddess, of the wrath of Peleus' son, Achilles). The generic word θεά ("goddess"—as opposed to Μοῦσα, "Muse") makes clearer the contrast between two different states of existence, mortality and immortality, and underscores the structural parallel between Achilles and his song; goddess and man bring both into being, since Thetis gives birth to the child of the mortal Peleus, and the goddess-Muse transmits the *Iliad* in some form to its mortal parent, the bard.[19] The goddess sings of divine wrath, but Achilles belongs to us, the mortal audience, more than to the listening gods on Olympus, because of that old man, his father Peleus, who fatally defines him in the poem's opening line. The bard, like Peleus, has a part in bringing to birth this blend of mortal weakness and divine ambition. It is he who translates Achilles to us.

Ordinary mortals cannot listen directly to the divine singing of Muses, who live in remote and inaccessible places. As with the Epicurean gods, their geographical remoteness bespeaks detachment from human interests and suffering. As Hesiod puts it in *Theogony* 61, they have a heart that is ἀκήδεα—"without grief" or perhaps even "without a capacity for grief." There is no room for grief or passion in a heart where song is *the* concern.[20] The bard, in contrast, while he shares

---

a man tolerate the girlish quarrels of early marriage—lest he discard the green grapes, thereby losing the pleasure of the ripe clusters.

[17] Calame 1977. In 1.104 he notes a distinction in the manner of performance: Apollo does not sing, whereas human bards both sing and play the lyre.

[18] Alcman in a famous fragment (26 *PMG*) contrasts himself as a slow-footed (old) man with blithe young girls in the chorus; the youth of the recurring generations of girl singers gives them a Muse-like permanence and creates an impression of unbridgeable distance. See Nagy 1990a:56, where he cites the famous σφραγίς to the Homeric *Hymn to Delian Apollo* (164ff.). The Delian maidens (described by Nagy as local manifestations of the Muses) identify the bard as a blind man from rocky Chios.

[19] Nagy 1979:184 remarks: "[Iliadic epic] is presented *by epic itself* as an eternal extension of the lamentation sung by the Muses over the hero's death (xxiv 60–61, 923–94)."

[20] Even in the extraordinary situation described in *Od*. 24, their formal dirge (θρῆνος) for Achilles is distinguished from the familial lamentation (γόος) of Thetis and the Nereids. The θρῆνος is a beautiful song that inspires tears in others, but there is no hint that the

in the authority of those distant goddesses, belongs in the suffering world.[21]

Direct contact between men and Muses, even if possible, is probably dangerous, which is why the poet is necessary. The Muses induce a distinctive pleasure that consists in part of a forgetfulness of the circumstances of everyday life; as *Theogony* 98ff. puts it, the poet, as θεράπων (servant) of the Muses, can bring oblivion even to the heart of a man who is newly bereaved. The innocent pleasure and temporary forgetfulness induced by song can spill over into dangerous intoxication, as Walsh has warned.[22] I suggest that it is the bard who prevents this from happening, as he mediates the dangerously enchanting message of the Muse, putting himself at risk in the process.

As Buschor once noted, the Sirens may be seen as a lethal "double" of the Olympian Muses.[23] The Sirens' song notoriously immobilizes its audience to the point of death and dissolution. This paralysis results when the listener forgets the loyalties that should pull a man back to the mortal world. The ghastly decay of the body visibly represents and completes his loss of identity, which is formed by the relationships with the people he has left at home: parents, children, friends, and even enemies. The nexus of loyalties and responsibilities that may be threatened by direct contact with Sirens can be subsumed under the heading αἰδώς, a Greek word meaning (among other things) "respect," "a sense of appropriateness."[24]

Like the Sirens, the Muses, in their single-minded devotion to pleasure, have little to do with αἰδώς or with the passions that may threaten it. Like the Sirens, the Muses invite mortals to participate in immortal pleasures, threatening a simultaneous loss of αἰδώς in the mortal heart. Men and women alike, when they forget or renounce αἰδώς, bring disgrace and fatal danger on themselves. Although the social responsibilities inherent in the term extend beyond the sexual realm, αἰδώς has a special

---

Muses themselves are actually grieving. They are professionals and make grief exquisite. See Alexiou 1974:11–13.

[21] See Bergren 1983:74–75 on the bard's appropriation of the Muses' authority.

[22] Walsh 1984:14–15.

[23] Buschor 1944. Bergren 1983:88 n. 6 supports his contention with further evidence of the connections between Muses and Sirens.

[24] Cf. the *Ajax* of Sophocles, and especially the claims made by Tecmessa on Ajax at 485ff. She uses the cognate verb αἰδεῖσθαι (in its aorist imperative αἴδεσαι) at 506 and 507 when she calls on Ajax to remember (i.e., consider or respect) his mother and father. The whole speech, with its appeal to Ajax's many responsibilities, is a lesson in αἰδώς. In *Pyth.* 4 itself Jason speaks of the sense of shame (αἰδώς) that will afflict the Fates, if kinsmen fight each other (146).

link with chastity in the female, as Segal has observed.[25] No mortal woman can act like a Muse—that is,'fix her gaze on something beautiful or desirable, and forget everything else—without bringing destruction in her wake, as the case of Helen testifies.[26]

The honest bard achieves a blend of enchantment and remembrance, educating his audience in αἰδώς as he simultaneously transmits the otherworldly message of the Muses.[27] On the other hand, dangerous and socially disengaged females—divine and human—can induce in an unprepared audience a loss of αἰδώς (and perhaps even of life or identity) by song and also by chemical means; one thinks of the intoxicating song of the Sirens and Muses, of Circe's λυγρὰ φάρμακα (baneful potions) and of Helen's φάρμακον νήπενθες (potion that banishes cares), which cause a man to lose emotional or moral contact with reality, even to the point of failing to react to witnessing a relative's violent death. I suggest that in *Pythian* 4 Medea functions as a kind of Muse, whose marvelous (but possibly destructive or disorienting) power must be handled adroitly by the poet.[28]

The Narrative of *Pythian* 4

The Medea of *Pythian* 4 is indeed a diva who has both magical song and drugs at her disposal.[29] She appears near the beginning of the poem as a formidable and divine singer, but later as the passionate Colchian woman who has succumbed to Jason's erotic magic. In fact, late in the poem we realize that the prophetic Medea of its opening must already have fallen under Jason's spell, but the poem contrives that we perceive the transformation as taking place during Pindar's telling of

[25] Segal 1973. He cites Hdt. 1.8.3 as an example of the implications of the word αἰδώς for female sexuality (26).

[26] In poem 16 (Campbell), Sappho measures Helen's great love in terms of the domestic network that Helen forgot, renounced, or abandoned: "Helen left her husband, and did not remember at all (οὐδὲ ... πά[μπαν] ἐμνάσθη) her child or her own parents."

[27] *Od.* 3.265ff. hints at this obligation on the part of the bard to maintain a sense of αἰδώς in his audience. Agamemnon chose a bard to watch over his wife during his absence from Greece—and Clytemnestra remained loyal to her husband until Aegisthus had the singer marooned on a desert island. It was after this—according to Nestor's narrative—that Aegisthus took Clytemnestra back to his house and found her willing.

[28] Segal 1986:177–78 suggests that Medea's potentially dangerous powers are neutralized by her position, framed as she is by the patriarchal order of Zeus and Apollo. He sees Pindar's appropriation of Medea as reflecting a traditional and patriarchal poetic.

[29] She is called παμφαρμάκου ξείνας (foreign woman versed in drugs) at 233, a passage that describes her help to Jason in harnessing the fire-breathing oxen.

the story. This illusion, and our developing awareness of Medea's role within the poem as a whole, evokes a sense of Pindar's own magical powers. The apparent metamorphosis undergone by Medea comments on the relationship between the *epinician* poet and *his* Muse, which is a transformation of the traditional relationship between the epic poet and Muse.

Medea's appearances in the poem fit within an exceptionally complicated structure that spans centuries of time and highlights a series of interconnected "heroic" moments. These moments include (1) the handing of a magical clod of earth to Euphamus, one of the Argo's crew, by a mysterious deity in Libya, during the return voyage from Colchis (this clod guaranteed a North African colony to his descendants, and the fact that it accidentally dropped out of the boat later on merely slowed—but did not stop—the destined colony, eventually founded by Battus); (2) the prophecy of Medea of this future colony, sanctioned by Delphi; and (3) the Delphic victory of Arcesilas, descendant of Euphamus and of Battus.

Pythian 4 begins with Pindar's instruction to a Muse to stand beside the victor, Arcesilas, in his hometown of Cyrene:

> Σάμερον μὲν χρή σε παρ' ἀνδρὶ φίλῳ
> στᾶμεν, εὐίππου βασιλῆι Κυράνας,
> ὄφρα κωμάζοντι σὺν Ἀρκεσίλᾳ,
> Μοῖσα, Λατοίδαισιν ὀφειλόμενον Πυ-
> Θῶνί τ' αὔξῃς οὖρον ὕμνων....

$$(1-3)$$

> Today my Muse you must stand beside a beloved man
> the king of Cyrene, rich in horses, so that
> together with Arcesilas, as he travels in procession,
>   Leto's children....

As we will see, this "relocation" of the Muse from her traditionally remote "otherworld," where she must be sought out by special devotees, to the familiar Greek and civic world of Cyrene parallels Medea's movement within the poem from distant Colchis to Hellas. Hesiod's encounter with the Muses was in the wilderness, a social and sexual no-man's-land where male and female can break out of their traditional roles, and often do.[30] At the same time, Pindar's overture to his Muse duplicates the transaction of marriage, where the alien female is brought

---

[30] See Carson 1990:144. Maenads, Amazons, and hunters (like Cyrene in Pindar's *Pyth.* 9) obviously resist the constraints on women imposed by society.

in to join in the procreative projects of a new home. She joins in a celebratory procession, she stands next to a dear or beloved man; she is to cause fruitful increase in his household as she is called on to "swell the favoring wind of songs" (1–3).

Pindar asks his Muse to sing a tribute to the children of Leto and to Pytho, where the Delphic priestess, close by Apollo, made a prophecy to Battus that repeated and endorsed one made by Medea on the island of Thera to the Argonauts on their shared return journey to Greece. The poem then segues into an extended quotation of Medea's prophecy. Thus Medea appears to engage in a hymnic/prophetic exchange with Apollo: she sings in anticipation of Apollo's prophetic message to Battus; this in turn inspires Pindar's Muse, who speaks to Apollo's ancient intervention in the Battiad dynasty, and of course to the recent victory, which also took place under Apollo's auspices, at Delphi. The stately exchange—Medea to Apollo to the Muse to Apollo—appropriately begins a poem structured by a complex antiphonal movement between scattered points in time: the very distant past of the Argo's voyage, the fairly distant past of the oracle to Battus and his ensuing foundation of Cyrene, and the recent history, and future, of Arcesilas, Cyrene's current king.

Medea's appearance near the beginning of the poem and within a triad of powerful, prophetic females (including also the Muse and the Delphic priestess) gives her considerable status. She is called ζαμενής (10), a word Pindar elsewhere uses of the prophetic Chiron and of the sun's mighty heat.[31] It seems a carefully chosen epithet for this prophetic queen of the Colchians. Indeed during this, her earlier manifestation in the poem, Medea seems to stand in the spectrum between prophet and singer, while she possesses additional magical powers of manipulation and healing.[32]

She "breathes forth" her oracular words from an "immortal mouth" (ἀπέπνευσ' ἀθανάτου στόματος, 11). As Pucci observes, the tongue is

---

[31] *Pyth.* 9.38; *Nem.* 4.13. Braswell 1988:*ad loc.* argues that the word means "spirited" rather than "inspired," as many previous editors have taken it. Pindar's own use of the word in connection with Chiron suggests that for him it does indeed have a prophetic connotation, however.

[32] I am indebted to Jenny Strauss Clay for this observation. ἐπέων στίχες (57) could characterize either epic verse or the hexameter prophecies enunciated by the Pythia, for example (for the meaning of the phrase, see n. 38 below). By the end of the poem the role played here by Medea—with all its complex and interrelated powers—has been fully taken over by the ambitious epinician poet and placed in the service of the man he is praising.

more usually the organ of voice production in epic, and the expression ἀπὸ στομάτων in the *Odyssey* describes only the song of the Sirens; in the *Iliad*, it is the poet's own mouth or that of Odysseus.[33] "Breathed forth" also is unusual when applied to words rather than to breath or smell, and recalls the inspirational breath of Hesiod's Muses; yet the prefix ἀπό is significant; the verb ἀποπνέομαι can characterize a last breath or *ex-(s)piring*.[34] In fact this "breathing forth" of an oracular statement (ἔπος) has a paradoxical doubleness whose significance emerges as the poem develops; Medea *is* a Muse of sorts, but also, as we later discover, her singing is that of a creature who has died and become a tool in the hands of another.

Her audience comprises the "demigod sailors who accompanied Jason the spear-bearer," whom she addresses appropriately as "sons of bold-hearted men and sons of gods." Curiously, Jason himself does not appear to be included in the group; certainly she does not single him out for special advice, as for example did Circe (Medea's aunt, incidentally), who in a somewhat similar situation in *Odyssey* 12 described Odysseus' future adventures and advised him, using singular imperative forms.[35] I will refer again to the Circe episode for purpose of comparison.

Medea's tone is lofty, oracular, and a little remote as she promises a city (Cyrene) to be founded out of Thera at some future time. As she explains the basis for this pronouncement, she describes their recent ship-hauling trek across Libya as having been undertaken because of her counsels—μήδεσιν ... ἀμοῖς (27). The word μήδεσιν (*mēdesin*) evokes the cerebral power witnessed in her name, Medea.[36] She has taught her fellow travelers how to adapt to an alien and uncompromising environment—a lesson that she surely will have to absorb herself when she arrives in Greece.

Medea explains that during the Argonauts' journey across North Africa, one of them, Euphamus, was handed a clod of earth by a mysterious divinity. This clod of earth predestined a member of his family to return to North Africa and found a colony there. Thus Pindar, with Medea as his mouthpiece, deftly transforms the presumption of

---

[33] See Pucci 1979; Segal 1986:134.

[34] *Il.* 4.524 (with θύμον). Pindar uses it at *Nem.* 1.47 in a causal sense—to make to give up the ghost.

[35] *Od.* 12.37ff. For Medea's genealogy, see Graf in this volume.

[36] The cognate verb μήδομαι means "to contrive" or "to plan skillfully." Braswell 1988:370–71 expresses skepticism regarding this wordplay—and also the ἰατήρ-'Ιάσων wordplay of line 270.

a foreign colony into a νόστος or return. The accidental dropping of this clod into the sea, according to Medea, would delay (but not prevent) the fulfilment of this magical promise. The expedition's moment of ineptitude—the loss of the clod of earth—Medea recounts as an event that took place in her absence. "I hear (πεύθομαι) that it was washed out of the ship, and went into the sea with the evening tide" (38–40). There is a disdainful distance marked between this knowledgeable, competent heroine/singer and the butterfingered crew. Thus Medea gives a double prophecy; what would have happened, had Euphamus been able to hang onto the clod of earth, and what was now going to happen—colonization of Cyrene in the seventeenth, instead of the fourth, generation.[37]

When Medea concludes speaking, Pindar characterizes her pastiche of prophecy, narrative, and commentary as "lines of epic verse" (ἐπέων στίχες, 57).[38] The dactylo-epiritic meter of *Pythian* 4 gives it an epic weight and sonority; the meter also allows Pindar here and later in the epyllion on the Argonautic voyage to demonstrate the power of lyric verse to contain epic and to turn epic's themes and tropes to its own purposes.[39]

Her audience's reaction to Medea is unlike Odysseus' reaction to Circe in *Odyssey* 12. Odysseus pipes up with a question; the Argonauts crouch or cower in fear (ἔπταξαν, 57). They later are motionless and silent. The verb πτήσσω applies frequently to animals and birds cowering in fright. It is a strong term, suggesting a potentially sinister metamorphosis worked by this other Circe.[40] At the same time it recalls

[37] The verb πεύθεσθαι (an older form of πυνθάνομαι, according to LSJ) in several poetic contexts appears to carry implications of oracular knowledge. For example, at Soph. *OT* 604 Creon exhorts Oedipus to *check* at Delphi as to the veracity of his report. Eur. *IA* 1138 is a question asked of Agamemnon by Clytemnestra regarding divine justice/punishment; in other words, divine insight would be required for a confident response. At Hes. *Th.* 463 the verb is used in the sense of having oracular knowledge (Cronus learns that he will be overcome by his son).

[38] See Braswell 1988:139: "This unique use of the phrase 'ἦ ῥα' in extant choral lyric is a genuine example of *color epicus* ... and as such entirely in keeping with the epic character of the ode." Braswell cites M. Leumann, *MSS* 33 (1975) 82, on the use of στίχες to link the Homeric feminine noun meaning "battle lines" and the later masculine form, which refers to lines of verse. At *Nem.* 2.2 Pindar uses ἔπεα to designate Homeric poetry (ῥαπτῶν ἐπέων ... ἀοιδοί), which is what I take the plural use to mean here also.

[39] Nagy 1990b:350ff,, 416, argues that lyric contains (a form of) epic within itself.

[40] The prophet Tiresias, to take a comparable prophetic figure, does not have this effect on Odysseus in *Od.* 11—despite the formidable import of his message, which includes information about Odysseus' own death. Menelaus' shock at hearing Proteus' words— αὐτὰρ ἐμοί γε κατεκλάσθη φίλον ἦτορ (but my dear heart was broken) at *Od.* 4.481 and

a familiar response to epic song—such as we encounter in Phaeacia at *Odyssey* 11.333–34 and 13.1–2, as a result of Odysseus' own songs: οἱ δ' ἄρα πάντες ἀκὴν ἐγένοντο σιωπῇ / κηληθμῷ δ' ἔσχοντο κατὰ μέγαρα σκιόεντα (they all were silent / and were held spellbound throughout the shadowy halls).

One might see Pindar's description of the reaction of Medea's audience as simply a stronger version of this formula. Yet there is a qualitative difference between being held spellbound and cowering motionless and in silence.[41] After the narrative of Odysseus and the prophecy of Circe, somebody does in fact speak and break the awed hush. The silence is impressive, but temporary. *This* Argonautic immobility recalls the Sirens' monstrous spell whereby men cannot move to save their lives. There is an irony in the fact that the poet Orpheus is numbered among this paralyzed throng; Pindar later names him (176), together with other members of the expedition, but doubtless his audience already would have known of his presence on board. Thus the poet whose song could move trees is himself immobilized.[42]

We do not hear of further reaction or of the end of Medea's spell. Directly following this dangerous silence Pindar interrupts in his role as epinician poet, apostrophizing Battus, the recipient of Delphi's oracle, and moving swiftly to the current victor, a winner at Delphi. Pindar promises to give the Muses both Arcesilas and the Argonautic voyage, a significant variation on the usual epic arrangement whereby the Muses grant the theme to the poet:

> ... ἀπὸ δ' αὐτὸν ἐγὼ Μοίσαισι δώσω
> καὶ τὸ πάγχρυσον νάκος κριοῦ...
>
> (67–68)

> I will hand him [Arcesilas] over to the Muses
> together with ram's pelt, all golden.

There follows a familiar epic invocation, as Pindar asks for information about the beginning of the voyage.

538—is explained in the first case (a perilous sea voyage must be undertaken) and is obvious in the second, which immediately follows the account of Agamemnon's murder. In contrast, Medea's speech, which is neither inherently fearful nor shocking, affects its audience in a way that is *not* immediately explicable.

[41] Cf. Soph. *Ajax* 164–171.

[42] Simon. fr. 567 *PMG* describes Orpheus' song as capable of enchanting fish and birds. Eur. *Ba.* 560ff. ascribes to Orpheus the power to move trees and wild animals.

τίς γὰρ ἀρχὰ δέξατο ναυτιλίας,
τίς δὲ κίνδυνος κρατεροῖς ἀδάμαντος δῆσεν ἅλοις;

(70–71)

What kind of embarking found them,
What danger bound them with powerful adamantine bolts?

Thus the poem incorporates a classically traditional stance toward the Muse—that of the bard as the passive vessel for information—within a framework that hints at a different relationship, in which the poem is a glorious concoction spontaneously offered as a tribute to the deities of song.

Of the earlier part of the Argonautic story as told by Pindar I will say little, except to point out a detail whose significance will shortly become clear: Pelias imposes a double task on the young hero, retrieval of the fleece *and* the recovery of the wandering soul of their dead kinsman, Phrixus.

...δύνασαι δ’ ἀφελεῖν
μᾶνιν χθονίων. κέλεται γὰρ ἑὰν ψυχὰν κομίξαι
Φρίξος ἐλθόντας πρὸς Αἰήτα θαλάμους
δέρμα τε κριοῦ βαθύμαλλον ἄγειν,
    τῷ ποτ’ ἐκ πόντου σαώθη
ἔκ τε ματρυιᾶς ἀθέων βελέων.

(158–62)

... You can dispel the wrath of the earth-dwellers
For Phrixus bids [us], having journeyed to the halls of Aeëtes,
to bring back (κομίξαι) his soul,
and to bring the fleecy pelt of the ram
on which he was saved, once, out of the sea
and from his stepmother's godless weapons.

The scholiast remarks on the passage that Pindar alone of the traditions known to him assigns this double task to Jason: a double return of what has been doubly lost.[43] This version gives the impression (substantiated by a scholiast's speculation) that the ram's fleece has been requested by Phrixus to assuage his restless soul.[44] The dead ram's and the dead

---

[43] See Drachmann 1910:135–36.
[44] See Kirkwood 1982:188: "χθονίων: 'those in the earth' is general enough to suggest both the dead (Phrixus in particular, as Pelias goes on to explain) and the underworld powers, whose ill will, Pelias seems to imply, is the source of the family's troubles."

man's νόστος will match, if not actually bring about, the restoration of the legitimate living heirs to the ruling house of Iolcus.

Medea reappears near the end of Pindar's extended narrative of the Argonauts' expedition. Upon their arrival in Phasis the Argonauts "violently mingled with the black-visaged Colchians" (κελαινώπεσσι Κόλχοισιν βίαν / μεῖξαν, 212–13).[45] The explanation for this surprising epithet is to be found in Herodotus (2.103–4), who explains the existence of a black-skinned people at Colchis as the result of the ancient conquests of Sesostris. It is likely that black-skinned Colchians did in fact exist and Pindar is referring to them.[46] The significance of his comment in this context is difficult to pinpoint, but a number of connotations spring to mind. Medea was a granddaughter of the Sun, and it was believed in antiquity that a dark skin was the result of being burned by proximity to the sun.[47] Further, Egyptian women were famous for their expertise in magic as early as the *Odyssey*, where we learn that Helen has learned skill in drugs from Polydamna, the wife of the Egyptian king Thon.[48] Finally, as Herodotus testifies in book 2 of his *Histories*, Egyptian mores and cultural norms were believed to be different from those of *all* the other peoples in the world. By calling the Colchians "black-visaged" and thus reminding his readers of their Egyptian origins, Pindar indicates the immense cultural divide that separated Medea's people from Jason's.[49]

----

[45] The verb μείγνυμι itself here seems to mingle two different things: sex and warfare. This first encounter between Greeks and Colchians gives an ominous sense of lethal intimacy.

[46] See Mokhtar 1981:36: "In the fifth century before our era, at the time when Herodotus visited Egypt, a black-skinned people, the Colchians, were still living in Colchis on the Armenian shore of the Black Sea, east of the ancient port of Trebizond, surrounded by white-skinned nations.... Herodotus, on the strength of commemorative stelae, erected by Sesostris in conquered countries, asserts that this monarch had got as far as Thrace and Scythia, where stelae would seem to have been still standing in his day." "Sesostris" has been interpreted as Ramses II (1301–1234 B.C.) and as a composite of Sety I (1313–1301 B.C.) and Ramses II; cf. Snowden 1970:290. Braswell 1988 is, I believe, being unfair to Herodotus when he claims that the historian's detailed and circumstantial account of the dark-skinned Colchians derives from a misreading of Pindar's epithet here, which he takes to mean "grim-faced."

[47] See, e.g., Lucr. 6.722.

[48] *Od.* 3.266–32. Snowden 1970:27, 276, cites a fifth- or fourth-century Kabeiric vase, now in the Ashmolean, portraying Circe (Medea's aunt) as a black woman.

[49] According to Hdt. 2.35 the Egyptians are to be sharply distinguished from *all* other people in their customs and laws—just as their climate and the vagaries of the Nile have rendered the country itself unique. Apollonius Rhodius, while describing at length the ancient Egyptian invasion of Colchis at 4.260–80, nonetheless presents Medea herself

Pindar moves directly from interracial conflict to the violent subjugation of Medea. As the two peoples engaged in mortal combat, "the queen of sharpest weapons yoked the *iynx*—the bird of madness—to a wheel." Only at the end of this procedure is this brutal goddess identified as Cyprogeneia, Cypriot-born Aphrodite.

πρῶτον ἀνθρώποισι λιτάς τ' ἐπαοιδὰς
ἐκδιδάσκησεν σοφὸν Αἰσονίδαν·
ὄφρα Μηδείας τοκέων ἀφέλοιτ' αἰδῶ, ποθεινὰ δ' Ἑλλὰς αὐτάν
ἐν φρασὶ καιομέναν δονέοι μάστιγι Πειθοῦς.

(217–19)

She it was who taught Aeson's son magic incantations
so that he might rob Medea of αἰδώς for her parents,
and a passion for Hellas might spin her with Persuasion's lash,
as she burned in her heart.[50]

Her passion for *Hellas*—rather than for Jason—emphasizes the geographical and cultural exchange that is the crucial result of her loss of αἰδώς. The *iynx* wheel essentially causes *movement* as a result of its sympathetic spinning; in this case it draws the singer out of her own magical realm and into the familiar world of Hellas. One can hardly overstate the importance of this immigration or of the passion that made Hellas so irresistible to Medea.

Pindar's account of the motivation behind Medea's transfer to Greece seems to borrow from two of the known strands of earlier tradition. Hesiod's heroine, described as Aeëtes' daughter, is led by Jason to

---

as white; she is credited with light-colored hair (ξανθὰς ἐθείρας, 3.829). Pindar makes no such distinction between Medea and her subjects, and we should not assume one. Euripides attributes white skin (πάλλευκος) to both Medea and Creon's daughter (see Boedeker in this volume).

[50] ἐπαοιδή (incantation[s]) is used by Pindar at *Nem.* 8.49 to describe song—and its power to take away the pain of bereavement. It appears at Soph. *Ajax* 582 as an incantation that may be said over a wound. On the nature of the wheel and whip, see Faraone 1993 and Johnston 1995b. Faraone argues that the *iynx* wheel and whip have connotations of torture and violence, and that, within the Greek magical tradition, this violence is felt to be essential in separating an otherwise respectable young woman from her home and responsibilities. I found this persuasive until I read Johnston, who argues that the burning is simply poetic convention for amatory passion and that the whip is a reference to the thong or string on which the magical *iynx* wheel spins. Thus the *iynx* effects not a torture spell but a powerful (and unscrupulous) use of magical persuasion. I think that Johnston's arguments are fully correct—but, as always, Pindar's pungent and complex language makes it difficult to confine or define his meaning very securely. For discussion of the *iynx* and its sound and movement, see also Johnston 1990:chap. 7.

Iolcus, where she "is subject to" him and bears him a son, Medeus.[51] In the *Corinthiaca*, Medea travels independently to Greece because she has more or less inherited the throne of Corinth.[52] Jason becomes king as her husband, through her. Pindar's Medea desires to go to Greece—but it is a desire that is imposed on her by Jason; she does not inherit a kingdom. Indeed, by talking of her loss of αἰδώς Pindar makes clear that Medea's ties with her own family are abruptly severed; her movement to Greece follows a complete rejection of her native responsibilities.[53]

Medea's autonomy, in other words, is seriously curtailed—although (paradoxically perhaps) her desires are very much part of the picture. If we glance briefly at the account of Herodotus in the opening section of his *Histories*—a narrative written in the years between the composition of *Pythian* 4 and Euripides' *Medea*—we see how different Medea's journey to Greece can appear, if viewed in a different context.[54] There Medea

[51] Hes. *Th.* 992–1002. The participle δμηθεῖσ' in line 1000, describing Medea's relationship to Jason ("and she was subject to Jason, shepherd of the people") may merely describe marital subjection, although at *Od.* 3.269, *Il.* 3.301, and in the Gortyn law code, for example, it refers to rape. Whichever is the case, the Hesiodic narrative leaves Medea in an entirely passive role.

[52] The scholiast ad *Ol.* 13.74 cites Eumelus' poem:

ἀλλ' ὅτε Αἰήτης καὶ Ἀλωεὺς ἐξεγένοντο
Ἡελίου τε καὶ Ἀντιώπης, τότε δ' ἄνδιχα χώρην
δάσσατο παισὶν Ὑπερίονος ἀγλαὸς υἱός.
ἦν μὲν ἔχ' Ἀσωπός, ταύτην πόρε δίῳ Ἀλωεῖ·
ἦν δ' Ἐφύρη κτεάτισσ', Αἰήτῃ δῶκεν ἅπασαν.
Αἰήτης δ' ἄρ' ἑκὼν Βούνῳ παρέδωκε φυλάσσειν
εἰσόκεν αὐτὸς ἵκοιτ' ἢ ἐξ αὐτοῖό τις ἄλλος,
ἢ παῖς ἢ υἱωνός· ὁ δ'ἵκετο Κολχίδα γαῖαν.

But when Aeëtes and Aloeus were born
Of Helios and Antiope, then the shining
Son of Hyperion divided the land in two, among his sons.
One part [the river] Asopos bounded; this he gave to godlike Aloeus.
The other part Ephyra [Corinth] acquired; this he gave in entirety to Aeëtes.
Aeëtes voluntarily entrusted it to Bounus, to guard,
Until he himself might come, or some other member of his line
Either a son or grandson. He himself arrived at the land of Colchis.

Pausanias' description of the coffer of Cypselus at 5.18.3 suggests more clearly that Medea's throne (in Corinth presumably) was hers independently of her marriage to Jason. The scene depicts Medea sitting on a throne, with Jason *standing* on her right and Aphrodite on her left, the caption reading "Jason weds Medea, as Aphrodite bids."

[53] Another lost archaic epic, the *Naupactica*, apparently included an account of Medea's murder of her brother Apsyrtus. This killing may be implied by Pindar's discreet reference to her loss of αἰδώς but it is not named. See Segal 1986:19–20 on this passage and its unsettling implications. Cf. also Bremmer, this volume.

[54] Hdt. 1.1–5. See Bergren 1983:76–78. The date(s) of the publication of the *Histories* are somewhat in doubt. Immerwahr 1985:426–28 suggests some time around 425 for a

is one of a series of women who traverse the space between Greece and the East in a vengeful interchange: Io (removed from Greece by Phoenicians), Europa (removed from the Phoenician town of Tyre by Greeks), Medea (removed from Colchis by the crew of an armed Greek merchant ship), Helen (removed from Greece by Paris). Both Io and Medea apparently were added spontaneously to cargo already acquired—through honest means—as plunder, although Herodotus, with his reference to an *armed* merchant ship, hints at bad initial intentions on the part of the sailors who took Medea. Although in the cases of Io and Medea the woman's removal or departure is appended to a trading expedition, the countertheft in each case retroactively identifies the *women* as the essential medium of exchange in his narrative.

For all his prefatory commitment to investigating the cause of Greco-Persian conflict (which he sees as originating in these interchanges of women), Herodotus cannot disentangle the various accounts of these events. Either the women were seized, in which case they function as the currency in a rough and ready "marital" exchange between East and West, or they traveled voluntarily, in which case the need for recompense is illusory. The function and value of these women (and the unexpected overvaluation of Helen, whose loss is anomalously avenged by means of a military expedition instead of a countertheft) undergo further shifts, depending on the reader of the situation. Greeks, Persians, and Phoenicians all have their various interpretations of the hostilities.

Pindar's version also places Medea within a context of earlier movement between East and West; Jason has set out to bring back to Iolcus the soul of his lost kinsman Phrixus and the Golden Fleece. As in the later, Herodotean account, Medea's movement to Greece is a by-product of an expedition designed for another purpose. Pindar's Medea does not appear as currency in this very differently designed program of exchange, however; rather she is a catalyst. She makes possible Jason's removal of the fleece (and presumably the exiled spirit) and ultimately the restoration of the (male) heir to the throne of Iolcus.

Pindar's Medea displays a far greater and more disturbing ambiguity than Herodotus' two-dimensional heroines. There is no doubt as to her willingness to travel, yet Pindar's powerful metaphors—of love's burning and persuasion's lash—bring into question the very notion of her will and suggest that she is helpless to resist. Her desire is for Hellas—a direct and linear journey—yet the violence of that desire spins

---

formal publication date, although it seems likely that they were written—and probably circulated informally—some time earlier, perhaps around 440 B.C.

her in chaotic circles. Her passion for Hellas, a desire more appropriate and necessary in Jason and his crew, is paradoxically the result of her pathological loss of αἰδώς, the same emotion that encompasses the sense of home and familial obligation underlying and motivating the return of all Greek mariners from Odysseus onward. Their return home (νόστος) is *her* dislocation from her race and family; their pursuit of what is theirs by birth—Hellas and the privileges of belonging there—is *her* disloyalty and madness. Although the spell transforms her from Jason's enemy into his ally and fellow traveler, Medea is still the very antithesis of what it means to be Greek.

Yet, as I said at the outset, Medea is also typical of all women, including Greek women, and exceptional only in the degree to which she represents female traits and dangerous potentialities. All of her "otherness"—the geographical, racial, and cultural difference she represents—serves to accentuate the most problematic and radical difference of all: gender. For the Greeks *all* women were no less than a race apart.[55] Medea most fully exemplifies the potential disloyalty present in all wives, living as necessary but suspect aliens in their husbands' houses. She is the ultimate risky import, defining Jason's exceptional heroic courage. At the same time, the act—biologically necessary, politically astute, or both—of "taking the outsider in" and adapting her (or him) to one's own's purposes defines *all* Hellenic males: Jason, Arcesilas, and Pindar himself.

The tool composed of an *iynx* bird bound to an *iynx* wheel, which instigates Medea's psychological metamorphosis into Jason's ally and lover, makes a sound to accompany the love incantation or song, just as the lyre accompanies epic song. Like the lyre, it is played by human hands as well as divine, and like the lyre it begins its existence as an animal. Both instruments have a destructive potential, but, as Segal has shown, the *iynx* wheel is destined to bring about a dangerous and unstable relationship.[56] Jason's magical "song" is fraught with risk for himself and for Medea.

Our perspective on Medea shifts as we watch her succumb to Jason's spell, moving from divine singer to the victim of Aphrodite and Jason. Whereas the earlier Medea gave the impression of detachment, concern with the distant future, and an Olympian lack of sympathy for human folly, this Medea is fully human and fallible in that she has a sense of αἰδώς to lose, and lose it she does. She is doubly conquered—on the

---

[55] See Loraux 1978.
[56] Segal 1973; cf. Johnston 1995b.

battlefield and as a victim of love. The former "Muse" who immobilized her audience has herself fallen victim to the poetic/magical skills of Jason and Aphrodite. Her own prophetic and pharmaceutical skills now serve Jason's purposes and not her own. Of course, she is still very formidable.[57]

Medea's final appearance in the poem is under the sobriquet Πελιαο-φόνον—"Death-of-Pelias" (250).[58] Jason stole away the "Death-of-Pelias" with her own help. This second metamorphosis of the Colchian princess seems to fall into a recurring pattern of such transformations whereby animate and independent creatures become tools in the hands of man: a wryneck becomes part of a magical tool, a tree serves as pillar or firewood in Arcesilas' house, the ram has become a Golden Fleece, and a clod of living earth, a distant colony. Medea is now a deadly weapon, even the very embodiment of Pelias' death. It is likely that Pindar knew of a tradition in which Medea murdered Creon and his daughter, and, most significantly and appropriately, Jason; Neophron's play and later that of Euripides, with their shocking presentation of the murder of the children, were additions (from a separate tradition) to an ancient tale of adultery and vengeance.[59]

In most versions of the Argonautic story their landing on Lemnos takes place *before* their arrival at Colchis.[60] In *Pythian 4* it occurs

[57] I differ from Segal in that I regard the poem's treatment of Medea as *deliberately teasing*, evocative of the destructive variants of the myth; it does not (and could not) control or repress the sinister elements of her story (cf. Segal 1986:70–71).

[58] The MSS are divided between Πελιαοφονόν (Killer-of-Pelias), sometimes written as two words (following Wackernagel), and Πελιαοφόνον (Death-of-Pelias). See Segal 1986:84, where he argues that "the Lemnian women's foreignness and murderousness are a displaced form of Medea's potential danger.... As in the case of Medea, their possible threat is neutralized and incorporated into a patriarchal monarchy by a sexual conquest at sea." I suggest that the Lemnian women's murderous past accentuates Medea's dangerousness rather than displaces it.

[59] See Graf and Johnston in this volume for the preexisting strands of the mythic tradition. See Page 1938:xxvi for the literary evidence; Hyginus seems to know of a pre-Euripidean version (*Fab.* 25): Medea made a poisoned crown of gold and gave it to her sons, telling them to give it to their stepmother. Creusa accepted the gift and perished in flames, together with Jason and Creon. There are hints of this variant at lines 163ff, 374–75 in Euripides, where Medea threatens Jason with death. On the subject of the death of the children see Page xxiii–xxv. It is clear from the accounts of Eumelus, Didymus, and others that these deaths are not originally related to Jason's infidelity. See Michelini 1989, who argues for retention of these disputed lines and discusses Neophron's play, which appears to have included Medea's decision to murder the children. On this last topic, cf. Manuwald 1983.

[60] Braswell 1988:347: "Already in antiquity readers had remarked on the oddity of Pindar's placing the Lemnian episode after instead of before the events in Colchis." Cf. the schol. *ad loc.*: "Not sequentially. For they landed on Lemnos not as they turned back,

afterward, with the result that the ἀνδροφόνων Lemnian women follow directly after Πελιαοφόνον Medea in the narrative (250, 252). Husband-slaughtering women, however successfully they may have been absorbed into the expedition, create an ominous echo. Surely Medea is truly like the *iynx*: not only threatening the person against whom she is used but implicating the magician himself in her destructive cycle. The removal of αἰδώς, which made possible her abandonment and betrayal of her kin in Colchis, has made Medea an unpredictable ally.[61]

Pythian 4 ends with advice to its recipient, Arcesilas, to recall from exile Damophilus, a former political rebel. Arcesilas is to be a timely healer (ἰατὴρ ἐπικαιρότατος, 270) in mending his city's wounds. Damophilus will return to his native land to support the regime, giving evidence of his honest heart—like good oak wood, hewn from the living tree, which burns serviceably in the hearth or stands as architectural support in the form of a pillar. The image speaks of the irremediable dissolution of death, that is, the tree's death. Yet Pindar advocates restoration from a treatable condition, the dissociation of exile. This metaphorical legerdemain seems to endow Arcesilas with the tremendous power denied even the great healer gods, Apollo and Asclepius: the power to restore life. Arcesilas will have the best of both worlds—handling his own tractable subject as an instrument, after having brought him back and rooted him in the living soil of home.

Pindar ends with a moving vision of Damophilus praying to return from exile:

> ἀλλ' εὔχεται οὐλομέναν νοῦ-
> σον διαντλήσαις ποτὲ
> οἶκον ἰδεῖν, ἐπ' Ἀπόλλω-
> νός τε κράνᾳ συμποσίας ἐφέπων
> θυμὸν ἐκδόσθαι πρὸς ἥβαν πολλάκις, ἔν τε σοφοῖς
> δαιδαλέαν φόρμιγγα βαστάζων πολί-
> ταις ἡσυχίᾳ θιγέμεν.
> μήτ' ὦν τινι πῆμα πορών, ἀπαθὴς δ' αὐτὸς πρὸς ἀστῶν·

---

but setting forth." Braswell explains the anomaly in terms of Euphamid political claims; their claim to Libyan sovereignty would be stronger if Euphamus sired his son *after* receiving the clod. Kirkwood 1982:195 had made a similar suggestion.

[61] Regarding αἰδώς, Goldhill 1986:14ff. suggests that Clytemnestra's transgressive use of language in *Agamemnon* comes back to haunt her in *Libation Bearers*. Indeed I would add specifically that Clytemnestra's appeal to αἰδώς (*Cho.* 896–97; τόνδε δ' αἴδεσαι, τέκνον / μαστόν, "Pity this breast, my child") fails because she herself has destroyed the web of trust and decency that binds society together. αἰδώς is not a concept to which she can appeal any longer.

καί κε μυθήσαιθ᾽, ὁποίαν, Ἀρκεσίλα,
εὗρε παγὰν ἀμβροσίων ἐπέων
πρόσφατον Θήβᾳ ξενωθείς.

(293–97)

But having purged to the end his destructive disease he prays
to see home again, and, as he indulges in convivial company by
    Apollo's stream,
to yield his heart again and again to youth, and among
wise citizens as he lifts the gorgeous lyre, to win peace,
neither bringing harm to anyone
nor being himself hurt by the townsfolk.
And he might tell, Arcesilas, of how he found
a source of immortal epic verse, when he
was lately welcomed as a guest in Thebes.

Pindar's invitation to Arcesilas—that he be a healer and bring home an alien and a singer to serve his political purposes—invites comparison with the mythic hero he had just described. The name "Jason" appears to be cognate with the verb ἰάομαι, "heal," and Pindar asks Arcesilas to play Jason to Damophilus' Medea. The implied parallel gives a faintly disruptive edge to Pindar's flattery since, as I have suggested, ineradicably embedded in the tale of Argonautic success is a hint of future disaster. Arcesilas will have to succeed in his taming of a dangerous alien where Jason notoriously failed.

Medea's shifting appearance in *Pythian* 4 also speaks to Pindar's own role, defining a poetic stance unlike that of the epic poet. The epinician poet, as he represents himself, is far from blind, old, and feeble: instead, he resembles the athletes he celebrates in being disciplined, ambitious, energetic, confident, and of course *first*. Pindar hands Arcesilas with Jason to the Muses in line 67; they do not give the theme to him. He openly avows his contribution to the song to be significant, whereas in Homer and Hesiod the poet's contribution—though crucial, as I have argued—is not explicitly defined. Significantly at 277 Pindar quotes Homer as saying that a good messenger brings great honor to every affair, but it is Pindar in his own voice who adds by way of commentary that even the Muse is increased or glorified (αὔξεται) by a true message. The poet can confer honor on the Muse, and the word describing this conferral is commonly used by Pindar to describe praise given to a

victor.[62] Thus Pindar's opening invitation to the Muse to stand beside
Arcesilas reflects his transfer of the Muse from her traditional role of
shaper of the song and thus outside its frame to a place within it. Like
Medea, she moves from being a singer to being a theme of song, from
supernatural force to cultural artifact.

At line 247, *before* the expedition to Colchis reaches its goal of finding
the Golden Fleece, Pindar pointedly changes from epic to epinician,
abandoning the epic high road as too well worn and pedestrian for his
swift feet:

> μακρά μοι νεῖσθαι κατ' ἀμαξιτόν· ὥρα
>   γὰρ συνάπτει· καί τινα
> οἶμον ἴσαμαι βραχύν· πολ-
>   λοῖσι δ' ἄγημαι σοφίας ἑτέροις.

(247–48)

> It is tedious to travel by the high road.
> The hour presses on, and I know a short route.
> To many others I am a leader in song.

Pindar's handling of the story is not just a shortcut but a precisely
crafted response to the Argo's challenge of a pioneering voyage in un-
charted waters. The poem incorporates and transforms moments of
epic within its own repressive Greek and civic ideology, as it moves
to its complex goal, and the figure of Medea enables Pindar to illustrate epinician's flexibility, power, and inclusiveness. As I suggest, the
unsung catastrophic end to her marriage with Jason forms an ironic
counterpoint both to Arcesilas' anticipated successful reabsorption of
Damophilus in Cyrenean politics and to Pindar's own poetic enterprise.
Jason ultimately may have failed in harnessing the supernatural abilities of Medea, but Pindar has not; he tames the dangerous Muse. Thus
Pindar fulfills the poet's ancient role of fostering αἰδώς in his audience,
with the intransigent and lethal Medea as his tool and inspiration, since
in persuading Arcesilas to *surpass* Jason and restore Damophilus he
reminds the ruler of his human and political responsibilities, even as
he enchants him with a song.

[62] See, e.g., line 3 of this poem, where Pindar (conventionally) asks the *Muse* to swell or
increase the breath of songs.

6

BECOMING MEDEA

ASSIMILATION IN EURIPIDES

Deborah Boedeker

URIPIDES' TRAGEDY of 431 B.C., it is agreed, gives Medea her canonical identity: the woman who kills her children in vengeance when her husband deserts her. Euripides may not have originated this plot—according to the first hypothesis of the play (which cites Dicaearchus and Aristotle), he followed the outlines of an earlier drama by a certain Neophron[1]—but it was his heroine who became the point of reference for later versions. Just how definitive the vengeful Euripidean Medea came to be is evident in Seneca's *Medea*, for example: early in the play the Nurse addresses the protagonist, "Medea . . .," and the response is simply, *Fiam*! (I shall be! 171). The Neronian audience understands what a threat that is meant to be.[2]

In Euripides' drama, however, such a character is not yet firmly established. Besides the deliberate infanticide, alternative Medeas were still possible. For example, Medea herself might kill Creon and the princess, but the children could be killed in retribution by the Corinthians.[3] Indeed, at the beginning of the play Medea is above all an object of pity, recently abandoned by the man for whom she betrayed home and family, and now about to be exiled. By the end of the tragedy, however, although in a sense Medea has destroyed herself, she has also acquired a profound and disturbing power, as commentators have recognized. "Medea the human being is dead; into her place has

I am grateful to Sarah Iles Johnston and the Press's anonymous readers for their helpful suggestions, as well as to commentator Gordon Kirkwood, my fellow panelists, and the audience at the 1991 APA panel on Medea, at which a version of this paper was first presented.

[1] For bibliography and recent discussion see Manuwald 1983:50–56 and Michelini 1989:115–35 (to which add also the detailed discussion in Séchan 1927:251–56, 273–74).

[2] For the very different process of "becoming Medea" in Seneca's play, cf. Nussbaum's essay in this volume.

[3] As happens in the epic *Oechaliae Halosis* fr. 4, for example (cf. schol. ad *Med.* 264).

stepped the victorious goddess of vengeance."[4] "[T]he energy she had wasted on Jason was tempered to a deadly instrument to destroy him. It became a *theos*, a relentless merciless force, the unspeakable violence of the oppressed and betrayed which ... carries everything before it to destruction. ..."[5] "[T]his crime was not one that human nature suffices to explain; it needed an energy, a superhuman force of hatred and determination, a complicity with the forces of destruction that, in nature and in life, represented for the Greeks the obscure face of the divine."[6]

What creates this powerful effect? In large measure, of course, it comes from Medea's murderous deeds during the course of the drama. But her compelling *persona* is enhanced also through the many ways Medea is described, both by herself and by other characters.[7] This paper will not offer a new interpretation of Euripides' tragedy but will merely try to analyze some of the poetic mechanisms that give the protagonist her overpowering presence.

First, with similes and metaphors Medea is compared to threatening beasts, legendary killers, and to natural elements such as rock, sea, or storm; she frequently compares herself to a beleaguered voyager. Second, inconspicuous and natural-sounding categories are often applied to Medea—simple terms such as γυνή (woman) or μήτηρ (mother), but as we shall see, Medea is gradually dissociated from such apparently obvious definitions of what she is.[8] Finally, Medea is subtly assimilated to several figures in her own story, such as Aphrodite, Jason, and the princess. In this essay I will suggest how these several kinds of

---

[4] Schlesinger 1966:51.

[5] Knox 1977:225.

[6] Rivier 1960:67–68.

[7] The abundance of metaphor and other imagistic language in a genre that can *show* as well as narrate is in some ways paradoxical. Stanford 1936:94, in his review of previous work on metaphor, cites Brinkmann 1878:122 on "how Drama delights in metaphor more than do Epic and Lyric as a general rule, because there is more *Leidenschaft* in drama, and metaphor thrives on passion and emotion." In a very different vein, de Jong 1991:173, analyzing dramatic narrative (messenger speeches), quotes de Romilly 1961:132, "Le récit insiste plus que le spectacle direct ne pouvait faire," and Pathmanathan 1965:6: "It is a commonplace of stage-craft that horror can be conveyed more effectively through the suggestive power of words or the imagination than actual spectacle." The present essay focuses on other kinds of "telling vs. showing" (de Jong's phrase), not through narrated action but through the variety of ways a dramatic character is described, including metaphor.

[8] See further Barlow 1989 on Medea's transcendence of female stereotypes. Sourvinou-Inwood's contribution to this volume explores in more detail the shifting categories of "normal woman," "good woman," and "bad woman" with reference to Euripides' Medea.

characterization cumulatively affect the powerful and canonical Euripidean *persona*.

Explicit Assimilation and Categorization

In the prologue and parodos the Nurse—sympathetic but intimately familiar with her mistress—describes Medea in a series of vivid images as a dangerous beast or natural force. These metaphors call into question the pathetic descriptions of a homeless woman, abandoned by her husband, about to be exiled, which the Nurse or Pedagogue develops in the same scenes.

In the opening monologue, the Nurse regrets that the desperate Medea pays no more attention to her friends' words than would "a rock or a wave of the sea" (πέτρος ἢ θαλάσσιος / κλύδων, 28–29). Significantly, the vehicles of comparison, rock and wave, are part of the larger story: the heroine is made as intractable as the very elements the Argo faced on its famous voyage. Other examples of such poetic interaction will recur often in the drama.[9]

Rocks and waves are of course common elements of comparison in Greek poetry, and not always negative ones.[10] Odysseus withstands the blow from Antinous' footstool "solidly as a rock" (ἠύτε πέτρη / ἔμπεδον, *Od.* 17.463–64); in Euripides' *Andromache*, Menelaus boasts that he will prove as unyielding as rock or sea (537–38). But the Nurse's image of Medea here closely resembles Patroclus' complaint to Achilles: his parents must have been "grey sea and steep rocks" (γλαυκὴ ... θάλασσα / πέτραι τ' ἠλίβατοι, *Il.* 16.34–35), so intransigent is the hero in the face of grave danger to his friends.[11] Medea's rock- or sealike toughness is only one of the ways in which she resembles her heroic male counterparts.

Medea's extreme hard-heartedness will be proved by her defining deed later in the play. In the final stasimon, hearing the children's death cries from inside the house, the Chorus apostrophizes Medea, "So

[9] Silk 1974 categorizes various forms of interaction between *comparandum* (or "tenor") and *comparans* (or "vehicle") in poetry, although not precisely this kind, which involves the larger context of the tenor (the whole Jason/Medea myth, rather than just the figure of Medea). "Interaction" is Silk's term for the various ways in which the "outward separateness" of tenor and vehicle can be modified (15).

[10] See Kurtz 1985:483 for parallels in epic and tragic diction.

[11] For further references to metaphorical uses of πέτρος and πέτρα in Homer and tragedy, see Bongie 1977:29 n. 8; Page 1938:67*ad* Eur. *Med.* 28–29.

then you *were* rock or iron" (πέτρος ἢ σίδαρος, 1279–80). The Nurse's characterization of a stony, intractable Medea has proved accurate, in the view of the shocked Chorus.

In contrast to what others say about her, however, Medea presents herself not as a natural force, against which no one can prevail, but as a *victim* of the sea, looking for a safe place to land. Unlike the women of the Chorus, for example, she can claim also to be plundered from a barbarian land, with no family to turn to, no place to change anchorage (μεθορμίσασθαι) from misfortune (252–58). Again, after Creon announces that she must leave Corinth, Medea describes herself as a beleaguered voyager, lamenting that her enemies are unfurling all their sails against her and she can find no place to disembark from disaster (278–79). As Creon departs, the Chorus sings a brief lament for Medea, taking up her own image of herself as hapless sailor: "a god has brought you to a wave of ills, Medea, with no way out" (ὡς εἰς ἄπορόν σε κλύδωνα θεός, / Μήδεια, κακῶν ἐπόρευσε, 362–63; cf. also 431–45, especially μεθορμίσασθαι, 442). In repeating this image the Chorus shows how fully it still accepts Medea's description of herself as a victim of greater powers, storm and sea. The audience, however, has already heard the Nurse compare Medea to those very powers.[12]

Shirley Barlow, in her study of Euripidean imagery, judges the nautical metaphors in this play to be overdrawn, stereotyped, and irrelevant.[13] But they can be seen to fit Medea and her story especially well, just as similar language suits the Nurse when she describes how they have been overcome with new troubles before they could "bail out" the old (ἐξηντληκέναι, 79). Through repeated nautical metaphors, Euripides reminds his audience that these veterans of the Argo are familiar with the sea and its dangers.[14] Here again is a set of metaphors that interact with the larger context of the story.

[12] When she has secured the support of Aegeus, Medea voices another nautical metaphor, consistent—given the changed circumstances—with her previous usage: now that the harbor (λιμήν) she sought has finally appeared, she will attach her cable to him (769–70). Another seafaring metaphor occurs when Medea argues that Jason should have told her about his "beneficial" new marriage beforehand: Jason, speaking to Medea like a captain addressing his recalcitrant crew, replies sarcastically, "You would have pulled your oar (ὑπηρέτεις) very well for this plan if I had told you about my marriage, you who even now can't rid your heart of great wrath" (588–90). See Kurtz 1985:396–98 for an Aeschylean parallel and for comments on Jason's self-righteous, ironic tone here.

[13] Barlow 1971:97–98, 105; similarly, Kurtz 1985:483. Apart from this criticism, Barlow says little about metaphors in *Medea*.

[14] Jason too describes himself in a nautical metaphor, with his self-aggrandizing image of the rhetorical navigator: to respond to Medea's vehement charges, he will have to be

Besides inanimate entities like rock or sea, the Nurse also compares Medea to dangerous animals, the kind that often figure in heroic similes. First, Medea has been "bulling her eye" at the children (ὄμμα ταυρουμένην, 92–93). Here Euripides adapts a memorable Aeschylean metaphor, famous enough to be parodied by Aristophanes (*Frogs* 804): Orestes recalls Apollo's frightening catalogue of what he will suffer if he does not avenge his father, attacking Agamemnon's killers in their own fashion, like a bull (ταυρούμενον, *Cho.* 275). The Nurse's description of Medea as bull-like again interacts with the Argo myth, as do her comparisons to rocks and sea. The metaphor recalls the fire-breathing bulls Jason had to harness to the plough in Colchis (cf. Pindar, *Pyth.* 4.224–29)—which Medea herself mentions in the next episode (478). The same Medea who once helped Jason survive her father's murderous bulls now glares bull-like at the products of her union with Jason.

The "glaring bull" metaphor is further developed a few moments later, when the Nurse tells the Chorus that she will try to bring Medea outside to speak with them, even though "she bulls out at her servants the glare of a lioness with cubs" (τοκάδος δέργμα λεαίνης ἀποταυροῦται δμωσίν), whenever anyone approaches to try to speak with her (187–89).[15] The parturient lioness's fierce glare introduces a note of maternal care that will of course prove ironic when applied to Medea. The protective overtones seem discordant even in this context, where the Nurse has just voiced her fear that Medea may "do something" to her children (92–93, 95), warning that the children should keep away from their mother in her angry mood (90–91, 101).[16]

Just as the Chorus eventually adopts the Nurse's view of Medea as rocklike, so too does Jason eventually come to see her as "a lioness, not a woman" (1342). Medea accepts this identification (1358–59), and perhaps acts the part when a moment later she reminds him that the children are dead, precisely because that word will "bite" him (δήξεται, 1370; cf. also δάκοιμι, 1344–45).[17] Previously Medea was the one "bitten"

a clever helmsman, making his way carefully, using only the edges of his sails against her tongue-lashings (522–25).

[15] I disagree with the judgment of Stanford 1936:33 that ἀποταυροῦται has "lost its original imaginative force" and therefore does not "mix" the lion metaphor here.

[16] But even after she discloses her plan to kill the children, Medea herself claims to be protecting them from her enemies (781–82, 1060–61, 1240–41 = [1062–63], 1378–83). Note too that in another version of the myth (Paus. 2.3.9), one of Jason's sons is killed by a lion. If this variant was known to Euripides' audience, the lion simile attested here would be another example of an image that interacts with the larger story of Medea and Jason.

[17] In an earlier scene she explains to the Chorus that she must kill the children, even though it will hurt her, in order that Jason be "bitten" (δηχθείη, 817). Another of Medea's

(δηχθεῖσα, 109–10) with misfortunes. Now the roles reverse, as she goes from being sufferer to inflicter of pain. So, too, Medea changes metaphorically from a lioness fiercely protecting her cubs to one that has killed her own children.

Jason adds a new vehicle of comparison at this point too, calling Medea more savage than that most famous threat to Greek sailors, the devouring, bestial Scylla.[18] The comparisons to Scylla would be especially appropriate if the audience, as seems likely, hears in them a reference to Jason's experiences on the Argo expedition. Such an echo would provide another interactive assimilation of Medea to an element "internal" to the larger story, suggesting that Jason finds Medea more dreadful than the kinds of dangers he faced on his great adventure. Scylla is associated with the Argo voyage tangentially in *Odyssey* 12.55–100, and later (closely following the Homeric tradition) in Apollonius' *Argonautica* 4.922–32.[19] Scylla's traditional role in the Argo voyage need not be pressed too far; at least it is clear that Jason, as one-time champion voyager, finally finds Medea more terrible than the worst threat a seafarer can imagine.[20]

The Nurse also describes her volatile mistress with a meteorological image. Medea, she fears, will soon "ignite" (ἀνάψει) with greater anger the "cloud of lament" (νέφος οἰμωγῆς) that rises from its beginning (106–8). The lightning suggested here develops an image latent in the Nurse's prediction that Medea will not cease her wrath until she "dashes down" someone (καπασκῆψαι, 94), for the same verb describes the action of lightning bolts. Medea will soon wish for a flash of lightning to

---

enemies will be metaphorically "bitten," in grimmer, more tangible fashion: in his speech describing the death of Creon's daughter, the Messenger says "her flesh poured from her bones ... through the 'unseen jaws' (γναθμοῖς ἀδήλοις, 1201) of Medea's poisons."

[18] In Seneca's *Medea*, the protagonist herself asks what Scylla or Charybdis is as threatening as she is (408–10).

[19] In *Od.* 12.55–100 Circe explains to Odysseus that on his homeward voyage he can try to sail either through the Planctai, or "Wandering Rocks," which only the Argo has ever negotiated safely (and that only thanks to Hera's protection of Jason), or past Scylla and Charybdis. The exact geography is unclear, but all three dangers are located near one another. In the *Argonautica*, Thetis agrees to Hera's request (4.825–32) that she help the Argo safely past Scylla, Charybdis, and the Planctai; Thetis directs the ship through the latter, but apparently in sight of Scylla and Charybdis (4.922–32). See Hölscher 1990:173–78 for further discussion of the relationship between this part of the Argo voyage and the *Odyssey*.

[20] Another Scylla, the Megarian maiden discussed by Graf (p. 24) and Newlands (pp. 196–200) in this volume, like Medea betrays her father for love of a foreigner who abandons her. Sarah Iles Johnston suggests to me that Euripides' audience may have heard echoes of her story in the references to the sea-monster Scylla here.

pass through her own head (διά μου κεφαλᾶς φλὸξ οὐρανία / βαίη, 144–45), but the drama ends instead with another role reversal, as Jason complains that the gods have "dashed" Medea's avenger on him (τὸν σὸν δ'ἀλάστορ' εἰς ἔμ' ἔσκηψαν θεοί, 1333).[21]

Defining Categories

Hearing Medea's cries and threats coming from inside the house during the parodos, the audience can well envision her as the threatening, intransigent, inhuman character the Nurse has suggested. But when she emerges to speak to the Chorus, the protagonist appears a model of decorum.[22] She describes herself to the women of Corinth not as beast, rock, or wave, but simply as a poor creature in many respects like themselves—a woman: "We women are the most pitiable species" (γυναῖκές ἐσμεν ἀθλιώτατον φυτόν, 231); like the women of Corinth, Medea suffers the unfairness, uncertainty, and restriction that is the female lot (228–51). She presents herself also as a typical woman (γυνή, 263), significantly, because she will devise evil when treated unjustly in her marriage (263–66).

Creon describes Medea only as a woman (γυνή, 290, 319, 337) wise in all manner of evils, angry at being deprived of her marriage, and capable of harming his daughter (282–89). As his lack of metaphors for her may indicate, he underestimates how violent her reactions will be. In his bitter first scene with Medea, Jason too assumes that he knows his wife well—all too well. Like Creon, he makes no attempt to describe her metaphorically, but only develops the theme of the typical (i.e., troublesome) woman: "You women are only concerned about your marriage beds, and so you consider even great advantages to be hostile. There ought to be a way to beget children without the female race: then there would be nothing bad for human beings" (573–75).

---

[21] In another conflation and reversal, Medea's decision to kill the children affects her with the same metaphorical suffering that she had threatened against Jason's house: the Pedagogue is surprised to find his mistress "poured out" (συγχυθεῖσ', 1005) in distress at the news that the children's gifts have been accepted. This is the very punishment Medea told the Chorus she would inflict on Jason's entire house (δόμον τε πάντα συγχέασ' Ἰάσονος, 794).

[22] Conacher 1967:35, 188, compares Medea's rhetorical control in this passage with that of Phaedra in the Eur. *Hipp.*: before they appear calmly before the chorus, both women are heard wildly crying inside the house. Cf. also Pucci 1980:61–77 on Medea's effective, if dubious, mode of argumentation.

Euripides' Jason has a well-defined concept of the female, a stereotype that will contribute to his undoing when Medea plays it against him two episodes later.[23]

Aegeus similarly uses very little figurative language for Medea. He does not try to compare her with anything else but accepts the pitiable picture she presents to him of a woman abandoned by her husband (cf. "then it is understandable that you grieve, woman," συγγνωστὰ μέν τἄρ' ἦν σε λυπέσθαι, γύναι; 703). Yet this γυνή will react like one of the great male heroes of epic and tragedy, a Homeric Achilles or a Sophoclean Ajax.[24]

Once her refuge is secured, Medea discloses to the Chorus her terrible plan for vengeance: she will not only kill Jason's bride and whoever touches her but will murder her own children as well. At this point, the protagonist presents herself clearly, and not for the first time,[25] in terms of male heroism, focused on achieving honor, vengeance, fame.[26] Although it will cost her dearly, she is willing to sacrifice her children to her heroic reputation (807–10).

Now the dismayed Chorus realizes that Medea is not merely a typical woman, however pitiable, vengeful, and resourceful. They even change the way they address her at this point. Previously, identifying with her suffering, they had called her "futile one" (ματαία, 152), "unhappy woman" (δύστανε γύναι, 357; cf. 442), "wretched one" (τάλαινα, 437), as well as "Medea" (268, 363). Now they call her simply "woman" (γύναι, 816) and warn that if she goes ahead with her plan, she will become a "most miserable woman" (ἀθλιωτάτη γυνή, 818)—as if by repeating the term that should define her, they hope to make her respond accordingly.

Throughout the following episode, as the audience knows, Medea feigns a change of heart in order to further her plan of vengeance. She admits she was foolish to oppose Jason's clever plan but, assuming something of his attitude toward her sex, she explains, "We are what we are—I won't say an evil—women" (889–90). Medea continues to

[23] On the ironies of that deception see Barlow 1989:163–64 and passim. In the schema developed by Sourvinou-Inwood in this volume, this concept corresponds to the male (i.e., normative Athenian) view of a "bad woman"—but note that Jason applies it generally in this context, as if all women fit the pattern.

[24] On Medea as (male) hero see Maddalena 1963; Bongie 1977; Knox 1977. On Medea's adoption of masculine values see further below.

[25] In their first confrontation, when Medea reminds Jason how she saved him, she uses the language of heroic epic: "Killing [the serpent] I offered you a saving light" (φάος σωτήριον, 482; cf. Achilles in Il. 18.102: οὐδέ τι Πατρόκλῳ γενόμην φάος).

[26] Maddalena 1963 and Knox 1977:197–99, among others, discuss Medea's heroic ethos in detail. For Medea's critique of that ethos, see Foley 1989:79; Rehm 1989:109–10.

adopt a stereotypical masculine perspective in her false dealings with Jason: as if she were a warrior or a head of state, she calls the children out of the house to celebrate the truce (σπονδαί) she has enacted with their father (894–98). Blind to Medea's manipulation of his misogyny, Jason is now willing to forgive her first reaction to the news of losing him: "For it is to be expected (εἰκός) that the female race (θῆλυ γένος) gets angry when a husband smuggles in (παρεμπολῶντος) a new marriage" (909–10).[27] Despite the mercantile metaphor he uses of himself, Jason seeks no analogies for Medea here; he still does not see *her* as anything but a typical member of the "female race." Medea hides behind the same facade when Jason notices the tears she is shedding over the children's future: "You! why do you wet your cheeks with fresh tears?" (922). She replies, "A woman is born a female thing, and tearful" (γυνὴ δὲ θῆλυ κἀπὶ δακρύοις ἔφυ, 928). She again uses his assumptions about the similarity and predictability of all women when she foresees that Jason will be able to persuade the princess to intercede on behalf of his children, "if she is like other women" (εἴπερ γυναικῶν ἐστι τῶν ἄλλων μία, 945).[28]

As the children depart, bearing the fatal gifts to the princess, the Chorus mourns for all concerned: children, princess, Jason, and Medea. Now for the first time they address Medea as a mother, starkly describing her situation in plain, unmetaphorical language: "I grieve with your pain, wretched mother of children, you who will murder your offspring because of the bridal bed, which your husband has lawlessly abandoned to live with another spouse" (996–1002). The Chorus assumes that it will be as "mother of children" that Medea too will suffer most in avenging the wrongs done to her. They hope that at the fatal moment Medea will act in accord with what they expect of a mother. As with γυνή (woman), the term μήτηρ (mother) occurs mostly in ironic or pathetic contrast to Medea's most "unmaternal" plans and behavior.[29]

In her great monologue, Medea uses vivid images to describe her suffering, specifically as woman and mother. Because she must kill her children, her maternal labors on their behalf are undone: "In vain,

---

[27] See Page 1938:139–40 on the reading and interpretation of line 910.

[28] This line, not implausibly, is attributed to Jason himself in most manuscripts. As it turns out, the princess will be persuaded by Medea's gifts far more than by Jason's request; see the Messenger's report, 1156–57.

[29] This contrast is greatly extended by significant alliteration (*Medea/mater*) in Seneca's portrayal of Medea; see Traina 1979 and Segal 1982.

children, I raised you, in vain I toiled and was racked with labors, bearing sterile pains in childbirth" (1029–31). She resolves nevertheless to accomplish her plans—in the male roles of sacrificer and avenging hero. Steeling herself to the task, banishing "cowardice" and "soft words" (1051–52), she describes the murder as a sacrifice (τοῖς ἐμοῖσι θύμασιν) and warns away all who should not be present (1053–55). After the Messenger describes the deaths of Jason's bride and Creon, Medea resolves for the last time to kill her children. She now speaks of herself as a warrior girding for battle and taking up the sword (ὁπλίζου, 1242; λαβὲ ξίφος, 1244), and at the same time as an "ill-fated woman" who will kill the children she bore and loves (1246–50, ending with δυστυχὴς δ'ἐγὼ γυνή). Through such conflicting categories Euripides emphasizes the paradox of a character who aspires to male heroism within the confines of what are presented as inescapably female concerns.[30]

In their earlier proleptic lament for Medea and her victims, we saw, the Chorus addressed the protagonist plainly as "wretched mother of children, you who will murder your offspring" (997–98). Now, as she goes into the house to carry out her plan, they struggle to describe her in other terms: Medea is a bloody avenging Fury (1260), a wanderer who survived the inhospitable Symplegades to labor in vain for her children (1261–64), a source of pollution and god-sent sufferings (1268–70). The Chorus's multiple reactions to Medea—sympathy, frustration, horror— are reflected in the different images they use at this desperate moment. They characterize her no longer as woman and mother, but as a dire supernatural power.

Even as they sing, from inside the house a child calls for help: "What shall I do? How can I escape my mother's hands?" (μητρὸς χέρας, 1271). His cry here reminds us what sort of "mother" this is. Searching for a precedent for her horrifying deed, they can think only of Cadmus' daughter Ino, another woman who killed her two children and wandered from her home. But Ino committed infanticide only because she was maddened by Hera;[31] furthermore, Ino "dying together, perished" (συνθανοῦσ' ἀπόλλυται, 1289) with her children. In these points the Chorus cannot really compare her with a consciously vengeful, plotting Medea. Moreover, Medea will survive the infanticide and escape aloft to Athens. Ultimately, the attempt to find a human precedent for

---

[30] The essays of Barlow 1989, Foley 1989, and Rehm 1989 focus in different ways on this idea, already adumbrated by Shaw 1975:261–63 and Dihle 1977:16–21.

[31] See Johnston's article in this volume for more on Ino, Medea, and Hera.

Medea fails.[32] Euripides' heroine is a figure explicitly without parallel: the single analogy the Chorus can think of ("one I've heard of, one woman of those in the past," μίαν δὴ κλύω μίαν τῶν πάρος / γυναῖκ'; 1282–83) turns out to be a woman very different from Medea.[33]

After the murders, Jason radically changes the way he speaks to and about Medea. He realizes that he did not know her before: "Now I understand, before I did not" (ἐγὼ δὲ νῦν φρονῶ, τότ' οὐ φρονῶν; 1329). Whereas previously he referred to her as a typical female, in the exodos he declares that she has done what no Greek woman would do (1339–40), and then denies that she is a woman at all. In his desperate insults just after she appears aloft in Helios' chariot, Jason calls her "a lioness, not a woman, with a nature more savage than Tyrrhenian Scylla's" (1342–43; cf. 1407). A few lines later Medea explicitly accepts this insult: "Call me, if you wish, lioness and Scylla who lives in the Tyrrhenian plain [or rock].[34] For your heart I have touched, as I had to" (1358–60).

Implicit Assimilation

Through the explicit comparisons of Medea to Scylla, lioness and bull, storm cloud and lightning, intractable wave and rock, and hapless or rescued voyager, as well as through the failed attempts to categorize her as woman and mother, Euripides gives us a protagonist who is not

[32] Newton 1985 points out that mythical exempla in other tragic choruses are used to persuade or console a character by showing that her situation is not unique. In most cases several exempla are provided, e.g., of evil women (like Clytemnestra) in Aes. Cho. 585–651 or of royal victims imprisoned by gods in Soph. Ant. 944–87. In the Medea, by contrast, the Chorus claims that they can think of only one example, and eventually conclude that she is not a good parallel. The Chorus could also have mentioned not only the maddened Agave but, more appropriately, the premeditative filicides Althaea and especially Procne, who kills her son in response to her husband's infidelity. Newton concludes that Euripides here suppresses other possible exempla in order to make Medea's action more emphatically unprecedented. Michelini 1989:125, 134, likewise finds that Ino serves as a contrast rather than a precedent for Medea. Cf. Mills 1980 for more on parallels with the myths of Ino and Procne.

[33] The Chorus might have found a better precedent in a goddess: Medea resembles Hera (often cast as a vengeful wife) more than Ino. Cf. Johnston's paper in this volume for possible connections between Corinthian Medea and Hera. A link between Medea and Hera is suggested also by Eisner 1979:159.

[34] As Gordon Kirkwood points out to me, Elmsley's emendation πέτραν for the daggered πέδον in 1359 [1326] would make this passage suggest again Medea's stoniness. The emendation is plausible in terms of content, as Scylla is everywhere associated with rocks, e.g., Od. 12.80–85, Aes. Ag. 1233–34. On Medea and rocks, see above.

simply what she appears to be. Moreover, through a subtle but cumulatively powerful poetic process that I shall call "implicit assimilation,"
his hard-to-characterize heroine takes on characteristics of other figures,
most of whom are central to the tragedy and its immediate background.
Two of these are her enemies, Jason and his bride; one is the goddess
who aided Jason on his adventures; another is the geographical threshold between Medea's past and present worlds. And one figure stands
outside the Argo myth but looms large in the imaginations of Euripides'
audience.

"How near we are now to the sword's nets!" (ἀρκύων ξίφους, 1278),
cries one of Medea's sons offstage. The image of murder by net and
sword, as if in hunting, recalls Clytemnestra in *Agamemnon*, who also
combines disabling net (the robe she casts over Agamemnon) with striking blade.[35] The comparison of Medea to Scylla, noted above, may also
evoke her famous Aeschylean prototype, for Cassandra, prophesying
to the bewildered Chorus, calls Clytemnestra "some Scylla dwelling in
the rocks" (*Ag.* 1233–34).

Further, Medea's manly decision to "sacrifice" her offspring (τοῖς
ἐμοῖσι θύμασιν, 1054) resembles the Aeschylean Agamemnon, who literally "dared to become the sacrificer (θυτήρ) of his daughter" (*Ag.* 224–25;
cf. 1417). And as we have seen, the Nurse's images of a bull-like Medea
(92, 188) recall the vengeful Orestes goring his father's killers (especially Clytemnestra herself) in the same trilogy. Compelling images
from three different phases in the *Oresteia*'s cycle of vengeance are col-
lapsed into the figure of Medea. This group of intertextual echoes from
the single most resonant set of Athenian tragedies suggests that Euripides is adding to the grotesque stature of his Medea by evoking the
series of kin murders, and especially the great murderess, of the famous
Aeschylean text.[36] Against Medea, however, there will be no avenging

[35] Both according to Cassandra's lyrical visions (e.g., δίκτυον, 1115; μελαγκέρῳ
λαβοῦσα μηχανήματι / τύπτει, 1127–28, where the sword is envisioned by Cassandra
as a "horn" with which the murderous beast gores her mate), and in Clytemnestra's own
scarcely more prosaic description of her deed (e.g. ἀρκύστατ᾽, 1375; παίω δέ νιν δίς, 1384).
Cf. also Aes. *Cho.* 999–1000, where Orestes, having killed Aegisthus and Clytemnestra with
a sword, displays their bodies covered by the robe with which Agamemnon was netted.
Euripides refers to this combination of weapons again in *Heracles*, where Amphitryon
predicts that Lycus will be caught "in the sword-bearing meshes of nets" (βρόχοισι
δ᾽ἀρκύων ... ξιφηφόροισι, 729–30). On the confusion of sacrificial and savage imagery
in the *Heracles* scene, which culminates in another kin-murder, see Seaford 1989:93–95.

[36] It is scarcely necessary to remind readers of the famous parodies of the recognition
scene in Aeschylus' *Choephoroi* in the *Electra* plays of Sophocles and Euripides, or of
the fact that Aeschylean tragedies were permitted to be reperformed in later fifth-century

Orestes or hostile Apollo;[37] however horribly she will both avenge and punish herself.

Medea also resembles in some ways the Symplegades, the "Clashing Rocks" that threaten to crush ships passing through the Bosporus. These rocks, which the Argo traversed safely on its way to and from Colchis, form the "uncrossable" threshold between Jason's and Medea's worlds; passing through them, albeit safely, marks the starting point of all their troubles (cf. 1–2, 211–13, 1262–64). *Medea* is our earliest text in which the rocks are referred to as "Striking-together" rather than "Running-together" (cf. σύνδρομοι πέτραι in Pindar *Pyth.* 4.208–9 and συνορμάδες in Simon. *PMG* 546) or simply as "Dark" rocks (cf. κυανέαιν σπιλάδοιν in Soph. *Ant.* 966). Although Euripides himself calls the legendary rocks by different names in other tragedies,[38] in *Medea* he uses only κυάνεαι Συμπληγάδες [πέτραι] (2, 1263). Possibly Euripides invented a new name for the rocks; more likely, he selected the most expressive variant for this tragedy. In several ways the rocks suggest his formidable Medea, who, in addition to the general "stoniness" of her temperament, shares with the Symplegades the ability to strike her enemies. By definition, the rocks destroy by "striking together" (συμ-πλήγνυμι); a recurrent image in the drama suggests the latent question of who will strike and who will be struck.[39] In the prologue, the Nurse describes Medea as "struck" (ἐκπλαγεῖσ', 8) with love for Jason. Jason himself of course safely escaped the Symplegades; now he insists that he is not 'struck' with desire for his new bride (ἱμέρῳ πεπληγμένος, 555–56). But Medea foresees that in the end he will die basely, "struck" (πεπληγμένος) in the head by a fragment of the Argo itself (1386–87). Moreover, reversing the image, the Chorus begs Medea to reconsider the "striking" (πλάγαν) of her own children (851–52). The stone-hard, love-struck heroine, brought by Jason from beyond the Symplegades, will be appropriately avenged: her betrayer (as well as his children) will ultimately be struck down.

Athens. Cunningham 1954:152 draws another parallel between Clytemnestra and Medea: both drop their "feigned and dissembling manners of speaking" and show "an utter but honest callousness" after the murders.

[37] And no pursuing Erinyes either, despite Jason's wish in 1389–90. See Sourvinou-Inwood's essay in this volume, p. 270.

[38] The rocks of the Bosporus are called κυάνεαι ἀκταί (dark cliffs) in *Andr.* 864 and κυάνεαι / σύνοδοι (dark junctions or constrictions) in *IT* 392–93; elsewhere, συγχωροῦσαι (together-coming) in *IT* 124–25 and συνδρομάδες πέτραι (together-running rocks) in *IT* 422, as well as ξυμ- or συμπληγάδες (*Andr.* 794; *IT* 241, 260, 355, 1389).

[39] In a common poetic process, described, e.g., by Barlow 1971:28, "Descriptive imagery of place becomes dramatic imagery." Barlow does not discuss the Symplegades in this context.

Medea is also identified with supernatural powers: she is called "avenger" (ἀλάστωρ, 1260; cf. 1059, 1333), "Fury" (Ἐρινύς, 1260), and a source of "pollution" as well (μίασμα; e.g., 1268–70). She threatens to become "a curse" (ἀραία, 608) to Jason. In addition to these explicit demonic analogies, many have recognized that with her diction, position on stage, and actions at the end of the play, Medea strongly recalls a Euripidean *deus ex machina*.[40]

In particular, Medea is assimilated in several ways to the Olympian goddess Aphrodite.[41] Perhaps the most obvious resemblance is their mutual role as Jason's savior. Medea twice claims that it was she who saved Jason's life (476–77, 515); Jason replies that he considers Cypris alone responsible for his safety, since Medea was compelled by Eros to do what she did for him (526–31). Euripides is here developing a tradition attested also by Pindar. In *Pythian* 4 (which Euripides apparently alludes to more than once in *Medea*),[42] Aphrodite comes to Jason's aid in Colchis, the most dangerous stage of his journey. Rather than help him directly, she teaches him to overwhelm Medea with love charms, as discussed by O'Higgins in this volume. The strategy is effective: driven by *erōs*, Medea helps Jason both to face her father's dangerous tasks and to recover the Golden Fleece (*Pyth.* 4.213–23).[43] Medea thus unwittingly serves in Pindar's poem, too, as an agent of Aphrodite.[44]

[40] For convincing arguments that Medea formally resembles a deity when she appears in Helios' chariot at the end of the play, see esp. Cunningham 1954; Knox 1977:206–13, 225.
[41] Apart from the analogies in Euripides' tragedy, a close relationship between the two is suggested also by the tradition that Medea founded the temple of Aphrodite on Acrocorinth (schol. to Pindar *Ol.* 13.32). See also Graf's and Johnston's contributions to this volume (pp. 39–41 and 46) for the hypothesis that as the myth became more Panhellenic, Medea's role was gradually assumed by the Olympian goddesses Hera, Artemis, and Aphrodite. Graf's argument, like the one presented here, assumes a degree of overlap between Medea and Aphrodite. Parallels between the two are also discussed in Clauss's essay in this volume, pp. 149–77.
[42] Cf. Braswell 1988:299 *ad* 216a, commenting on the resemblance between *Pyth.* 4.216 μαινάδ᾽ and *Med.* 432 μαινομένᾳ κραδίᾳ. Other resemblances in diction between *Pyth.* 4 and *Medea* (not cited by Braswell) include στερεᾶν ὀδυνᾶν (*Pyth.* 4.221) / στερρὰς ... ἀλγηδόνας (*Med.* 1031), and φαρμακώσαισ᾽ ... δῶκε χρίεσθαι (*Pyth.* 4.221–22) / χρίσω φαρμάκοις (*Med.* 789).
[43] In *Pyth.* 4.230, the Golden Fleece is even called στρωμνά, the normal term for "bedding." For the tradition that the fleece served as marriage couch for Jason and Medea, cf. Braswell 1988:*ad loc.*
[44] In *Pyth.* 4.218 Medea is made to lose her αἰδώς for her parents (see O'Higgins' essay in this volume). Even Charles Segal, who emphasizes Pindar's quite positive treatment of Jason, notes that here the hero is acting "rather as a seducer than as a husband"

Further, Euripides' Medea is, like Aphrodite, much concerned with the marriage bed (λέχος).[45] The Nurse, Chorus, and Medea herself all blame Jason for deserting his bed for a new one (140, 156, 265, 286, 489, etc.). Medea envisions herself murdering bride and groom precisely "where their bed is laid out" (ἵν' ἔστρωται λέχος, 380); later, a falsely repentant Medea tells Jason that instead of resenting his new marriage she really ought to "stand by the bed" (παρεστάναι λέχει, 887, cf. 1026–27) in attendance on his new bride.[46] Jason tells Medea that she would approve of his new marriage "if the bed did not grate on you" (568, cf. 1290–92). Like Euripides' Hippolytus in a play performed three years later, Jason wishes that men could get children in some other way, so that the female race would not be needed (573–74).[47] After the children's murder, Jason asks Medea, "Did you think it right to kill them because of your marriage bed?" and Medea counters, "Do you think that is small pain for a woman?" (1367–68). Medea and Aphrodite further resemble each other in the ways they deal with those whom they would overpower. Like Aphrodite's inescapable golden bow and arrows, anointed with desire (χρυσέων τόξων ... ἄψυκτον οἰστόν ... ἱμέρῳ χρίσασ', 633–34; cf. also the weapons of Eros, 530–31), Medea's weapons—the gifts she sends to the princess[48]—are also golden (πλόκον χρυσήλατον, 949; cf. also 978, 984, 1160), inescapable (cf. 9887–88, 1190–

(1986:19–20). Medea's betrayal of father and homeland is never criticized by Pindar, but in Euripides' version this decision is frequently lamented by Medea, and finally even by Jason (1329–32). Aphrodite's influence on Medea is perhaps to be inferred in another Pindaric ode, where Medea is said to have "made a marriage for herself apart from her father" (Ol. 13.53–54). Similarly, in Pherec. FGrHist 3 F 105 Medea is made to serve the interests of Hera: the goddess wants the expedition to Colchis to take place so that Medea will come to Iolcus and destroy Pelias, who has offended her.

[45] In Medea itself, for example, Aphrodite is explicitly associated with λέκτρα and λέχη (639–41) when the Chorus prays for safety and moderation in married love.

[46] For a detailed (to my mind somewhat exaggerated) interpretation of the thematic centrality of the bed for Euripides' Medea, cf. Rohdich 1968:59–66.

[47] Cf. von Fritz 1962:323–24 on Euripides' general tendency to treat more vigorously a few years later a theme adumbrated (but initially misunderstood) in an earlier tragedy. (von Fritz does not refer to Med. and Hipp. in this discussion.)

[48] Further evidence of Medea's "divine" attributes may be seen in the fact that these gifts are twice called δωρήματα (789, 1188), an unusual word otherwise reserved in Euripides for the (desirable) "gifts" of a god—in fact usually of a goddess—or for offerings made at a hero's tomb. Cf. Allen and Italie 1954:s.v. "δώρημα." Apart from three uses in Medea, the word is attested only six times in the extant plays and fragments of Euripides. (Medea's gifts are more often called by the unmarked term δῶρα: e.g., 784, 947, 958, 973, 1003, 1154, 1165.) The only other attestation of δώρημα in Medea occurs, interestingly, when the Chorus is praying to Aphrodite for moderate rather than excessive love: "May Moderation cherish me, the finest δώρημα of the gods" (635–36).

94), and anointed (cf. χρίσω, 789) with fatal drugs.[49] Further, as we saw in connection with the Symplegades, erotic love typically "strikes" its victims (including Medea: cf. 8, 556); Medea's victims will also be "struck" (the children, 851–52; Jason, 1386–87).

Jason's deprecating attitude toward sexual motivation would scarcely please Aphrodite.[50] He does not reject marriage, of course, but insists that he uses it only deliberately, for practical ends; as we have seen, he emphatically denies being "struck with desire" (555–56). Even Medea, who earlier sneered at Jason's alleged lust for Creon's daughter (e.g., 623–24), comes to view his *erōs* as wholly pragmatic: "He is in love," she tells Aegeus, "with acquiring connections to tyrants!" (ἀνδρῶν τυράννων κῆδος ἡράσθη λαβεῖν, 700). So much for the realm of Jason's savior goddess: he disdains it, boasts that he is immune to its allure, and would wish away her whole sphere of sexual difference and procreation.

In this tragedy, Aphrodite does not avenge her slighted dignity, as Euripides will later have her do against a different character in *Hippolytus*. Rather, it is Medea who takes over some of the goddess's attributes and modes of action.[51] In a broad sense, as Helene Foley has recently formulated it, "the story of [Medea's] revenge takes on a pattern typical of divine rather than human action."[52] The divine *persona* that Medea most closely resembles, I would add, is the one who once (according to Jason, at least: see 526–31) caused her to fall in love with the man who now betrays her.

---

[49] So too in Pindar *Pyth.* 4, Medea prepares protective φάρμακα (drugs) with which to anoint Jason against the harsh pains of the fire-breathing bulls (φαρμακώσαισ' . . . δῶκε χρίεσθαι: *Pyth.* 4.221–22). As Braswell notes in his commentary, the Pindaric Aphrodite too uses magic: the wryneck or *iynx* (ἴυγγα . . . μαινάδ᾽ ὄρνιν, 214–16) and the incantations (λιτάς τ᾽ ἐπαοιδὰς, 217) with which Jason will charm Medea. In *Pyth.* 4 Medea is at first the victim, but soon the manipulator, of φάρμακα. See Braswell 1988:305 *ad* 221–22: "Medea, herself a victim of magic, now assumes her more familiar rôle of *pharmakis*." Cf. also Giannini 1980:142–43.

[50] Shaw 1975:260 notes Jason's use of and disregard for Aphrodite. Shaw concludes (264) that Jason learns too late to revere the goddess, but I see no evidence for this tragic learning on Jason's part.

[51] As if to emphasize the parallels between goddess and protagonist, an early red figure Lucanian hydria (ca. 400 B.C.) by the Policoro painter shows Aphrodite and Eros seated alongside a depiction of Medea in her dragon chariot with the children's corpses, and Jason grieving nearby; for description and illustration see *LIMC* 6.1 (1992) 391 (3.b.35) and 6.2 (1992) 198 (Medeia 35).

[52] Foley 1989:77. Foley however does not argue that Medea specifically resembles Aphrodite. On Medea's resemblance to a vengeful goddess such as Aphrodite in *Hipp.*, see also Grube 1941:61 and *passim*.

Medea is also assimilated to several human characters in her myth. Creon's daughter, for one, bears many points of resemblance to the protagonist—at least as she was at an earlier stage of her life. Although Medea prefers to emphasize the difference in their descents (e.g., 405–6), both women do come from ruling families (cf. τυρανν- of Medea in 119, of the princess in 877, 957, 967). The princess quite naturally is called νύμφη (bride, young woman; 556, 785, 1179, etc.); surprisingly, so is Medea, even after years of marriage (150, 163). Both have the pale skin of feminine beauty, described with the rare word πάλλευκος ("all-white": παλλεύκῳ ποδί of Creon's daughter, 1164; πάλλευκον δέρην of Medea, 30);[53] both turn aside a "white cheek" in distress (λευκὴν ... παρηίδα; 923, 1148).

The connections between Medea and Jason's new bride extend beyond similarities of status and appearance. The princess looks eager (πρόθυμος, 1146) for Jason when he enters her chamber; Medea declares she was "more eager (πρόθυμος) than wise" when she followed Jason to Hellas (485). When Jason asks her to let Medea's children stay in Corinth, the princess will be persuaded (πείσειν, 942–44; cf. 962–64) to do something against her father's (and her own) interest (cf. 940–41, 1154–55); indeed, she will become the death of her father. Medea herself of course was once persuaded by Jason to betray her father and leave her country (πεισθεῖσ᾽, 802). Medea alludes to both women's susceptibility to Jason when she ironically assures her husband that if his new bride is "like other women," he will no doubt be able to persuade her to do what he asks (944–45). Most strikingly, the princess is killed while, and because, she is wearing Medea's heirloom gown and golden diadem, brought to her by Medea's own children. All these similarities combine to suggest that just as Homer's Achilles kills a Hector wearing Achilles' own armor, Medea too is killing an image of herself. Finally, as she suffers the torments inflicted by Medea's gifts, the bride imitates, in a more horrible way, some of what Medea herself suffered as a result of Jason's new marriage, groaning wretchedly (δεινὸν στενάξασ᾽ ἡ τάλαιν᾽, 1184) as Medea often did before (e.g., 149–50).[54]

---

[53] In the attested works of Euripides, πάλλευκος occurs only here and in two other contexts: *Hec.* 500 (of the heroine's pale head) and fr. 472.16 (of clothing).

[54] Further, in the Messenger's graphic description, "the flesh poured from [the princess's] bones like tears of pine" (σάρκες δ᾽ ἀπ᾽ ὀστέων ὥστε πεύκινον δάκρυ ... ἀπέρρεον, 1200–1201); less spectacularly but similarly, Medea's friends note that her "skin is wasted away" (χρώς ... συντέτηχ᾽, 689), and that she "wastes away her life in tears" (συντήκουσα δακρύοις χρόνον, 25, cf. also 141, 158–59).

All these comparisons involve not only verbal echoes but also distinct similarities of situation. The person Medea plans to kill reflects herself as she was when vulnerable to Jason's self-serving persuasion. Medea evidently wishes that this naive version of herself had never existed: "I went wrong at the time when I left my father's house, persuaded by the words of a Greek man, who with god's help will give me justice" (800–802). By the end of the drama, in the view of many interpreters, the mortal, womanly Medea has somehow died.[55] Her murder of a mirror image of herself surely suggests (or accomplishes) such a demise.

Worst of all, Euripides' Medea resembles Jason, the very man whose values and methods she professes to scorn.[56] "For me, may a bitter life not be 'happy,' nor 'prosperity' a thing that grates on my mind" (598–99), she once retorted after Jason explained how his new marriage was supposed to bring a good life (559–60) and security (595–97) to the whole family. Nevertheless, she soon not only adopts some of Jason's ways of speaking and acting, but will even explicitly accept a life of pain in order to achieve her goals of honor and vengeance (818–19, 1046–52, 1244–50).[57]

In declaring that Medea has actually profited from coming to Hellas, Jason argues that she has become famous—and as far as he is concerned, no other attribute is worth as much as this (539–44).[58] Medea appears to disagree with him at this point, but soon she also highly values a heroic reputation: in order to be "best famed" (εὐκλεέστατος) she will harm her enemy, even by killing her own dear children (807–10) and thereby bringing herself great sorrow (e.g., 1246–50, 1361–62). It has

---

[55] Among recent interpretations: see Schlesinger 1966:51. Walsh 1979:298–99 labels Medea's infanticide "a kind of suicide." Michelini 1989:134 calls Medea's victory over Jason "a triumph that is also a kind of annihilation."

[56] So too Walsh 1979:296: "Gradually ... Medea entirely assumes Jason's principles and negates the position she had taken against him earlier." This reversal has frequently been noted by critics of the play, at least in passing. Strohm 1957:3, 6–9, notes briefly the reversal that takes place between Jason and Medea, comparing their first encounter in the tragedy with their last, a comparison extended by Schlesinger 1966:35–37. Burnett 1973:22 mentions the resemblance between Medea and Jason; so does Barlow 1971:130, inasmuch as both Jason and Medea want to touch the "soft skin" of the children. See also Foley 1989:79, citing some of these scholars: Medea "can tragically imagine no other self or self-defense to imitate than that of her oppressors."

[57] Pucci 1980:155, 162–63, and passim, finds that Medea suffers the same pain as Jason, and takes over his role as "master." Foley 1989:79: "by pursuing her heroic code she ends by imitating even her despised immediate oppressors and harming herself."

[58] Bergson 1971:14–16 compares Jason's highest values, fame, and lack of material worries with those of Solon fr. 13.3–4 West. He also notes (pp. 20–21) how Medea's high valuation of glory makes her resemble her enemy Jason.

been pointed out that Medea is here succumbing to what René Girard calls "mimetic desire": "By thinking only of her enemies Medea dooms herself to think just like them."[59] This kind of tragic mimesis is found elsewhere in Euripides' plays, notably in *Hippolytus*, where, as Robin Mitchell has recently shown, Hippolytus resembles both the Phaedra whom he condemns in disgust and the Theseus who unthinkingly condemns him, carrying on a pattern of "reciprocal revenge."[60]

Unlike Seneca's formidable sorceress, who annihilates a weak but sympathetically paternal Jason who is clearly no match for her,[61] Euripides' Medea destroys her husband in part by adopting his own methods. Her resemblance to Jason extends at one point even to an uncanny echo of his rhetoric, when she repeats to Aegeus that in her he has "found a find" better than he knows (εὕρημα ... ηὕρηκας, 716; cf. Jason's εὕρημ' ηὗρον to Medea, 553).[62] More generally, even before complaining that he has deceived her with false supplication (496–98), she does the same to Creon, begging him to allow her an extra day in Corinth (338–39); later she sends the children to supplicate Jason's bride with gifts (969–73). Although she regrets that she succumbed to Jason's persuasion (800–802), Euripides' Medea habitually uses her own persuasive powers, deployed earlier against Jason's enemies (e.g., 9; cf. 486–87) but now against Jason himself (776–83) and his bride (964–65).[63] Similarly, she complains that he has betrayed her (e.g., 488–89), but at the same time she readily admits that she previously betrayed her father, family, and country (e.g., 483, 502–3). What Medea hates most in Jason, it turns out, is in large part his reflection of what she herself has become.

There are other points of resemblance between Medea and Jason. For example, by the end of the tragedy he replaces her as the sufferer, while she becomes the cause of suffering (cf. πάσχω of Medea in 37–39, 161, 207, etc.; of Jason in 1353, 1406). Medea was "bitten" by Jason's betrayal, as we have seen above; correspondingly, he will be "bitten" by her infanticide (817, 1370). So, too, Medea began the action by calling

---

[59] Rehm 1989:109–10.

[60] Mitchell 1991, esp. 103–11. See also the important study of Hippolytus in relation to *eros* and the feminine in Zeitlin 1985.

[61] Seneca's Medea, for example, does not have to worry about finding an asylum, in contrast to Euripides' character (cf. her concerns in 386–91). Curley 1986:198–99 attributes a certain similarity to Seneca's Medea and Jason, arguing that both of them "share their guilt and an aggressive, controlling stance towards the universe" (198). The resemblance between Euripides' antagonists, however, seems to me far more elaborate.

[62] For Jason's self-acclaimed rhetorical skills, see 522–25, 944.

[63] Cf. Boedeker 1991:96–101 on Medea's command of supplication and persuasion.

gods to witness her afflictions at his hands (160–61; cf. 22, 148, 168–69, 207), and Jason ends it with a similar cry (1410–11). The positions of husband and wife have reversed, but their resemblances have become more apparent.

Conclusion

How do all these kinds of resemblance help to establish the *persona* of Medea? First, she is characterized primarily by two kinds of images. A series of nautical metaphors, used by Medea and those in sympathy with her, depict her as a voyager, an exile, needing and then finding a new place to anchor: a metaphorical voyage succeeds and subsumes the traditional Argonautica. Next, a familiar set of similes and metaphors applied to Medea suggest her intractable, violent, "heroic" nature: a bull, a lioness, lightning, a wave of the sea, a rock, the sailor's fiend Scylla. Most of these images, perhaps all of them, are interactive metaphors of a certain kind, using vehicles of comparison that play a role in the larger story of the Argo as well as describing Medea within this tragedy. This phenomenon gives satisfying unity to the drama, as well as interesting resonance with other segments of the myth.

Beyond the factor of poetic unity, however, is the question of how characters see Medea at different times in the dramatic action. Male characters (Creon, Jason, Aegeus) at first do not describe her in metaphorical terms, sympathetic or hostile; they view her merely as a troublesome or unfortunate woman. Only after the murders does Jason see Medea differently, speaking of her then in terms much like those used by the Nurse in the prologue: her metaphorical descriptions prove all too accurate.

Second, the most obvious categories of definition show how inadequate they are for classifying Medea. Unquestionably she is a "woman" and "mother," but the conventional expectations those terms evoke are grossly mistaken, especially regarding her behavior toward her children. This discrepancy produces irony and pathos when Medea as woman and mother argues with her more masculine, heroic self. Further, Medea's familiarity with conventional perspectives on her defined status allows her to manipulate Jason by playing with his stereotyped view of her female nature.

Third, Medea is implicitly assimilated to other figures by mutual resemblances in diction and action. The Chorus' attempt to find a parallel with Ino fails, but the audience could see how Medea resembles or even transcends her Aeschylean counterpart: in shared metaphors as in her vengeful murders, she recalls Clytemnestra and the other kinmurderers of the *Oresteia*. This intertextual assimilation, repeated several times in the tragedy, enhances the stature, and horror, of Euripides' protagonist by borrowing from the emotional impact of one of her most memorable tragic predecessors.

In addition to Medea's echoes of another figure from Athenian tragedy, she is assimilated to several figures that appear in her own myth—even in this version of it. This is the subtlest but perhaps most interesting of Euripides' comparative strategies. Medea once worked under Aphrodite's compulsion to save Jason; now, with Aphrodite-like weapons, she takes upon herself the role of a vengeful goddess whose honor has been offended. In doing this, she kills a mirror image of herself: a beautiful royal bride, naively eager for Jason, who will cause suffering and loss for her father. Moreover, to carry out her plan, Medea adopts the self-serving, devious strategies she charges Jason used against her and replaces him as chief inflicter of harm. Striking down those close to her, she resembles the dangerous "Striking Rocks" that separated her world from Jason's.

By an elaborate process of mutual assimilation, Medea effectively displaces Jason from the saga of which he was hero.[64] Taking so many images and modes of action to herself,[65] she gradually assumes the methods of the natural, supernatural, and human powers that seemed to prevail over her, until at the end of the tragedy there remains only the composite, immense figure that has now become "Medea," to Jason's horror and the amazement of the Chorus.

Unlike Seneca's frightful sorceress with her superfluous powers,[66] Euripides' protagonist acts with almost surgical precision. First, she

[64] I argue this in more detail in Boedeker 1991:104–9.

[65] The multiplicity of images and categories applied to Medea partially explain the dizzying effect described by Pucci 1980:155: "Medea, finally, appears to us as a righteous avenger whose passion leads her to tragically unjust and deceptive deeds, or as a monstrous character who grasps at any possible motivation to bring herself to satisfy her hatred, or as a frenzied mother whose experience of suffering has led to a monomaniac urge, and granted her demonic powers. All these features and many more characterize Medea *simultaneously*, without any discriminating sign, and prevent us from delineating a closed picture of her consciousness."

[66] Seneca's Medea proclaims her superabundance of power to the frightened Nurse: *Medea superest—hic mare et terras vides ferrumque et ignes et deos et fulmina* (Medea survives— here you see sea and lands and iron and fires and gods and thunderbolts, 166–67). She is prepared to take on the whole world, not just Jason and his allies: *sternam et evertam omnia*

annihilates her enemy root and branch by destroying (only) his new connections, his chance for future offspring, and the children who have been born of his marriage with Medea—thereby undoing that marriage and all the deeds and sufferings it entailed. Further, all Medea's victims are, in part, images of herself: her fellow-tyrant and fellow-parent Creon,[67] her own dear children, the husband whose masculine values she has come to adopt, the bride who so closely resembles the young Medea. In all these ways, Euripides keeps his protagonist and her vengeance tremendously concentrated. Later dramatic versions of the myth may emphasize how Medea is most *unlike* other figures in the play. Euripides, by actively assimilating his heroine to characters and other elements internal to her story, gives his protagonist an almost unbearably focused power and allows her action a certain claim to reciprocal justice.

Of course this Medea is like no one else. But at the same time she does resemble many powerful elements in her traditional story. Moreover, she subtly assimilates her antagonists: she takes over their identities (as with Jason), or they hers (as with the princess). She destroys her enemies by becoming more like them, ruins them for being too much like herself. Ultimately Euripides' Medea expands to the point where she obliterates the other characters in her myth, fully transcending—and eradicating—her own once-limited identity as woman, wife, mother, mortal.

(I shall throw down and overturn everything, 414), *invadam deos et cuncta quatiam* (I will assault the gods and make everything shake, 424–25; cf. 527–28 for her human enemies).

[67] The resemblance between Medea and Creon as rulers is elaborated in some later *Medea* dramas, e.g., those of Seneca (cf. 203–6) and Jean Anouilh.

7

CONQUEST OF THE

MEPHISTOPHELIAN NAUSICAA

MEDEA'S ROLE IN APOLLONIUS'

REDEFINITION OF THE EPIC HERO

James J. Clauss

Helper-Maiden or Hero?

BOOK 3 of the *Argonautica*, with its gripping portrayal of Medea falling desperately in love, is so complete and compelling that many, if not most, readers virtually ignore the rest of the epic.[1] Because the poet focuses so much attention on Medea and her plight and because the Colchian princess contributes so much to the success of the expedition, some have even claimed, not unreasonably, that in the course of the poem Medea usurps the role of the hero of the Argonautic expedition.[2] Though attractive, such an interpretation does not explain away the fact that however one interprets Jason's character, Apollonius assigns him the traditional role of the hero: he is the one enjoined to complete the contest (ἄεθλος) of retrieving the Golden Fleece from Colchis,[3] and, in order to win the fleece, of yoking and driving the brazen bulls and killing the crop of earthborn

---

I would like to acknowledge the thoughtful advice of those colleagues who read this paper at various stages: Mary Whitlock Blundell, Catherine M. Connors, Michael R. Halleran, Stephen E. Hinds, and my co-editor Sarah Iles Johnston.

[1] Ovid's comment to Augustus that book 4 of the *Aeneid* shared a similar popularity (*Tr.* 2.531–36) offers an interesting parallel.

[2] For instance, Beye 1982:120–32; Pavlock 1990:19–68; and De Forest 1994. Cf. Barkhuizen 1979, who argues that the erotic, not the heroic, holds primacy of place in the poem in general.

[3] As the expedition to Colchis is called: 1.15, 841, 903, 2.877, and *passim*.

men.[4] Despite the obvious differences between the Apollonian and the Homeric heroes,[5] Jason, like his archaic predecessors, longs to attain glory (κῦδος) through the success of his contest.[6] The invocations of books 1 and 3 are instructive in this regard: at 1.1–4 Apollonius introduces his topic as the glory of ancient men who sailed after the fleece, and at 3.1–5 he asks Erato to tell how Jason brought back the fleece through the love of Medea. Moreover, the poem concludes with a farewell to the Argonauts—there is no mention of Medea (4.773–81). In the openings of books 3 and 4, on the other hand, Medea is presented as the victim of love (3.3–5) or panic (4.1–5). Medea's contribution to the expedition in the role of "helper-maiden," modeled on Nausicaa in the *Odyssey*, does indeed affect how we understand Apollonius' articulation of the Argonautic hero; she does not, however, usurp his role.

Before examining Medea's role, particularly in book 3 of the *Argonautica*, I would like to look briefly at Jason; for his mode of action will not only set him apart from other heroes of the ancient epic tradition but will also require a higher level of assistance on Medea's part.

When the Argonauts first met on the beach at Pagasae, Jason invited them all to choose the best man as their leader. His description of the optimal captain is significant:

> Ἀλλά, φίλοι, ξυνὸς γὰρ ἐς Ἑλλάδα νόστος ὀπίσσω,
> ξυναὶ δ᾽ ἄμμι πέλονται ἐς Αἰήταο κέλευθοι,
> τούνεκα νῦν τὸν ἄριστον ἀφειδήσαντες ἕλεσθε
> ὄρχαμον ὑμείων, ᾧ κεν τὰ ἕκαστα μέλοιτο,
> νείκεα συνθεσίας τε μετὰ ξείνοισι βαλέσθαι.
>
> (1.336–40)

> But, my friends, our return back to Greece is a matter of common concern
> and our journey to the palace of Aeëtes is also of common concern.
> Accordingly, sparing no one's feelings, elect now the best man
> among you as leader. To him will fall the consideration of all the
> details: the initiation of conflicts and treaties with foreign peoples.[7]

---

[4] As the contest in Colchis is also styled: 3.4–7, 502, 522, 720, 1407, and *passim*. Heracles' labors, typically called ἄεθλοι, are also so named in the *Argonautica*; cf. 1.1318, 1347.

[5] *Pace* M. Campbell 1994:*ad* 3.422f.

[6] Cf. 1.206, 351, 1292, 4.205. As a point of comparison, κῦδος is what Zeus wins through his thunderbolts (1.510) and what Idas boasts he can achieve through his spear (1.467).

[7] The text I use is that of Vian and Delage 1974, 1980, 1981; all translations are my own, unless otherwise specified.

The leader that Jason envisages is not a man of exceptional strength (βίη) or cunning (μῆτις)—the kind of hero one finds in the *Iliad* or *Odyssey*— but a good organizer. In particular, the best of the Argonauts must settle conflicts (νείκεα) and arrange treaties or agreements (συνθεσίαι) with foreigners. What immediately follows this speech is equally significant: Heracles, the quintessential archaic and classical hero, refuses to be named captain despite his unanimous election by the men and thereby implicitly rejects this definition for himself.[8] The hero Apollonius offers is not independent like Heracles, who completes his contests by himself, but thoroughly dependent on the assistance of others. And indeed, following the accidental abandonment of Heracles, the only way that the expedition can succeed in the face of Aeëtes' superior power is through the help of another equally powerful agent. That helper is Medea, a foreigner with whom Jason will forge a deadly agreement.

And the Greatest of These Is Love

Apollonius begins the second half of the poem by invoking Erato, the Muse of love poetry. The wording warrants close attention:

> Εἰ δ' ἄγε νῦν, 'Ερατώ, παρά θ' ἵστασο καί μοι ἔνισπε
> ἔνθεν ὅπως ἐς 'Ιωλκὸν ἀνήγαγε κῶας 'Ιήσων
> Μηδείης ὑπ' ἔρωτι. Σὺ γὰρ καὶ Κύπριδος αἶσαν
> ἔμμορες, ἀδμῆτας δὲ τεοῖς μελεδήμασι θέλγεις
> παρθενικάς· τῷ καί τοι ἐπήρατον οὔνομ' ἀνῆπται.

(3.1–5)

> Come now, Erato, stand alongside me and tell me
> how Jason brought the fleece back to Iolcus
> through the love of Medea. For you were allotted a share
> in Aphrodite's dispensation; you charm unmarried young women
> with your cares. For this reason you have acquired an erotic name.

Contrary to Homer's practice Apollonius sets himself and the Muse on the same level. Erato is asked to stand alongside the poet and to tell how Jason attained the fleece. Why Erato? She knows how to sing of love.[9] Apollonius, like his hero, would appear to need a "helper-maiden" to assist him with a topic that is foreign to his chosen genre: Aphrodite and

---

[8] For a discussion of this episode, see Clauss 1993:61–66.

[9] On the name Erato and a suggestion regarding Apollonius' model, see M. Campbell 1983:1–7.

the charming of unmarried (literally "unconquered") young women, a subject more appropriate for love poetry. This mixing of genres finds a ready parallel in the opening of the poem (1.1–5)[10] and provides an appropriate introduction for book 3, which treats the anxiety of love as a crucial element in the completion of a heroic contest. For, as Apollonius puts it, it is "through the love of Medea" that the expedition succeeds. By calling upon Erato, Apollonius, following the Hellenistic penchant for programmatic introductions, alerts the reader to his literary gambit.[11]

There remains one additional point to make with regard to the charming of "unmarried young women" (ἀδμῆτας παρθενικάς). Homer uses the phrase in a slightly different form (παρθένος ἀδμής, Od. 6.109, 228) only of Nausicaa.[12] The imitation suggests that the love story to follow will owe something to the Homeric portrait of Nausicaa, as indeed it does. Moreover, the transformation of the rare Homeric phrase might in itself suggest that what follows will be an innovative adaptation of the Phaeacian episode, which, as noted by many, it is.[13]

This highly suggestive introduction leads into the delightful and seemingly amusing episode in which Hera, Athena, and Aphrodite conspire to have Medea fall in love with Jason. Comments on this episode—in particular on the exchange among the goddesses and Aphrodite's encounter with her petulant son Eros—tend to focus on the realistic portrayals of the goddesses as Hellenistic women at court and of Eros as an overindulged child.[14] Playfulness is an essential ingredient of the one and only Olympian scene in the poem, but it has tended to overshadow the mordant symbolism that lies behind the comedy of manners. Hera, Jason's divine patron, wants her favorite to succeed and so she consults Athena, the goddess of war and protector of heroes. Athena is stumped (3.21). The implication of the consultation is clear: military action is not feasible for Jason against the likes of Aeëtes (15). It

[10] See Goldhill 1991:286–300; Clauss 1993:14–25.

[11] On metaliterary aspects of the invocation, see Fusillo 1985:367; Grillo 1988:25–27; cf. also Händel 1954:93 and Feeney 1991:90–93. Moreover, a good parallel for this blending of heroic and erotic imagery is provided by Hunter 1987:136. Finally, on the theme and importance of love in the *Argonautica*, see Zanker 1979.

[12] Cf. Hunter 1989:*ad* 4–5

[13] E. g., Huber 1926:84–86; Beye 1982:122–29; Hunter 1989:26–30; Goldhill 1991:303.

[14] See, for instance, Wilamowitz 1924:2.181–83; L. Klein 1931:32–33; Huber 1926:39–41; Zanker 1987:205–7; M. Campbell 1983:10–19; Feeney 1991:77–78. Most recently, M. Campbell 1994 offers a detailed analysis in his commentary.

is at this point that Hera suggests a visit to Aphrodite's house to persuade the goddess to send her son, Eros, to charm (θέλξαι) Medea; she
will give Jason the drugs he needs to acquire the strength to face Aeëtes'
contest and thereby the opportunity to retrieve the fleece (25–29). As
stated in the invocation of book 3, success depends on the charming
(θέλγεις) of young unmarried women.

Apollonius modeled Hera and Athena's visit of Aphrodite on Thetis'
visit of Hephaestus in *Iliad* 18. In both cases the goddesses go to the
home of Hephaestus in need of a favor. There are, however, several
important differences. First, Hera and Athena encounter not Charis
(Hephaestus' wife in the *Iliad*) but Aphrodite (his two-timing wife in
the *Odyssey*).[15] Second (and more significant), Hera and Athena ask not
Hephaestus but his wife Aphrodite to cause Medea to fall in love[16] so
that Jason can succeed in Aeëtes' challenge and return with the fleece.
Moreover, Thetis had asked for armor for Achilles so that he could fight
against Hector. This striking contrast between text and subtext reechoes
the juxtaposition of epic and erotic topics seen in the invocation.

There exists another contrast between the two passages. In the *Iliad*,
Thetis asked for new weapons and the poet described the golden armor
in considerable detail. While it is not the object of Hera and Athena's
visit per se, Apollonius supplies a golden artifact and a detailed description: a ball made by Hephaestus (3.131–41). The substitution of
a plaything for a shield, so typical of Alexandrian sensibilities, complements the thematic blending of amatory and military themes.[17] Yet
the amusing portrait of a wicked boy and a distraught mother has
blinded many readers to the grim significance of the scene. The golden
ball, longed for by an attractive but dangerous boy, is not merely a
transformation of the Iliadic shield or, what is more to the point, an
Olympian analogue for the Golden Fleece.[18] It is also emblematic of the

[15] Demodocus' story of the illicit love of Aphrodite and Ares is amusingly alluded to
in the present scene: not only does Hephaestus' absence from home for reasons of his
work (3.41–43) recall the god's trick to catch his adulterous wife in bed, but also Eros'
threat to use his bow on Aphrodite herself anticipates her future escapade with Ares.

[16] Hera's request for Aphrodite's assistance was suggested by the goddess's similar
request of Aphrodite in *Il.* 14, when she wanted to seduce Zeus. Here too, Hera wants
help with a seduction; cf. Hunter 1989:*ad* 79–82.

[17] In book 1.721–73 we find the same blend in the description of Jason's cloak, which he
wears as he goes to meet (and eventually make love to) Hypsipyle. The ecphrasis clearly
recalls that of Achilles' shield, which he carries in his climactic battle against Hector. On
ecphrasis in general in the *Argonautica*, see Thiel 1993, although his analysis of the cloak is
problematic (cf. *AJP* 116 [1995] 326).

[18] As well argued by T. Klein 1980–81.

universe: a sphere with five parallel circles (κύκλα: the equator, trop-
ics, and arctic circles) intersected at two points (ἀψῖδες: the equinoxes)
by a spiral (ἕλιξ: the zodiac).[19] The implication of the bribe is bleak.
Once Eros makes Medea fall in love with Jason, the universe will be
in the hands of a completely amoral and capricious power. As an
indication of how terrifying Eros is, even Aphrodite fears his unpredictable power (3.91–99). Moreover, to win his good will she must offer
a golden gift. Medea too will offer a golden object, the fleece, to satisfy
her eros.[20]

Charming the Unconquered Maiden

Diplomacy

Before approaching Colchis and King Aeëtes, Jason holds a meeting in
which he suggests the use of diplomacy to see what Aeëtes' reaction
to their request will be:

> Ὦ φίλοι, ἤτοι ἐγὼ μὲν ὅ μοι ἐπιανδάνει αὐτῷ
> ἐξερέω, τοῦ δ' ὔμμι τέλος κρηῆναι ἔοικεν.
> Ξυνὴ γὰρ χρειώ, ξυνοὶ δέ τε μῦθοι ἔασιν
> πᾶσιν ὁμῶς· ὁ δὲ σῖγα νόον βουλήν τ' ἀπερύκων
> ἴστω καὶ νόστου τόνδε στόλον οἶος ἀπούρας.
> Ὧλλοι μὲν κατὰ νῆα σὺν ἔντεσι μίμνεθ' ἔκηλοι·
> αὐτὰρ ἐγὼν ἐς δώματ' ἐλεύσομαι Αἰήταο,
> υἷας ἑλὼν Φρίξοιο δύω τ' ἐπὶ τοῖσιν ἑταίρους,
> Πειρήσω δ' ἐπέεσσι παροίτερον ἀντιβολήσας,
> εἴ κ' ἐθέλοι φιλότητι δέρος χρύσειον ὀπάσσαι,
> ἦε καὶ οὔ, πίσυνος δὲ βίῃ μετιόντας ἀτίσσει.
> Ὧδε γὰρ ἐξ αὐτοῖο πάρος κακότητα δαέντες
> φρασσόμεθ' εἴ τ' ἄρηι συνοισόμεθ' εἴ τέ τις ἄλλη
> μῆτις ἐπίρροθος ἔσται ἐεργομένοισιν αὐτῆς·
> Μηδ' αὔτως ἀλκῇ, πρὶν ἔπεσσί γε πειρηθῆναι,
> τόνδ' ἀπαμείρωμεν σφέτερον κτέρας, ἀλλὰ πάροιθεν
> λωίτερον μύθῳ μιν ἀρέσσασθαι μετιόντας.
> Πολλάκι τοι ῥέα μῦθος, ὅ κεν μόλις ἐξανύσειεν
> ἠνορέη, τόδ' ἔρεξε κατὰ χρέος, ᾗ περ ἐῴκει,
> πρηΰνας·

(3.171–90)

[19] See Lendle 1979 and Pendergraft 1991.
[20] Boedeker in this volume reveals a comparable association between Aphrodite and
Medea in Euripides' play.

Friends, what I myself prefer to do,
I shall make clear; the final decision, however, is up to you.
The expedition is a matter of common concern, so too our ideas
are a common concern for all equally. Let the one who withholds
    his thoughts and plans
know that he alone deprives this group of its return.
The rest of you, arm yourselves and stay here quietly along the ship.
I shall go to Aeëtes' palace,
taking with me the sons of Phrixus and two other comrades.
Meeting him face to face, I'll approach him first with words
to see if he might be willing to give us the Golden Fleece out of
    friendship,
or if not, relying on his strength, he might refuse our request.
In this way, learning in advance from him himself of our rebuff
we can decide whether we shall engage him in battle or find some
    other
plan that will prove helpful should we refrain from war.
Let us not resort to *violence* before giving diplomacy a chance,
especially since we are asking for his prized possession. It is better
first to approach him and win him over through persuasion.
Often what sheer strength can achieve only with great difficulty
persuasion easily accomplishes as a matter of course, armed with
the appropriate ingratiating flourishes.

The speech calls to mind Jason's first address to the Argonauts on the
beach at Pagasae where he observed their need for unity of action
(1.336–40, quoted above). In addition to providing a new starting point
for the action,[21] the repetition of this theme underscores Jason's brand
of leadership and heroism: making deals with foreigners. Moreover,
Apollonius expresses Jason's two other alternatives to diplomacy in a
significant way: either Aeëtes will turn to violence (βίη), forcing the
Argonauts to respond in kind, or they will have to devise some clever
plan (μῆτις). As it happens, Jason himself neither faces Aeëtes in battle
nor himself devises a clever ruse. Rather, his ability to make deals with
foreigners, to make a bargain for another's strength and cunning, is the
key to his success.

Arrival

As Jason, accompanied by Telamon, Augeias, and the sons of Phrixus,
proceeds across the plain of Circe, Hera sends a mist upon the city

[21] See Clauss 1990:138–39.

of Colchis to prevent their approach from being seen (3.210–14). As many have observed, Apollonius recalls Odysseus' approach to Alcinous' palace (*Od.* 7.14–17, 139–40, 143).[22] Moreover, the description of Aeëtes' palace (3.215–41) comes appropriately from Homer's description of Alcinous' (*Od.* 7.81–135).[23] Yet Apollonius also has other Homeric passages in mind. Once the men enter the city, they notice four fountains: one flowing with milk, one with wine, one with oil, and one with water. The water fountain was unusual in that it ran hot and cold at different times (3.221–29). The four fountains in Colchis call to mind Hermes' visit to Calypso's cave with its four fountains (*Od.* 5.68–73a) and the dual temperatures allude to the two sources of the Scamander River, a detail mentioned by Homer in the scene depicting Achilles' pursuit of Hector (*Il.* 22.148–52). Finally, the configuration of rooms in the palace (3.325–48) comes from Homer's description of Priam's palace when Hector returned to Troy (*Il.* 6.242–50).[24]

This preface to Jason's first encounter with Medea is highly suggestive. First, as in the case of Jason's previous encounter with Hypsipyle, the reader is asked to see Medea as a combination of Circe, Calypso, and Nausicaa: the Circean plain recalls the first; the four fountains, the second; and the overall imitation of the Phaeacian episode, the third.[25] Second, recollection of the Scamander's two streams not only imports into the Argonautic text its association with the climactic battle between Achilles and Hector, but also brings along the poignant comment that at this spot the Trojan wives and daughters used to clean their clothing (εἵματα σιγαλόεντα, *Il.* 22.154) before the war. Nausicaa met Odysseus when engaged in the same activity near a body of water (εἵματα ... σιγαλόεντα, *Od.* 6.26).[26] By inviting the reader to see a link between these two passages, Apollonius again invokes the thematic blend of martial and amatory motifs. Third, allusion to the episode in which Hector returned home and spoke to Hecuba, Helen, and Andromache makes the Colchian palace an ominous setting for Medea, who will tell her sister Chalciope that she fears for her sons, who have been for her brothers, nephews, and companions (3.731–32), thus recalling Andromache's statement to Hector that he is father, mother, brother, and husband to

---

[22] E.g., Gillies 1928:*ad* 211; Hunter 1989:*ad* 210–14; Rengakos 1993:65–66; and most recently M. Campbell 1994: *ad* 210–14.

[23] Roux 1963:84–87 also sees evidence of contemporary palace architecture—Ptolemaic in particular—behind Aeëtes' home.

[24] Cf. Hunter 1989:*ad* Ap. Rhod. 3.235–48.

[25] On the Lemnian episode, see Clauss 1993:106–47.

[26] The collocation of these two words occurs only here in the *Iliad* and the *Odyssey*.

her (*Il.* 6.429–40).[27] The striking difference between the heroines and their situations, however, is that while Andromache does not succeed in persuading Hector with this line of reasoning and will in time lose her husband, Medea not only successfully manipulates Chalciope but in so doing gains the opportunity to meet with and ultimately marry Jason. The ingenuous Andromache fails and the guileful Medea succeeds.[28]

Jason's arrival at Colchis suggests the presence of a "helper-maiden" who will, like Nausicaa, facilitate his return home with a treasure. Yet the interplay of other subtexts invites the reader to see Jason as attractively vulnerable as Odysseus, but also as potentially destructive as Achilles. Medea at this point has yet to show what kind of Nausicaa she will be.

The Meeting

Once the embassy made its way into the palace, Medea was the first to see them. Apollonius informs us that Hera had kept Medea home for this purpose (3.250–52). As Hunter points out, Apollonius neatly inverts the Odyssean model: "Whereas Nausicaa had to be sent out in order to meet Odysseus, Medea has to be kept at home for Jason's arrival."[29] As Medea sees the sons of Phrixus, she screams. Although Apollonius does not say why, her reaction is due, no doubt, to the unexpected sight of her nephews, who returned to Colchis with Jason. Ironically her scream turns out to be an appropriate reaction to the sight of the man who is about to change her life irrevocably and for the worse.

Apollonius describes the onset of passion appropriately as a wound from Eros' arrow (3.275–98). In a brilliant adaptation of this erotic theme, the poet portrays the wounding in a manner reminiscent of the shooting of Menelaus by Pandarus in *Iliad* 3, the incident that destroyed the possibility of achieving a peaceful settlement of the Trojan War through a duel.[30] Not only is the thematic blending of martial and amatory themes in play, but the recollection of the Iliadic model again strikes

---

[27] Apollonius returns to this famous Iliadic passage later when he has Medea say to Jason prior to their departure from Colchis that she is his daughter, wife, and sister (4.368–69).

[28] The entire constellation of martial and erotic episodes might well have been suggested by the simile in which Odysseus is compared to a lion as he approached Nausicaa and her friends (*Od.* 6.130–34); see Beye 1982:122, who notes the "charming blend of eroticism and military parody" in this Odyssean scene.

[29] See Hunter 1989:*ad* 250.

[30] Lennox 1980 offers a thorough reading of this scene and its Iliadic model.

an ominous note: the Argonautic archer likewise threatens to wreak bloody havoc.

Medea recedes from the poet's gaze for the moment as the Argonauts are introduced to Aeëtes and the purpose of their journey is revealed. After learning that Jason has come for the fleece, Aeëtes not unreasonably suspects a plot against his throne; there was, after all, an omen warning against a conspiracy among his kinsmen (3.597–605). At this point, Aeëtes proposes an impossible mission as the price for the fleece: yoking the fire-breathing bulls, sowing the field of Ares with dragon teeth, and dealing with the monstrous crop (401–21). Jason, in the presence of the king and his people, has no alternative but to accept a contest that he has no hope of surviving. He clearly lacks the strength and cunning to succeed, while the only Argonaut capable of succeeding in Aeëtes' trial—Heracles—was abandoned in Mysia. Nonetheless, Jason will ultimately succeed against the bulls and the crop of the dragon teeth with Medea's assistance.

Love

Following the challenge, Jason returns to the Argonauts and Medea, to her room, her mind filled with thoughts of love (3.451–52). Apollonius has her replay the previous scene over and over in her mind, as Jason's words still ring in her ears (454–58).[31] This is the segue to the first of Medea's three monologues:

Τίπτε με δειλαίην τόδ᾽ ἔχει ἄχος; Εἴ θ᾽ ὅ γε πάντων
φθείσεται ἡρώων προφερέστατος εἴ τε χερείων,
ἐρρέτω.... Ἦ μὲν ὄφελλεν ἀκήριος ἐξαλέασθαι.
Ναὶ δὴ τοῦτό γε, πότνα θεὰ Περσηί, πέλοιτο,
οἴκαδε νοστήσειε φυγὼν μόρον· εἰ δέ μιν αἶσα
δμηθῆναι ὑπὸ βουσί, τόδε προπάροιθε δαείη,
οὕνεκεν οὔ οἱ ἔγωγε κακῇ ἐπαγαίομαι ἄτῃ.

(3.464–70)

Why has this anxiety made me so distraught? Whether he is the
best of all heroes who is about to be destroyed or the worst,
let him go to Hell. Yet, I would like him to escape unharmed.

[31] Scholars have tended to focus on Apollonius' psychological portrait of Medea in love (e.g., Carrière 1959; Paduano 1972), which I shall avoid in this paper, focusing instead on the various literary subtexts and a determination of how they affect our understanding of Medea's role, particularly in book 3.

Yes, may it turn out so, august goddess, daughter of Perses:
may he escape death and return home. But if it is his fate
to be killed by the bulls, may he learn this first,
that I for one take no pleasure in his bitter destruction.

Again Apollonius poses indirectly the question that was seen as a major theme of book 1: who is the best of the Argonauts?[32] In her present state, however, for Medea the question is irrelevant. So charmed by Eros is Medea that to her it does not matter whether Jason is an Achilles or a Thersites.

Yet the nature of the hero reemerges as a central issue in the following scene among the Argonauts (3.472–575). As they return to the group, Argus suggests that they employ Medea's assistance: through her drugs, the contesting hero (840) will not experience fear. Following Jason's description of his contest and the expression of willingness of several other Argonauts to take it on, Argus repeats his suggestion. As soon as he finishes speaking, a dove, pursued by a hawk, falls into Jason's lap while the pursuing hawk impales itself on the Argo. Mopsus immediately marks the significance of this event: Aphrodite approves of Argus' suggestion, which, as it turns out, confirms the prophecy of Phineus (cf. 2.423–25). Apollonius highlights the novelty of the decision to turn to love by having Idas, "caricature du héros épique" (Vian and Delage 1980:127 ad 3.557), rail against the prospect, recalling Heracles' reproach to the Argonauts on Lemnos (cf. 1.865–74):

Ὦ πόποι, ἦ ῥα γυναιξὶν ὁμόστολοι ἐνθάδ' ἔβημεν,
οἳ Κύπριν καλέουσιν ἐπίρροθον ἄμμι πέλεσθαι·
οὐκέτ' Ἐνυαλίοιο μέγα σθένος, ἐς δὲ πελείας
καὶ κίρκους λεύσσοντες ἐρητύεσθε ἀέθλων.
Ἔρρετε, μηδ' ὕμμιν πολεμήια ἔργα μέλοιτο,
παρθενικὰς δὲ λιτῇσιν ἀνάλκιδας ἠπεροπεύειν.

(3.558–63)

You damned fools! Surely we have come here in the company
    of women,
we who call upon Cypris to be our savior.
You no longer look to Enyalius' great power, but to doves
and hawks in order to avoid heroic contests.
Go to Hell! Care no more for the deeds of war
but seduce defenseless young girls with your prayers!

---

[32] As argued in Clauss 1993.

Two modes of action collide, and in this case it is not strength versus cunning but strength versus Eros, and Eros will have the upper hand. As it turns out, Jason's ability to arouse passion will prove to be as successful as Achillean strength or Odyssean cunning.

While Argus confers with Chalciope about the possibility of having Medea assist Jason, Medea falls asleep and experiences a revealing dream: she imagines that Jason came not to acquire the fleece but herself, that she herself undertook Pelias' "contest" (ἀεθλεύουσα), that an argument arose in which she had to decide between her father and Jason, and that she chose Jason (3.616–32). As Hunter observes, Medea's dream is modeled on the one Athena sent to Nausicaa (*Od.* 6.25–40).[33] Nausicaa was instructed in her dream by the image of a friend to go to the shore to launder the clothes, and it is here that she meets and assists Odysseus. Comparison of the two dreams reveals another instance of the programmatic contrast between erotic and epic themes seen above: Nausicaa dreams of meeting a husband; Medea dreams of taking on a heroic contest. As in the case of Nausicaa, Medea's dream represents an important stage in the awakening of her passion. Her subconscious desire so revealed not only makes her true feelings clear, at least to the reader, but her dream also opens the way for her assistance of Jason. In effect, she has already decided for Jason and against her own father.[34]

From the language she uses, Medea would appear to have usurped Jason's role. She envisages herself as the contestant and the one who handles an argument, both terms that have been associated primarily with Jason in the poem prior to this point. This does not necessarily mean, however, that she has now become the hero of the epic.[35] Apollonius was following the lead of Euripides in having his "heroine" identify with her beloved in a subconscious state. Much as Phaedra does in Euripides' *Hippolytus* (198–231), Medea, freed in sleep to express her true thoughts, reveals her subconscious desire for the object of her passion by assuming the role of that very person.[36] Once she is

[33] Hunter 1989:*ad* 626–32.

[34] The imitation of *Od.* 18.188–89 and 19.516–17 in 3.616–18, noted by Hunter 1989:*ad loc.*, brings in Penelope as another model: a married woman who nonetheless longs for her husband or at least a husband. As Hunter notes, like Medea, Penelope had to consider whether or not to abandon her family and pursue reawakening sexual desires (cf. *Od.*19.524–29).

[35] See Vian and Delage 1980:*ad* 623.

[36] Such assimilation is also at play in Euripides' *Medea*, as Boedeker demonstrates in this volume.

awake, at the completion of her second monologue Medea more aptly identifies her role as that of helper:

> Ἔμπα γε μήν, θεμένη κύνεον κέαρ, οὐκέτ' ἄνευθεν
> αὐτοκασιγνήτης πειρήσομαι, εἴ κέ μ' ἀέθλῳ
> χραισμεῖν ἀντιάσῃσιν, ἐπὶ σφετέροις ἀχέουσα
> παισί· τό κέν μοι λυγρὸν ἐνὶ κραδίῃ σβέσοι ἄλγος.

(3.641–44)

Nonetheless, assuming the heart of a bitch,[37] I shall actively make trial of my sister, to see if she will ask me to help out in the contest, making my excuse anxiety for her sons. This might extinquish the pain in my heart.

Use of the phrase "to help out" (χραισμεῖν) makes it clear that Medea, at least in her own mind, does not see herself as the hero undertaking the contest but as the "helper-maiden." Nonetheless her dream reveals something about the nature of her help that pertains to Jason's heroic contest: once she agrees to participate, the work of yoking the bulls, plowing the field, and dealing with the deadly crop will prove to be easy (3.624). The Medean helper-maiden differs markedly from the Nausicaan model in the degree to which she can help. As we shall see, Medea can turn a weak Jason into a powerful Heracles. Moreover, unlike Nausicaa, Medea will not allow the hero she helps to leave without taking her along.

Shame

Another significant difference between the two helper-maidens involves their reactions to how their assistance might be viewed by their respective societies. Similar to Phaedra in *Hippolytus*, Medea's debilitating passion (ἔρος) struggles with her sense of shame (αἰδώς), a struggle that begins at 3.649, after she first thought of approaching Chalciope, and lasts until she gives Jason both the drug and instructions on how to use it; only after this does she loses all shame (δὴ γάρ οἱ ἀπ' ὀφθαλμοὺς λίπεν αἰδώς, 3.1068).[38] It is shame then that keeps Medea from approaching Chalciope, reducing her to the condition of a young bride whose groom dies before they consummate their marriage and who

---

[37] Regarding this phrase, Hunter notes that behind Medea stands also a "Helen model" (1989:*ad* 641–42 and p. 29, 1993:67).

[38] Hunter 1989:*ad* 766–68, 811–16, notes the Euripidean influence.

fears revealing her physical longing for her dead husband (3.648–64).[39] When a servant sees Medea's distress and reports it to her sister, Chalciope rushes to her side and questions her. Medea is at first silent out of shame, but eventually proceeds with her ruse, forced by passion (681–87). What she has to say to Chalciope is utterly shameless: she pretends that her dream involved harm coming to her sister's children and so she can seem to give Jason the help he needs out of sororal piety (727–39).

Alone again, Medea confronts her sense of shame for the last time. After reviewing her options, she gives voice to her frustration, bringing the issue to its climax:

> πῶς γάρ κεν ἐμοὺς λελάθοιμι τοκῆας
> φάρμακα μησαμένη; ποῖον δ᾽ ἐπὶ μῦθον ἐνίψω;
> τίς δὲ δόλος, τίς μῆτις ἐπίκλοπος ἔσσετ᾽ ἀρωγῆς;
> ἦ μιν ἄνευθ᾽ ἑτάρων προσπτύξομαι οἶον ἰδοῦσα;
> δύσμορος· οὐ μὲν ἔολπα καταφθιμένοιό περ ἔμπης
> λωφήσειν ἀχέων· τότε δ᾽ ἂν κακὸν ἄμμι πέλοιτο,
> κεῖνος ὅτε ζωῆς ἀπαμείρεται. ἐρρέτω αἰδώς,
> ἐρρέτω ἀγλαΐη·

(3.779–786)

> How might I devise some use for my drugs
> without my parents finding out? What story shall I concoct?
> What ruse or what device will there be to mask my assistance?
> Seeing him alone, apart from his companions, shall I address him?
> What misery! Once he is dead I do not expect
> an end to this suffering. He will turn out to be
> my undoing the moment he loses his life. To Hell with shame!
> To Hell with reputation!

Medea longs to save Jason but her sense of shame and her concern for her reputation prevents her from acting upon this desire.

As seen above, shame (αἰδώς) referred to Medea's inability to express her inner feelings before another (Chalciope in her room) and will cause her to hesitate to speak to Jason at the temple of Hecate on the next day. The emotion arises from the need to keep one's most intimate feelings private. Yet Medea also dismisses concern for her reputation (ἀγλαΐη, literally "splendor"). If she helps Jason,

---

[39] The simile has received much scholarly attention: see Wilamowitz 1924:2.210 n. 1; Faerber 1932:18; Fränkel 1950:123–25; M. Campbell 1983:39–40. Ardizzoni 1976 vigorously argues against a sexual reading of the widow's plight.

she acknowledges that she will not escape the notice of her parents or other Colchians and will in this way bring shame (ἤσχυνε) on her family:

ἀλλὰ καὶ ὣς φθιμένη μοι ἐπιλλίξουσιν ὀπίσσω
κερτομίαις· τηλοῦ δὲ πόλις περὶ πᾶσα βοήσει
πότμον ἐμόν· καί κέν με διὰ στόματος φορέουσαι
Κολχίδες ἄλλυδις ἄλλαι ἀεικέα μωμήσονται·
ἥ τις κηδομένη τόσον ἀνέρος ἀλλοδαποῖο
κάτθανεν, ἤ τις δῶμα καὶ οὓς ἤσχυνε τοκῆας,
μαργοσύνῃ εἴξασα.

(3.791–97)

But even so they will utter all forms of insults
after my death and every city far and wide will resound
with the tale of my fate. And making frequent mention of me,
Colchian women everywhere will hurl embarrassing taunts at me:
"She died because she cared so much for some foreign
man! She brought shame on her home and parents,
giving in to lust!"

Unlike αἰδώς, which is internal, ἀγλαΐη is exterior and societal, the direct result of not following the dictates of one's inner sense of shame. Euripides' Phaedra summarized well these two types of "shame" that apply to Medea's situation: "There are two sorts: one is not evil and the other is a burden for families" (δισσαὶ δ' εἰσίν, ἡ μὲν οὐ κακή, ἡ δ' ἄχθος οἴκων, Eur. *Hipp.* 385–86).

In her instructions to Odysseus about how to approach the city and her parents, Nausicaa fears what the Phaeacians might think and say of her cavorting with a foreign man. She even criticizes any young woman who would bring shame on her family by such an association:

καὶ δ' ἄλλῃ νεμεσῶ, ἥ τις τοιαῦτά γε ῥέζοι,
ἥ τ' ἀέκητι φίλων πατρὸς καὶ μητρὸς ἐόντων
ἀνδράσι μίσγηται, πρίν γ' ἀμφάδιον γάμον ἐλθεῖν.

(*Od.* 6. 286–88)

And I shall blame another woman who might do some such thing:
she who, against the wishes of her father and mother,
consorts with a man before the day of her public marriage.

Comparison of these two responses to public opinion underscores Medea's complete helplessness and loss of shame. Moreover, she cannot even muster the courage to kill herself, as Phaedra managed to do.[40]

The Tryst

After having resolved to assist Jason, Medea anxiously awaits the dawn, when she will go the temple of Hecate to meet Jason.[41] Her maids prepare a mule-drawn wagon and accompany Medea to the trysting place, following behind her. As she goes, Apollonius compares her to Artemis:

Οἵη δὲ λιαροῖσιν ἐφ' ὕδασι Παρθενίοιο,
ἠὲ καὶ Ἀμνισοῖο λοεσσαμένη ποταμοῖο,
χρυσείοις Λητωὶς ἐφ' ἅρμασιν ἑστηυῖα
ὠκείαις κεμάδεσσι διεξελάῃσι κολώνας,
τηλόθεν ἀντιόωσα πολυκνίσου ἑκατόμβης·
τῇ δ' ἅμα Νύμφαι ἕπονται ἀμορβάδες, αἱ μὲν ἀπ' αὐτῆς
ἀγρόμεναι πηγῆς Ἀμνισίδος, αἱ δὲ λιποῦσαι
ἄλσεα καὶ σκοπιὰς πολυπίδακας· ἀμφὶ δὲ θῆρες
κνυζηθμῷ σαίνουσιν ὑποτρομέοντες ἰοῦσαν·
ὣς αἵ γ' ἐσσεύοντο δί ἄστεος, ἀμφὶ δὲ λαοὶ
εἶκον ἀλευάμενοι βασιληίδος ὄμματα κούρης.

(3.876–86)

Just as at the warm streams of Parthenius,
or after bathing in the river Amnisus,
the daughter of Leto, standing on her golden chariot,
drives the hills, drawn by swift deer,
going far off to receive an offering of a hecatomb, plumed in rich
    smoke.
Nymphs accompany her: some coming together from
the spring of Amnisus, others leaving
the groves and many fountains on the hilltops; as she moves
wild animals crouch and surround her, whining obsequiously.
In this way the group hastened through the city; and the people
    all about
gave way, avoiding the eyes of the king's daughter.

[40] When Apollonius states that Medea is ultimately swayed by the many pleasures of life, he has in mind Phaedra's statement that people who act contrary to their good sense do so because of the many pleasures of life (Eur. *Hipp.* 382–85), as Hunter 1989:*ad* 811–16 rightly notes.

[41] On this episode, see M. Campbell 1983:56–61.

There the young women will while away the time, singing and collecting flowers until Jason arrives.[42]

As has long been observed, Medea's journey to meet Jason parallels Nausicaa's to the beach where she will encounter Odysseus.[43] The Phaeacian princess travels by mule-drawn cart (*Od.* 6.72–73) and her maids likewise follow on foot behind her (cf. 6.318–20). Instead of picking flowers, Nausicaa and her friends play ball and it is while they are at play that Homer compares Nausicaa to Artemis:

> Οἵη δ᾽ Ἄρτεμις εἶσι κατ᾽ οὔρεα ἰοχέαιρα,
> ἢ κατὰ Τηΰγετον περιμήκετον ἢ Ἐρύμανθον,
> τερπομένη κάπροισι καὶ ὠκείῃσ᾽ ἐλάφοισι·
> τῇ δέ θ᾽ ἅμα νύμφαι, κοῦραι Διὸς αἰγιόχοιο,
> ἀγρονόμοι παίζουσι, γέγηθε δέ τε φρένα Λητώ·
> πασάων δ᾽ ὑπὲρ ἥ γε κάρη ἔχει ἠδὲ μέτωπα,
> ῥεῖά τ᾽ ἀριγνώτη πέλεται, καλαὶ δέ τε πᾶσαι·
> ὣς ἥ γ᾽ ἀμφιπόλοισι μετέπρεπε παρθένος ἀδμής.

(*Od.* 6.102–9)

Just as Artemis passes through the mountains, shooting her arrows—
either along the peaks of Taygetus or Erymanthus—
rejoicing in the pursuit of boars and swift deer.
Together with her, the nymphs, daughters of aegis-bearing Zeus,
gather to play, and Leto's heart beats happily.
High above them all Artemis holds her head and face,
she is easily conspicuous, despite the beauty of all.
In this way the unmarried young woman surpassed her maids.

Allusion to the Phaeacian episode once again accentuates the difference between the two characters. In the *Odyssey*, the simile focuses on appearance by implying that Nausicaa surpasses her friends in stature just as Artemis does her accompanying nymphs; in the *Argonautica*, the simile underscores Medea's quasi-divine status, for wild animals are often depicted as fawning on the "Mistress of the Animals" (πότνια θηρῶν).[44] The simile is doubly appropriate in Medea's case: in addition to anticipating the reaction that the people of Colchis have to their

---

[42] On the sexual undercurrents of this activity, see M. Campbell 1983:60–61.

[43] E.g., Gillies 1928:*ad* 874; Vian and Delage 1980:137 *ad* 869. In addition to the influence of the well-known Odyssean scene, Hunter 1989:*ad* 869–86 and Paduano and Fusillo 1986:*ad* 876–86 also note the influence of Callimachus' *Hymn to Artemis* (cf. 110–12).

[44] In lines 883–84 Apollonius has in mind the Homeric *Hymn to Aphrodite* (69–74), where Aphrodite is described in terms reminiscent of the πότνια θηρῶν; see Vian and Delage 1980:137 *ad* 869 and Hunter 1989:*ad* 883–84.

princess—all fear to look into the eyes of the young woman (3.885–86)—Artemis is linked in myth and cult, and is sometimes synonymous, with Hecate, whom Medea serves. Thus, rather than focusing on the beauty or stature of the helper-maiden, the simile emphasizes Medea's terrifying power. In this way and at this point, the demonic side of the Argonautic Nausicaa begins to emerge.[45]

As Jason goes to meet Medea at the temple of Hecate, Hera makes him even more attractive:

Ἔνθ' οὔ πω τις τοῖος ἐπὶ προτέρων γένετ' ἀνδρῶν,
οὔθ' ὅσοι ἐξ αὐτοῖο Διὸς γένος οὔθ' ὅσοι ἄλλων
ἀθανάτων ἥρωες ἀφ' αἵματος ἐβλάστησαν,
οἷον Ἰήσονα θῆκε Διὸς δάμαρ ἤματι κείνῳ
ἠμὲν ἐς ἄντα ἰδεῖν ἠδὲ προτιμυθήσασθαι.
Τὸν καὶ παπταίνοντες ἐθάμβεον αὐτοὶ ἑταῖροι
λαμπόμενον χαρίτεσσιν·

(3.919–25)

Never was such a hero seen among the men of days long past—
neither among those born from Zeus himself nor those
who sprung from the other immortals—
as Jason on that day after the wife of Zeus made him
a wonder to speak with and to behold.
The Argonauts themselves marveled as they saw him
radiating with grace.

Similarly, Athena enhances Odysseus' physical appearance after he is bathed and puts on the clothes that the "unconquered maiden" (*Od.* 6.228) provided:

τὸν μὲν Ἀθηναίη θῆκεν Διὸς ἐκγεγαυῖα
μείζονά τ' εἰσιδέειν καὶ πάσσονα, κὰδ δὲ κάρητος
οὔλας ἧκε κόμας, ὑακινθίνῳ ἄνθει ὁμοίας.
ὡς δ' ὅτε τις χρυσὸν περιχεύεται ἀργύρῳ ἀνὴρ
ἴδρις, ὃν Ἥφαιστος δέδαεν καὶ Παλλὰς Ἀθήνη
τέχνην παντοίην, χαρίεντα δὲ ἔργα τελείει,
ὣς ἄρα τῷ κατέχευε χάριν κεφαλῇ τε καὶ ὤμοις.

(*Od.* 6.229–35)

[45] On the dual nature of Medea in the *Argonautica*, cf. Belloni 1981; Newlands in this volume discusses this feature of the myth in Ovid's *Metamorphoses*. In the past, scholars have focused on the inconsistency between the young girl one finds in book 3 and the witch in book 4: e.g., Wilamowitz 1924.2:213–14; L. Klein 1931:231–33; Otis 1964:61–96; and Collard 1975. This negative appraisal of Apollonius' handling of the character of Medea, however, has been successfully countered by others: e.g., Phinney 1967; Valgiglio 1970; Paduano 1972:63–84; Beye 1982:158–61; and, most recently, Hunter 1987.

Athena, Zeus' daughter, made him
taller and more robust to behold, and down from his head
she sent thick locks of hair, similar to hyacinth blossoms.
Just as when a man rims a silver object with gold—
the artist whom Hephaestus and Pallas Athena have taught
all kinds of skills—and the completed work is graceful,
so too the goddess surrounded his head and shoulders with grace.

The result of Odysseus' sudden transformation is immediate. Nausicaa, like Medea, wishes to have the hero as her husband (*Od.* 6.244–45).

Yet, once again, an interesting difference between Nausicaa and Medea emerges from a closer comparison of the wider contexts of these transformations. While there is no possibility that Nausicaa will ever betray her own sense of shame or her family, she never hesitates to speak freely with Odysseus, even when she is moved by his beauty. Medea, on the other hand, though a powerful sorceress, is unable to speak when she sees Jason, described as beautiful yet deadly like the appearance of the star Sirius (3.948–74).[46] Mention of this star recalls the climactic duel between Achilles and Hector in which Priam compared the fire in Achilles' eyes to the destructive Dog Star.[47] The thematic coupling of love and war in the Colchian episode is now fully realized: Jason, the "love-hero," to use Beye's term,[48] is engaged in his own particular kind of contest, that of infatuating and making deals with foreign women. Whereas Nausicaa's incipient love provided Odysseus with the opportunity to return home, where his real contest lay, Medea, just as she imagined in her dream and as their use of the fleece as a marriage bed implies (cf. 4.1141–46), represents Jason's real conquest; she is completely charmed by Jason's beauty and, upon his first request for the drug that will enable him to complete his task, hands it over (3.1012–13). To conquer Medea is to win the fleece, the opposite of the usual folktale motif, which has the young hero perform the contest to win the bride.[49] At this point, Jason has conquered the maiden.

[46] Hunter 1989:*ad* 956–61 aptly notes that the simile, an adaptation of *Il.* 22.25–32, corresponds to the simile in *Od.* 6 in which Odysseus, approaching Nausicaa, was compared to a hungry lion; see above n. 28.

[47] Hunter 1989:*ad* 964–65 notes not only that Apollonius had earlier alluded to this same scene but also that the Iliadic model, the duel between Hector and Achilles, becomes in Apollonius what Hector said it could not be: "an exchange of words between a young man and a girl" (*Il.* 22.126–28).

[48] Beye 1969.

[49] See Thompson 1955:H310–59. Beye 1982:137 refers to this scene as Jason's *aristeia.*

The sequence of allusions to the Phaeacian episode now comes to a climax. Aware that Medea is in love with him, Jason initiates the conversation by addressing her in an obsequious tone (3.974); in this we observe his "heroic" skill in action. Jason's opening words to Medea are a reversal of Odysseus' to Nausicaa.[50] At *Odyssey* 6.149–69, Odysseus expresses *his* awe before the Phaeacian princess, whom he likens to a goddess; Jason, on the other hand, asks Medea not to hold *him* in such awe (3.975–79). The same Argonautic speech contains another significant alteration from its Odyssean model. Jason concludes his first address to Medea with a promise of gratitude:

> Ὣς καὶ σοὶ θεόθεν χάρις ἔσσεται, εἴ κε σαώσεις
> τόσσον ἀριστήων ἀνδρῶν στόλον. ἦ γὰρ ἔοικας
> ἐκ μορφῆς ἀγανῇσιν ἐπητείῃσι κεκάσθαι.

(3.1005–7)

In this way you will earn the thanks of the gods if you save
so great an expedition of heroic men. For you seem to me,
to judge from your beauty, to abound in gentle courtesy.

Odysseus in his fairwell to Nausicaa promises something quite different:

> Ναυσικάα θύγατερ μεγαλήτορος Ἀλκινόοιο,
> οὕτω νῦν Ζεὺς θείη, ἐρίγδουπος πόσις Ἥρης,
> οἴκαδέ τ' ἐλθέμεναι καὶ νόστιμον ἦμαρ ἰδέσθαι·
> τῷ κέν τοι καὶ κεῖθε θεῷ ὣς εὐχετοῴμην
> αἰεὶ ἤματα πάντα· σὺ γάρ μ' ἐβιώσαο, κούρη.

(Od. 8.464–68)

Nausicaa, daughter of great Alcinous,
May Zeus, the thundering husband of Hera, bring it about that
I return home and see my day of return.
Thus, even there I shall pray to you as a god
for all the days of my life. For you, dear child, saved my life.

Jason says that Medea's kindness saved not him but the whole expedition, and for this she will earn the thanks of the gods.[51] Odysseus, on the other hand, acknowledges that Nausicaa saved him and for this reason he will look upon her as a god. The alteration of the model calls attention to the difference between the archaic and the Hellenistic

[50] Cf. Hunter 1989:*ad* 975.
[51] Jason will repeat this line of thinking at 3.1122–27.

heroes: Odysseus' admiration and praise are directed outward toward Nausicaa, while Jason's panegyric, though expressed to Medea, emanates from his high opinion of himself, his crew, and his expedition. In short, Odysseus sees Nausicaa's assistance as the act *of a god;* Jason solipsistically treats Medea's assistance as an act *for the gods.*

In this context Medea hands the drug over to Jason, completely charmed by his beauty and words. She also instructs him in its use.[52] The instructions (3.1029–51) recall those given by Circe to Odysseus to prepare him for his underworld experience (*Od.* 10.516–40, 11.23–50),[53] and it is at this point that the Circean side of Medea begins to surpass the Nausicaan—once Medea, after finishing her instructions, loses all sense of shame (3.1068, cited above).

The Agreement

Now able to speak her mind more directly, Medea asks Jason to remember her:

> Μνώεο δ᾽, ἤν ἄρα δή ποθ᾽ ὑπότροπος οἴκαδ᾽ ἵκηαι,
> οὔνομα Μηδείης· ὡς δ᾽ αὖτ᾽ ἐγὼ ἀμφὶς ἐόντος
> μνήσομαι[.]

(3.1069–71)

> Remember, if ever you make it back home,
> the name of Medea, and so I shall remember you
> when you are far away.

She repeats this request following Jason's reply, this time with a threat:

> ἀλλ᾽ οἷον τύνη μὲν ἐμεῦ, ὅτ᾽ Ἰωλκὸν ἵκηαι,
> μνώεο, σεῖο δ᾽ ἐγὼ καὶ ἐμῶν ἀέκητι τοκήων
> μνήσομαι. Ἔλθοι δ᾽ ἧμιν ἀπόπροθεν ἠέ τις ὄσσα
> ἠέ τις ἄγγελος ὄρνις, ὅτ᾽ ἐκλελάθοιο ἐμεῖο·
> ἢ αὐτήν με ταχεῖαι ὑπὲρ πόντοιο φέροιεν
> ἐνθένδ᾽ εἰς Ἰαωλκὸν ἀναρπάξασαι ἄελλαι,
> ὄφρα σ᾽ ἐν ὀφθαλμοῖσιν ἐλεγχείας προφέρουσα
> μνήσω ἐμῇ ἰότητι πεφυγμένον. Αἴθε γὰρ εἴην
> ἀπροφάτως τότε σοῖσιν ἐφέστιος ἐν μεγάροισιν.

(3.1109–17)

---

[52] On the significance of the drug, see Clark 1968.

[53] As has been observed; see Vian and Delage 1980:141 *ad* 1029; Paduano and Fusillo 1986:*ad* 1026–62; Hunter 1989:*ad* 1029–51.

Make sure that you remember me when you return to
Iolcus, and I shall remember you, despite my
parents. But I hope that a rumor might come to me from afar
or some bird carrying a message, should you forget about me;
or better, that raging storm winds carry me in person
over the sea from here to Iolcus
so that I might reproach you face to face
and remind you that you escaped thanks to me. If only I might show up
unexpectedly at that time before the hearth in your palace.

The desire to be remembered is modeled on Nausicaa's similar request
of Odysseus:

Χαῖρε, ξεῖν', ἵνα καί ποτ' ἐὼν ἐν πατρίδι γαίῃ
μνήσῃ ἐμεῦ, ὅτι μοι πρώτῃ ζωάγρι' ὀφέλλεις.

(*Od.* 8.461–62)

Farewell, dear guest, and may you remember me once you are in
    your native land,
and that you owe me first the thanks for saving your life.

Nausicaa never acted in a way that compromised her shame, interior or
exterior, and her integrity remains intact. Medea, on the other hand, no
longer has any shame to lose; she has indeed given her soul to Jason
together with the drug (3.1015–16). Thus, if Jason forgets her and her
benefaction, she will have sacrificed herself—her soul, her self-esteem,
her standing in her family and community—for nothing.

In response to her first request to be remembered, Jason, like Odysseus, swears that he will not forget his helper's benefaction (cf. *Od.*
6.464–68, quoted above):

Καὶ λίην οὐ νύκτας ὀίομαι οὐδέ ποτ' ἦμαρ·
σεῦ ἐπιλήσεσθαι, προφυγὼν μόρον, εἰ ἐτεόν γε
φεύξομαι ἀσκηθὴς ἐς Ἀχαιίδα μηδέ τιν' ἄλλον
Αἰήτης προβάλῃσι κακώτερον ἄμμιν ἄεθλον.

(3.1079–82)

I believe full well that I shall never forget you, day or
night, if, escaping death, I actually
make it back to Greece unharmed and Aeëtes does not
impose another contest upon me even worse than this one.

Familiar with the subsequent history of this love story, the reader
must wince at the irony of hearing Odysseus' words in Jason's mouth.

Nonetheless, Jason would seem to be sincere, since, as the poet tells us, moved by Medea's tears he too finds himself, temporarily at least, in the grip of love (3.1077–78).[54] He concludes this speech with a wish that Aeëtes might become reconciled to him and enter into a formal friendship, just as Minos did with Theseus (1100–1101), and thus hints at marriage. Medea immediately seizes upon this point and, in making an important contrast between the Greek and Colchian worlds, she unwittingly characterizes both Jason and herself accurately:

'Ελλάδι που τάδε καλά, συνημοσύνας ἀλεγύνειν·
Αἰήτης δ᾽ οὐ τοῖος ἐν ἀνδράσιν οἷον ἔειπας
Μίνω Πασιφάης πόσιν ἔμμεναι, οὐδ᾽ Ἀριάδνῃ
ἰσοῦμαι. Τῶ μή τι φιλοξενίην ἀγόρευε[.]

(3.1105–08)

I suppose this is considered proper behavior in Greece: to honor
   contracts.
But Aeëtes is not like Minos, the husband of Pasiphaë,
as you describe him, nor am I like
Ariadne. So don't speak of formal friendship.

From her limited perspective—she does not know the whole story of Theseus' love for Ariadne—Greeks may make and keep contracts among themselves; Aeëtes does not.[55] More significantly, she immediately grasps the import of Jason's wish: he speaks of making formal contracts with foreign peoples. Moreover, he is even about to offer her a deal: if she comes to Greece, he will marry her and love her until they die (3.1120–30). Medea replies by saying that she is no Ariadne. On the surface, her statement merely acknowledges that she will not be allowed to sail away with Jason by Aeëtes, as Minos was said to have allowed Ariadne to do with Theseus. The reader knows, however, that Ariadne, abandoned by Theseus, had to endure her fate passively; Medea will not allow Jason to abandon her both within and beyond the compass of the poem—that is, without a struggle. Medea is no Ariadne.

Following Jason's offer of marriage, Apollonius summarizes the situation succinctly and effectively:

---

[54] Vian and Delage 1980:36–37 gives a positive reading of Jason's proposal and overall an upbeat interpretation of Jason's "héroïsme et humanité" (32–35); Vian approaches Jason's character similarly, though from a different angle, elsewhere (see 1963, 1978).

[55] As Hunter points out (1989:ad 1100–101), the situation that Jason faces with Aeëtes is the reversal of the experience Odysseus had with Alcinous, who wishes to have the Ithacan as his son-in-law before he even knows who he is.

Ὣς φάτο· τῇ δ' ἔντοσθε κατείβετο θυμὸς ἀκουῇ,
ἔμπης δ' ἔργ' ἀίδηλα κατερρίγησεν ἰδέσθαι.
Σχετλίη, οὐ μὲν δηρὸν ἀπαρνήσεσθαι ἔμελλεν
Ἑλλάδα ναιετάειν· ὣς γὰρ τόδε μήδετο Ἥρη,
ὄφρα κακὸν Πελίῃ ἱερὴν ἐς Ἰωλκὸν ἵκηται
Αἰαίη Μήδεια, λιποῦσ' ἄ(πο) πατρίδα γαῖαν.

(3.1131–36)

Thus he spoke, and her soul drowned in his words.
Nonetheless she shuddered at the thought of the unexpected that
    was yet to come.
Poor woman, she was not going to refuse to live in Greece
for long. For this was Hera's plan:
that, leaving her fatherland, Aeaean Medea
come to holy Iolcus to be the death of Pelias.

While Medea swoons at the offer of a life together with Jason, she is also overcome with anxiety over the possible ramifications of her actions.[56] These lines thus provide a transition between books 3 and 4. In book 3 we have seen the effect that Eros has on the unconquered maiden; in book 4, Apollonius will study the effect that fear exerts on the witch (a topic that lies beyond the scope of this paper). Medea, Apollonius tells us, will make it to Greece so that Hera can have her vengeance on Pelias.

Jason has the last word in this scene and in the cluster of allusions to Odysseus' encounter with Nausicaa:

Ὥρη ἀποβλώσκειν, μὴ πρὶν φάος ἠελίοιο
δύῃ ὑποφθάμενον καί τις τὰ ἕκαστα νοήσῃ
ὀθνείων· αὖτις δ' ἀβολήσομεν ἐνθάδ' ἰόντες.

(3.1143–45)

It's time to move along. I fear the gradual approach of
sunset and that some outsider might learn of all our plans.
We shall come back here to meet again.

In the Odyssey, it was Nausicaa who worried about being seen with a stranger by the locals (6.273–96).[57] A clever reversal once again reveals just how different the two situations are. In the place of a young girl's concern for her honor, Apollonius sets the hero's fear of compromising his contest. This meeting is after all Jason's real contest: charming the

---

[56] When we last see Medea in this episode, she is in the same ambiguous state; cf. 3.1149–62.
[57] Cf. Hunter 1989:ad 1143–45.

unconquered maiden. After his victory, he returns to his comrades joyously (3.1148); Medea retreats to her room in a state of confusion (1149–62).

The Mephistophelian Nausicaa

Book 3 ends with the successful completion of Jason's heroic contest.[58] Twenty-four hours elapse between the gift of the drug and the contest. During that time, Telamon and Aethalides fetch the dragon's teeth and Jason performs the rites described by Medea. Aeëtes' arming scene, followed by Jason's, suggests that a duel between Aeëtes and Jason will ensue. Moreover, imitations of Iliadic passages throughout the event give Jason's actions an archaic and larger-than-life coloration:[59] Medea's power has temporarily made Jason a hero comparable to the heroes of old, particularly Heracles, as a passing comment regarding the might of Aeëtes implies:

> τὸ μὲν οὔ κέ τις ἄλλος ὑπέστη
> ἀνδρῶν ἡρώων, ὅτε κάλλιπον Ἡρακλῆα
> τῆλε παρέξ, ὅ κεν οἷος ἐναντίβιον πτολέμιξε.

(3.1232–34)

Not any other among the heroes
would have resisted him [sc. Aeëtes] ever since they left Heracles
far behind. He alone would have fought him face to face in battle.

Jason proceeds to yoke the bulls, sow the dragon teeth, and destroy the earthborn offspring.[60] Hera's plan and Eros' intervention have been successful. Jason ultimately secures, as Heracles in the course of the epic will do in North Africa (4.1432–49), a golden object that hangs in a tree guarded by a serpent.[61] Although scholars in recent times have correctly observed that Jason falls short of an Achilles or an Odysseus

---

[58] Although, as Vian and Delage 1980:3 correctly notes, the conclusion of the book puts the spotlight on Jason's ἄεθλος, its execution is largely anticlimactic; just as Medea foresaw in her dream, the contest was going to prove to be very easy (3.624). Such a treatment of what was, in most accounts, the central contest of the expedition (as in the *Naupactica*, frs. 4–5 Davies, and Pindar *Pyth.* 4.220–41) was more than likely unique in its day.

[59] See Hunter 1989:*ad* 1278–407.

[60] That the warriors should be called "earthborn," γηγενέες (3.499 and *passim*), calls to mind the Γηγενέες that were sent by Hera against Heracles on the island of Cyzicus (cf. 1.989–1011).

[61] See Feeney 1987.

with whom he is implicitly compared throughout the poem, we must nevertheless keep in mind that like Heracles, he succeeds. At issue is no longer who the hero of the *Argonautica* is—that much is clear—but rather how this hero operates. And Medea plays a crucial role in the evaluation of Jason's brand of heroism and indeed of heroism in general.

In his first encounter with Medea, Jason prayed that Aeëtes might become reconciled to him and enter into a formal friendship, just as Minos was said to have done with Theseus (3.1100–101). To this Medea replies: "In Hellas, I suppose, it is considered appropriate behavior to honor contracts" (συνημοσύνας, 3.1105). Jason responds by making a promise of marriage, which he reiterates at 4.92–98 and 190–205. As Apollonius had Jason expressly state at Pagasae, the best among them is the one who can handle quarrels and agreements (συνθεσίαι) among foreigners. Medea's consenting to meet with Jason and give him the drug and necessary instructions is called an agreement (συνθεσία, 3.821). Medea refers to Jason's assent to marry her and bring her back to Greece as an agreement (συνθεσίαι, 4.390, 1042; see also Alcinous' agreement to allow Medea to stay with Jason on condition that they were married, 4.1176). Moreover, Jason's bargain with Apsyrtus, Medea's brother, to keep the fleece but hand Medea over to a local king for judgment is likewise called an agreement (συνθεσίαι, 4.340, 378, 404, 437, 453). Thus, Jason's success is due not only to his ability to settle quarrels, a prominent feature of book 1, but especially to his skill at forging agreements, as is evident in books 3 and 4.[62]

Apollonius presents Jason in Colchis as a transmogrified Odysseus who makes his way back home aided by a surrogate Nausicaa. When Odysseus landed on Phaeacia, he was in sore need of help. His divine protector, Athena, intervened to have Nausicaa meet and take an interest in him. She provided instruction as to how to approach her parents, Alcinous and Arete, and this enabled Odysseus to secure safe passage home. Much like—or rather more than—Odysseus, Jason needs help. In fact, the parallels between these two heroes continue beyond book 3 during Jason's return to Iolcus: like Odysseus he too encounters Circe on Aeaea; sails past the Sirens, Scylla, Charybdis, the Planctae, the cattle of the sun; and spends time on the island of the Phaeacians, where he meets Alcinous and Arete.[63] Yet a crucial difference exists between

[62] On book 1, see Clauss 1993:79–85, 198–210. Hunter 1993:63–64 briefly touches on the theme of agreements and their betrayal.

[63] On the relationship between the *Argonautica* and the *Odyssey*, see Meuli 1921; Dufner 1988.

the two heroes: Odysseus forgoes marriage with Nausicaa in order to return to Penelope; Jason continues to need Medea's help, if he is to return home with the Golden Fleece. Medea, then, although presented in such as way as to recall Nausicaa, emerges as a more powerful and indispensable "helper-maiden."

Odysseus was renowned for his adaptability (he is typically described as "clever"—πολύτροπος and πολύμητις) and, although—unlike Jason—assisted at different times by various women and goddesses, nonetheless he possesses the strength and especially the cunning needed to succeed on his own. Jason, on the other hand, is often called ἀμήχανος or ἀμηχαέων—"clueless"—and cannot possibly succeed without the help of others, divine and mortal. Nausicaa helped Odysseus because of her budding interest in him but backed off because he longed to return to his wife; Medea, in contrast, is forced to sail with the Argonauts out of fear, and, try as he may, both in Colchis and on the way back to Greece, Jason cannot shake the helper-maiden from Hell. In short, Apollonius has completely inverted the Odyssean pair of hero and helper-maiden by setting a resourceful (πολυφάρμακος) Nausicaa opposite a helpless (ἀμήχανος) Odysseus.

In the opening of the epic Apollonius described Jason as a man of the people (δημόθεν, 1.7). Despite his moment of glory, Jason is no Heracles, with whom he is implicitly compared in the poem, but is, as a man of the people, all too ordinary.[64] In essence, he is a good-looking young man who attracts women, young (Hypsipyle and Medea) and old (Hera in disguise and Iphias, the aged priestess of Artemis); and, in addition to settling quarrels, he has a knack for making agreements among foreigners. Once the Argonauts lose Heracles, Jason and his men are on their own. Their only avenue of success is to enlist the aid of a helper who can turn a weak and helpless Jason into an invincible Heracles, even if only for a few hours. Jason is the best among the Argonauts precisely because he is the only one physically attractive and diplomatically skillful enough to make a deal with a Mephistophelian Nausicaa. But such deals are soon regretted. Just before their return to Iolcus, Medea reveals the full extent of her power when the Argonauts encounter the bronze man, Talus, on Crete, and Medea casts a spell on him from afar.[65] The poet intervenes with the following comment:

[64] See Clauss 1993:23–25.

[65] Paduano 1970–71 offers a fine analysis of this episode; for a more recent treatment from a different angle, see Dickie 1990.

Ζεῦ πάτερ, ἦ μέγα δή μοι ἐνὶ φρεσὶ θάμβος ἄηται,
εἰ δὴ μὴ νούσοισι τυπῇσί τε μοῦνον ὄλεθρος
ἀντιάει, καὶ δή τις ἀπόπροθεν ἄμμε χαλέπτει.

(4.1673–75)

Father Zeus, my mind is greatly amazed at the thought that
death confronts us not only through disease and bloodshed,
but even harasses us from afar.

What began as an impossible mission for an ordinary man has in
the course of its success turned into a hideous nightmare. Being no
Heracles, Jason followed Odysseus' model in seeking the help of a
Nausicaa. Being no Odysseus, Jason needed someone more powerful
than Nausicaa, and, through the intercession of Hera, he finds, and
makes a deal with, a being who does not need a club or spear to destroy
her enemies; her malignant thoughts and fiendish prayers are sufficient
(4.1659–72). As Jason discovers, the cost of achieving mythical heroism
in a postmythic world is an irrevocable deal with a Hecatean power.
But what makes Medea's role both so fascinating and chilling is not
simply Apollonius' deft handling of the love theme in an epic context,
to which the preface of book 3 adverts, but rather the grim ramifications
of this love. As the daughter of Aeëtes and priestess of Hecate, Medea
possesses the ability to create a Heracles or destroy a man of bronze.
Yet she would not have lost her soul, together with her shame, if she
had never known such an all-consuming, self-destructive passion. In
the world of the *Argonautica*, Eros is a more destructive force than either
strength or cunning, and its destructiveness can work on behalf of or
even against the object of desire, as Jason will one day learn. Even more
unnerving, we learn that as a result of Aphrodite's bribe, Eros, a wanton
brat completely lacking in any scruples, now possesses and controls the
universe.

Heroes like Heracles are, according to Apollonius, as distant and hard
to envisage as the new moon (4.1477–80). For a culture so concerned
with realism, it must have been evident that the only way the deeds
of a Heracles or Achilles or Odysseus could ever be replicated was
through the help of some magical or divine power.[66] In the *Argonautica*
Medea plays this role. Seen from this angle, the choice of the Argonautic myth for an Alexandrian epic becomes all the more understandable. The traditional story, especially filtered through the Euripidean

[66] Cf. Valgiglio 1970:328.

lens,[67] gave Apollonius the opportunity to explore the impossibility—or even absurdity—of Heraclean heroism in a postmythic world in which anyone who attempts a heroic contest requires an invincible "helper maiden." In addition to this, in his choice of the Argonautic tale the poet has created an ironic setting for Jason's particular brand of "heroism," which entails the settling of quarrels and forging of agreements with foreigners. At the conclusion of the poem, the reader, left to supply the ending of the Argonautic story, must be aware that the best of the Argonauts will ultimately fail to settle the quarrel he has with Medea over the breaking of his old agreement with her and the forging of a new one with another foreign bride.

As I hope to have shown, Medea's role in the *Argonautica*, book 3 in particular, is that of helper-maiden, not hero. The nature and degree of her assistance to the hero is crucial: helping Jason as she must if he is to succeed, Medea underscores his difference from Odysseus, and hers from Nausicaa, and thus affects how we respond to the epic and its hero. Regarding the helper-maiden herself, Medea's difference from Nausicaa reveals yet another feature of her "otherness" that others in this vo<lume have observed and commented on in various ways. The Phaeacians, despite their physical separation from the Greek world, are—roughly speaking—within that world culturally: they play the same games, worship the same gods, and, when hospitable, honor their guests, like Nestor, Menelaus, and others, with banquets and gifts. Nausicaa's cultural imperatives are likewise the same as those one would expect of a young Greek woman: do the laundry, move about attended by other women, be hospitable, and don't cavort with foreign men. Medea, on the other hand, is portrayed by Apollonius as a manipulative, powerful, and threatening foreign woman who, among other things, does not do laundry. Thus, the systematic imitation of Nausicaa's words and experiences sets Medea's foreignness in relief by placing in the background the icon not merely of a Hellenic woman, but of one who was best known for her virtue and restraint. Thus, as the passionate and terrifying Medea does things that call Nausicaa to mind, the reader becomes more keenly aware of the "other" that is within Medea.

---

[67] On Medea's portrayal in the *Argonautica* as a "prequel" to Euripides' play, see, e.g., Dyck 1989; Knight 1991. Rosenmeyer 1992, in his penetrating analysis of decision making in the *Argonautica*, offers a strong argument for the influence of lyric deliberation both in Medea's monologues and throughout.

8

THE METAMORPHOSIS OF

OVID'S MEDEA

Carole E. Newlands

THE MEDEA of Ovid's *Metamorphoses* is the result not only of interaction with the rich tradition of Greek and to a lesser extent Roman literature, but also of interplay with the author's own earlier poetry—with Medea's letter to Jason in *Heroides* 12 and his lost tragedy *Medea*.[1] His treatment of Medea in *Metamorphoses* 7.7–424 represents his third and final attempt to elucidate this complex myth, and here, unlike his major Greek predecessors Euripides and Apollonius of Rhodes, who focus respectively on the mature Medea at Corinth and the young Medea at Colchis, he tells her story in a linear narrative that runs from her first meeting with Jason in Colchis to her final departure in disgrace from Athens.

In the opening essay of this volume, Graf demonstrates the disparate nature of the individual episodes of Medea's life. Ovid's treatment of Medea in the *Metamorphoses* exacerbates that disparity, for it is neither predictable nor uniform. For instance, while Ovid refers in only four lines to the events at Corinth, including the murder of Medea's children (7.394–97), he treats at length material largely suppressed by Euripides in which Medea's magical powers are central: Aeson's rejuvenation (159–293) and the murder of Pelias (297–349). Furthermore, Ovid's linear narrative lacks the psychological unity that Euripides and Apollonius in book 3 of his *Argonautica* achieve with their focus on one time and place. Instead, in the *Metamorphoses* Ovid passes abruptly from a sympathetic portrayal of Medea as love-sick maiden to a tragi-comic account of her career as accomplished *pharmaceutria* (witch) and murderess.[2] The Medea of *Metamorphoses* 7 is not a coherent, rounded

---

[1] On Ovid's lost tragedy see Nikolaidis 1985:383–87.

[2] Thus Anderson 1972:262 introduces the first story that clearly presents Medea to us as a witch: "The Medea we see here has very little to do with the love-torn girl we have watched earlier. Now she is an accomplished witch, delighting in her powers and

character. Her role as Jason's wife and the mother of his children is traditionally a powerful and complex one. But the young Medea who bares her soul at the start of Ovid's narrative becomes in her maturity a one-dimensional figure of evil that arouses neither sympathy nor revulsion.

In *Metamorphoses* 7 Ovid offers an implied contrast to his own procedure in *Heroides* 12, a poem that takes the form of a retrospective letter written by Medea to Jason on the eve of her slaughter of their children. The epistle skillfully combines the two temporal and spatial frameworks of Euripides and Apollonius—mother and girl, Corinth and Colchis. By giving Medea control over the narrative, Ovid is able to smooth over the inconsistencies in her character.[3] The few hints of Medea's dreadful powers in *Heroides* 12 do little to detract from her self-representation as an unjustly injured wife and lover, the victim of an ungrateful Jason.[4] The letter plays upon the notion of

---

rather amusing us by her skill. Except for a momentary conversation between Jason and Medea, we hear nothing of the passionate love which is the theme of 7.9–99, of Apollonius 3 and Euripides' tragedy; here we remain in the make-believe world of marvel created in 7.100ff." For a different view see Rosner-Siegel 1982:231–43. Rosner-Siegel divides the myth into three stages, each marked by a change of character and moral deterioration: Medea and Jason, Medea and Aeson, Medea and Pelias. His interpretation depends upon the hypothesis that Medea's failure to keep Jason's love explains the contrast between the youthful and the mature Medea, but the change in Ovid's Medea resists a single interpretation. Jason is virtually absent from the second half of the myth in which Medea appears as an autonomous figure of supernatural powers and moral questions remain implicit, not explicit.

[3] See the discussion of *Her.* 12 in Verducci 1985:66–81, who comments: "Medea's epistle to Jason is the only literary artifact preserved from antiquity in which the mature, demonic Medea of Euripides' play speaks with the same voice as the young, sympathetically engaging Medea of Apollonius Rhodes' *Argonautica*. What is most surprising in this diminutive fact of literary history is not that no other author attempted what Ovid did, but rather that Ovid, against so many odds, succeeded. The agency for the reconciliation of the youthful and the mature Medea accomplished in Ovid's *Heroides* 12 is memory . . ." (71). H. Jacobson 1974:109–23 likewise sees the poem as a unified composition, generated by the idea of presenting Medea's entire career from her point of view, but unlike Verducci, he finds the poem plagued by a dull uniformity. On the authenticity of *Her.* 12 as an Ovidian composition see Hinds 1993, esp. 9–21, on the epistle's relationship to *Met.* 7.

[4] Interestingly, H. Jacobson 1974 and Verducci 1985 have entirely different responses to Medea's letter. Jacobson sees Medea's letter as a futile attempt to cover up her true "contemptible personality" (119). While accepting that Medea does engage in some distortion, Verducci argues that "throughout *Heroides* 12 we sympathize with Medea, and must sympathize with her, because however distorted her memory of the past, she does not seem to lie. She is not hypocritical. She is not covert. All that she relates is so suffused with emotion that the narrative of past events is a secondary product of what she tells us she wishes, regrets, or suffers" (79–80).

Medea as the abandoned woman, a sympathetic elegiac type, and not as *pharmaceutria*.

The humanization of Medea undertaken by Apollonius and continued by Ovid in *Heroides* 12 does not square well, however, with the strong tradition concerning Medea's evil supernatural powers. By representing both disparate branches of the tradition in the *Metamorphoses*, Ovid thus shows that the tradition as a whole is problematic, for how in fact can the love-stricken Medea who cannot control her own nature be reconciled with the Medea who controls and even alters nature with her drugs? How does the trembling maiden become the murderess? Only, it seems, by suppressing one branch of the tradition, as Ovid has his Medea do in *Heroides* 12. By juxtaposing in the *Metamorphoses* the two Medeas of literary tradition, the sympathetic girl and the wicked sorceress, Ovid invites reflection on the difficulties and dangers involved in the rewriting of myth.

The dissonant structure of the full Medea story has one clear advantage, however. It removes some of the moral pressure from Medea herself. Questions concerning marriage, love, betrayal, and woman's marginal status tend to be engulfed by the horror of Medea's act of infanticide. Ovid's cardboard figure of evil does not invite reflection on such questions, nor does she arouse strong emotions. But Ovid does find a way to explore the urgent moral issues that are involved in the Medea story without the preexisting biases that result from her overdetermination as a figure of evil: the foreign enchantress and the bad mother. He surrounds the myth of Medea with other myths about women and marriage, allowing him to explore in different ways questions of female power that are elided in the Medea of *Metamorphoses* 7. Recurrent themes in the myths of Procne, Philomela, and Tereus (6.424–676), Scylla and Minos (8.1–151), Procris and Cephalus (7.694–862), and Boreas and Orythia (6.677–721) are filial duty, marriage, betrayal, the exercise of power through violent crime, and, connected to all these themes, the problem of a woman's physical and psychological displacement. There are other tales about marriage in the *Metamorphoses*, but the four I will proceed to discuss are so closely related to the myth of Medea—by means of their structural relationship to one another, the family connections between the protagonists, and their shared thematic concerns—that they can conveniently be called a "marriage group."[5]

[5] The recent study of *Met.* 2.549–835 by Keith 1992 argues for the importance of the structurally and thematically related sequence as a formative principle of Ovidian narrative. I obviously differ here from Otis 1966:chap. 6, who groups together the tales

Through these myths Ovid alerts us to the complex issues surrounding a woman who violently resists dispassionate scrutiny. In the *Metamorphoses* he offers not one Medea but different figures of a single type—a woman who is so driven by passion that she oversteps cultural conventions and acts independently of her traditional male guardian, whether father or husband.

This paper will explore two aspects of the narrative of Medea in *Metamorphoses* 7: first its bipartite structure and then its narrative relationship to the other "marriage tales" that form a cluster in books 6, 7, and 8. As Medea is removed from her family and known ways to a strange and unfamiliar land, her physical and psychological displacement is echoed in the dissonant structure of the Ovidian narrative. The human issues surrounding such displacement are most fully played out in the surrounding myths that form, as it were, a magnetic field of which the Medea of *Metamorphoses* 7 is the center.

Young Medea

In the first part of Ovid's narrative (7.1–158), the young Medea is presented as a sympathetic character. The account of her falling in love with Jason is conveyed in large part through her first dramatic soliloquy in the poem (11–71). Here her intimate feelings and inner moral struggle are revealed. Medea is introduced as a young girl caught

---

of Procne and Scylla with those of Byblis, Myrrha, and Ceyx and Alcyone because of their generic affiliations with tales of amatory pathos. Otis excludes the tale of Procris and Cephalus from this group because its martial context approximates it to epic; its content, however, a lament for a lost love, is a classic elegiac theme. Cf. Pöschl 1959 and below, n. 39. The Ceyx and Alcyone myth (*Met.* 11.410–78), which Otis regards as the "resolution" to the tales of amatory pathos, stands structurally and thematically apart from the others. Alcyone is not displaced by marriage and her husband does not betray her trust: his departure from home on a mission unrelated to his love for his wife motivates the tragedy. Conversely, Scylla's tale does belong: although she does not marry Minos, she *desires* marriage with him, and her actions and thoughts are directed to that end. I thus classify this myth not as a "digression," (cf. the generic classification of Pechillo 1990) but as an important variant in the marriage group. Larmour 1990 argues that parts of one story in this group are woven into another because Ovid could not engineer a metamorphosis, or wished to avoid repetition of a hackneyed theme, but Ovid shows himself often capable of transforming a well-known myth into something vital and engaging. G. Jacobsen 1984 points out the similarities between the Apollo-Daphne myth and the Tereus-Procne myth. In recalling these similarities, however, Ovid also demonstrates the difference between gods and humans: both are aroused by *amor* but only the latter suffer.

in an extremely difficult situation and unable to cope with the new emotions that threaten to overwhelm her:

> concipit interea validos Aeëtias ignes
> et luctata diu, postquam ratione furorem
> vincere non poterat, "frustra, Medea, repugnas:
> nescio quis deus obstat" ait.
>
> (9–12)[6]

> Meanwhile, Aeëtes' daughter harbours burning emotions;
> she struggled a long time to conquer her mad passion with reason,
> but finally said, "it's useless, Medea, to fight back:
> some god is against you."

Medea debates these rival claims of reason and passion, *ratio* and *furor*, in her soliloquy without any clear resolution; the chiastic arrangement of lines 19–20, *aliudque cupido, / mens aliud suadet* (your desire and your mind urge you in different directions), reflects the inner bind in which she finds herself.[7] Her debate hinges on the fact that she is in love with a foreigner who is, moreover, her father's enemy. To help Jason means to betray her country and her father. Medea makes no claim to special knowledge or powers that can help her cope with an overriding passion; rather her opening remark, *frustra, Medea, repugnas* (it's useless, Medea, to fight back; 11), draws attention to the theme reiterated throughout this passage: her helplessness in the face of a love that she recognizes is forbidden by duty to her father and her fatherland.

That same helplessness and vulnerability is projected into her imagined future with Jason. Thus, as she anticipates her fears of the dangerous voyage back to Greece, she consoles herself with the thought that her lover's embraces will drive away her fears: *nempe tenens, quod amo, gremioque in Iasonis haerens / per freta longa ferar: nihil illum amplexa verebor* (Of course I shall be carried far across the sea holding what I love / and clinging to Jason's lap: I shall be afraid of nothing when I clasp him to me, 66–67). This from a woman whose task it will be to keep Jason safe from terrors as great or greater than the Argonauts encountered on their voyage! Medea is sympathetically portrayed as she reveals her innermost thoughts. Her comment, *video meliora proboque, / deteriora*

---

[6] Text for the *Metamorphoses* is that of Anderson 1988; commentaries are those of Bömer 1976–77 and Anderson 1972. Translations are my own.

[7] At least, as Anderson 1972 points out in his note on line 11, Medea's attempt to resist her desires, fruitless though it may be, makes her far more sympathetic than the gods, who show no moral compunction when they fall in love.

sequor! (I see and approve the better course, / I follow the worse, 20–21), echoes Euripides' Medea, who at lines 1078–79 of the Greek play claims that she recognizes the rational course, but her anger will not let her take it. Euripides makes Medea speak these words before she kills her children; her failure to do what she clearly sees is reasonable and right is therefore appalling. But the transferal of these words to the youthful, untested Medea makes them disarming, a sign of her love rather than her barbarism.[8] Her irrational passion drives her to help, not to harm. Medea emerges in the first part of *Metamorphoses* 7 not as a being with supernatural powers that can control the universe, but as a struggling young girl who knows what is "right" but is impelled by her passion to act otherwise. In speaking to herself, Medea is also speaking directly to her readers, who are thus invited to engage in her personal dilemma.

In keeping with Medea's sympathetic portrayal as an innocent and vulnerable young woman, her powers of witchcraft are not mentioned in her soliloquy. Medea is a victim of passion, not the controller of powerful forces. When Medea sees Jason in a seemingly unplanned encounter in Hecate's grove, we are made to see how ironically slender are the inner claims of *pietasque pudorque* (filial duty and modesty, 72) when confronted with a powerful love.[9] Her moral collapse is swiftly conveyed in the appropriate imagery of fire: *et iam fortis erat, pulsusque resederat ardor, / cum videt Aesoniden, exstinctaque flamma reluxit* (And now she was resolute, and the fire of her passion, beaten down, had sunk low, / but when she sees Jason, the flame that had been extinguished flared anew; 76–77). Fire, the very element over which Medea will exercise control as she protects Jason from the fire-breathing bulls, is here applied to Medea's psychological state, over which she clearly has no control as she switches suddenly from propriety to passion.

In the *Argonautica*, Medea's representation as love-stricken young girl is combined with her superior knowledge of magic, for at her meeting place with Jason, Medea prescribes elaborate magical rituals for him to perform prior to his encounter with the brazen bulls (3.1029–51). In the *Metamorphoses* Ovid compresses the giving of the important

<hr/>

[8] On the importance of Eur. *Medea* 1078–79 for the philosophers see Dillon in this volume, and his conclusion: "Medea remains for the philosophers a dangerous, barbarian woman, occasionally to be pitied (Epictetus), but generally to be condemned as the paradigmatic example of a disordered soul" (p. 218).

[9] Ovid omits the role of the sister in persuading Medea to meet with Jason, thus focusing solely on Medea's inner feelings. Cf. Ap. Rhod. 3.664–741; Ovid *Her.* 12.62–66.

charms to Jason into two perfunctory, paratactic lines: *Creditus accepit cantatas protinus herbas / Edidicitque usum laetusque in tecta recessit* (He was believed and immediately received the charmed herbs / and learned their application and happily returned home, 98–99). Ovid emphasizes instead Medea's insistence upon an oath promising Jason's protection and marriage (89–98). She remains a sympathetic figure even in her capitulation to Jason and *amor*, for although she insists upon the oath she is frankly aware of the power of her own self-deception, which she is helpless to stop: *quid faciam, video, nec me ignorantia veri / decipiet, sed amor* (I see what I am doing, so love, not ignorance of the truth, / will ensnare me; 92–93). Medea's open recognition of her human weakness makes her an endearingly vulnerable character at this point of the story. Her implicit magical powers cannot help her control her agonized feelings, and thus they play little part in the initial presentation of her character.[10]

The human terms in which Medea's dilemma is presented are made more vivid by the absence of nearly all divine or supernatural elements in this first part of the narrative. Ovid makes no mention here of Medea's role as priestess of Hecate. Medea's meeting of Jason at the goddess's ancient altar, *ad antiquas Hecates Perseidos aras* (74), provides us with the sole mention of Hecate. Nothing is made here of Hecate's associations with magic and witchcraft, although the description of the altar's surroundings in a secluded, shady wood at line 75 could have led to some demonstration of the goddess's or Medea's supernatural powers. Instead, with the unusual patronymic *Hecates Perseidos* (Hecate, child of Perses), Ovid alludes obliquely to Medea's close family connections with Hecate. According to one well-known tradition Perses was Aeëtes' brother and the father of Hecate.[11] An adjective such as *triformis* (triple-formed) would have more clearly associated Hecate with the supernatural.[12] The epithet *Perseidos* instead brings to the fore the competing claims of family and love. Medea betrays her family at a place consecrated to a family member.[13]

---

[10] Thus Rosner-Siegel 1982:236 comments that "this lack of information and detail with regard to magic, and the use of the magical herbs by Jason and not by Medea, once again stress Medea's characterization so far in the narrative as a normal, mortal woman in love. Her witch-character remains, for the moment at least, only in the background."

[11] On the family connections between Hecate and Medea see Bömer 1976–77:ad 74.

[12] When Jason swears to be true to Medea, he invokes Hecate in this ritualistic context as *triformis* (goddess of three forms, 7.94).

[13] In *Her.* 12.67–70 Jason and Medea meet at the grove of Diana. Although Diana is one aspect of Hecate, the choice of the name of the goddess associated with virginity

Moreover, the gods play no apparent part in motivating the love affair. In the *Metamorphoses*, we hear nothing of the machinations of Aphrodite and Eros that in the *Argonautica* prompt Medea to fall in love.[14] Indeed, the gods show no interest in either Medea or Jason and are not mentioned as active participants in the drama.

Like Medea, Jason appears stripped of his associations with the divine. This is most notable on his first appearance in the poem, when Medea meets him at the altar of Hecate. Apollonius, drawing upon Nausicaa's encounter with Odysseus in book 6 of the *Odyssey* (229ff.), describes Jason's appearance as greatly enhanced by Hera (3. 919–26), a motif that Vergil powerfully reinforces in Dido's first encounter with an Aeneas gift-wrapped by Venus in book 1 of the *Aeneid* (587–93). But Ovid chooses to deny this convention. It is simply by chance, *casu* (84), not by divine agency, that Jason happens to look more handsome than usual when he meets Medea (84). Moreover, whereas Apollonius' Jason is made to look as if he were semidivine (3.919–27), and Vergil's Aeneas is compared to a god, *deo similis* (1.589), we are told that Ovid's Medea thinks that Jason looks like a god but that she is mad to make this assumption: *nec se mortalia demens/ora videre putat* (the crazed girl thinks she sees a face that is not mortal, 87–88). As we have seen, her love involves self-deception, as Medea herself realizes when she blames love, not ignorance, on her ensnarement (92–93, quoted above). Nonetheless she persists in it. Jason is not given any direct speech in this encounter; we see him through Medea's eyes, a factor that reinforces the obsessive and one-sided quality of her passion.

In its omission of divine agencies and its subjective focusing upon the heroine, the first half of the Medea narrative provides a psychological study of how human passion involves contradictory emotions and voluntary self-deception. Even in the following episode, when Jason meets the fire-breathing bulls (100–48), Medea's magical powers remain in the background; she is cold with fear lest Jason not succeed

---

is ironically appropriate to a scene in which Medea, described as *puellae simplicis* (naive girl, 89–90), is manipulated by Jason into believing he will be always faithful to her in marriage.

[14] In Apollonius' *Argonautica*, as soon as Jason enters Aeëtes' palace, Eros, bribed by his mother with the promise of a new ball, shoots an arrow straight into Medea's heart (3.275–84). Ovid's Medea opens her soliloquy with the remark *nescio quis deus obstat* (some god is against you, 12), an opening attempt to rationalize emotions that her subsequent speech reveals as purely internalized.

(134–38).[15] The climax to the quest for the Golden Fleece—the slaying of the dragon and the return voyage to Greece—is passed over in one long sentence (152–58), a sign that love and the exploration of feelings are more important in this narrative than actions and magical powers. The first half of the Medea story in *Metamorphoses* 7 does not prepare us for the following parts of the narrative, in which Medea, now Jason's expatriate wife, appears as an accomplished witch and scant attention is paid to her feelings or to motives for her deeds. This second section falls into four episodes: the myth of Aeson's rejuvenation (159–293), the myth of Pelias' murder (297–351), Medea's journey to Corinth and Athens (351–403), and the debacle with Theseus (404–24).

Medea the Witch

The first and longest of these episodes marks an immediate contrast to what has gone before. While admittedly a good deed, the rejuvenation of Aeson is presented in a way that emphasizes Medea's extraordinary powers and her remoteness from ordinary humans. Her reply to Jason's request that she give some of his life span to his father reveals little emotion for her spouse, who was the focus of her previous speeches:

> "quod" inquit
> "excidit ore tuo, coniunx, scelus? ergo ego cuiquam
> posse tuae videor spatium transcribere vitae?
> nec sinat hoc Hecate, nec tu petis aequa, sed isto,
> quod petis, experiar maius dare munus, Iason.
> arte mea soceri longum temptabimus aevum,
> non annis renovare tuis, modo diva triformis
> adiuvet et praesens ingentibus adnuat ausis."

(171–78)

> "What criminal words have fallen from your lips, husband?"
> she said. "Do I appear to have the power to transfer to anyone
> the span of your life? Hecate would not allow this; besides,
> you do not make a reasonable request. But I shall try
> to give a greater gift than you seek, Jason.
> We shall try to renew my father-in-law's long life

---

[15] There is nothing spine-chilling or horrific about Medea's recourse to a supplementary spell and secret arts (137–38). Vague and unspecified, her magical arts here function much as the superstitious muttering of a prayer in moments of crisis.

by my art, not by your years, provided the triple-formed
goddess helps and by her presence assents to my great experiments."

Medea speaks for the first time of her art (176) and of her close relationship through magic with Hecate, here called "triple-formed" (177).
Her refusal to take away years from Jason's life span seems not to be
motivated by love.[16] Having abandoned her own father, she is moved
first by Jason's filial piety (169–70). Her reply to him elaborates a second
motive, her ambition as witch: she desires to try something even greater,
maius ... munus (175). Medea wants to test her powers as witch. She
is like a heart surgeon who refuses to do a transplant but insists upon
the impossible, the rejuvenation of the heart itself.

In this narrative, speech is directed toward the proposal or description of magical ritual, not toward the individuation of feelings. Medea's
longest speech here is a ritualistic prayer to various deities to help
her with her magical spells (192–219). Attention is focused not upon
Medea's thoughts but upon her incantatory words and her superhuman actions. Here, where we see Medea for the first time practicing
her supernatural craft, Ovid plays up her new appearance as a witch.
The previously fearful maiden now shows no fear of the dark and silent
woods, and she reveals her distance from the world of ordinary mortals
by filling the nocturnal silences with ritualistic triple howlings, *ternisque
ululatibus* (190).[17] Ovid goes into tremendous detail—112 lines in all—in
describing the magical rituals involved in Aeson's rejuvenation (179–
287). The excess of detail is part of the humor of Ovid's portrayal of
Medea as witch. When he comes at last to her cauldron (264–84) and
begins to itemize at length its exotic and horrible ingredients—foreign
vegetables, snake skins, deer's liver, and crow's head among them—he
indicates that his patience is exhausted with the length and oddity of the
list by mockingly concluding that she added a thousand other nameless
items (275). This hyperbole establishes his segregation as narrator from
Medea. Whereas previously he provided close insight into Medea's
feelings, he now preserves an ironic distance tinged with humor. He
plays here with the idea of the witch and gives us no further insight into
Medea as a person. Through his focus on externals in this second part
of the narrative, Ovid pays scant attention to the motives for Medea's

---

[16] Cf. Rosner-Siegel 1982:238, who sees this speech as demonstrating Medea's "misguided love." But Medea says nothing of *amor* here.

[17] Cf. *Met.* 14.405 where, in a rather pat piece stereotyping the witch's craft, Circe
(Medea's aunt) summons Hecate *longis ... ululatibus* (with lengthy howlings).

deeds and permits no further glimpses into her inner thoughts. His Medea has become remote and fantastic.

Apart from the speech with which the myth of Aeson's rejuvenation opens, Medea has no further conversation or interaction with Jason. Although traditionally the mature Medea's relationship with Jason is of prime importance, in *Metamorphoses* 7 her relationship with him and his family members disappears from the story.[18] Apart from the brief reference to the infanticide at Corinth (394–97), we hear nothing further of Medea the wife and nothing at all of Medea the mother; she appears exclusively as a witch. Jason plays a very minor role in the entire second part. His speech requesting new life for Aeson is his only one (164–68), and thereafter he drops out of the narrative. Thus in the following story of the murder of Pelias (297–351), Ovid breaks with precedent by excluding Jason from any involvement in the deed. Although other sources, including *Heroides* 12, insist that in the murder of Pelias Medea was merely the instrument of Jason's desire for vengeance, no motivation is provided in the *Metamorphoses* for Medea's masterminding of Pelias' murder beyond the weak transitional disclaimer with which Ovid crosses from the story of rejuvenation to that of Pelias' murder, *neve doli cessent* (her purpose was to prevent any lack of treachery, 297).[19] Here then, since Jason plays no part in setting the crime in motion, Medea seemingly acts alone purely for malice's sake. She is detached from the family context that in Euripides' *Medea* plays a crucial role in articulating her moral dilemma.

Medea was moved by Jason's piety toward Aeson and the thought of her filial dereliction, but no such thoughts influence her contrivance of the murder of Pelias by his daughters. Although she is called *Aeëtias* for the second time in *Metamorphoses* 7 (326), a reminder of her disobedience to her father in a story in which she persuades others to violate their filial bonds,[20] the sensitivity with which the question of a daughter's duty is handled in the first part of the Medea myth is not found here. As Frécaut has pointed out, much of the story focuses on the gullibility of the

---

[18] The rejuvenated Aeson's feelings are perfunctorily described without reference to feelings of gratitude for Medea or indeed to her emotions (293–94).

[19] Cf. Apollod. 1.9.27; Hyg. *Fab.* 24; Ovid *Her.* 12.129–32.

[20] The patronymic *Aeëtias* (daughter of Aeëtes) was first used at the start of the myth to introduce Medea's passion, *concipit interea validos Aeetias ignes* (meanwhile Aeëtes' daughter harbors burning emotions, 9), and was obviously chosen with care: a reminder of the central obstacle to Medea's passion, her father Aeëtes, is placed in the middle of the two words describing her powerful feelings.

daughters of Pelias, not on the moral failings of Medea.[21] The question of filial *pietas* devolves upon them, not upon the one-dimensional Medea, and because of their grimly comic folly in trusting Medea, the story lacks a tragic dimension and moral complexity. The narrator's distance from Medea in this act of evil is articulated in the choice of epithets he applies to her. Here for the first time he calls her the "Colchian" (296, 301, 331, 348).[22] The repeated use of this epithet serves to associate Medea with the foreign and outlandish, to distance her from common human experience as she performs her act of malice. Here too for the first time she is called by a clear term of reproach, *venefica*, "poisoner" (316).[23] The choice of epithets for Medea in the myth of Pelias again serves to remove the reader from any close identification with her. She appears as a foreign barbarian, dissociated from any cultural or familial ties with Greece.

As a witch Medea has clearly undergone a form of metamorphosis. Like many of the metamorphosed characters in Ovid's *Metamorphoses* she has lost her human characteristics, but unlike them she has retained her human form. Her flights in her chariot drawn by winged serpents assimilate her to the divine rather than the human world. Like Ovidian divinities, she operates by a different code of behavior from human beings. Her opening soliloquy debating the rival claims of passion and reason calls upon the reader to judge her in moral terms. But we cannot do so in the second half of the myth, for she increasingly appears as airborne, a sign of her literal and metaphorical removal to another plane of existence. Euripides' *Medea* ends with Medea's removal from the scene of tragedy by an airborne chariot, which appears in the play for the first time as a device providing closure. The appearance of her chariot in Ovid's narrative of Aeson's rejuvenation (218–23), early in her tale, distances Medea physically and psychologically from the human world with its moral frames of reference. Her psychological metamorphosis is accompanied by her physical removal from the world of land-bound

---

[21] Frécaut 1989:67–74 centers much of his discussion of the myth on the daughters of Pelias rather than on Medea. For him, the story lacks a deep sense of tragedy, for the daughters are not individualized. Instead, the story has a moral that is directed at them, "rien n'est si dangereux qu'un ignorant ami" (nothing is as dangerous as an ignorant friend, 74).

[22] The first reference occurs in the last line of the brief transitional episode, the rewarding of Bacchus' nurses (294–96), that articulates the two contrasting tales of Aeson and Pelias.

[23] The term *venefica* is used, e.g., by Hypsipyle at *Her.* 6.19 to describe (and condemn) Medea.

humans. In the second half of the myth, Medea is no longer presented within the same ethical framework as at the beginning.

One-dimensional characters cannot sustain a reader's interest for long. Not surprisingly, Medea as witch becomes of decreasing importance in the text. In the myth of Pelias she shares the stage with Pelias' foolish daughters. In her subsequent aerial journey over places connected with obscure metamorphoses, she chiefly takes on the role of observer (351–401). Corinth, the focal point of so much suffering in Euripides' play, is simply one stopping point in a long, learned journey. Instead of building up to the climactic events at Corinth, Ovid's myth of Medea winds down with a zigzag course that serves, in large part, as a narrative device by which a number of other myths involving metamorphoses can be told (351–401).[24] The first thing Ovid has to say about Corinth, the city in which Medea's most dreadful deeds were performed, is that there was a tradition there that the first people sprang from magic mushrooms (392–93). Thus the normally climactic events there are subordinated to the etiological import of Medea's journey and are given no more than a quick summary that ascribes the minimum of motivation for Medea's slaughter of her children:

> sed postquam Colchis arsit nova nupta venenis
> flagrantemque domum regis mare vidit utrumque,
> sanguine natorum perfunditur impius ensis,
> ultaque se male mater Iasonis effugit arma.

> (394–97)

> But after the new bride burned from the Colchian poisons
> and the Isthmus saw the king's home blazing,
> the impious sword is drenched with children's blood,
> and the mother, evilly avenged, flees Jason's weapons .

The syntax here makes Medea directly responsible only for the final act, that of flight. Beyond the brief reference to *nova nupta* (the new bride, 394) and the oblique phrase *ultaque se male mater* (the mother evilly avenged, 397), any reference to Medea's motives, such as Jason's betrayal of Medea, is conspicuously absent. The four lines dealing with what is traditionally the emotional climax of the Medea myth thus became basically a further item of antiquarian lore. In the next episode, which tells of Medea's attempted poisoning of Theseus at Athens, no explanation at all is given for her malice toward the Greek hero (398–424).

---

[24] Thus Bömer 1976–77:*ad* 286.

Instead, the bulk of the narrative focuses on an etiological explanation for the poison, which, Ovid reports, originated from Cerberus' foam-flecked jaws when Hercules dragged him from the Underworld (406–19). At the emotional highpoints of Medea's story—her killing of her children and attempted killing of her stepson—antiquarian interests are instead preeminent and preclude attention to the thoughts, the motives, and the troubled desires that intimately concern Medea in the myth's first half.

The emphasis upon a fantastic journey at the end of the myth rather than at the beginning marks the disruption of the traditional order of the tale and is in keeping with Medea's own displacement. She has in a sense appropriated the Argonauts' role, but at the wrong time and the wrong place in the story. The journey of the Argonauts was a traditional and important precursor to the myth of Medea's love for Jason, but at the start of book 7 Ovid, intent on pursuing Medea's feelings, rather pointedly passes over their fabulous adventures with the brief words *multaque perpessi* (having endured many things, 5). In the second part of Ovid's treatment of the myth, Medea herself undertakes a journey to bizarre, outlandish places. The girl once fearful of traveling across the sea to Greece is now transformed into a witch fearlessly crisscrossing the Mediterranean world. The reversal of the expected order of the journey points to the reversal of Medea's role from vulnerable girl to fearless adventurer. The emphasis in the journey, however, falls not upon Medea but upon the narratives embedded in the peripatetic frame. Ovid's version moves outwards from almost exclusive focus upon Medea and her feelings to a diffuse set of stories in which Medea is chiefly important as an observer, while her infamous crimes are only cursorily described.[25]

By splitting the Medea of the *Metamorphoses* into two incompatible types, Ovid suggests the difficulties and inconsistencies involved in the rewriting of tradition. The complex workings of Medea's psyche are replaced by her complex ritualistic activities and journeys. The focus shifts dramatically from internal to external events. The themes of filial and conjugal obligations that are significantly raised in the first part of the myth are not pursued in the second half, where there is virtual silence on Medea's role as wife and mother. We are invited to view Medea from two dramatically opposed perspectives, the first closely involved with her character, the other far removed. Anderson notes that in Ovid's

[25] Schubert 1989 makes an interesting attempt to trace links between each of the stories of metamorphosis and that of Medea and Jason.

Metamorphoses a person's actual physical change is usually preceded by a psychological transformation, often due to the effects of love.[26] But Ovid does not explain the reason for Medea's transformation into a sorceress and semidivine, evil being, a metamorphosis that occurs well before the drastic events at Corinth. Only the disjunctive narrative mirrors the physical and psychic displacement of Medea herself.

Absent from the second half of Ovid's myth of Medea are the suffering and personal tragedy that mark the life of the Medea who is presented as primarily wife and mother. Ovid's Medea is a figure of supernatural power for whom conjugal and maternal obligations are minimal. She successfully escapes from her evil deeds. Thus the story of Medea in *Metamorphoses* 7 does not come to a definite conclusion. Rather, Medea disappears abruptly from the text as she flees from execution and Athens in one line (424), and the focus of the narrative subsequently shifts to events in that city.

The open-ended nature of Medea's story invites further reflection on issues that are elided or suppressed in Ovid's version. As a woman with supernatural powers, Medea is exceptional in her avoidance of physical punishment. Although ultimately she is excluded from human society, the Medea of *Metamorphoses* 7 eludes human judgment, for she is removed from the complex moral issues that traditionally sustain her story. Far different is the case for the women whose stories surround hers in books 6, 7, and 8. As mere mortals, their assertion of power inevitably leads to personal disaster and loss of identity. The tales that surround the myth of Medea examine the "missing link" in the Medea story, namely the intricate motivating factors that push a woman to violent crime and personal destruction.

Procne

The first of these interrelated stories is the myth of Procne, Philomela, and Tereus (6.424–676). Like Medea, Procne is guilty of infanticide. This crime, which is so cursorily treated in *Metamorphoses* 7, forms the climax of Procne's story. Here in book 6 Ovid explores at length the complex factors that drive to such an extraordinary act a woman who, unlike Medea, possesses no extraordinary powers and has no criminal background. At issue are Procne's marriage to a foreigner and his

[26] Anderson 1963.

betrayal of her conjugal trust. Like Medea, Procne marries a foreigner, the Thracian Tereus, but whereas Medea moves from a barbarian land to civilized Greece, Procne moves from civilized Greece to a barbarian land.[27] The results of her displacement, however, are equally disastrous. Ironically, although her marriage, unlike Medea's, is arranged by an approving father (426–28), paternal wisdom and approval do not lead to a happier conclusion.

Like Jason, Tereus betrays his wife for another woman. But he does so in an apparently irredeemable way: Philomela, the woman in question, is his sister-in-law; he rapes her; he mutilates her; he imprisons her in the woods; he then lies to his wife, saying that Philomela died on the voyage. Ovid condemns Tereus early on in the narrative with the exclamation, *pro superi, quantum mortalia pectora caecae / noctis habent!* (gods above, how much darkness human hearts contain; 472–73), and Tereus is labeled impious (482) for his violation of the kinship bonds requiring that he honor his father-in-law and sister-in-law as well as his wife. Tereus betrays not only the kinship bonds that should have made rape of his sister-in-law taboo but also the fundamental trust between husband and wife. The breaking of such trust is an important issue in the myth of Medea that Ovid virtually ignores; here in the myth of Procne he explores its disastrous consequences.

At first justice seems to be all on Procne's side, for Tereus is given no excuse for his actions. Unlike Medea, who marries Jason with blood on her hands and betrayal on her conscience, Procne starts her life with Tereus unblemished. But when Tereus violates the kinship ties that forge a link between Procne's new home and her old, Procne is in a sense displaced. Social categories are confused, as the raped Philomela recognizes when she accuses Tereus of upsetting their fixed family relations with one another: *omnia turbasti* (you have messed everything up, 537). With the fabric of her marriage rent asunder, Procne acts out her displacement in the most terrible fashion. A case of obvious right and wrong, with the husband irrefutably the guilty party, becomes a very different matter with Procne's slaying of her own child.

Unlike Euripides' Medea, Procne shows little compunction about using her son as the instrument of her vengeance. Ovid merely touches on Procne's dilemma between love for her son and love for her sister

---

[27] See the discussion of Joplin 1984, which explores the dynamic between civilized and barbarian in the myth. By marrying Procne, the barbarian Tereus has successfully "invaded" Athens and appropriated the princess for himself (31–33).

in a short speech in which Procne debates their rival claims (631–35). The collapsing of the social categories that stabilize marriage is demonstrated in her rejection of her maternal *pietas* (629) for a perversely redefined concept of conjugal duty: *scelus est pietas in coniuge Tereo* (for Tereus' wife, crime is a duty, 635). Conjugal duty here means killing one's offspring, an exercise of female power that defies the normative nurturing roles of wife and mother. Procne's paradoxical statement bluntly presents a moral dilemma to which there are no easy answers. The reciprocal obligations of conjugal *pietas* demand that a crime answer her husband's crime. But Procne the wronged wife thus becomes guilty of dreadful impiety.

Like Ovid's Medea, Procne undergoes a drastic metamorphosis of character. The sweet dutiful wife becomes the implacable murderess of her child. But we are at least given an explanation for Procne's empowerment in terms of Tereus' destruction of the marital and familial bonds that traditionally constrain her. On learning of her husband's betrayal, the deferential wife of the start of the myth, *blandita viro* (440), becomes a wild, barbaric woman, *terribilis Procne* (595). She is likened first to a Bacchante (590–600) and then to a tigress as she drags her own son to his death: *nec mora, traxit Ityn, veluti Gangetica cervae/lactentem fetum per silvas tigris opacas* (immediately she dragged Itys away, like a tigress by the Ganges dragging / through the impenetrable woods an unweaned fawn, 636–37). The simile is resonant of Tereus' rape of Philomela, in which he is described as a wolf (520–26) dragging to the dark woods a lamb or dove (527–30), a gentle, vulnerable young creature like the fawn to which Itys is now compared.[28] The comparison of Procne to a wild beast implicates Tereus in his wife's metamorphosis. Once the civilized accord and trust of her marriage is destroyed, she takes on a man's role and becomes like the barbarian Tereus in her vengeance. Indeed she surpasses Tereus in her impious cruelty, for whereas he mutilates his sister-in-law, she kills her own son. Moreover, whereas he cuts out Philomela's tongue, a savage enough act, Procne dismembers her son's body, cooks it, and serves it up to Tereus as a meal in a ghastly inversion of her wifely role. In this horrific meal, Tereus' confusion of social categories reaches its tragic

---

[28] Though Philomela is transformed like Procne into a resolute and savage avenging fury. After Procne has stabbed Itys to death, Philomela performs the additional and unnecessary act of cutting his throat (642–43) and even hurls the boy's head at Tereus (657–60). Her hair, sprinkled with blood (658), suggests her change of roles from victim to killer. My concern here, however, is with the connections between Medea and Procne.

climax. The ultimate similarity of Tereus, Philomela, and Procne in their use of violence is confirmed in their transformation into birds that perpetuate the cycle of violence in Tereus' endless pursuit, the women's endless flight (667–74).[29] As a swallow, with plumage perpetually stained with the marks of blood (669–70), Procne loses her complex human identity and becomes frozen in the ambiguous role of guilty victim.

Unlike Medea, Procne is at first a dutiful daughter. She marries the man her father chooses for her. But like Medea, she becomes metamorphosed into a powerful woman who operates outside all civilized bounds of restraint. The clear boundaries between male and female roles in society are blurred as Procne kills her son. Having no links with divinity, she is punished for her impious transgression. Although Procne's crime has a clear motivation, the motivation does not match the enormity of her vengeance. Ovid thus reveals the complex factors at work in an act of infanticide and our response to that act. Procne is an innocent wife who is unjustly injured, yet the sympathy that she gains is severely tested by the bloody meal she cooks for her husband. In Procne, Ovid offers a morally ambiguous picture of a woman who answers her betrayal by her husband with a violent crime.[30]

Through Procne Ovid explores the themes that are acutely compressed in his version of the Medea myth—betrayal, vengeance, and infanticide—and reveals their troubling complexities. As a version of the Euripidean Medea, Procne serves as an appropriate vehicle for exploring the difficult situation of the woman whose displacement from her homeland through marriage, followed by subsequent betrayal, leads to her repudiation of the traditional roles of womanhood. Her behavior is not complicated by the fact that she is semidivine with a criminal record. The moral ambiguities of her infanticide are instead explored in consistently human terms.

[29] Anderson 1972:ad 667 points out that the versions of Apollodorus and Hyginus make the metamorphosis of the women the result of the gods' intervention. Ovid, in contrast, by omitting the gods and by making the birds recall the crimes they have committed, suggests there is no escape here. Joplin 1984:45 takes this approach further and sees the metamorphosis as ironically meaning no further change: "in the final tableau all movement is frozen. Tereus will never catch the sisters, but neither will the women ever cease their flight. In such stasis, both order and conflict are preserved, but there is no hope of change."

[30] Joplin 1984:45: "The women, in yielding to violence, become just like the man who first moved against them. . . . And as literary tradition shows, the end of the story overtakes all that precedes it; the women are remembered as more violent than the man."

Scylla

Betrayal and the empowerment of women are the themes that likewise
preoccupy the myth of Scylla (8.1–151) and are explored through Scylla's
relationships with her father and with the man she loves, King Minos.
As in the myth of Procne, the moral balance in the story shifts, although
in a different direction. Initially unsympathetic, Scylla becomes less so
as troubling questions are raised about the responsibility of Minos to
the young woman who has granted him victory. When a woman helps
a man by morally culpable means, does he then have any responsibility for her fate? This question, which is ignored in Ovid's version of
the Medea myth and yet is crucial to any judgment of Jason's abandonment of Medea, is made of central importance in Ovid's treatment
of Scylla.

Through the dramatic soliloquy, the same medium he uses in the
myth of Medea, Ovid explores the theme of the woman in love with
an unsuitable foreigner (44–80). Like Medea, Scylla is young and in
love with a handsome warrior from abroad who is her father's enemy. Like Medea, she thinks she can secure marriage with the foreigner by betraying her father. The betrayal takes a similar form, the
theft of an important talisman—in this case not a Golden Fleece but
her father's purple lock of hair. Ovid's perspective on the lovelorn
maiden has undergone a metamorphosis, however. Unlike Medea,
Scylla is obsessed exclusively with her own feelings rather than at-
tending to the ethical issues at stake, as is clear from her opening
question: *"laeter" ait "doleamne geri lacrimabile bellum,/in dubio est"*
("it's uncertain," she said, "whether I should be happy or sad that
this lamentable war is going on"; 44–45). For her there is no moral
decision to be made. Instead of debating the rival claims of reason
and passion, of duty and love, as Medea did, she discusses with herself the best strategy for securing Minos as her husband. Her father
is a nuisance, an obstacle best out of the way: *di facerent, sine pa-
tre forem!* (if only the gods could make me fatherless, 72). Indeed,
she abandons all morality with her decision to take the law into her
own hands: *sibi quisque profecto/est deus* (anyway, everyone is her
own god, 72–73).[31]

---

[31] See Anderson 1972:*ad* 44–80 and on the psychological intricacies of Scylla's monologue; Larmour 1990:138–41 on the sexual resonances of Scylla's words and their similarity
in thought to those of Phaedra, Minos' daughter.

Scylla's callous maneuverings and casuistical arguments throw into sympathetic relief Medea's troubled moral sensibilities in the first part of *Metamorphoses* 7. Scylla's cutting of her father's lock of hair is presented as a violent deed that approximates parricide, for she claims that she is in effect offering Minos her father's head, not just his hair (93–94). The betrayal of her filial duty, an issue that is kept to the background in the Medea myth, here explicitly involves a criminal, impious act. With this desperate measure, Scylla finds a way of cutting through the cultural and political norms that deny her a voice in choosing her own husband. Unlike Medea, however, she has no ties with the divine world, and she lacks the encouragement of Minos. Her one powerful act renders her powerless. Swift retribution comes in the form of Minos' curse, which, in banishing her from land and sea, anticipates her final loss of human identity through metamorphosis into a bird. The physical and psychological isolation that finds tragic expression in her neurotic obsession with Minos becomes her permanent lot.

Like Procne and Medea, Scylla ends up as a woman displaced and devoid of kin. Also like them, she is not a passive victim. Abandoned by Minos, she harangues him with words and then tries physically to flee through the waters to him. As a displaced and abandoned woman, does she then command greater sympathy than in the first part of her story? I think so. Once again Ovid has engineered a metamorphosis of our perceptions of the female protagonist.

Medea's passion for Jason is reciprocated because Jason needs her help to secure the Golden Fleece. Minos in contrast recoils with horror from the lock of hair that Scylla offers him as a pledge of her love (92). Nonetheless he takes full military advantage of Scylla's betrayal and sacks her father's city. The second part of the Scylla myth suggests that Minos' high-minded rejection of Scylla is, in some ways, as morally questionable as Jason's exploitation of Medea. Here then Ovid explores another aspect traditionally important in the Medea myth, the betrayal of the woman to whom the beloved owes his success. As Graf argues, Apollonius builds his story of Jason, Medea, and her father upon a familiar Hellenistic model, the "Tarpeia-type," to which the story of Scylla also belongs.[32] In the second part of Ovid's tale of Scylla, however, we see the female protagonist from a different perspective, in the role of the deserted lover. She has undergone a typological metamorphosis

[32] See Graf in this volume, pp. 23–25. On the connections with Tarpeia see also Bömer 1976–77:13.

from a Tarpeia to an Ariadne, herself the daughter of Minos, whose story of abandonment directly follows Scylla's (8.169–82).[33]

When Scylla addresses Minos directly as he sails away from her, we are invited to view her with some sympathy. She is as frighteningly isolated as if, like Ariadne, she were abandoned on a desert island. She has nowhere to go to, nobody to turn to. Her homeland hates her; the neighboring lands fear her example (113–18). She is cast out, an orphan of the world, *exponimur orbae / terrarum* (117–18). She reveals at last a moral sensibility, for she openly admits her guilt and expresses repentance for her crime (125–30). Like Ariadne's, Scylla's speech is a mixture of special pleading and abuse. Indeed, several of Scylla's complaints against Minos—her abandonment by her lover, her social ostracism and geographical isolation, his ingratitude and inhumanity— are found in *Heroides* 10, the letter of Ariadne written supposedly as Theseus speeds away from the shore of Naxos.[34] However, Scylla emphasizes to a greater extent her beloved's obligation to her. In this important regard she comes closer to the Medea of *Heroides* 12, whose letter, a litany of reminders to Jason that his successes are due to her, leads to the expected conclusion that he should not abandon her. Scylla calls herself *meritorum auctor*, the agent of Minos' success (108), for, in her view, he owes his military conquest of Megara to her. He has exploited her action while expressing the utmost distaste for it. We are thus offered a different, more sympathetic perspective on Scylla when she appears in the role of abandoned heroine, who, through the speech that Ovid gives her, vents her feelings about Minos' departure without her (108–42).

Of course, like the deserted heroines' complaints in the *Heroides*, Scylla's words are not to be accepted uncritically. Her speech serves to show that her story is not a simple one of right and wrong, however. Ovid prepares the way for the substance of Scylla's complaints by hinting at the moral ambiguity of Minos' own position.[35] Refusing

---

[33] On the links of Ovid's Scylla with Catullus' and Ovid's own Ariadne and Vergil's Dido, see Anderson 1972:333.

[34] Each heroine addresses her departing beloved from the shore; each anguished speech begins with the despairing cry *quo fugis?* (*Her.* 10.34, *Met.* 8.108); each woman complains of her banishment from her father (*Her.* 10.65, *Met.* 8.115–16) and from all the world (*Her.* 10.93–98, *Met.* 8.113–18); each reminds her lover of the service she has performed on his behalf (*Her.* 10.99–110, *Met.* 8.108–13); and each accuses her hard-hearted lover of an inhuman birth (*Her.*10.131–32, *Met.* 8.131–33).

[35] Earlier versions of the Scylla myth make Minos drown Scylla as she clings to the prow (Apollod. 3.15.8) or drown herself (Hyg. *Fab.* 198), a possible misunderstanding, according to Anderson 1972:334, of Minos' throwing her into the sea. Ovid then has

to take the purple lock as a pledge of love from Scylla, Minos expresses his horror at the thought that such an abomination as this girl should touch Cretan soil:

> di te submoveant, o nostri infamia saecli,
> orbe suo, tellusque tibi pontusque negetur!
> certe ego non patiar Iovis incunabula, Creten,
> qui meus orbis est, tantum contingere monstrum.

(97–100)

> O infamy of our age, may the gods remove you
> from their world, and may earth and sea be refused you!
> Of course I shall not allow Jupiter's birthplace, Crete,
> which is my world, to touch such a monstrosity.

The climactic noun *monstrum* (100) used to describe Scylla lends irony to Minos' seemingly high-minded refusal to take her home, for Minos' home is famous for its family monsters—as Scylla will remind him with her taunting references to Pasiphae's perverse mating with a bull (131–37). Indeed, the next occurrence of the word *monstrum* refers to the Minotaur itself (156). The phrase with which Scylla describes herself, *meritorum auctor*, somewhat ironically recalls the description of the victorious Minos as *iustissimus auctor* (the excellent agent of justice, 101), for the traditional view of Minos as judge is counterbalanced by the reminder of the different tradition about Minos as king of perversions.[36] Minos' high-minded position can hardly be sustained by his own ugly history of family betrayal, of which we are amply reminded in the following story of the Minotaur (152–82). By letting Scylla speak her thoughts about what she perceives as her betrayal by Minos, Ovid opens

---

certainly removed the charge of murder from Minos. It is in his artistic interests, of course, to conclude the tale with a metamorphosis, one moreover of a female whose rejection of civilized norms is symbolized, as with Procne and Medea, in her departure from the earth. Rather than presenting Minos as a callous murderer, Ovid skillfully suggests the moral complexity of his rejection of Scylla. Cf. Anderson 1972:*ad* 101–3: "Ovid consistently retains our sympathy with Minos, who undertook a just war, treated Scylla justly, and now deals with the Megarians with just conditions."

[36] Minos lurks in a more unsavory role in the background of the preceding story of Procris and Cephalus. According to Apollod. 3.15.1 and Antoninus Liberalis *Met.* 41.4–5, Procris cured Minos of unusual sexual problems, in return for which he gave her a javelin. In Ovid's version Procris' loving husband Cephalus does not tell this story, telling only *quae patitur pudor* (what decency allows, 7.687), a hint of the less reputable material that is suppressed in his account. Note that Ovid refers to the donor of the javelin as *muneris auctor* (agent of the gift, 686). The phrase *auctor* is not used again until book 8, with reference there to Minos. See Anderson 1972:*ad* 7.687; Ahl 1985:204–11.

up to moral uncertainties a story of a rather conventional type, the girl who betrays her country for love. Like Medea, Scylla is both the betrayer of her father and the betrayed. We find here the same slippage of moral categories as in the myth of Procne. Ovid thus adds complexity to the theme of betrayal by woman and by man. Although Scylla betrays her father, moral perfection is by no means all on the side of Minos, who cannily takes advantage of her betrayal. In Ovid's hands the theme of betrayal, like that of infanticide in *Metamorphoses* 6, resists moral absolutes.

Lacking special powers and status, Scylla is a more open and potentially a more sympathetic vehicle than Medea for the exploration of the moral implications of betrayal. Presented at the end as a victim of her passion and naïveté rather than as a mere traitor, she is a forceful example of the woman condemned and ostracized for an impious crime for which society allows no extenuating circumstances. Her metamorphosis into a bird is a form of solution to her tragic displacement—at the expense of her human identity. Like Procne she ends her life as a bird hunted by a vengeful male relative, for her father is also transformed into a bird, the predatory sea eagle (145–47). Scylla's one powerful act condemns her to both perpetual victimization and perpetual guilt, for she becomes a bird that bears its name from the cutting of the fatal lock (150–51). Scylla is suspended in an endless cycle of pursuit and flight, without hope of forgiveness from her father or of respite. The marginalization of the woman who disobeys social norms and attempts to seize power for herself is here displayed in an extreme and unresolved form, with the cycle of paternal vengeance and filial rejection endlessly repeated.[37]

Procris

On the surface, the story of Procris and Cephalus, which concludes book 7, is of a very different type from the three I have discussed thus far.[38] The story is told from the male perspective, and it is a man, not a

[37] Anderson 1963:15 shows how Scylla's metamorphosis as *ciris*, literally "the cutting bird," is psychologically related to her desires as lover to plunge down into the Cretan camp (39–40) and to glide on wings to Minos to confess her ardor (51–52): "When her metamorphosis takes place, then, her bird-shape commemorates her love and the crime to which it led (150–51)."

[38] Otis 1966:176ff. discusses the story and its departure from Hellenistic sources; Anderson 1990 discusses its relationship to the version in *Ars Am.* 3.687ff.

woman, who has lost his object of desire.[39] In addition, this story tells of a marriage that results from a father's arrangement and the mutual love of a couple, as the narrator Cephalus is at pains to say: *pater hanc mihi iunxit Erechtheus, / hanc mihi iunxit amor* (her father Erechtheus united her with me, / love united her with me; 697–98). For once, the two necessary ingredients for a marriage come together. Scylla and Medea had *amor* but not the father's consent; Procne had the father's consent but we hear nothing of *amor*.

Like the marriages of Medea and Procne, however, the marriage of Procris and Cephalus is severely tested when Cephalus is abducted by the dawn goddess Aurora shortly after the wedding (700–713). Different versions of this story tell of a series of complications that result from this abduction, among them Procris' own sexual liaisons.[40] In his account of his married life, Cephalus, presumably respectful of his royal audience and protective of his wife's memory, tells only what modesty permits (687) and emphasizes his wife's chastity (734–36). The presence of Procris in the text is carefully controlled by Cephalus' words, through which she appears as the honorable object of his desire, not as the angry, sexually independent woman portrayed by other writers.

Cephalus' self-representation in his narrative is likewise carefully controlled. Although he betrayed Procris with Aurora, he argues that throughout his enforced abduction he remained faithful to Procris in his heart: *Procrin amabam: / pectore Procris erat, Procris mihi semper in ore* (I stayed in love with Procris: / Procris was in my heart, Procris was always on my lips; 707–8). Unlike the marriage of Jason and Medea, the marriage of Procris and Cephalus survives its first betrayal, the first assault upon the necessary trust between man and wife, for the couple are eventually reconciled. This first testing of their trust, however, leads to a second testing that proves fatal to Procris. After hunting in the woods, Cephalus calls in a sensually evocative manner upon a breeze, *aura*, to visit him. Procris' suspicions are aroused by the name *aura*, so resonant of *Aurora*. Like the other women discussed by Ovid in the "marriage tales," she decides to act for herself and find out the truth of her suspicions by spying upon him in the woods. But

---

[39] Pöschl 1959 likens Cephalus as narrator to the elegiac love poets, particularly Propertius and Catullus in their most deeply felt poems.

[40] According to Apollod. 3.15.1, Procris achieves an independence comparable to Medea's through her success at sexually ensnaring a royal male and concocting a magical potion, in this case a beneficial one used to cure Minos of ejaculating deadly serpents. See also Antoninus Liberalis *Met.* 41; Hyg. *Fab.* 89; Anderson 1972:*ad Met.* 7.687.

although previously she had hunted with Diana during her separation from Cephalus (746), as a wife she is extremely vulnerable when she leaves the home for the wilderness and crosses into the man's realm of action. The javelin she gives Cephalus when she abandons her hunting for a wife's role is the instrument of her death, for Cephalus kills her, thinking she is a wild beast hiding in the bushes. The resemblance in sound between *aura* (breeze) and *aurora* (dawn) implies that the first dislocation of their marriage has led tragically to its end. Cephalus catches Procris' final breath on his lips, *infelicem animam nostroque exhalat in ore* (she breathes out her unfortunate spirit upon my lips, 861), in a literal and unhappy rendition of Cephalus' obsessive murmurings of Procris' name in Aurora's presence, *Procris mihi semper in ore* (Procris was always on my lips, 708). Like Medea, Procris is the victim of sexual betrayal.

Despite its auspicious start and its survival of the first serious challenge to their marital trust, the marriage of Procris and Cephalus ends in tragic failure like the rest. The woman is again the victim of betrayal and misunderstanding, clearly so since the details of Procris' independence from Cephalus that dominate the other versions of this myth are here suppressed. *Amor* is evidently not enough. The marriage of Procris and Cephalus tragically founders upon the issue of trust. Procris' suspicions are false but not, given the couple's past history, baseless. The marriages of both Procne and of Medea collapse when the trust between husband and wife is broken, just as Scylla's imagined relationship with Minos is destroyed when he refuses her pledge of trust in him. And once again, a woman's independent act is self-destructive.

The story of Procris and Cephalus has an important function within the group of tales that surround the myth of Medea in that it offers a thorough investigation of inequality between the male and the female experience of love. Unlike the other marriage tales, it is told from the man's perspective. It shows that the man as well as the woman can be cast in the role of the lover deserted by his beloved as well as the role of the murderer (no matter how inadvertent) of close kin. But unlike Procne, Medea, and Scylla, whose desertion or betrayal leads to their ostracism and ultimate loss of human identity, Cephalus does not destroy his life or halt his career in any way because of his slaying of his wife, and he tells his tragic story while on a diplomatic mission that turns out successfully.

The nature of that mission is important to our interpretation of his narrative. Cephalus is asking King Aeacus and the inhabitants of

Aegina for military help against his enemy, King Minos. According to Apollodorus and Antoninus Liberalis, Minos was one of Procris' lovers in Cephalus' absence.[41] Ahl has persuasively argued that Ovid's Cephalus cannily suppresses the salacious details about his wife's relationship with Minos because of his diplomatic need to recruit from his audience military help against Minos.[42] If so, Cephalus' story is shaped not just by his heartbreak and feelings for Procris but by his political needs. While offering a pessimistic view of the course of true love, his story forms a contrast with the surrounding "marriage tales," for Cephalus does not undergo any metamorphosis through sorrow for his wife. His grief remains a private matter that does not impinge upon the public realm, and he is not ostracized for killing his wife. By living on to tell his story and by thus assuming the role of narrator, Cephalus stands in sharp contrast to the marginalized, lovelorn women whose independent feelings or actions redound disastrously upon them. Cephalus' violent act has caused him sorrow but has in no way destroyed him. Cephalus continues to live and to thrive after Procris' death; he is not in any way displaced. The difference between his fate as injured lover and that of Procne, Medea, Scylla, and his own wife Procris emphasizes the tragic difference between men and women not only in social standing but also in the experience of love.

In *Ars Amatoria* Ovid observes that women are by nature more easily deranged than men.[43] His treatment of deranged women in the *Metamorphoses* provides a different, sustained view of women as the prisoners of social conventions that fail to protect them, at the same time as these women are denied legitimate means of expressing their desires and feelings. Their violent acts are a product of the very culture that attempts to prevent such acts. The story of Procris and Cephalus therefore invites reflection upon the social inequities that make women Medeas, the victims of their own tragic and temporary empowerment.

Orythia

The final tale of this group that I wish to examine, that of Boreas and Orythia (6.675–721), likewise describes the experience of love and

---

[41] Cf. n. 36 above.

[42] See Ahl 1985:204–11. Such a view modifies that of Pöschl 1959, who sees Cephalus as a sufferer in love like Propertius.

[43] *Ars Am.* 1.269–350.

courtship largely from a male perspective. Although generally regarded as a lighthearted appendage to the myth of Procne, Philomela, and Tereus, it takes a comically subversive look at the major themes that are concentrated in the "marriage tales": the power of the father, the rituals of courtship, conjugal trust, and female victimization. We are invited to read the myth of Boreas and Orythia in relation to the other marriage tales in books 6, 7, and 8 through the explicit connections Ovid makes between this story and that of Procris and Cephalus as well as that of Procne. Orythia's father succeeded Procne's father to the throne (6.675–80); Orythia's sister is Procris, as we are reminded in both tales (6.681–83, 7.694–97). The marriages of the two sisters, however, run an entirely different course from the start. Cephalus' marriage has the approval of Procris' father; but fearing all foreign suitors after Procne's tragic experience, he rejects Boreas' suit for Orythia. The god therefore forcefully abducts Orythia, but instead of abandoning her, as happens with most divine rapes, he makes her wife and mother, *coniunx* and *genetrix* (6.711–12). The formality of these terms suggests the legality of their arrangement. Together Boreas and Orythia raise two fine sons who become a credit to their parents as Argonautic heroes. Unlike Itys, Procne and Tereus' son, these children grow into manhood. We are told, moreover, that they resemble both parents (713), a crucial point, for it is Itys' too close resemblance of his father that impels Procne to murder him (621–22).[44] This then is the only marriage in this cluster of tales that takes a normative course, and yet it does so by dispensing with all the civilized formalities involved in cementing male and female relationships.

Like Cephalus, the male god Boreas is basically in charge of his own story and offers his own perspective on the rituals of courtship. Unlike most of the other gods of Ovid's mythical world, Boreas has attempted to observe the formal etiquette of courtship; with eloquent pleas he has approached the father, not just the girl, before finally resorting to rape. Ovid gives Boreas a long speech in which the god justifies his resort to violence on the grounds that his prayers to Orythia's father and blandishments have gone unheeded (6.687–701).[45] His problem lies not with Orythia, whose opinion is never made known and who apparently is never consulted, but rather with Orythia's father, who categorically

[44] See Anderson 1972:237 on the sources and Ovid's treatment of this tale.

[45] Anderson 1972:*ad* 690–701 comments on the rhetorical skill and wit of Boreas' speech, which he delivers in the role of *exclusus amator*. Although he claims his proper sphere is *vis* (physical force) not speech (*Met.* 6.689–90), he is comically made very articulate here.

fears and rejects all Northerners (682). Boreas' speech is a sort of comic paraclausithyron in which Boreas plays the role of *exclusus amator,* the excluded lover. But unlike the unhappy lover of elegiac poetry, Boreas has the divine power to achieve his goal. The god decides to cut through the red tape of courtship and marriage proposals; he will simply make Erechtheus his father-in-law, not beg him to be one (700–701). His defiance of cultural conventions at the start of the relationship, rather than at its end, leads surprisingly in this case to a stable marriage.

The father's role is here undercut. In the other stories I have considered, the father is a source of familiar if ineffective values, displaced from which the female suffers tragically. Aeëtes and Nisus seemingly know nothing of their daughters' illicit passions; Orythia's father alone tries actively to oppose the foreign suitor. Nonetheless, he too fails to prevent his daughter marrying a man not of his choosing. Yet in this case his failure ironically results in the children that a father naturally hopes for in a daughter's marriage. The civil protocol of oaths and promises by which fathers hope to sanctify marriage and protect their daughters is here rejected in favor of violent action—with socially normative results! Boreas, in his role of Northern Jason, proves the father's opposition not only ineffective but misguided. He subverts the rituals of courtship, oaths, promises, and patriarchal power that are the usual substance of the institution of marriage. In his comically inflated speech Boreas spells out here what the other tales imply: passion and force rule in human affairs as in divine ones. He gives humorous voice to what the other myths have shown, the fragility of cultural conventions in the face of the unpredictability of human experience and the strength of human passion. Carefully constructed social institutions and hierarchies are all subject to flux and metamorphosis.

Boreas succeeds, however, not just because Orythia's father is ineffective but because he does not have a Medea to oppose him. Indeed, Orythia is the antitype of Medea. Unlike Medea, Scylla, Procne, and Procris, she has no voice in this story and takes no independent action. Her passivity ensures her survival, whereas the women who protest male power are socially ostracized, destroyed, or metamorphosed. If power in a woman is generally dangerous and destructive, then it is easy to see why Orythia survives. She does not threaten or subvert male authority, as do Procne, Medea, and Scylla. From the point of view of Boreas, she is the perfect wife—a silent woman.

Seen in contrast to Orythia, Medea, whose myth directly follows, appears highly vocal. Her inner debate in the first half of the myth

is replaced in the second half by her incantatory spells, her *carmina*.
Indeed, Medea's incantatory spells serve as the female counterpart of
Boreas' physical power. The special powers Boreas gains through force,
vi tristia nubila pello,/vi freta concutio nodosaque robora verto (by force I
drive away the storm clouds, / by force I whip up the seas and overturn
knotted oaks; 6.690–91), are achieved by Medea through her verbal
charms: *stantia concutio cantu freta, nubila pello/nubilaque induco* (I whip
up the calm seas, I drive away the clouds / and I enshroud the sky
with clouds; 7.200–201). Her incantation corresponds to his physical
force in its power to uproot oaks (6.691, 7.204–5) and to agitate the
spirits of the dead, the *manes* (6.699, 7.206). Medea reveals speech as the
characteristic source of female power. Yet, as *carmina* her incantations
are connected with poetry, which in the ancient world is primarily a male
activity. The female appropriation of *carmina* is threatening to social
order. Thus whereas Boreas' power secures him domestic harmony,
Medea's power sets her apart from human society and relationships.[46]
Like the story of Procris and Cephalus, the story of Boreas and Orythia
illustrates the difference between the male and female experience of
love and power.

In the other stories of the "marriage group," too, speech is an important but dangerous aspect of female power. Tereus fears Philomela's
speech, so he rips out her tongue. She continues to express herself ver-
bally only by weaving her tale into a tapestry that will inflame her sister
Procne to madness. This, like Medea's spells, is called a *carmen* (6.582),
and Procne unrolls the horrific story (*evolvit*), like an ancient scroll.[47]
Words are also deceptive. Scylla and Medea both talk themselves into
pursuing their mad passion; Procris tragically misunderstands the song

[46] Wise 1982:21 argues that "the relation of language to the magician's powers of
metamorphosis connects Medea's incantations with poetic activity." As Ovid emphasizes
the destructive aspects of Medea's transforming, magical powers, he shows his awareness
of the destructive power of both types of *carmen*. See O'Higgins in this volume, pp. 103–
26, on Medea's function as a kind of Muse in Pindar *Pyth.* 4. O'Higgins notes that
our perspective on Pindar's Medea alters in the course of this poem. But unlike in the
Metamorphoses, Medea is presented first as a divinely inspired singer and subsequently
as a human and fallible victim of Jason's and Aphrodite's superior arts.

[47] Joplin 1984:53, who interprets Philomela's weaving as a sign of female resistance to
male attempts at silencing woman's voice, asks us to celebrate "not Philomela the victim
or Philomela waving Itys' bloody head at Tereus" but rather the woman who in the act
of weaving uncovers her voice's potential "to transform revenge (violence) into resistance
(peace)." Yet unfortunately what we remember in this story is the effect of that weaving
upon Procne and its incitement to violence, not peace. Cf. the remarks of Joplin, n. 30
above.

to *aura* that Cephalus sings to the breeze.[48] The dangerous power of words, their frequent slippage in meaning, reflects back upon Ovid's procedure in the myth of Medea whereby he lays bare the inconsistencies between the two parts of the tradition that he himself rewrote in *Heroides* 12 and, presumably, his own lost *Medea*.

The Fractured Woman

In Ovid's rewriting of the myth of Medea, the inconsistencies between the figure of Medea as girl and as witch are particularly sharp. Indeed, Ovid plays up the difference between the two figures. Who then is his Medea? Ovid offers us not one figure but refracted images that vary according to the different perspectives from which the reader is invited to survey them. Although the cause for Medea's sudden change is nowhere developed, the stories of Procne, Procris, and Scylla provide us with different standpoints from which we can recognize how complex are the motivations and consequences involved in the power struggles between men and women. Medea, Procne, Procris, and Scylla all provide broken, refracted images of one complex type, the displaced woman who suffers because of the loss or lack of a husband's or lover's affection and trust and who actively seeks redress. But only Medea is removed from human experience through divine and magical connections. In the stories that surround the Medea myth, Ovid investigates in more consistently human terms the social and moral ambiguities that involve the love-torn woman who chooses to speak and act independently.

Ovid then stands in relation to tradition much like a cubist painter who fragments his subject into disparate parts. Otis sees the *Metamorphoses* in terms of large sections of similar themes enclosed by framing devices.[49] Departing somewhat from this image, I suggest that like a cubist painter, Ovid wants to dispose of the frame. Rejecting organic form in favor of a certain degree of thematic fragmentation and dislocation, Ovid offers us not one canonical Medea but many perspectives on the central idea of the powerful woman.

In the *Metamorphoses* Ovid adds complexity to the story of Medea by juxtaposing it with stories that are simultaneously similar and different.

---

[48] Ahl 1985:206–7 points out that Cephalus admits at *Met.* 7.821–23 that his words were open to misconstruction.

[49] See above, n. 5.

Like Medea's rejuvenating brew, which has different effects depending on the situation in which it is used, myths are elusive, shifting bodies of knowledge that offer partial truths in their particular context. By articulating Ovid's myth of Medea with the myths of Procne, Scylla, Procris, and Orythia, Ovid uses his awareness of the mutability of myth and tradition to good effect by offering us varying studies of the female as victim and criminal. Her shifting representations in the marriage group call attention to the variety of human experience and the elusiveness of moral and social categories. Ovid thus typically offers no single moral judgment. This complex of stories does clearly display the difference between the female and the male experience of love, however, and it thereby leads to some disturbing implications. The violent man rarely suffers from his acts of violence; indeed, like Boreas, he may benefit from it. The violent woman, however, is ostracized and condemned. Medea is a byword for the unnatural mother. Ovid's marriage group of tales illustrates how society both denies a woman power and rejects her when she uses it; at the same time these tales illustrate how fragile social conventions are and how ineffective they are to either protect or restrain a woman.

By presenting us with two very different Medeas, who cannot be reconciled except, perhaps, by stepping outside the boundaries of the myth to other similar tales, Ovid reworks the story of Medea into an open-ended form that offers divergent perspectives on the problems of marriage, betrayal, and power. Comedy is juxtaposed with tragedy, and overall Ovid offers compassionate insight into a vilified type of woman. There is however no resolution to this story of sexual and social differences; significantly Medea does not die but simply disappears from Ovid's text. If judgments are to be made, the onus ultimately falls upon the reader, for Ovid, I believe, would have concurred with the remark of a very different writer, Jane Austen, who concludes *Northanger Abbey:* "I leave it to be settled by whomsoever it may concern, whether the tendency of this work be altogether to recommend parental tyranny, or reward filial disobedience."

PART III

UNDER PHILOSOPHICAL INVESTIGATION

9

MEDEA AMONG THE PHILOSOPHERS

John M. Dillon

THE "ARGUMENT from the poets," that is, the tendency to buttress one's arguments by adducing characters or situations from the great store of Greek mythology, as portrayed by Homer, Hesiod, or any of the lyric or tragic poets, is deeply ingrained in the psyche of educated Greeks. Among philosophers this habit is just as ingrained as with everyone else. Even Plato, who had officially little love for poets and their tales, as a literary artist cannot avoid allowing his characters, including Socrates himself, to make frequent appeals to the poets to buttress all sorts of points they are making, serious and otherwise.[1] Aristotle, too, has frequent recourse to this source of exempla and illustration.[2]

The Stoics in turn, it seems, observed this time-honored practice. The philosopher Chrysippus, in particular, was notorious for the copiousness with which he employed quotations from the poets to support his philosophical positions.[3] As regards one such usage of his we are

---

[1] E.g., even in the *Republic*, where Homer is very much under attack, we find him appealed to at 5.468 as an authority for giving special honor to the most valiant among the youth, referring to *Il.* 7.321, where it is said that Ajax "was rewarded with the long cut of the chine." Cf. also *Phd.* 65b (ref. to Epicharmus and possibly others); *Symp.* 119a (ref. to Euripides *Hipp.* 612).

[2] E.g., *Met.* 1009b28 and *De An.* 404a30 (a rather loose reference to Homer, which does not occur in the text available to us); *Met.* 1076a4 (ref. to *Il.* 2.204); *EN* 2.9.1109a31 (ref. to *Od.* 12.219—advice of Circe to Odysseus, wrongly attributed to Calypso); *Pol.* 1.1.252b8 (ref. to Eur. *IA* 1400); *Pol.* 1.1252b23 (ref. to *Od.*9.114–15).

[3] Diogenes Laertius tells us (7.180) that Chrysippus "padded out his writings by arguing repeatedly on the same subject, setting down anything that occurred to him, making many corrections and citing numerous authorities; so much so that in one of his works he copied out nearly the whole of Euripides' *Medea*, and someone who had taken up the volume, being asked what he was reading, replied, 'The *Medea* of Chrysippus.'" Galen speaks scornfully at *Hipp. et Plat.* 3.3.25, p. 190, 22ff. De Lacy of Chrysippus filling up his work *On the Soul* with quotations not only from Homer and Hesiod but also from "Orpheus, Empedocles, Tyrtaeus, Stesichorus, Euripides, and other poets"; and Philodemus, in his work *On Piety,* chap. 13 (= *SVF* 1.1.539) talks of Chrysippus "in the second book of his work *On Gods* attempting to reconcile the views attributed to Orpheus

particularly well-informed by Galen, who subjects it to extended criticism in the course of his vast work *On the Doctrines of Hippocrates and
Plato*. Galen is here concerned to defend the Platonic doctrine that the
human soul possesses an irrational part or element as well as a rational
one; he attacks the Stoics, and Chrysippus in particular, for denying this
and maintaining that the soul is unitary and that the ruling element, or
ἡγεμονικόν, is involved in every decision taken and acted on by the
human being.[4]

To reinforce his position, Chrysippus turned, as was his wont, to
the poets—first to Homer, but then, it seems, to Euripides and in
particular to *Medea*. The passage from Homer is the famous one from
book 20 of the *Odyssey* (17–21) in which Odysseus rebukes his heart
(κραδίη), which constitutes an example of the rational element in the
soul quelling an irrational impulse. From the *Medea*, on the other hand,
Chrysippus chose the equally famous passage (1078–79) where Medea
acknowledges the subjugation of her reason to her passion (θυμός): "I
understand the evils I am going to do / But anger (θυμός) prevails over
my counsels." Galen[5] declares himself to be at a loss to comprehend how
Chrysippus felt able to make use of passages which seem so clearly to
refute his own doctrine, but in this he is being either somewhat obtuse
or somewhat disingenuous. I quote his remarks at *Hippocrates and
Plat*. 3.3.13ff.:

> Plato, I think, recalls these words [*sc.* those of Odysseus in *Od.* 20] most
> opportunely in the fourth book of the *Republic* [441 B.C.], but Chrysippus
> most inopportunely; and even less apposite is his quotation of the lines
> which Euripides had Medea speak, when in her soul, too, reason was
> contending with anger. She knew what an unholy and terrible thing
> she was doing, when she set out to kill her children, and therefore she
> hesitated and delayed and did not immediately carry out the act she had
> started to do. Then anger dragged her again to the children by force,
> like some disobedient horse that has overpowered the charioteer;[6] then
> reason in turn drew her back and led her away, then anger again exercised
> an opposite pull, and then again reason. Consequently, being repeatedly

and Musaeus, and those of Homer and Hesiod and Euripides and many others to his own
doctrines."

[4] For a good account of the Stoic doctrine of the soul, and of their theory of action,
see Rist 1969:chap. 14 and now Annas 1992:37–120.

[5] *Hipp. et Plat*.3.3.13–22, p. 188, 15ff. De Lacy. Cf. also 4.2.27, p. 244, 2ff. and 4.6.19–
27, p. 275, where he discusses Chrysippus' use of the passage again. For a most useful
discussion of Chrysippus' use of *Medea*, see Gill 1983:136–49.

[6] A reference to the myth of Plato *Phdr*. 246ff.

driven up and down by the two of them, when she has yielded to anger, at that time Euripides has her say: "I understand the evils I am about to do / but anger prevails over my counsels." Of course she knows the magnitude of the evils she is going to do, being instructed by reason; but she says that anger overpowers her reason, and therefore she is forcibly led by anger to the deed, quite the opposite of Odysseus, who checked his anger with reason.

Euripides has made Medea an example of barbarians and uneducated persons, in whom anger is stronger than reason; but among Greeks and educated people, such as Odysseus, as the poet presents him, reason prevails over anger. In many instances reason is so much stronger than the spirited part of the soul that a conflict never arises between them; the one rules, the other is ruled. This is the case with persons who have reached the ultimate goal of philosophy. In many other instances, however, anger is so much more powerful than reason that it rules and governs everywhere; this is seen in many barbarians, in children who are naturally inclined to anger, and in no few beasts and beastlike men.

There are times, on the other hand, when neither of the two is so much stronger that it immediately pulls the other its way, but they oppose each other and fight it out, and eventually one of them prevails—reason in Odysseus, anger in Medea—inasmuch as they are two parts of the soul, or, if not parts, certainly powers of some sort.

But Chrysippus, who holds that they are not parts of the soul, and that the soul has no irrational powers separate from reason, nevertheless does not hesitate to mention the lines spoken by Odysseus and Medea that clearly refute his doctrine. (tr. De Lacy, slightly altered)

Now Galen is here being rather silly, I fear. Obviously Chrysippus is not going to quote this passage of *Medea* if he thinks that it tells against his own position. On the contrary, he must have thought that it supported him. We do not unfortunately have Chrysippus' own words in this connection, but from what we know of his doctrine we can, I think, reconstruct his argument. His position was that any action of a rational being is the result of an impulse (ὁρμή), and this impulse is in turn the result of an assent (συγκατάθεσις) to an impression (φαντασία). The soul may be perverted in various ways by bad education or even by physical causes, but it is still the whole soul that decides, when the chips are down. For Chrysippus, impulses are in all cases decisions (κρίσεις)—often very bad decisions, but decisions nonetheless. His point is presumably that Medea, even though she may try to shift responsibility by blaming her θυμός, nevertheless makes a *decision*, and that is an act of her whole soul. Galen is refusing to recognize this.

Chrysippus' use of the passage is that followed later by Epictetus at the end of the first century A.D. He quotes Euripides at *Discourses* 1.28.7, where he is discussing the passion of anger and asserting that, just as it is impossible to assent to an impression that one does not believe to be true, so, in the domain of action, one cannot perform an act unless one believes it on the whole to be the best of various alternatives. Once again, it is worth quoting at some length:

> Well now, in the sphere of actions, what have we corresponding to the true and the false here in the sphere of perceptions? Duty and what is contrary to duty, the profitable and the unprofitable, that which is appropriate to me and that which is not appropriate to me, and whatever is similar to these.
>
> Cannot a man, then, think that something is profitable to him, and still not choose it?
>
> He cannot.
>
> How of her who says, "I understand the evils I am going to do, / but anger prevails over my counsels"?
>
> It is because the very gratification of her passion and the taking of vengeance on her husband she regards as more profitable than the saving of her children.
>
> Yes, but she is deceived.
>
> Show her clearly that she is deceived, and she will not do it; but so long as you do not show it, what else has she to follow but that which appears to her to be true?
>
> Nothing.
>
> Why, then, are you angry with her, because the poor woman has gone astray in the greatest matters, and has been transformed from a human being into a viper? Why do you not, if anything, rather pity her? As we pity the blind and the lame, why do we not pity those who have been made blind and lame in their governing faculties? (trans. Oldfather 1926–28, slightly emended)

We see Epictetus here, in his characteristic fashion, elaborating on the doctrine of Chrysippus on this question. Anger may be said loosely to overcome reason, but the human being cannot perform an action (πρᾶξις) in the proper sense, unless he or she has assented to it. And that is an act of the whole soul.

We can see, then, how *Medea* 1078–79 was employed to illustrate the Stoic doctrine on the soul. However, it is Galen's interpretation of the passage, not surprisingly, that prevailed among later Platonist philosophers. What we see, in a whole series of later Platonist texts, is this passage of *Medea* being trotted out, in company with one or more other Euripidean proof texts, to illustrate precisely the Platonic theory of the tripartite soul, and thus the possibility of an irrational element in the soul overcoming the reason.

We may start with the *Didaskalikos*, or *Handbook of Platonism*, of the rather shadowy author long known as Albinus, but to whom I prefer, with John Whittaker, to return his manuscript name of Alcinous.[7] In chapter 24 of his work (p. 177, 4ff. Hermann), a section on the parts of the soul, he introduces Medea as an exemplum to illustrate the existence of the θυμός as distinct from the reason (followed by Laius, from Euripides' lost *Chrysippus*, to illustrate the distinctness from reason of ἐπιθυμία, or desire): "One can see in the character of Medea the spirited element in conflict with reason: 'I know the evils I am going to do/ but anger prevails over my counsels.' And similarly in the case of Laius, when he abducted Chrysippus, we see desire struggling with reason; for he speaks as follows: 'Alas, alas, for mortals this is an evil sent from God/when one sees the good, but makes no use of it' " (Eur. fr. 841 Nauck).

The Latin commentator on Plato's *Timaeus*, Calcidius (fourth century A.D. or even later, but still essentially dependent on Middle Platonist sources), in chapter 183 of his work (p. 210, 5ff. Waszink) includes a long excursus on Fate, which arises out of his commentary on *Timaeus* 41. There he adduces the same two proof texts that Chrysippus is attested by Galen to have made use of, Homer *Od*. 20.17–18 and our *Medea* passage, to illustrate the different degrees to which θυμός may dominate or be dominated by reason. Clearly by now the fact that Chrysippus used these passages to buttress his argument for a unitary soul has been quite obscured (perhaps due to the efforts of Galen himself), and the proof texts retained to serve the opposite purpose.

Down to the end of antiquity, *Medea* 1078–79 goes on being employed in philosophical circles to serve various purposes, some relatively frivolous. We find it being used by Plutarch, in his essay *On Compliancy*, apropos writing recommendations for those that one knows one should not recommend. Lucian (*Apologia* 10) parodies it to excuse himself for taking a government job in Egypt, after he had written a slashing satire against taking employment in great men's houses—excusing himself, jokingly, by reason of his destitution: "But *poverty* prevailed over my counsels!"

---

[7] See Whittaker 1990. A translation of, and commentary on, this work by me has recently appeared from the Oxford University Press in the Clarendon Later Ancient Philosophy series (1994).

On a rather more serious level, we find it made use of in the second century by such varied figures as the rhetor Aelius Aristides (*Or.* 34, 50, p. 249, 14–15 Keil), the church father Clement of Alexandria, in his *Stromata* (2.15.63.3); and later, in the fourth to the sixth centuries, by Synesius, in his essay *On Kingship* (10, p. 22, 18–19 Terzaghi), and Hierocles, in his *Commentary on the Golden Verses of Pythagoras* (p. 32, 6–7 Köhler). The great Neoplatonic commentator Simplicius makes use of it three times in commenting on Epictetus (*Epict.* 1 p. 18, 50–51; 5, p. 30, 39–40; 6, p. 33, 22–23 Dübner), giving it a Platonist gloss, as opposed to that of Epictetus, and once in his *Commentary on Aristotle's Categories* (p. 237, 13–14 Kalbfleisch).[8] Somewhat later again, the passage (or more exactly, 1079–80) turns up in Stobaeus' *Anthology* (3.20.37, p. 547, 4–5 Hense), under the rubric "On Anger," as well as in the *Prolegomena to Plato* of the late commentator Elias (p. 10, 3–4 Westerink), and, for all I know, in the work of many Byzantine writers during the centuries that followed.

This passage was not, of course, the only part of Euripides' *Medea* to attract the attention of philosophers. We have, as noted above (n. 3), the tantalizing report in Diogenes Laertius' *Life of Chrysippus* that Chrysippus transcribed so much of the play in one of his works that it was derisively termed "the *Medea* of Chrysippus." What use he made of the rest of the play, however, we have no idea, although one might speculate. But we do find Epictetus elsewhere in his *Discourses*, under the rubric "How ought we to adjust our preconceptions to individual instances?" (2.17.19–22), making a more general reference to Medea as an excellent cautionary example of one who did not make this philosophic adjustment. Again, he deserves quoting at length:

> Why is it that when you want something it does not happen, and when you do not want it, it does happen? For this is the greatest indication of discontent and misery. I want something, and it does not happen; and what creature is more wretched than I? I do not want something, and it does happen; and what creature is more wretched than I?
>
> Medea, for example, because she could not endure this, came to the point of killing her children. In this respect at least hers was the act of a great spirit. For she had the proper conception of what it means for anyone's wishes not to come true. "Very well, then," says she,[9] "in these

---

[8] In this latter passage it is used to support a point about the ambiguity of meanings. When Medea says that she "knows" (μανθάνω) the evil she is going to do, she cannot mean this in the full (Platonic) sense, but only in a superficial sense. Otherwise she could not have acted against her knowledge of the good.

[9] Here, as Oldfather notes in the Loeb edition, Epictetus is loosely paraphrasing lines 790ff. of the play.

circumstances I shall take vengeance on the man who has wronged and insulted me. So how can this be accomplished, and what good will I get out of his being in such an evil plight?[10] I kill my children. But I shall be punishing myself also. Yet what do I care?"

This is the falling into error of a soul of great vigor. For she did not know where the power lies to do what we wish—that we cannot get this from outside ourselves, nor by disturbing and deranging things. Give up wanting to keep your husband, and nothing of what you want fails to happen. Give up wanting him to live with you at any cost. Give up wanting to remain in Corinth, and, in a word, give up wanting anything but what God wants. And who will prevent you, who will compel you? No one, any more than anyone prevents or compels Zeus."
(trans. Oldfather 1926–28, slightly emended)

This is splendidly futile advice to offer a character like Medea, but Epictetus is in no way deterred by that. She serves very well as an extreme exemplum for the point he wishes to make. Her attitude to life is the antithesis of that of the ideal Stoic sage, and we know what that drives her to do. He concedes the greatness of her nature (μεγαλοφυῶς κατά γε τοῦτο), but it is a nature that has undergone dreadful distortion—he speaks of her state of mind as ἔκπτωσις ψυχῆς μεγάλα νεῦρα ἐχούσης (the falling into error of a soul of great vigor)—and this increases her paradigmatic value. Her judgment may be wildly astray, but she still makes a judgment, and that involves an assent of her soul as a whole, not the overcoming of λογισμός (reasoning) by θυμός. This, too, must surely have been Chrysippus' point in adducing Medea as an example, even if Galen professes not to understand this.

What I hope is demonstrated by this rather brief survey are the interesting adventures of, in particular, the passage 1078–79 of *Medea* as a proof text in philosophical discussions of psychology, ethics, and the problem of free will and determinism down through later antiquity. That it should have had this history is all the more interesting because of the possibility that has been mooted in modern times:[11] that Euripides, in presenting Medea's dilemma in this form, and indeed in allowing

---

[10] I here transpose two sentences in the text, καὶ τί ὄφελος τοῦ κακῶς οὕτως δι-ακειμένου and πῶς οὖν γένηται, since the manuscript order seems quite illogical. Whether or not I am right, it is interesting that Epictetus, as an orthodox Chrysippean Stoic, represents Medea as making a *judgment* —no matter how misguided—about what is for her own greatest good, i.e., revenge on her husband.

[11] E.g., Snell 1948:125ff.; Dodds 1951:186f. Euripides allows characters to utter similar sentiments, it may be noted, also in frs. 220, 572, 840, and 841 Nauck (the last mentioned above, as quoted by Alcinous).

Phaedra to make a speech of similar import in *Hippolytus* (373–87), is posing a direct challenge to the extreme intellectualist theory (associated with the name of Socrates) that it is impossible to do wrong willingly. This notion has been widely dismissed,[12] but in view of both Euripides' well-attested interest in contemporary philosophical theories and the persistent gibes of comic poets about his association with Socrates,[13] I am unwilling to reject it absolutely. At any rate, ancient philosophers in later generations took up the challenge that they discerned being laid down here by Euripides—though it is only Simplicius, in fact, in the passage from the *Categories* commentary mentioned above (p. 216), who is recorded as addressing the dilemma directly. For our other authorities, it is used as a proof either (for the Stoics) that all voluntary actions are performed by the whole soul, or (for the Platonists) that there is an irrational part of the soul that militates against the reason. Medea remains for the philosophers a dangerous, barbarian woman, occasionally to be pitied (Epictetus), but generally to be condemned as the paradigmatic example of a disordered soul.

As for Euripides himself, he was plainly interested both in abnormal psychology and in the springs of action in general, but it is not my purpose in this essay to add further to the vast body of criticism of that great playwright.

---

[12] Not only that, but a prevalent opinion among Euripidean scholars, going back to Bergk 1884:3.512 n. 14 seems to be that 1056–80 is an actor's interpolation in *Medea* (though possibly introduced from another play or plays of Euripides). James Diggle, for instance, in his new OCT of Euripides, brackets the whole passage, and other scholars have proposed lesser excisions. If this were provable, it would add a nice touch of irony to the circumstance that 1078–79 took on such importance in later times, but I must say that it seems to me a rather extreme proposal. See on this subject the useful articles of Reeve 1972 (for deletion); Lloyd-Jones 1980:51–59 (delete just 1159–63); and Kovacs 1986, who gives a most lucid discussion of the evidence, as does Michelini 1989, who is in favor of retention. I am indebted to Judith Mossman for information on the current state of this controversy.

[13] Cf. Diog. Laert, 2.18, 22.

10

SERPENTS IN THE SOUL

A READING OF SENECA'S *MEDEA*

Martha C. Nussbaum

1

IMAGINE, FIRST, the ending, staging it in your mind as the audience for Seneca's recitation-dramas would have staged it: She appears on the steep slope of the palace roof. The man she loves stares up at her. He sees her looming over him (995), radiant and boiling, wrapped in the red light of her grandfather the Sun.[1] (She wrapped his helpless bride in a cloak that ate her flesh with snaking flames [818–19].) She will not die of this light. Fire is her patrimony, as snakes are her familiars. She calls down to him to lift his swollen eyes her way (1020)—knowing, perhaps, that never has her beauty appeared to greater advantage. He is witnessing a triumph. It is the triumph of love. And now bleeding, innocent limbs of children come hurtling through the air, the last "votive offering" (1020) of passion.

It is his passion too. For although the Chorus prefers to acquit him, describing him as "accustomed in fear, and with a reluctant right hand, to caress the breasts of an unbridled partner" (103–4), Jason knows, or should know, otherwise. Only a moment before, in a desperate attempt to save the last child, he appealed to her in the name of the desire that bound and binds them, insisting that his erotic life has been with her alone, and not with the virtuous person who died. Her reply acknowledges that they have indeed been intimate very recently—even while he was contracting marriage with a decorous virgin; even, in fact,

"Serpents in the Soul" is an abridged version of chap. 12 of Nussbaum 1994. That chapter contained a longer analysis of the implications of Stoic ethics and is to be read in conjunction with chap. 10 ("The Stoics on the Extirpation of the Passions"), where a fuller analysis of the Stoic theory of passions is presented.
[1] Medea's relation to the Sun is given much emphasis in the play: cf. 28–36, 207–10, 510–12, 570ff. For a good discussion of this, see Fyfe 1983:82.

while she was deploying the "whole tribe of snakes" (705) to get rid of this person. For Medea thinks it possible that she may even now be pregnant by him. She proposes a simple gynecological experiment to ascertain the facts, and to correct them: "If even now in my uterus (*matre*)[2] there lies concealed some safety deposit (*pignus*) from you, I shall examine the inside of my abdomen with a sword and draw it out on the iron" (1012–13). She is not suggesting that she might make a cut across her abdomen; she is too victorious for self-harm. No: enraged by the knowledge that he has been in her, she retaliates with the wish for a murderous vaginal penetration, one that will pierce where he pierced, cancel his penetration with one controlled and managed by her alone—one that will restore her to the health of self-sufficiency. "My kingdom has come back," she exults. "My stolen virginity has come back.... Oh festal day, oh wedding day" (984–86). Both of them have extended themselves out into the uncertain world. Both have valued undependable things. Now she stabs him in the body of his living child (cf. 550); he stabs her by placing in her a possible new child, a pledge of *erōs* (erotic love)—a pledge that can be redeemed only by violence. Neither preserves integrity; neither is free of pain; neither is free of evil.

And then, flying through the bright air, a chariot appears for her, drawn by two scaly snakes equipped with wings (1023–24). "This is the way I make my escape," she calls, taking the reins (1022). "A road in the heavens is open for me." Charioteer and serpents, they ascend. Eyes streaming, swollen, he looks after her, weeping for his wife, for his children, for all that he has loved and she has killed. Weeping, too, if he is that honest, for the murders they have done together, for the passion he felt and feels. "Go aloft through the deep spaces of heaven," he calls to her, for the last time. "And bear witness that where you travel there are no gods" (1026–27).

What does this awful nightmare have to do with us? Seneca's claim is that this story of murder and violation is our story—the story of every person who loves. Or rather, that no person who loves can safely guarantee that she, or he, will stop short of this story. The Aristotelian holds that we can have passionate love in our lives and still be people of virtue and appropriate action: that the virtuous person can be relied upon to love the right sort of person in the right way at the right time, in the right

---

[2] For the figure, see also Costa 1973; Miller 1917, Ahl 1986. The word picks up the literal use of *mater* at 1007: "Seek the beds of virgins, abandon mothers."

relation to other acts and obligations.[3] Medea's problem is not a problem of love per se, it is a problem of inappropriate, immoderate love. The virtuous person can avoid this problem. The Chorus of Euripides' *Medea*, which persistently treats their heroine as an abnormal being (*pace* Sourvinou-Inwood in this volume, Edd.), doomed to live out the fate belonging to an overly intense nature, subscribe to this comforting thought: "Excessive passions, when they come, bring neither good fame nor virtue to men. But if Aphrodite comes in the right way at the right time, there is no other god who is so delightful" (627–31). Seneca sternly tells us here that this distinction is empty. There is no erotic passion that reliably stops short of its own excess. That very way of caring about an external uncontrolled object yields uncontrol in the soul.

Again, the Aristotelian tells us that we can have love in our lives and still get rid of cruelty and murderous rage. Euripides' Chorus prays to Aphrodite not to stir up hostility and aggression, but to "honor beds without strife" (639–40). The Aristotelian virtuous person is mild, not prone to vindictiveness (*EN* 4.5, esp. 1126a1–3). Seneca's argument will tell us that this, too, is a hollow prayer. Given the nature of the beliefs that ground the passions, and given the contingencies of life, one can never safely guarantee that love will not give birth to murder. For the love may come to have an impediment; someone may assail or oppose or damage it. And then love itself—its own evaluative exaltation of its object—provides rage with its most exquisite fuel. *Veniet et vobis furor* (rage will come to you too).

Finally, the Aristotelian claims that you can have an acceptable amount of personal integrity inside a life of love. You can form passion-

[3] Aristotle provides Seneca not only with an opposing philosophical position but also with a view close to many of the intuitions of his audience concerning the role of emotions in the good life. Here I mean to describe a general Aristotelian position on love, analogous to Aristotle's explicit position on anger. That it is close to Aristotle's position concerning φιλία (friendship) that has an erotic component has been successfully shown by A. Price 1989. The Stoics clearly credited the Peripatetics with a general across-the-board position that emotions should be moderated, not extirpated (see esp. Sen. *Ira;* Cic. *Tusc.* 4). The closeness of the "Aristotelian" position to that of Euripides' Chorus confirms its popular credentials. For Greek Stoic views of *erōs*, see *SVF* 3.397–99, 650–53; the definitions contain an apparently rejected form of *erōs* (longing for bodily intercourse). Seneca's *On Marriage* (fragments in Haase 1893–95) similarly condemns all erotic passion, even toward one's spouse. Intercourse is grudgingly permitted for reproduction only. Musonius Rufus joins in the attack on passion, holding that pleasure should never be the goal of intercourse. But he paints a more favorable picture of marriage as a "partnership" (κοινωνία) and "living together" (συμβίωσις) in which man and woman "strive together and breathe together." He urges marriage on the philosopher. (See "On Intercourse," "On the End of Marriage," and "Is Marriage an Impediment to Philosophy?" in Hense 1905.)

ate attachments and still regard yourself as your own to govern, your selfhood as inviolate. Seneca will argue that this, too, is evasion. Love itself is a dangerous hole in the self, through which it is almost impossible that the world will not strike a painful and debilitating blow. The passionate life is a life of continued gaping openness to violation, a life in which pieces of the self are groping out into the world and pieces of the world are dangerously making their way into the insides of the self; it is a way of life appropriately described in the imagery of bodily violation, implosion, explosion; of sexual penetration and unwanted pregnancy.

This play explores these arguments and the connections among them. In so doing, it shows us the shape of the life of passion and its characteristic conception of the self, and, over against these, the structure of Stoic self-sufficiency, seen as the cure for such a life. It claims to be our story; this claim must be assessed in connection with the Stoic claim that the basic assessable action is not a movement in the outer world but a movement in the world of the heart, a movement of thought, of wish, of desire. The play claims, then, that none of us, if we love, can stop ourselves from the wish to kill—and that a wish to kill is itself a murder. The erotic soul of Plato's *Phaedrus*, inspired by desire for its beloved, ascends toward truth and knowledge, a winged chariot driven by a charioteer and drawn by two powerful horses. Passionate love creates a beautiful harmonious movement, as the noble character of the horse representing the soul's emotions forms a partnership with reason and gives reason new motivational and cognitive power.[4] Seneca's winged chariot (absent from Euripides, but prominently stressed in this play) reveals to us, he claims, the true nature of the erotic: the human agent is drawn along toward heat and fire by two scaly serpents, whose sinuous and ignoble movements mimic the movements of the two lovers' bodies in the grip of passion, whose silent murderous ferocity is emblematic of the murderous wish of passion itself.

Such arguments against Aristotelianism can be found in Stoic prose works as well; but they are worked out with particular power and

---

[4] Plato's *Phaedrus* is a work well known and much valued by Roman Stoics. At *Ep.* 24.6, Seneca points out that Cato, his paradigmatic Stoic hero, read Plato's *Phaedo* just before his death; and Griffin 1976: chap. 11 shows that Seneca, too, modeled his own death on the death of Socrates. This shows us that Seneca's relation to Plato was so deep and internal that the text became a way of expressing the most profound commitments of his life. For other Stoic or Stoic-related uses of the Platonic chariot and horses, see Plut. *Mor.* 446: Arius Didymus *Ecl.* 2.89.4–90.6; Posidonius frs. 31, 166; Philo *Legum Allegoriarum* 2.94, 3.118; Galen *Hipp. et Plat.*4.2, p. 244 De Lacy, 4.5.18, and cf. 3.3.15, 3.3.5–6.

vividness in the plot and the language of this tragedy. And the Stoics, unlike the other Hellenistic schools, have a high regard for tragedy, giving it cognitive importance,[5] arguing that it can frequently display the human significance of a philosophical argument more clearly than prose writing. Epictetus argues that among the literary forms tragedy is the one best suited to arguing against the passions. "For what else are tragedies but the sufferings of human beings who have been wonder-struck by external things, set down and displayed in the customary meter?" (*Discourses* 1.4.26). And again, "Look how tragedy comes about: when chance events befall fools" (2.26.31). Such poems can toughen our souls by showing in an unavoidable way the consequences of the life of external wonder. As it happens, Seneca's *Medea* provides a clear expression of the strongest and least circular of the Stoic arguments against passion.

2

She is justified: yet she does monstrous things. From the play's opening lines, this doubleness is stressed. Medea calls, first, on the gods of lawful marriage; on Juno Lucina, guardian of the marriage bed, protector of childbirth (1–2); and upon all the gods by whom Jason swore binding oaths to her. Then, "with ill-omened voice" (12), her anger invokes a darker group of deities: "chaos of endless night, kingdom of the world below, unsanctified spirits of the dead" (9–10). Last of all, with a cry in which the demand for justice is inseparable from the lust for revenge, she calls the Furies:

> Now, now be near, goddesses who avenge crime, your hair foul with writhing serpents, grasping the black torch in your bloody hands— be near—as once, dread spirits, you stood about my marriage bed. Bring death to this new wife, death to her father, to all the royal line. (13–18)

We cannot avoid feeling the justice of her anger. She calls the Furies because she has a right to call them. She has loved Jason long and

---

[5] This is true of Chrysippan Stoicism and its later continuers, especially Seneca and Epictetus. Posidonius, because of his belief that the soul has a separate irrational part, seems to have adopted a noncognitive view of the moral importance of poetry and music. See also the fragments of Diogenes of Babylon's *On Music* preserved in Philodemus' polemic (*SVF* 3.221–35). The evidence on Stoic views of poetry is assembled usefully in De Lacy 1948; see also Dillon in this volume.

loyally. She has risked for him; she has sacrificed home and family; she has even committed crimes. They have lived together for years; she has borne him legitimate children. And now he betrays his oaths, his lawful marriage, his wife, for the bed of a rich and well-connected younger woman. Well might the Furies bear a black and bloody torch to that marriage feast. It is, as she says, *fas*[6]—lawful and right—that she should call awful penalties down upon their union.

And yet we cannot help feeling, too, the foulness of this revenge, the awfulness, especially, of calling out powers of Hell against a more or less innocent woman, whose only crime was to agree to receive Jason's disloyal affections. The Furies, by themselves, evoke this double response. For as described they are legitimate avengers of a real guilt; yet they are also foul and hideous. They bring their blackness, their serpents, to the soul of the one who, with whatever justice, invokes them.[7] Later, as she invokes the whole tribe of serpents to give her poison to use against Creusa, Medea herself becomes similar to these Furies—as, hair loosed, neck arched and head darting, she calls once again upon Hecate (800–801).

This mingling of justification and horror is essential to Seneca's plot—indeed, to several of his plots. His heroines are not criminals to begin with; they are made criminals by love. His tragedies parade before us a series of loyal loving wives who are abandoned in middle age by opportunistic husbands—usually for a younger woman, sometimes for money, always with callous disregard for the wife's long years of service. The wife's intense, unabated love then produces an upheaval that leads to tragedy—usually through evil action by the wife against rival, or husband, or both. Deianira, Phaedra, Clytemnestra, Medea: by leading us again and again through variants on this same plot, obsessively reworked, Seneca forces us to see that it is the one who loves properly, loyally—the one who really understands what it is to value a commitment to an external object—who will be most derailed by a loss. It is precisely because these women genuinely care about that external item, stake their whole being on it, that they are driven mad by grief and anger. He shows us that a betrayal that comes from outside, though through no fault of the woman's own, can still produce evil in the woman's soul. And by dwelling on the plight of the aging wife, the collapse of a marriage of long standing, he reminds us that, the structure of erotic passion being as it is, such betrayals

---

[6] For an excellent treatment of the ambiguities of this speech, see Fyfe 1983.

[7] On the connection between Furies and moral darkness in Vergil, see Putnam 1990.

and such losses will frequently occur to people who have passion in their lives.

Seneca displays Medea as shrewd, strong, regal, honest. He links her in the choral lyrics with great explorers and heroes of the past— with Orpheus, Hercules, Meleager, and others. He gives her speeches expressing an accurate sense of the wrong done to her and a determination that her proud spirit will respond to calamity in an appropriate way. "Fortune can take my wealth, but not my soul" (176)—a statement that conjures up a whole tradition of Stoic heroism. She sees her murderous acts as appropriate, in some sense correct, responses to her loss: "Do it now, my soul—you must not lose your virtuous act in secrecy" (976–77, just before killing the children). And above all, he depicts her as one who understands how deeply her own virtue, her selfhood, is identified with externals—in such a way that, injured and invaded by fortune, she is not herself any longer. She can be made Medea again only by a revenge that removes the obstacle. "Medea," the Nurse calls to her as she suffers. "I shall become Medea," she answers (171). And when, rejecting all her previous crimes as petty, she conceives of a great deed to bear the power of her grief, she then can say, "Now I am Medea: my wits have grown through suffering" (910). In suffering she has understood what it means to lose what she wants; therefore she has understood what she herself is and stands for. At the end, throwing the murdered children down, she calls out to Jason, "Do you recognize [or acknowledge] your wife (*coniugem agnoscis tuam*)?" (1021). Several passages link her name alliteratively with other words; the list reveals a nature poised between greatness and monstrosity. We have *monstrum, maius, mare, malum, magnum, immane.* The greatness and the evil seem more than incidentally linked.

3

If we are going to read this play as an extension of Stoic ethical arguments,[8] we need to begin by establishing that its representation of the passions is indeed Stoic. As we have already seen, Medea's emotions—love, grief, anger—fundamentally involve the assignment of high value to external objects and situations. Her love for Jason, for her children, for her power and position: all these are the main-

---

[8] There have been many attempts to trace these connections. See, e.g., Marti 1945, 1947; Pratt 1948, 1983; Egermann 1940; Dingel 1974; Rosenmeyer 1989.

springs of her action. The point is made just as clearly in the characterization of Jason, who considers his children to be his very "reason
for living, the comfort of my heart, exhausted by care. Sooner could
I part with breath, with limbs, with the light" (547–49). This judgment is, of course, the basis for his ensuing grief. As Medea says
when she hears it, "He is trapped: there is a space wide open for a
wound" (550).

But this much is common to all ancient thinkers on passion; we
need to do more to show the play's Chrysippan credentials. And we
can do more. The identity of emotion with belief or judgment is in
fact prominently stressed. Medea's passions are not shown as coming
from some part of her character to which the rational judging part is
opposed. They are inclinations of her thought or judgment itself—of
her whole personality, conceived of as housed in the rational part.[9]
When the Nurse urges her to keep her ill wishes hidden, she replies:
"Light is the grief that can deliberate prudently and conceal itself: great
sufferings do not hide" (155–56). Grief is depicted as an entity capable
of deliberation, of choice whether to hide or not; it is not something that
stands in a certain relation to thought, it is a form of thought. Later
she speaks of her "angry soul" as "decreeing" or "judging" something
"within her" (917–18).

Conflict, too, is shown in the Chrysippan way—not as the struggle of
contending forces, but as an oscillation or fluctuation of the whole personality. The most remarkable example of this approach is in Medea's
long speech of deliberation at 893ff. First she goads her soul to anger,
reminding herself of Jason's wrongs (893–909). When she has fully embraced the judgment that she has been wronged, she declares herself
identical with her anger: *Medea nunc sum* (Now I am Medea, 910). Anger
now shows her the way: the final stroke of vengeance must be the killing
of the children. But the thought of the children now causes her heart
to change its course. "Horror strikes my heart, my limbs are numb with
cold, my breast trembles. Anger has left its place; the angry wife is
driven out, and the mother has entirely come back" (*materque tota coniuge expulsa redit*, 928). She pours out her horror at child murder. Then
the thought that they are Jason's children returns. Now the oscillations
become extremely rapid:

---

[9] See Gill 1983 and Knox 1977 on Euripides' play. Chrysippus apparently found Stoic
psychology in Euripides (see Dillon in this volume, Edd.); Seneca's drama presents the
Chrysippan view in a far more explicit way.

Let them die, they are not mine, let them perish.—They are my own,[10] they are free of crime and fault, they are innocent—I acknowledge it—and so was my brother. Why, soul, do you totter back and forth (*titubas*)? Why is my face wet with tears, and why do anger and love draw now here now there (*nunc huc nunc illuc*) my oscillating self (*variam*)? A double tide tosses me; I am uncertain of my course—as when rushing winds wage savage war, and from both sides conflicting currents lash the sea, and the fluctuating waters boil, even so is my heart tossed on the waves (*fluctuatur*). Anger puts love to flight; mother-love, anger. Grief, yield to mother-love. (934–44)

The oscillation continues. She embraces her beloved children. Then the tide of anger returns with the thought of Jason's wrong. "Again grief grows and hate boils, and the Fury of old takes my hand. Anger, where you lead I follow" (951–53).

This is not only a marvelous account of a deep torment; it is also a compelling argument for the intuitive rightness of the Chrysippan view. The depth of Medea's conflict is shown in the fact that it is, precisely, an oscillation between two positions of the mind and heart, each of which represents a way in which Medea sees the world and her children in it. One minute they appear to her as inexpressibly dear and wonderful—as innocent, as special, as hers. The next minute they strike her as pieces of their father and tools to wound him with. Her entire soul is tossed back and forth; it rocks, it verges now this way now that. In two other scenes of deliberation, the Chorus's *nunc huc nunc illuc* is literally acted out, as Medea's physical pacing back and forth mimes the turnings of her soul. She "runs now here now here (*huc et huc*)" with a frenzied motion (385); she "turns her step now this way now that, like a tigress robbed of her young" (862–63). We become convinced that Medea's conflict is grave precisely because her whole soul is carried on the flood; what is going on here is a struggle of reason concerning what to view as most important. The account is intuitively compelling; it is also too emphatic in its emphasis on Chrysippus' view to be accidental.

---

[10] I have punctuated this utterance slightly differently from the way chosen by Zwierlein 1986b, Costa 1973, and Miller 1917, who all write: *occidant, non sunt mei;/pereant, mei sunt, crimine et culpa carent*, etc. Ahl 1986 translates that punctuation. On that reading, the shift takes place later, after *sunt*, and the thought is, "Let them die because they now belong to Creusa, and let them perish just because they are mine (and therefore also Jason's)." I find this less plausible, because throughout Medea has linked anger and the desire for revenge with the thought that the children are Creusa's, while connecting love and shrinking from vengeance with the thought that they are hers (cf. 920–25, 929–30).

But more strange and striking yet, and our most conclusive proof of this play's Chrysippan origins, is its depiction of relationships among the passions. To someone who reads this play straight through for the first time, nothing is more shocking and surprising than the way in which the names of different passions replace each other. Jason describes Medea this way: "And see, at the sight of me she starts up, she bursts into rage, she displays her hate before her—the whole of her grief is in her face" (445–46). Later, in the passage we have just discussed, Medea says of her own feelings: "Anger puts mother-love to flight; mother-love, anger. Grief, yield to mother-love" (943–44). In both of these passages the word "grief" appears where we should expect "anger"—or, rather, the anger and the grief are so close, so commingled, that what first manifests itself as one shows itself a second later as the other.[11] The Loeb translator Miller, perplexed, translates *dolor* in the second passage by "wrath." But such passages should not be normalized. For it is not surprising that love, anger, and grief are this close, if the Stoics are right about what these passions are. Medea's passionate love, her anger, and her grief are all identical with judgments that ascribe high and nonreplaceable value to Jason. They differ only in the precise content of the proposition. Grief focuses on the fact that this beloved man is lost to her; anger, on the fact that he is gone because he has betrayed his oaths and deserted her; love, simply on how valuable he is. It is not surprising, in Medea's situation, that these judgments should lie close to one another in the heart.

What we see as we watch her is that one basic condition—the condition of ascribing so much importance to this unstable external being—naturally takes on a kaleidoscopic multiplicity, as she goes through the various judgments that are part of this condition. The Nurse describes it well:

> Her cheeks flaming, she draws deep sighs, she shouts aloud, she weeps floods of tears, she shines with joy; she shows the form of every passion.

[11] This closeness of the passions, evident in other Latin poetic texts as well (in Vergil above all) has even affected the sense of the word *dolor*, so that in quite a few passages it appears to mean "being wounded" in the sense of "feeling resentment," and thus lies very close to anger. See, e.g., *Aen.* 1.25, 2.594, 5.608, 7.291, 8.220, 8.501, 9.66. This complicates but does not negate my point. We would expect the Stoic thesis to link what ordinary nontechnical discourse keeps separate only if it were a theory very much at odds with ordinary beliefs and life. I have argued that it is not, and the tendency in nontechnical discourse of *dolor* to hook up, on occasion, with *ira* should, I think, be taken as evidence of the intuitive strength of the view. I am grateful to Michael Putnam for discussion on this point; and I have been helped by the subtle account of *dolor*, *amor*, and *ira* in Putnam 1985.

She stops threatens seethes complains groans. Where will she incline the
weight of her soul? Where will she place her threats? Where will this
wave break? Madness swells beyond all bounds. (387–92)

The soul in love has gone outside of its own bounds into the world. It is
swollen up like a wave that can break now on the side of joy, now on
that of murderous rage or of grief. (And her joy here may be joy at the
thought of murder.) Once she cares about this man that much, there
is no passion into which she will not go. The change from grief to love,
from anger to joy—this is hardly in her power but lies with him, with
the power she has given him over her life and thought. (Indeed, the
only way she can get from grief to joy without his help is to do several
murders.) And the play's claim is that the same is true of the relation
between love and anger. If he and Creusa act so as to threaten what
she values most in the world, then the very commitment of soul that
is her love will turn into rage and hate directly.

I have said that these points are evidence of Stoic doctrine. I have
also said that I find them compelling and psychologically true. There
is too much highly specific use of Stoic ideas to be mere coincidence,
especially since our author is a Stoic philosopher. But the play is not a
mere tract or handbook, nor is Seneca just paying lip service to an idea.
The conviction and power of this dramaturgy is the work of someone
who has found in the Stoic doctrine a true way of seeing human life.

4

So much for the depiction of passion. Now we must see how Seneca
uses this psychology to construct a case against love—a case that might
even convince the Aristotelian, antecedently convinced of love's truth
and value. One can accept the Stoic analysis and depiction of passion
without accepting their case for extirpation, though clearly the analysis
helps them both to show that extirpation is possible and to convince us
that it is necessary. Seneca has accepted the analysis; he also presses
in a powerful way the case for extirpation, developing the strongest of
the Stoic anti-Aristotelian arguments.

No confirmed Aristotelian who reads this play will be convinced
that Medea's love is simply an error of judgment, an acceptance of
beliefs about Jason that are false. Seneca has not rested his case upon
falsity. Indeed, in order to persuade the reader that the argument is

evenhanded, he has, if anything, shown Jason to be a more appealing figure than he was in Euripides.[12] By stressing that his motive was sincere love for his children and fear for their safety, not greed or callousness, Seneca gives him a new humanity and dignity. Both here and in the continual reminders of his past heroism and strength, we see a figure who is believably worthy of Medea and her judgments, worthy of her loving wish for his life: "May he live on—if possible, my Jason, as he was—if not, still may he live remembering me, and keep safely the life I gave him" (140–41). Indeed, as we have already suggested, Jason is a figure who in many ways invites our identification. Like most members of the audience, he is a split being with a double allegiance. On the one hand, he shows a sensitivity to morality and a fearfulness before moral laws that Medea increasingly loses. His first and final speeches are about the gods of morality (431ff., 1026–27). He speaks of moral shame (504), of loyalty (*fides*, 1003), of a desire for reasonable discourse and an end to anger (537, 558–59). It is as a moral being that he shrinks (or so the Chorus sees it) before Medea's ferocious passion (102–4). On the other hand, he is a hero, and as such is persistently linked with *erōs* and *audacia*, with bold exploits that have Medea as their fitting prize (364), since they break through the laws of nature. In both aspects, Jason wins the reader's sympathy; we are convinced both by his erotic nature and by his moral concern, and we sense the same double allegiance in ourselves.[13]

Seneca grants, then, that this is a good case of love, no obvious delusion or distortion. But with that his argument has only begun. For all three of the noncircular arguments against Aristotle are here worked out with subtlety. We should remember that much of the drama's force derives from the way they are interwoven.

First we have, throughout, ample evidence of the painful and debilitating feeling of passion. Love, anger, and grief are repeatedly described as very violent movements, stronger than "any force of fire or of swelling gale" (579ff.). This violence of movement results in a weakened and unstable condition of the soul. This weakness is most evident in the case of Jason, who, from his first entrance, has clearly lost the vigor and intensity of his heroic days. He is a man exhausted, drained, burned out: "I yield," he says, "worn out by troubles" (518). And the same is true of his wife. Medea, from the time when she first appears, is enervated, longing for "the ancient vigor" of her spirit (41–

---

[12] Cf. McDonald's discussion of Jason in Theodorakis' *Medea* in this volume, Edd.

[13] On Jason's character, see Maurach 1966; Pratt 1983:25; Herington 1966.

42).[14] She feels that she is being drawn here and there in a way she does not comprehend: "unstable, distracted as I am, I am carried in every direction" (123–24). She is riding a wave; nobody knows where it will break (392). Above all, she feels an agonizing passivity; she is "snatched away headlong by mad passion" (850–51), not knowing "what my fierce soul has decreed within me" (917–18); "I follow," she says to her anger, "where you lead" (953). Passages like these show the experience of emotion to be a disturbing and awful one for the person who, in Aristotelian fashion, is attached to practical reason, planning, and control. How can a figure this commanding, this capable of heroic virtue, endure to be at the mercy of forces like these, her soul blown before the wind?

The repeated suggestion that the passions may operate beneath the level of consciousness deepens Seneca's argument against Aristotle; for can the experience of a life in which the most important things are decided at a level to which the agent has incomplete access be anything but excruciating to one who is trying to live a life "in accordance with practical reason"? Aristotle has let the emotions into the good life without understanding how they operate, without understanding how little they are transparent—and how much passivity, therefore, they bring to the life that lets them in. The Stoic, on the other hand, watches over himself "like an enemy lying in wait" (Epictetus *Ench.* 48.3)—for his zeal for his moral perfection, taken together with his belief in the moral relevance of thought and desire, means that he cannot afford to let down the guard of moral scrutiny for even a moment.[15]

This leads us directly to the argument from integrity. Medea, like a good Stoic hero, values control; she defines her selfhood in terms of certain aims and activities that are very important to her, and she views it as a diminution of her selfhood if these things should be invaded or controlled by another. But she loves. And any person who loves is opening in the walls of the self a hole through which the world may penetrate. Seneca's tragedies are full of images of the loss of bodily integrity—images in which, through an agent's loves and needs, pieces of the external world get taken into the self, there to exert an

---

[14] For these symptoms of passion, cf. *Phaedra* 360ff., especially 374–78: "She goes with an unsteady step, wasted now in strength. Her energy is not the same, and the ruddy glow of health does not shine on her bright face."

[15] Cf. Rabbow 1954, who perceptively speaks of the Stoics' "Wille zur ethischen Totalität."

uncontrolled disturbing power.[16] Thyestes, victim of Atreus' revenge, eats his children and discovers inside his own entrails a horrible substance that both is and is not his own and himself: "What is the uproar that stirs up my entrails (*viscera*)? What just trembled inside? I feel a burden I cannot carry, and my breast groans with a groaning that is not my own (*meumque gemitu non meo pectus gemit*)" (*Thy.* 999–1001). His boundaries have been invaded by the consequences of *erōs* and anger. Seneca's interlocking word order (*meum ... non meo*) shows us the horrible confusion of self and not-self that these attachments bring about. Oedipus, who could have had a tranquil life had he not killed in anger, had he not felt erotic passion, discovers his crime and feels that he must dig into himself to root out the eyes in which these passions have lived: he digs out (*scrutatur*) his eyes with "hooked fingers" (*Oed.* 965), snatching them from "their furthest roots deep within" (968). In language unmistakably laden with the imagery of his sexual penetration of the woman from whose womb he came, he tears "the hollows and empty recesses," his "hand fixed deep inside." In *Phoenissae* he goes still further, wishing to reach beyond the eye into the brain itself: "Now dip your hand into brain; complete your death in that part where I began to die" (180–81). Desire is so deep in his insides that only a fatal assault on his own brain can restore his self-sufficiency. The invasions and corruptions of self that come with passion can be corrected only by further violations. Desire is the beginning of the death of the self.

In *Medea* we see these remarkable visceral images worked out with consistency and power. Seneca's language, far more graphically physical than the language of Greek tragedy, reminds us that a life given over to love cannot avoid having holes in it. And once there is a hole there is, as Medea says, "a space wide open for a wound" (550). Later on, her sword does in fact enter the body of the still-living child; it enters Jason at the same time. "Here, where you forbid me, where you suffer pain (*qua doles*), I shall plunge my sword" (1006). On her side, as we have seen, the sexual love she still feels for Jason is felt as an unwanted pregnancy; her desire is to root it out, to destroy the piece of him that grows in her. Her image of success is the fantasy of restored virginity.

Seneca's violence forces us to confront the issue of integrity in a way that no calm didacticism could. For it reminds us of the physical feeling of passion and of pain—of the way we do feel struck by the external world in a very physical way, as a piercing of our private bodily space.

---

[16] In what follows I am much indebted to Segal 1983a, whose translations I follow for *Thy.*, *Oed.*, and *Phoen.*; see also Henry and Henry 1985.

Struck, therefore, when things go wrong, with a pain that is from the world but yet indwelling—that thus has enormous power of dislocation, mutilation. The Aristotelian likes to imagine herself as stably balanced by good character, taking steady aim at the target of virtuous action. Seneca argues that if the passions and the commitments that ground them remain inside this life, it cannot have that constancy. Instead, it must be in a dangerous oscillation between gaping passivity and a violent rejection of intrusive externals: between raw bleeding skin and tough scar tissue, between rape and violent abortion, between being mutilated and mutilating.

And lest we think that reactive passion, once aroused, can be made moderate or gentle, Seneca saturates this drama with evidence of passion's excesses. Only a light grief, Medea has told us, can be ruled by reason (155); since she has loved intensely she will know no moderation, no mean (*modum*) in hate (397–98). "How difficult it is to turn the soul from its anger when once it is aroused," she says in language that recalls Chrysippus (203–4). The Nurse, observing, describes her: "It is monstrous how her grief grows and feeds its own fire" (671–72).

Two images that recur throughout the play make the Chrysippan idea clear: that of the bridle and that of the wave. Medea's sexuality, said the Chorus, is "unbridled." Later on, they realize that this implies an equal excess in reactive anger: "Medea does not know how to bridle her anger or her love" (866–67). And in the great chorus in which they compare the anger of disappointed love to all the most violent of natural forces, they conclude, "Blind is the fire of love when fanned by anger; it does not want to be ruled, it does not tolerate the bridle" (591–92). If the image of the bridle emphasizes the ardent speed and force of the passions, the wave image emphasizes the inexorability of their violence, once begun. Her wave will surely break (392), her mad passion "overflows" (*exundat*, 392). To the imagery of water the Chorus adds images of fire, wind, and flood-bringing rain (579ff.).

We have seen how the play draws the different passions together; we have seen how Seneca's version of the argument from integrity draws them even closer. We have seen Medea's excesses. Seneca completes his argument by showing that—as we by now expect—the excesses of passion are mixed excesses. What we have here is a love that has itself, while still being love, turned murderous. "Where is this blood-stained maenad carried headlong by ferocious love?" the Chorus asks (*praeceps amore saevo*, 849–50). Medea herself makes an even more paradoxical claim. Speaking of the past, of her murder of her brother, she says,

"And no crime did I do out of anger (*irata feci*); it was unhappy love that raged" (*saevit infelix amor*, 135–36). The text has frequently been emended by critics who are troubled by the conjunction of love and ferocity.[17] It is deliberate.

Later the Chorus generalizes the point, in a passage to which we have referred:

> No violence of fire or swelling gale, no fearful force of hurtling spear, is as great as when a wife, bereft of her marriage, burns hot with love and hate (*ardet et odit*) ... Blind is the flame of love when fanned by anger. It cannot be ruled, it does not endure the bridle. (579ff.)

In such passages we are confronted with a love itself turned violent. Anger is only a stimulus. The primary strength of frenzy comes from love itself, unhappily blocked. Love is not a gentle, lovely passion (or not only that—for we should not forget Medea's wish for Jason's good); it is the strongest form of violence in nature, a fire that burns now for our wonder, now for terror. The difference is made by fortune; we are passive to it. Nor can we, if we once give ourselves to that flame, in any way prevent it from consuming innocent others. Now we know the deepest reason why the Aristotelian cannot say, "I shall have love in my life, but I shall get rid of murderous rage." It is because it is love itself that rages and does murder.

5

We can now confront the play's central image—the image of the snake. Snakes are, from the beginning of the play, the emblems of Medea, of her love, of the crimes of her love. We see them first writhing in the hair of the Furies who, having avenged against Medea the earlier crimes of her love, are now prepared to help her bring destruction to Creusa her rival (13ff.). Her imagination depicts a vengeance that is itself snakelike: "wounds and slaughter and death creeping along the limbs" (47–48). And (as often in Latin poetry) the thought of the snake is linked with the thought of flame—similar in its lethal suddenness, in its fluid supple shape. The destruction of Corinth is to come by flame;

---

[17] See Zwierlein 1986a, 1986b; he keeps *saevit*, defending it against various proposed emendations (such as *suasit*, *movit*, and *fecit*), with references. Especially pertinent is Vergil *Aen.* 4.531–32: "Ingeminant curas rursusque resurgens / saevit amor magnoque irarum fluctuat aestu."

and its witness will be Medea's grandfather the Sun (28ff.). Later in the play, as we have seen, Medea herself becomes a maenad with snakelike neck and loosened hair (752ff., 800–801). The play's central episode is the long scene of incantation, in which Medea calls forth all the snakes on earth and in the heavens. Fierce, powerful, with forked tongues darting, winding their coils, they leave their hidden places at the sound of her songs and gather to do the will of her ferocious love. Out of their bodies she extracts poisons that contain "hidden seeds of fire" (832). These devour Creusa's vital organs, as "the snaking flame burns her inmost marrow" (818–19). At the play's end, after being hounded by the angry Furies of her brother, who bear whips made of snakes (958–61), she escapes through the aid of other snakes. The snake-drawn chariot that carries her toward the sun is, as we have seen, Seneca's ironic replacement for the *Phaedrus'* stirring and beautiful image.

But what are snakes here? We have said that they represent her love; her anger; the anger of her love: its cycle of passion, crime, and retribution; its final triumph. But how do they represent it? What does the image of the snake—or the dual image of snake and flame—tell us about Seneca's view of this love? Snakes are a pervasive source of imagery in Latin poetry, as Bernard Knox showed in his classic article "The Serpent and the Flame."[18] And Seneca explores many of the traditional associations: the ferocity of snakes, their silent deadly power, the concealed nature of the threat they pose to innocent life.[19] (The Chorus tells us that not even Idmon, who knew fate well, could guard against a serpent's sudden bite on the Libyan sands [653].) Snakes are sinuous and indirect in motion; they come out from hiding and touch their victim all at once, intrusively, tongue hungrily darting. They are a most appropriate symbol of erotic passion as this play depicts it. Three centuries later, Augustine tells us why the Devil, bringing sin into the Garden of Eden, chose the serpent as his bodily form: "because, being slippery, and moving in tortuous windings, it was suitable for his purpose" (*Civ. Dei* 14.11). His purpose, of course, being the awakening of sexual lust in the garden's previously virtuous and will-governed

[18] Knox 1950, who collects many examples of snake imagery and of the linking of images of snake and flame. He refers also to the "serpent catalogue" in Vergil G. 3.414–39 and to the elaborate description of a serpent in *Culex* 163–97.

[19] For other references to snakes in Seneca, see Motto 1970. The passages in the prose works stress the poisonous character of snakes, their ferocity, their unpredictability (e.g., *Ira* 1.1.5–6, 1.16.5, 1.17.6; *Clem.* 1.25.4, *QNat.* 2.31.2). But *Clem.* 1.17.1 says of a different sort of animal, "No animal is more recalcitrant of temper, no other needs such skill in handling." That animal is the human being.

inhabitants. The snake is the suitable form for the threat posed by erotic desire to the will and to morality.[20] It is appropriate that Lucan's poem depicts the snake as the deadliest foe of the Stoic hero Cato, as in the remarkable "catalogue of snakes" he records the dangers faced by Cato in the desert.

In our play, Seneca, far more explicitly than Vergil or Lucan, plays upon the snake's sexual associations, both female and male. Transforming Medea into a snake, he links the serpent with woman's hair and with her writhing movement. And in the great catalogue of snakes in the incantation scene, he reminds us that the snake is also an emblem of the sexual power of the male. Making her serpentine offering to Hecate, Medea includes "the members that rebellious Typhoeus bore when he attacked the power of Jove" (773–74). Miller translates *membra* with "these serpent limbs." And in fact if we look to the mythographer Apollodorus (a likely source for Seneca in this and other passages), we find these limbs described as follows: "And growing from his thighs he had extremely large snakes, whose coils, stretching out and up toward his head, sent forth a great deal of hissing" (1.6.3ff.). So, at the moment when she prepares the murder of her rival, she is haunted, as if in a dream or hallucination, by the image of Jason's erotic power—which she depicts as something wondrous and at the same time dangerous, linked with mythic strength and with guilt, something that rebels violently against the gods of morality. To Hecate she offers these members.

Up to a certain point, then, Seneca is true to Stoic tradition in his depiction of the snake (and, through it, of love) as undependable, violent, lethal, the deadliest enemy of virtue and order. Most of the snakes in the catalogues are dangerous foes of the gods and heroes. The Hydra was Heracles' most difficult labor; Python dared to attack Apollo and Diana when they were still innocent babies in the womb (a prefiguring of Medea's fantasized abortion); Typhoeus assailed Zeus himself. And yet, when we read this catalogue we feel that the serpents of this play are not the same as that hideous tribe who threatened Lucan's Cato in the desert. There the vile properties of each variety of serpent are given a detached naturalistic description, and we see them come to life vividly as actual base animals, with no higher power or function. Here, by contrast, snakes take on a mythic and quasi-divine

---

[20] See also Freud 1955: chap. 6, section E, which argues for a universal significance for snake imagery. The multiple meanings of the Romans' snake imagery are paralleled in the remarkable catalogue of snakes in the *Mahabharata*. For one excellent account of snake imagery in Indian erotic traditions, see Doniger 1973.

power; and they have a beauty that we cannot in any simple way despise. Medea's magic, working through and with snakes, has been able to change the laws of nature, to alter the seasons, to reorder the heavens. It has created not chaos but a counterorder. And the snakes that answer to her songs are no mean or vulgar beasts: "Now now," she cries, "It is time to set in motion something higher than common crime" (692–93).

In the lines that follow, she calls down the snakes of heaven and of age-old myth: the constellation Draco, coiling its way between the two bears; the immense power of Ophiouchus; the daring of Python; the snake heads of Hydra, cut off by Hercules, "which renew themselves with their own slaughter" (*succisa serpens caede se reparans sua*, 702); and finally, the serpent who guarded the Golden Fleece. The presence of these snakes of legend suggests to us that the power of *erōs* is no petty evil but an age-old cosmic power, a divine force connected with regeneration and birth, as well as death and slaughter. It is, we might say, a force that comes from a countercosmos set outside of, but just as powerful as, the cosmos of the gods, a cosmos that claims our reverence as well as our fear. It is the image of *erōs* that we find, in fact, in Euripides' *Medea* and memorably in Sophocles' *Antigone*, where *erōs*, though capable of inspiring injustice, is "seated from the beginning of things beside the great laws of right" (797–800).

We might think at this point that Seneca is simply recalling to us the age and the power of irrationality and its attendant evils, telling us that such ugliness creates ongoing and powerful obstacles to virtue in any human life. But I think that matters are not so simple. For these snakes, unlike Lucan's, are not—or not all—hideous. The winged chariot at the play's end soars into the bright air with grace and power. We are, I think, to imagine it as brilliantly colored, gleaming in the sun. The first snake who answers Medea's incantations has properties both hideous and wonderful:

> Here a fierce snake (*saeva serpens*) draws his huge body along; he darts out
> his forked tongue and seeks those to whom he can come bringing death;
> hearing her song he stops in awe, wraps his swollen body into writhing
> knots and compels them to coil in circles (*cogitque in orbes*). (686–90)

This snake is lethal and erotic; he also has an affinity for poetry or song. (Seneca's alliterative poetry has, too, an affinity for him.) And, as he silently winds himself into *orbes*—Seneca's frequent word for cosmic order[21]—compelling fluid matter to take on form, we feel we are present at the creation of a world. The world it creates, Medea's countercosmos, is, furthermore, fertile and benign. When she describes how she has altered nature there are no images of blight. Instead there is harvest in winter, flowers in summer, light in the forest, sun and moon blazing together. Here, clearly, the snake has stood for birth and flourishing.[22]

Finally, consider the snake Draco, lying "like a vast rushing river" (694) in the starry heavens. What we are to imagine as Medea says of him "let that serpent descend" (695), what we would have to see before us if ever this scene were to be visually represented, is the sudden descent into Medea's earthly room of a snake whose tremendous body is made out of the stars of heaven. We would see its winding splendor shooting down toward us. And then the entire room, our entire world, would explode around her, around us, in a blaze of flickering light. It is an unmistakable and extraordinary image of sexual pleasure. It captures the beauty and value, as well as the intensity, of erotic experience. And by putting the snake of heaven before the spectators or listeners, in their room (so to speak) as well as Medea's, it makes the experience theirs, it recalls to them that it is theirs. There is nothing like this in Lucan, where disgust remains supreme and Cato's straightness distances itself ever more from the snake's subversive power. Seneca has invited the power of the snake into the heart of his play. It has arrived, illuminating the world with irresistible splendor, creating (subversively) a counterworld to the world of Stoic virtue. He lets us know that these beauties are inseparable from the snake's death-dealing properties; but he shows as well that a virtue that leaves this out leaves out something for which one would, perhaps, commit a murder. In short: he allows each spectator to see, and be gripped by, the value of *erōs*. She is suddenly bitten; the "snaking flame" penetrates to her inmost marrow.

This reading is confirmed by the play's final lines. Medea triumphs: this is itself a subversive thought. For in a universe ruled, as the Stoic

[21] The word, according to Busa and Zampolli 1975, occurs in Seneca's works 165 times, of which 45 occurrences are in the QNat. In Medea the word occurs in four other passages. At 5 it is the natural world-order as recipient of the sun's light. At 98, it designates the circle made by the horns of the moon as they enclose a full circle of light; at 372 it is used of the entire world of nature, now traversable by human daring; at 378, it refers to the new "worlds" that will be discovered by that daring.

[22] This aspect of Seneca's portrait of the erotic life is neglected by the otherwise impressive analyses of Regenbogen 1927–28 and Henry and Henry 1985, who lay all stress on disorder and chaos.

universe is ruled, by right reason, such audacity should not get off scot-free. (Seneca is very fond of, and elsewhere obsessively retells, the stories of Icarus and of Phaethon, whose unhappy endings give a properly moral warning against such ambitiousness.)[23] But the ending is given by the traditional plot; so perhaps we should discount it. What we cannot discount are Jason's final lines, lines that have been found anomalous and shocking even vis-à-vis the Greek and Roman mythic tradition, and that surely are far more so when placed at the end of a Stoic drama. "Go aloft through the deep spaces of heaven," he calls, "and bear witness that where you travel there are no gods" (1026–27). Here Jason expresses, of course, his sense of injustice: her triumph seems incompatible with the gods' judgment on her acts. Since he is only partially encased within the narrow world of Stoic moral judgment—since, indeed, he mirrors the likely position of the spectator, caught between that moralism and an intuitive human sense of the worth of externals—he cannot help seeing her escape as a triumph and cannot help feeling that this matters. But the way Seneca chooses to have him express this thought is very strange. Costa remarks, "*Nullos esse deos* is not a characteristic complaint in Greek tragedy, even in Euripides: rather the sufferer asks, 'How can the gods allow these things to happen?' "[24] T. S. Eliot writes, "The final cry of Jason to Medea departing in her car is unique; I can think of no other play which reserves such a shock for the last word."[25] The shock is, of course, deepest within a Stoic view of the world. For in that view, god is everywhere. There is no space in the universe that is not inhabited by divine reason. No matter where Medea goes, her rage and her love will be judged bad by reference to the will of god, which is to say, with reference to perfect moral virtue. The universe is thoroughly moralized, and everything must be either good or evil: if

---

[23] For Icarus, *Ag.* 506, *Oed.* 892ff., *Her. O.* 686; for Phaethon, *Phaedra* 1090, *Her. O.* 677, 854, and the Chorus at *Medea* 599. At 826, Medea tells us that she got her fire from Phaethon: so she is his survivor, so to speak. On Vergil's use of the Icarus story in *Aen.* 6, with some very pertinent reflections on *dolor* and pity, see Putnam 1987.

[24] Costa 1973:159–60. Rosenmeyer 1989 oddly translates as "the gods are dead"; but his remarks about the relationship between Medea's passion and an upheaval in the world order (200–201) are suggestive and apposite.

[25] Eliot 1950:73. Cf. Pratt 1983:89, who remarks, perceptively, that Medea has become "anti-god." This is much better, I think, than Lawall 1979's association of Medea with chaos and unshaped wild nature. Dingel 1974:108ff. argues that since the gods support Medea they cannot be real gods. Fyfe 1983 argues that we are meant to see Jason as deluded: Medea is an instrument of the natural order's vengeance. I find this the least successful part of her otherwise valuable paper.

not good, therefore evil. And Seneca explicitly told us that the region beyond the moon is as serene—and as good—as a wise man's heart (*Ep.* 59.16). Jason's line, by contrast, tells us that the moral universe has a space in it. Not every place is full of gods. For the serpent chariot takes the loving soul to a realm in which god and god's judgment on passion do not exist. There is a place, then, beyond virtue and vice, health and disease—a place, as Nietzsche would say, beyond good and evil.

6

Seneca's play now begins to have the suddenness, as well as the passion, of the snake; it takes us by surprise, weaving its path between the moral world and the world of love. Like the poetic snake who loved Medea's song, it arranges its coils into a cosmos, it creates a world—and, like that snake, it has a forked tongue and asks to whom it should come bringing death. We do not know whether its intended victim is passion or Stoic morality itself. To conclude our depiction of the play's serpentine doubleness, and make the case for finding these ambiguities in it stronger still, we turn to the Chorus and its remarkable ode on the Golden Age and humanity's fall from purity. Unlike the Euripidean Chorus, Seneca's is not sympathetic to Medea. Throughout it is the sober voice of Stoic morality, counseling the extirpation of passion, the containment of daring—a life that stays at home with its own virtue, never overstepping the limits of nature. Yet I believe that we will find that the very language Seneca gives it for its central sermon contains a critical judgment upon that morality; and in this judgment is contained a profound criticism of traditional portraits of the Stoic hero. Like the ode on the human being in *Antigone,* though apparently without that ode's admiring side, this chorus begins with a story of man's invention of the art of sailing.

> Too daring (*audax nimium*), the man who first in a fragile bark broke through the treacherous seas and, seeing his lands disappear behind him, entrusted his life to the light winds: who, cutting the waters in a doubtful path, could trust to a slender plank, drawing too slight a line between the circumstances of life and death. (301–8)

Soon this account of human daring is contrasted with a purer and more moral world:

Pure (*candida*) were the ages our fathers saw, crime being far removed. Each person inactive (*piger*), keeping to his own shore, grew old in his ancestral fields, rich with only a little, knowing no wealth except that which his fatherland bore. (329–34)

Both before and after this portrait of a "Golden Age," the Chorus goes on to indict the daring (*ausus*) of early explorers who broke through limits previously set up in the laws of nature (*foedera mundi*, 335), wrote new laws for the winds, and afflicted the sea (depicted, in Stoic fashion, as a living, morally demanding presence) with blows (337); the chronicle of excessive exploration culminates in their observation that the prize for the Argo's voyage was Medea, a danger worse than the sea (*maiusque mari Medea malum*, 362). The ode concludes with a bitter reflection that appears to move from the mythical times of the play straight into Roman contemporary life:

> Now, in our time, the sea has ceased resistance and suffers any law we give it.... Any little bark now wanders anywhere on the deep. Every boundary has been removed (*terminus omnis motus*); cities have set their walls in new lands, and the world, now open to travel throughout (*pervius orbis*), has left nothing in its earlier seat.... There will come a time in the distant future when Ocean will loose the bonds of things, when the huge earth will be revealed, when Tethys will uncover new worlds (*novas orbes*), and Thule will not be the limit of the lands. (365–79)

This ode[26] presents us with a contrast between two conceptions of the good life and two associated conceptions of the self, one of which it apparently blames and one of which it apparently praises. On the one side we have the audacious life of the human being who values external goods and who expends effort and ingenuity to get to the objects of his or her desires. Since this life is clearly linked with Medea and her scheme of value, and with the erotic Jason of the old days, we might call it the erotic life. This life values unstable things like possessions, love, worldly achievement, renown. It is imagined in terms of outward movement, of adventuring. The *audax* self is dynamic, extending itself beyond itself, spreading exuberantly out over pieces of the world. Its relation to nature and natural law is frequently adversarial—it bursts

---

[26] On this choral ode, see especially Henry and Henry 1985:51–52; Segal 1983b; Lawall 1979.

through boundaries, it joins lands that are supposed to be separate, it lets no limit stand.[27]

On the other side is a purer self: this self stays at home content with few externals because it does not value these things. It is morally unsullied, pure white (*candida*); crime is far off.[28] It is the Stoic self, which has all its goods at home, because all good is placed in virtue. It respects, because it doesn't want not to, the limits in nature.

Most commentators have seen this passage as a depiction of an ideal "Golden Age." Costa, for example, says that it "clearly belongs in the category of the many accounts of that ideal early existence which we find in Greek and Latin literature." He mentions Hesiod, Vergil, and Ovid.[29] But we can see, if we examine these sources (and others), that Seneca is criticizing these traditional stories in a predictably Stoic fashion. The typical stress of Golden Age stories is on the ready availability, without risk or labor, of valued external goods. The earth itself bears fruit; it is spring all year long; abundance requires no toil; there are no diseases, no old age, no pain. The age is golden because people have all good things at home with them—but the good things are the usual externals, and the myth therefore requires an alteration in the behavior of nature. There is no seafaring here not because, as in Seneca, there is no desire for the goods that are achieved by seafaring, but because nature herself gives these very same goods in abundance right where we are. Of course to a Stoic this emphasis upon the value of externals is deeply misguided. The thing that is wrong with human life, the thing that prevents people from having all good things with them as they are, is vice; so the only way to imagine a Golden Age correctly is to imagine an age without vice, without passion, without the false belief in the value of externals. This is what we have here.[30] These people stay at home inactive because they do not misguidedly long for the things that are far away.

What we must, however, notice as we read the ode again is the ambivalence with which this ideal existence is depicted. The word *piger* is not a term of praise in Roman literature. It is consistently

---

[27] However, we see no sign that this self is committed to chaos. Instead, it pursues orderly projects, discovering new spheres for human practical reason.

[28] Compare *innocuae vitae* of *Her. F.* 125ff., on which see below, and *vitio carens* of Hippolytus' praise of the woodland life free from greed (*Phaedra* 482ff.).

[29] See Vergil *G.* 1.125 (notice that this Golden Age contains no poisonous snakes); Hes. *Op.* 109ff., Aratus 110–11, Catullus 64.6ff., 38ff.; Ovid *Met.* 1.94ff., Tib. 1.3.37ff. See Costa 1973:*ad loc.*; Lovejoy and Boas 1935, esp. 263ff.; Konstan 1977; S. Blundell 1986.

[30] Cf. also Hor. *Carm.* 1.3, much closer to this passage than other Golden Age descriptions are; and *Epode* 16 should be compared as well.

pejorative, generally opposed to *labor* and to *virtus*. Seneca uses the word (with its relatives, *pigritia* and *pigrescere*) fifty-six times in his writings.[31] It is neutral only in a few cases, where it has a complement introduced by *ad* and means "slow to do X," "sluggish at X-ing"—where X is not always something good. But without *ad, piger* is pejorative. When it designates sluggish movement in nonhuman nature, or in the physical life of human beings, there is almost always, even here, something ominous going on. A sluggish river has water that damages the fertility of crops (*Phaedra* 15); sluggishness of limbs is a sign of plague (*Oed.* 182); fresh air prevents a stagnant sluggish atmosphere from forming (*QNat.* 5.18.1); the air beneath the earth is sluggish and foul, so that, released by earthquakes, it causes plague (*QNat.* 6.27.2); an oozing swamp surrounds a sluggish or stagnant pool (*Oed.* 547); and so forth: "stagnant" is frequently the best translation. In the moral world, things are clearer still, as Seneca consistently reproves stagnation of soul. "I will give no pardon to the sluggish (*pigris*), to the careless, to the babblers," he proclaims (*Ira* 3.24.2). "Morally vicious (*inhonesta*) is all timidity and worry, is sluggishness (*pigritia*) in any action" (*Ep.* 74.30). Mix *pigritia* in with a virtuous act and it loses its virtuous character (*Ep.* 66.16). The job of a philosophical teacher is to draw forth mental powers that were previously hidden and sluggish (*Ben.* 6.16.7). So *piger* in Seneca, as in other Roman writers, Stoic and non-Stoic, is a word unambiguously opposed to major virtues, especially those connected with work and striving. It is a word that the Stoic, in order to have a convincing conception of virtue (especially at Rome), needs to be able to set over against his own idea.

But can he consistently do so? Our passage suggests deep doubt. The presence of *piger* on the side of Stoic virtue suggests to us that the Stoic ideal, while pure and blameless, is strangely lacking in effort, daring, and activity—qualities deeply valued by the entire Roman tradition of virtue. The life of a Stoic paradise is indeed a sluggish or lazy life—as it must, perhaps, be, if it cares deeply for nothing outside itself.

The one other apparently positive use of *piger* in Seneca confirms this story. The Chorus in *Hercules Furens* has praised the simple life of the country, where needs are few and people "have the undisturbed quiet (*tranquilla quies*) of a life free from harming (*innocuae vitae*)" (159–60). They have contrasted this life with the "immense hopes and trembling fears" (162–63) of the city, where people live for unreliable external

---

[31] Cf. Busa and Zampolli 1975:s.v.

goods. They have, once again, praised *secura quies* (175) and reproved the "too brave heart" of Hercules (*nimium ... pectore forti*, 186). They now give a summary of their moral advice:

> Let glory speak of someone else to many lands. Let babbling report praise him through every city, and lift him up, an equal to the stars of heaven. Let someone else go lofty (*sublimis*) in a chariot. As for me, let my land protect me beside an unknown hearth. The inactive (*pigros*) live on to old age; and the mean lot of a small house rests in a lowly but secure place. But high-spirited virtue falls from a lofty height (*alte virtus animosa cadit*). (192–201)

Again, being *piger* is linked with Stoic goals of security and quiet, and with a lack of blameworthy concern with externals. Again, it is connected with moral blamelessness, again opposed to heroic daring. But here, even more clearly than in *Medea*, we discover what the ideal of moral purity rejects: the courage of Hercules, the glory of great deeds out in the world, and high-spirited virtue itself.

Seneca, in these plays, sees more deeply than most Stoic writers when he comprehends that you cannot have traditional Roman heroism and have Stoic virtue too. Stoic writers would like to think that you can, and they write as if these elements can be combined. Lucan's Cato—ever watchful, effortful, *audax*—exemplifies, along with his Stoicism, some elements of Roman virtue to which any reader of the poem will be deeply attached. "The virtue of Cato, unwilling to stand still, dares (*audet*) to entrust his men to unknown lands" (9.371–72). His *audax virtus* (302) does not know how to keep inactive (294–95). In crossing the Libyan desert he hopes to get the better of Nature (302). "I seek as my comrades," he says, "those who are attracted by danger itself." Without these qualities Cato could hardly be a Roman hero. Seneca's point here (directed, presumably, not only at others but at some of his own views) is that this sort of heroism is not available to the good Stoic, even though Stoics like to think that it is. The good Stoic may not be altogether inactive; but because he lacks the passionate love of externals he will not undertake bold projects out in the world, or endure labor and risk for their sake. Instead of the grand old words *audax* and *labor*, we must now honor the words *candidus* and *piger*—the latter now assuming a new positive meaning. This is a profound change in the ideal of the hero. A later ode denounces for excessive daring and boundary violations a whole list of heroes usually thought great—the

Argonauts first, then Hercules, Meleager, and several Homeric heroes. The good Stoic wants none of this life.

But when the spectator sees how limp and unheroic this newly bounded life is, contrasted with her intuitive images of greatness, she is likely to be ambivalent toward it and erotically drawn to Medea's greatness of soul. (Jason the erotic voyaging Argonaut is a far more sympathetic figure than the tame and moralizing Jason we see in most of this play; indeed, it is clearly Seneca's intent to juxtapose these two Jasons, not always to the advantage of the latter. We might add that the only time when the stage figure of Jason inspires love is when he declares his love of his sons, his grief on their account, his fear on their behalf. These are not Stoic sentiments.) Nor can we, further, escape the fact that this very ode (unlike, for example, Horace's condemnation of progress in *Carm.* 1.3) depicts the *audacia* it condemns with unmistakable élan. The lines about future exploration allegedly depict a nadir to which our audacity will eventually lead us. But they have an exuberant tone that sits ill with Stoicism. In the margin of his copy of the play, Ferdinand Columbus wrote, "This prophecy was fulfilled by my father Christopher Columbus in the year 1492."[32] He feels in the lines not moral condemnation but a prophecy of high achievement. I think he saw something that is really there.

We can venture even further. In this Stoic Golden Age, characterized by moral blamelessness, we do not even get a very rich conception of moral virtue. *Candida saecula* have no dark blot; but it is not clear what else they do have. The image makes us think of a blank space. *Procul fraude remota*, too, is negative and weak. (Compare *vitio carens, Phaedra* 483; *innocuae vitae, Hercules Furens* 159. The wise man is free from wrongdoing, ἀβλαβής—Diogenes Laertius 7.123). We see here no positive concern for social justice, no generosity to one's fellow human beings, no courage for friends or country. For—as Aristotle keenly saw when he told us that the gods lack moral virtue—the great moral virtues all require some high evaluation of uncontrolled external things. What courage can there be, if poverty, slavery, loss of loved ones, and even death are not to be counted evils and there is no fear to manage? What commitment to justice can there be, if the goods distributed within society have no real human worth? Again, what generosity? The only virtue that can exist here fully is, perhaps, σωφροσύνη—construed as knowing and keeping one's proper place in the scheme of things. The

---

[32] See Costa 1973:*ad loc.*

traditional anthropomorphic gods cannot have the virtues because they control all good things; like the men of the traditional Golden Age, they want these goods, but they command them fully. The Stoic, this play suggests, has a similar problem with the virtues, because what he doesn't control he defines as nongood and learns not to want. The result is the same; the Stoic is indeed godlike. This life, then, begins to look strangely *piger* not only in terms of traditional standards of heroism but also with regard to its own ostensible scheme of valued ends. Virtue, it seems, may itself be erotic.

What we have discovered, then, is that there are two selves, two pictures of selfhood in the world, two pictures even of morality, and that we must choose between them. This choice is not simple, but tragic. If we go for *erōs* and *audacia* we get crime and murderous anger; if we go for purity, we get flatness and the death of heroic virtue. We get the death of tragedy too, since what tragedy is, we recall, is "the sufferings of human beings who have been wonderstruck by external things." This play can be a tragedy only by having characters who are not Stoics;[33] and I think we can say that even then it succeeds in being tragic only because it shares to some extent their loves and their wonder—only because it depicts the choice to follow Stoicism as itself a certain sort of tragedy inside of us, brought about by the demand of our moral being for unsullied purity and lives free from harming.

Who, then, is Seneca? we feel like asking. And what is Senecan tragedy? Seneca is, as would be no surprise to anyone who has worked on him, an elusive, complex, and contradictory figure, a figure deeply committed both to Stoicism and to the world, both to purity and to the erotic—a figure who sits at home and who is carried loftily in his chariot. The tensions between his career and his thought are many and famous. They have been set forth with convincing precision of argument by Miriam Griffin in her fascinating study.[34] What is less frequently discussed is the fact that these tensions surrounding the value of worldly striving work themselves into the writing as well. Griffin perceives the writing's paradoxical character: "If one were asked to characterize as briefly as possible the distinctive Senecan outlook, one would probably point to his morbid asceticism and his realistic

---

[33] In a fragment of *On Marriage*, Seneca writes, "Everything that fills up tragedies, everything that overturns cities and kingdoms, is the struggle of wives and mistresses" (Haase 1893–95).

[34] Griffin 1976.

humanity."[35] Seneca's intense interest in progress and striving made him attach to the work and effort of philosophy a value that is hard to reconcile with Stoicism. This interest in daring, courage, and striving—which itself has deep roots in (especially Roman) Stoicism—actually turns out, and is here seen by Seneca to be, in a deep and tragic tension with some fundamental principles of Stoic morality. This tragedy discovers and explores that tension, taking Seneca further in his criticism of Stoic purity than he is willing to go in any prose work.[36]

It is, perhaps, no accident that it is in poetry that this ambivalence should have come out most powerfully, no accident that it was in tragedy that this critique should have been made. For tragedy is, as Plato in banning it already saw, profoundly committed to the values that Plato and Stoicism wish to reject. It is a dangerous form for the Stoic to attempt. Like Medea's serpent, it has a way of sneaking up on Stoic morality with its own sense of drama, its own ways of appealing to the imagination and memory of its audience, its own scheme of values. The real danger posed by literature to philosophy is nowhere more evident than here, inside this play: for in the very act of turning tragedy into a Stoic argument, Stoicism has bitten itself.

7

The message to the Aristotelian is, then, that there is no combining deep personal love (especially, but probably not only, erotic love) with spotless moral purity. If you set yourself up to be a person who cherishes all the virtues, whose every act is done justly and appropriately, toward the right person in the right way at the right time, you had better omit erotic love, as the Stoics do. And you had better omit, as well, any form of love in which you and your good are deeply vulnerable, any love on which you have staked your εὐδαιμονία (human flourishing). If you admit such love, you will almost surely be led outside the boundaries of the virtues; for this one constituent part likes to threaten and question all the others. And then the very perfectionism of the Aristotelian, who so wants all of life to fit harmoniously together, will produce rage upon

[35] Griffin 1976:177.

[36] This might be a chronological point, but it certainly does not need to be, especially in light of the fact that philosophical writing and action-guiding belief are in continuing tension, it seems, throughout Seneca's life (see Griffin 1976). The dating of the tragedies is highly uncertain in any case. And changes of feeling and thought about important matters are not always unilinear; we recall Seneca's account of the heart's oscillations.

rage—angry violence toward one's own violence, a sword aimed at one's own aggression.

On the other hand, if we leave love out, as the play also teaches us, we leave out a force of unsurpassed wonder and power, whose beauty is incommensurable with and no less than that of morality. It can never reside harmoniously inside morality, as one component inside a harmonious life-plan; but leave it out and you will have a life that is not fully good. So, either way we live, we will be, it seems, imperfect.

As we consider this conclusion, we are assisted by an aspect of Stoic ethics that has so far not figured in my account:[37] its emphatic concern for the causal history of each story of human wrongdoing, as developed in connection with the concept of mercy. This narrative attitude supplies the Seneca of *De Ira* and *De Clementia* with a partial antidote to rage at human imperfection. In mercy, as Seneca describes it, the soul turns itself away from the strict punishment of each defect, even when a fault is present, understanding the difficulties the person faced in his or her efforts to live well. Here we have a source of gentleness to both self and other, even when wrongdoing has been found. A Stoic pupil will be urged to assume this merciful attitude to the lover who has wronged her—imagining patiently and vividly, in the manner of one watching a play, the difficulties and obstacles both social and psychological that contributed to the wrongdoing, until rage gives way to narrative understanding. She will also, and just as urgently, be asked to take up this attitude to herself, understanding the reasons for her resentments and evil impulses and thus relaxing the harsh punishments she is inclined to mete out to her own soul.

In the spirit of that narrative project, then, I return to the end of Medea's story, as it might be told to such a pupil. Medea appears on the steep slope of the palace roof. The man she loves stares up at her. He sees her looming over him, radiant and boiling, wrapped in the red light of her grandfather the Sun. That light both threatens and transfigures. The straight order of the daily world, imperiled, shines with amazing beauty. In terror, in passionate desire, he lifts his swollen eyes to the snakelike flames; for never has her beauty appeared more wonderful. And now, flying through the bright air, a chariot approaches, drawn by two scaly snakes equipped with wings. He sees their sinuous and sudden movements, their noiseless coils glistening. As she takes the reins, their twisting motion becomes one with her hair and with the

---

[37] See Nussbaum 1993, 1994: chap. 11.

movement of her body. Jason sees them as the doubles of her body and of his own, wrapped around one another in passion. Excessive winged fluid lethal, symbols at once of death and potency, of murder and of birth.

Charioteer and serpents, anti-Platonic symbols, they ascend. Medea, fully identified with her passion, goes off from our world into the sun, from the place of moral judgment to the place where there are no gods. Jason, pulled equally by morality and by love, by identification and by judgment, by the compunctions of piety and the splendor of the serpent, is as if split into two, as the mind of the spectator is also split in two. The moral Jason weeps, condemns, repudiates. He distances himself from Medea's flight, saying, "Where you travel, there are no gods." But now we recall, we see in our mind, that there are two serpents in the sky. The serpent Jason, twining in ecstasy around his partner, moves himself, winged, reborn, beyond the gods, beyond the Stoic universe in which gods dwell everywhere. Deep in the cosmos, in that once silent country beyond the chaste Stoic moon (while children die on the earth), there now appears a flickering hot light, an irregular, snaking motion. We are witnessing a triumph. It is the triumph of love.

PART IV

BEYOND THE EURIPIDEAN STAGE

11

MEDEA AT A SHIFTING DISTANCE

IMAGES AND EURIPIDEAN TRAGEDY

Christiane Sourvinou-Inwood

Medea as a Special "Other"

$\mathbb{A}$N IMPORTANT modality of exploration of the central Athenian self, the male citizen, is through the exploration of those others that are not self, among whom the most important is the woman.[1] A figure with rich potential as a locus for such explorations is a woman whose otherness was multifaceted, Medea. In this essay I shall investigate some dramatic and iconographical explorations focused on the figure of Medea in the fifth and fourth centuries, reconstructing their ancient meanings and thus the perceptions that articulate them.[2]

Euripides' *Medea* played a focal role in the articulation of certain aspects of Medea, and so I shall explore the ways in which the character of Medea is constructed in this tragedy and the ways in which it relates to what is perceived as female normality. I shall then investigate the impact that this tragedy made on the perceptions of Medea as they are articulated in the images.

"Euripides *Medea:* The Construction of Medea" was delivered at the meeting of the Classical Association in Oxford in April 1992. I am grateful to Robert Parker, Chris Pelling, and Oliver Taplin for their comments and to J. J. Clauss for performing the onerous task of drastically abbreviating the paper. I am indebted to the Trustees of the British Museum for figures 1–2 and 4–5 and to the Cleveland Museum of Art for figure 3.

[1] Cf. Zeitlin 1990.

[2] On the myth of Medea and its iconography, cf. Page 1938:xxi–xxx, lvii–lxviii; E. Simon 1954, 1961; Meyer 1980; Zinnerling-Paul 1979; Vojatzi 1982:13–22, 91–100, 118–24; Sourvinou-Inwood 1979:22–58, 1990a; M. Schmidt 1992:386–98.

Euripides' *Medea*: The Construction of Medea

I begin by reconstructing—as far as possible—the ways in which the Athenian audience in 431 B.C. made sense of *Medea*. Any attempt to recover Euripides' "intentions," besides relying on a fuzzy concept that is far from providing the whole story relevant to a text's meanings, is a much more speculative operation. Hence my focus is on how the original audience made sense of the text. This is problematic enough, since the audience of 431 was not uniform and coherent. Nevertheless, there were common parameters, created by cultural and genre assumptions shared by the tragedian and his audience, which determined the tragedian's selection and the audience's meaning creation; it is these parameters that we need to reconstruct in order to use them to help shape appropriate perceptual filters.

In my view, Medea's character was constructed in the course of the tragedy by means of a series of shifting relationships to certain conceptual schemata representing the cultural norm. First, she was seen through a "normal woman" model, as this was perceived in normative ideology and constructed in the play. The precise details of this schema were not fixed, nor are they accessible to us; but its main parameters were set into place by the normative ideology of the *polis*. The second conceptual schema to which Euripides' Medea has a series of shifting relationships in the course of the play was "good woman" as constructed by male ideality, a schema that is the positive polarization of "normal woman." The final schema that came into play was "bad woman," a schema that the construction of Medea's character in the play helps define further. In the course of the play, these schemata are activated in complex ways. Medea and the other female characters are constructed, and audience response toward them is directed, through a series of shifting relationships to the three schemata.

Thus, for example, Medea is sometimes seen as "zoomed" to the schema "good woman" or as distanced from the schema "normal woman."[3] All the schemata were complex, and my definitions necessarily address only the basic core of Athenian perceptions pertaining to the normative discourse about women. A good woman is devoted to the interests of her husband and children and she possesses

[3] These shifting relationships are, we shall see, complex; I disagree with those who view Medea and the other characters simply in terms of inversions and reversals of earlier expectations (cf., e.g., McDermott 1989:65–70).

αἰδώς (shame). Women's epitaphs reflect the society's established values and provide a glimpse into this schema. Among the virtues for which women are praised in their epitaphs, the most commonly mentioned are ἀρετή (generic goodness) and the fame of ἀρετή;[4] σωφροσύνη (self-control);[5] the fact that she loved and pleased her children and/or husband or both;[6] and her diligence and thrift.[7] The perfect model of a good woman was constructed by Euripides in Alcestis. A bad woman is the opposite of that positive norm; a bad mother is a bad woman par excellence. The boundaries between normal woman and good woman are fluid, since normality tends to be positively colored in the collective representations.

These three schemata were important crystallizations of the ancient assumptions that helped direct audience response. I set them out as points of reference to minimize the intrusion of subjectivity and cultural determination. Since Medea was a bad woman in myth, and thus in the audience's assumptions, and since this knowledge was activated by the tragedy, the "bad woman" schema inevitably came into play in the audience's reception; but it is partly subverted. For the schemata are manipulated to produce greater complexity. One possible way of expressing this modality of construction of "character" is by saying that these ever-changing relationships are created through the deployment of a series of what I call "zooming devices" and "distancing devices,"[8] generated through the interaction of textual elements with the audience's cultural assumptions. Thus, for a modern audience the description "he was a slave owner" would negatively distance the character from "normal man," while for ancient Greeks this would be a neutral description. In considering how the character of Medea is constructed through the deployment of these devices I shall proceed linearly, from beginning to end, for I am trying to reconstruct the original audience's process of meaning creation.

The first presentation of Medea is through the τροφός (nurse) and is thus framed by this figure's *persona:* distanced from the central male self, because a slave woman, but positive insofar as nurturing. Thus

[4] E.g., *CEG* 2.513, 493, 510.
[5] E.g., *CEG* 2.525; 516; 479; 486.
[6] E.g., *CEG* 2.530, 536.
[7] E.g., *CEG* 2.537.
[8] I first used these terms in a paper on Sophocles' *Antigone* to describe the textual devices deployed to manipulate the shifting relationships between the audience's world of the *polis* and the world of the play; see Sourvinou-Inwood 1989:136.

the sympathetic presentation would have made sense: it is articulated by someone whose viewpoint is removed from the central male self and yet is not negatively charged. What she says in her first reference to Medea (6–10) distances Medea negatively from a "normal woman" model in three ways: first, she is a foreigner from Colchis; second, she was struck by love of Jason (about which, more below); and finally and most strongly negative, she persuaded Pelias' daughters to kill their father. Thus she is the instigator of a parricide and subverter of the father-daughter relationship. But the next words of the τροφός zoom Medea positively toward the male ideal of a normal woman: Medea complied with Jason in all things, and this—the woman not disagreeing with the man—is the chief salvation of the οἶχος (house). The positive zooming continues in another modality in 17–29, in which Medea is presented as the unhappy and dishonored victim of a faithless and opportunistic husband, a situation comparable to that of many a normal woman in the real world. But in 31–35 we have a very strongly negative distancing device: the reference to Medea's betrayal of her homeland, her father, and her father's οἶχος, which recalls her brother's murder for the sake of a man. A woman who betrayed her father and killed her brother for the sake of a future husband she chose herself is a bad woman. In Athenian eyes, Medea's union was a transgressive form of marriage.

Medea's betrayal of her natal family is one element in her *persona* as subverter of the woman's role in the family that was repeatedly activated in the course of this play. Line 36 distances Medea even more strongly from a "normal woman": she loathes her sons and does not rejoice at seeing them—the latter, weaker formulation has the function of evoking the behavior of a normal woman in order to distance Medea explicitly from it. Thus this verse presents Medea as a bad woman. A stronger version of the same distancing device is generated by Medea's own hostile words toward her sons at 113–14 and by the nurse's response, which contains also a different type of distancing device:[9] the Nurse presents Medea's temper and behavior as a version of those of τύραννοι (monarchs), thus distancing the world of the play as well as Medea from the normality of the democratic *polis*. One of the effects of this distancing is to put her in a different perspective, that of virtual normality for a remote and (for fifth-century Athenians) negatively colored group, and thus

---

[9] The type proposed in Sourvinou-Inwood 1989:136 and described briefly above.

partially to deconstruct the "bad woman" facet of Medea's constructed character.[10]

The parodos begins at 131. From now on the Chorus provides another point of reference for the operation of the distancing and zooming devices. The Chorus' dramatic *persona* will also be constructed through devices situating it in relation to "normal woman," "good woman," and "bad woman." Their structural position is both central and marginal: in the world of the play they were citizens, and thus central when contrasted to Medea; but their sex made them marginal. In the Athenian audience's eyes, the fact that they were foreign women further distanced them from the normative self of the Athenian male. With their first significant statements, the Chorus expresses sympathy for Medea and presents her desertion by Jason as a misfortune that commonly afflicts women,[11] and thus zooms Medea's distress and her negative reaction to it to the normal woman experience. Then Medea distances herself negatively at 166–67 through her statement that she killed her brother and betrayed her father, which zooms her to the "bad woman" schema. This juxtaposition of a typical unjust situation for normal women with Medea's *persona* as a bad woman here suggests that in her case her misfortune was correlative with her character as a bad woman.

Just before Medea's entrance at 213 the Chorus frames her positively by stressing that she was the victim of an injustice, begging for divine vengeance from the gods that police oaths. Her address to the Chorus contains unimpeachable normal woman statements concerning reputation, making it clear that her reputation among the Corinthian women is important to her. She is thus zoomed toward the normal woman schema. In lines 230–51 she utters her famous statements about the wretched condition of women. It is very difficult to reconstruct their effect. Clearly, the Chorus' subsequent reaction shows that in the world of the play the women of Corinth, whose *persona* so far has been that of normal women, show no disagreement with these sentiments; on the contrary, their approval of Medea's revenge indicates that they agree. The audience is presented with the viewpoint of one woman who is not

---

[10] Here the term "deconstruct" does not indicate that one thing undermines another in the sense of denying its validity or mitigating it: the first remains valid, but next to it another, different and sometimes antithetical, perspective is presented that is also valid— though in some cases less so than the first, which is dominant; meanings are created through a complex interaction between the two perspectives.

[11] I read κοινὸν τόδε at 157 (cf. Page 1938:*ad loc.*).

exactly ordinary, but a viewpoint with which "normal" women would agree. So how did the male audience make sense of these verses? The question is virtually impossible to answer.[12] It is likely that different reactions were possible, and that the response of different segments of the audience ranged from a perception of these utterances as subversive nonsense, spoken by a self-confessed "bad woman," to a certain empathy. Such empathy would be possible for those who underplayed the fact that the sentiments were uttered by Medea; and in any case, her *persona* as a bad woman has so far been only lightly constructed in the play. However, the statement at 250–51, that she would rather fight in war three times than give birth once, would have been generally perceived as subversive, since it challenges important tenets of the normative ideology of the *polis*. Indeed, in the verses that immediately follow Medea distances herself from the Chorus and normal women by pointing out the differences between them: they are in their own country and they have friends and their father's house, while she is ἄπολις, in a foreign land, without mother, brother or kin. In the world of the play, this attracts the Chorus' sympathy and thus obtains their cooperation in her plans; but in the world of the audience it evokes the acts committed by Medea that characterize her as a "bad woman."

Aegeus' arrival and the expression of his disapproval of Jason's behavior confirm the women's assessment of that behavior as wrong. For Aegeus, as an Athenian king and the future father of Theseus, was positively colored in the eyes of the audience. Thus Aegeus' disapproval of Jason's behavior has the effect of zooming Medea toward the normal woman schema. But Aegeus' oath at 749–51 not to expel Medea from Athens would inevitably have evoked for the Athenian audience the mythological knowledge that Aegeus and/or Theseus, the son whose birth was called to mind by the discussion of Aegeus' childlessness, had in fact later expelled Medea for plotting Theseus' death. This recollection would have distanced Medea from the normal woman schema by lightly suggesting her future role as murderous stepmother, a prefiguration of her role as murderous mother.

[12] The one thing we know about the reception of the play by its original audience is that when he produced *Medea, Philoctetes, Diktys,* and *Theristai Satyroi,* Euripides came third after Euphorion and Sophocles. We cannot be sure what this meant about the reception of each play, but it is unlikely that any individual play had been received with great enthusiasm. However, *Medea* clearly had a very strong impact in popular perceptions (cf. Knox 1983:272; on its influence on Medea's imagery, see the following two sections).

At 791–810 Medea is negatively distanced from the normal woman schema; indeed she constructs herself as the negatively polarized version of "bad woman," when she announces that she intends to kill her sons. This is the exact opposite of the "good woman," whose first duty and loyalty was owed to her sons. The Chorus is immediately distanced from her through their strong disapproval. Her monologue, whatever text we accept for its disputed parts,[13] generates a series of zooming and distancing devices, which function in the same fashion as those discussed above; unfortunately space does not allow me to pursue this here. The conclusion of the play offers an even more striking view of their working.

After 1316 Medea appears in the chariot given her by Helios and drawn by dragons. She is either on the roof of the σχηνή (stage) or in the μηχανή (crane), certainly high up and out of reach. As Knox noted, she is in the place, and performs a role, reserved for gods in Attic tragedy.[14] Her words to Jason at 1317–22 stress further this supernatural distancing. Throughout the play Medea was a more or less ordinary woman, the victim of male power, zoomed to and distanced from the two poles of feminine behavior that were crystallized into the schemata normal woman and bad woman; she had ended up in an extreme version of the latter, killing her sons and wreaking havoc on her husband's οἶκος and the male power establishment.[15] Given Greek social values she should now be defeated and punished. Instead, she is dramatically distanced from normal women and zoomed toward the divine. But her bad woman *persona* does not disappear when she appears on the chariot: it continues to be constructed and elaborated by Jason, who brings out many aspects of this *persona*, including her betrayal of father and country, the murder of her brother, and the murder of their sons. His claim at 1339–40 that no Greek woman would ever dare do these things distances this polarized bad woman from the Greek normal woman and the world of the audience. Jason crystallizes the negative distancing by comparing Medea to a lioness and the monster Scylla. But the audience's knowledge that some Greek women did do such things, activated here by Jason's

---

[13] I follow Page's text and take 1056–80 (except 1062–63) to be genuine; Diggle 1984 athetizes 1056–80; cf. the comments and discussion in Kovacs 1986:343–52.

[14] Knox 1983:280–81.

[15] The shift from victim to agent is not unique to Medea; as Segal 1990:113 notes, in *Hecuba, Medea, Ion,* and *Bacchae* there is abrupt reversal of a female character from victim to agent.

assertion to the contrary, as earlier when similar views were expressed by the Chorus, may perhaps have slightly deconstructed some of this distancing.

Then Medea is in some degree zoomed toward the normal woman's voice—albeit within the visually articulated distancing framework that partly undermines such zooming—when she evokes her "wronged woman" character at 1366. To Jason's implicit accusation that murdering the children was a disproportionate response, she answers by expressing the view that it is not a slight annoyance for a woman if her husband takes another wife. This statement would have activated the audience's knowledge that marriage is the whole foundation of a woman's life. Thus, when Jason responds by stating that to a σώφρων (self-controlled) woman it is indeed only a slight annoyance, at least some of the audience would have perceived him to be expressing a male ideal that was offensive to a normal woman.

Medea is firmly distanced to the divine sphere at 1378–88 when she announces the institution of a festival, as gods do in tragedy. When she prophesies a bad end for Jason and announces she will go to Athens and marry Aegeus, the audience knows this will indeed happen. Her announcement would have evoked for the Athenian audience a mythological and ideological nexus that had been lightly adumbrated before: her unsuccessful attempt to kill her stepson Theseus. Her punishment was expulsion; she then went on to become the ancestor of the fifth-century Athenians' most significant "other," the Medes, a genealogy that made Theseus' victory over her a mythological paradigm of the victories over the Persians.[16] This zoomed the story nearer to the audience's own world, their own *polis* in the heroic past. Medea and the Persians were defeated, but the Athenian male par excellence was seriously endangered. What is worse, this bad woman got away with everything. Her distancing to the divine sphere created the ideological space in which Medea escaped punishment. But this does not neutralize her *persona* as a bad woman, and thus it does not wholly neutralize the fact that in this tragedy a bad woman escapes punishment. This viewpoint is crystallized in, and activated by, Jason at 1405–14 when he stresses that Medea, a bad woman in the extreme, is getting away with everything, while he has suffered dreadfully. Medea's disappearance after his words emphasizes further her divine *persona*. This disappearance is followed by the floating epilogue, which is not, as some have

---

[16] See below on images of Medea.

thought, inapposite.[17] It answers Jason and articulates the ultimate un-
knowability of the will of the gods. The verses acquire their full import
in context: here they make possible the meaning that the success of
Medea's revenge and escape was the will of the gods, and that this was
correlative with Jason's betrayal of his oaths.[18]

The notion explored in this play—that when women turn into "bad
women," they use the weapons of the weak, which are both deceitful
and violent, and hurt men where they are vulnerable to women, in the
οἶκος—was articulated in many myths. What is different here is that
the play has explored the great disadvantages of the position of women
and has come near to hinting that the so-called bad women have a
point: given that position, if men break oaths and abuse their power
over women, it will be their own fault when catastrophe follows, and
the gods will not necessarily favor their cause. Such vengeful action
by the women is wrong, but in some strange way it has a certain sort
of rightness; for the gods appear to have willed Medea's success and
Jason's suffering.

The play places these explorations at a safe symbolic distance. Their
relevance to the world of reality was constructed through a series of
zooming and distancing devices that brought the world of the play
and Medea nearer to that of the audience and then distanced it again
at crucial moments. Thus the deployment of distancing and zooming
devices made it possible to manipulate the character's shifting distances
in such a way as to conduct these explorations, and also articulate the
notions "bad woman" and "bad mother," at a safe symbolic distance.
For it is through these devices that Medea, the extreme personification
of "bad woman," also becomes at certain points a sympathetic character. This has two important consequences: first, she is an effective
dramatic character, and second, she can generate a certain empathy
both for herself and for the position of women in general in a way
that does not appear to threaten the central male self of the audience.
This construction of Medea's character, a process involving shifts from
normal woman to bad woman and the management of symbolic distances, can help us understand how Euripides' Medea and the Procne

---

[17] McDermott 1989:111–12 and Kovacs 1993:65–67 also consider the epilogue significant.

[18] Kovacs 1993, published after this paper was first presented, expresses a not dissimilar
view regarding the role of the gods. The notion that *Medea* ends in moral chaos is culturally
determined, dependent on a particular type of reading and on modern perceptions of a
simpler "moral order."

in Sophocles' *Tereus* (*TGF* fr. 583) display a "strange combination of infanticide and programmatic speech about the lot of women."[19] Certain things could only be safely uttered by a truly bad woman. But, at least in *Medea*, when she utters them Medea speaks with a normal woman's voice and arouses sympathy. The situation, the play suggests, is not as ideal and unproblematic as normative ideology indicates; and if things go wrong, men also suffer. One should not simply blame women for this; it is not inconceivable that they may have a point.

Images of Medea before 430

I shall now consider Medea's images and their relationships to Euripides' *Medea* and to its construction of Medea proposed in the previous section, examining first the images produced before ca. 430. Since tragedy is one major focus of this exploration, I am concentrating on the representations that are more directly relevant to Medea's tragic articulations: Athenian and South Italian images.

The earliest known representation of Medea in Greek art is on the chest of Cypselus, a Corinthian work known to us only through the literary sources, which showed Medea sitting on a throne with Jason on her right and Aphrodite on her left; the epigram "Jason marries Medea, Aphrodite commands" accompanied the image.[20] The iconographical schema, like the epigram, represented Medea as a bride; it may have evoked the divine facet of her *persona*.[21] She is certainly represented as a supernatural being on four Attic black figure lekythoi of ca. 530 that depict a bust of Medea flanked by two snakes (figure 1).[22] I shall now consider her Athenian narrative images in the sixth century and in the first seventy years of the fifth.

First, the Argonauts' cycle. Only in one nexus of scenes from this cycle is Medea represented: her rejuvenations, of which the most

---

[19] Knox 1983:289.
[20] On Medea on Cypselus' chest, cf. Paus. 5.18.3; Schefold 1966:77–78; E. Simon 1961:951; Vojatzi 1982:91–92; Neils 1990:631 no. 10; Schefold 1992:193.
[21] Cf. Vojatzi 1982:92.
[22] M. Schmidt 1992:nos. 3–6, one of which, BM 1926.4–17.1, has the inscription *Medeia*, the authenticity of which had been doubted by Beazley, but has now proved genuine (cf. Schmidt no. 3); cf. also E. Simon 1961:952; on the iconographical schema cf. especially Vojatzi 1982:93–94.

1. Bust of Medea Flanked by Two Snakes. Lekythos, London, British Museum 1926. 4–17.1.

frequently represented was her deception of the Peliades,[23] popular in Attic art in the later sixth and fifth centuries.[24] One of the preferred

---

[23] On this subject cf. E. Simon 1954:207–11, 1961:952–53; Zinnerling-Paul 1979:412–19; Schefold 1978:100–106; Vojatzi 1982:94–100, 119–23; Meyer 1980; Bol 1989:77–78; Schefold 1992:193–94; Halm-Tisserant 1993:38–43.

[24] We are told (Paus. 8.11) that Micon painted images of the Peliades. Pollitt 1990:142 n. 21 thinks that these images belonged to Micon's painting of the Argonauts in the Anakeion in Athens (Paus. 1.18.1). If this is right, the painting did not only represent the Argonauts themselves and would have included Medea. Robertson 1977:160 suggested that the death of Talos on the column krater recently discovered in Montesarchio near Benevento (cf. below n. 27) may have been derived from a wall painting of the time and circle of Micon and Polygnotus.

2. Medea's Rejuvenation of a Ram. Hydria, London E 163.

images of this myth is the rejuvenation of the ram, the event that persuaded Pelias' daughters to kill their father (figure 2). These images emphasize the rejuvenation of the animal, and thus the success of Medea's magic and her *persona* as a powerful witch, rather than the murder of Pelias. That murder is more to the fore in the second category of preferred images of this myth,[25] which shows the preparations for Pelias' slaughter and includes images of the Peliades leading their father to his death. Representations of other rejuvenations, such as Jason's, are

---

[25] On this category, see Schefold 1978:102–6; Vojatzi 1982:95–97; Meyer 1980:29–34.

rarer;[26] they involve various versions of the boiling cauldron schema seen in the images of the deception of the Peliades.

Of the other parts of the Argonaut myth, I know of only one surviving representation earlier than 430 in which Medea is depicted: the death of Talus on the column krater recently discovered in Montesarchio near Benevento dating from between 440 and 430,[27] in which Medea is represented as an ordinary woman, wearing Greek dress and holding a bowl. Medea is never shown helping Jason against the dragon at this time, as she is in the literary sources and in South Italian vase painting. This is not simply the result of the rarity of Jason scenes in Attic art; for in the two Attic scenes in which Jason is shown with the dragon, it is Athena who is shown helping him, while in the South Italian images it is Medea.[28]

After Medea escaped from Corinth, she went to Athens, married Aegeus, and, according to one variant, had a son with him called Medus.[29] When Theseus arrived from Troezen to claim his inheritance Medea realized that he was Aegeus' son and persuaded Aegeus, who had not recognized him, to kill him—first by sending him to fight against the Bull of Marathon, and then, when he defeated the bull, by attempting to poison him. At the last moment Aegeus recognized the sword that he had left behind under the rock at Troezen and thus realized that Theseus was his son. Medea was expelled from Attica and went to the East, where she, or her son Medus, reigned in Media or gave their name to the land (or both).

In the years following the Persian Wars this story was articulated as a mythological representation of the Greek victories over the Persians, with special reference to the Athenian victory at Marathon. Medea's role in Theseus' fight against the bull, which is one of the mythological themes that became a paradigm for those victories, is expressed in a series of images of this fight. They include Medea in ordinary Greek dress holding a *phialē* and jug, which she will use in the preparation and serving of the poison during her second attempt against Theseus' life.

[26] Figure 2 represents the hydria London E 163. For the images of the rejuvenation of Jason, see Neils 1990:637, nos. 58–62; 77–79. On this and Medea's other other rejuvenations, see Vojatzi 1982:98–99, 123–24; Zinnerling-Paul 1979:416–17; E. Simon 1954:208–9; Bol 1989:76–77; Halm-Tisserant 1993:25–48.

[27] Neils 1990:no. 55; cf. Robertson 1977:158–60.

[28] Cf. Zinnerling-Paul 1979:419; Vojatzi 1982:91.

[29] For the myth of Medea's dealings with Theseus, see testimonia and discussion in Sourvinou-Inwood 1979:22–28, 33–35, 48–55, 1990a:412–13.

No representation of the poison attempt or recognition is known from the period before 430, although a series of Roman terra-cotta reliefs depicting the attempted poisoning may reflect an Attic original of the third quarter of the fifth century.[30] The images of Theseus attacking a woman with a sword represents the expulsion of Medea from Attica. I discussed elsewhere Bologna PU 273 (ca. 430),[31] on which Medea is represented in Greek dress; the dominant aspect of her *persona* is that of Theseus' stepmother, which here also evoked her connection with the Persians and helped create the complex meanings pertaining to war and patriotism.

To sum up, the most popular of the Argonaut cycle subjects in which Medea is represented in Attic art is her deception of the Peliades, which shows her as a witch and a subverter of family relationships. She is not shown together with Jason as a part of a married or courting couple, as in the Cypselus chest; nor is she shown helping him in his confrontation with the dragon. Only in the destruction of Talus is she shown as a helper in the Argonautic expedition. The rejuvenation of Jason, shown a few times, is somewhat ambivalent, for it evokes the slaughter of Pelias, to which it is iconographically and thematically close. In the Theseus myth Medea's role is wholly negative, and Theseus' victory over her represented a victory over a variety of negative representations threatening to the Athenian male self.

In the large majority of these scenes the iconographical schema through which Medea is represented is not differentiated from that of "normal woman," that is, "Greek woman." In some scenes her character as a sorceress is indicated explicitly by the fact that she is shown holding a chest, which in her hands would be identified as her box of poisons.[32] Her maximum distancing from normal woman in these narrative scenes, though much less distanced than on the lekythoi mentioned above, is on the neck amphora London British Museum B 221,[33] where Medea is differentiated from the Peliades through the fact that she is wearing a *polos*, a hat associated with deities and also women who are somehow connected with deities. Thus in most narrative scenes Medea is distanced from normal woman, but not radically, while in a few non-narrative scenes she was distanced very strongly.

---

[30] See references, description, and commentary in Sourvinou-Inwood 1979:31.

[31] *ARV* 1268.1; Add. 356. See Sourvinou-Inwood 1992.

[32] Cf., e.g., Schefold 1978:pls. 29.2, 30.1; see Vojatzi 1982:96.

[33] *ABV* 321.4; Add. 87.

Images of Medea from
ca. 430 to the End of the Fourth Century

"Old" Subjects

I begin with the subjects that had also been represented before 430. Of the scenes from the Argonauts' cycle, the Peliades episode loses its centrality. To my knowledge, there are no representations of Medea and the Peliades in Attic vase painting that can be firmly dated after ca. 430[34] and there are no representations of this myth or of any rejuvenation theme in South Italian vase painting. But there is an important representation of this theme on an Attic relief, part of a set of four of which we only have Roman copies,[35] the original of which is to be dated 420–10. In this image Medea is wearing an oriental tiara, chiton, peplos, and χάνδυς (a short Persian overgarment).[36] She is holding her drug box. As for the other episodes, in Attic art the death of Talus is represented twice, on the volute krater Ruvo, Jatta 1501, by the Talus Painter,[37] and on the calyx krater fragment from Spina near the Talus and Pronomus Painters, on which enough of Medea is preserved to show that she is seated and holding her box of poisons and a knife.[38] Scenes of Medea and Jason in Colchis, the winning of the Golden Fleece, and events in Corinth become popular themes on South Italian vases.[39] The representation of the confrontation with the dragon is the most popular episode;[40] other representations include the meeting of Jason and Medea, the yoking of the bulls, and the presentation of the fleece to Pelias.

When we turn to the Theseus cycle, we find that some Attic representations of Medea in the Marathonian Bull episode show her in

---

[34] Two belong to the third quarter, one to the 430s: Meyer 1980:nos. I Va 20 (calyx krater formerly on the Swiss market) and I Va 21 (pyxis Louvre CA 636) (cf. Meyer 1980:12–13).

[35] See E. Simon 1954:209–10, 1961:952; Robertson 1975:374, 684 n. 34 with bibliography; Hofkes-Brukker 1967:43; Zinnerling-Paul 1979:17–18 fig. 8 and n. 28 with bibliography; Meyer 1980:38–50.

[36] See Schoppa 1933:52. Cf. also Losfeld 1991:284–85.

[37] For the volute krater, see *ARV* 1338.1; Add. 366. For the calyx krater, see Robertson 1992:257 fig. 260, 1977:159.

[38] The fragmentary bell krater by the Dinus Painter in Gela (Neils 1990:no. 11; Trendall and Cambitoglou 1978:37–38) does not represent Medea and the Argonauts but Medea, Aegeus, and Theseus (cf. below).

[39] Cf. Neils 1990:nos. 12–13, 16–17, 37–42, 57. On Medea on South Italian vases, cf. also Zinnerling-Paul 1979:423–27.

[40] Neils 1990:nos. 37–42.

oriental dress, others in Greek.[41] A fragmentary bell krater by the Dinus Painter in Gela shows Aegeus with Medea in oriental costume at the departure of the ship carrying Theseus to Crete.[42] This does not represent a different version of the myth, according to which Medea had not been thrown out of Attica by the time Theseus started on his expedition against the Minotaur; rather it is an iconographic creation,[43] in which the narrative and the emblematic modes are intertwined. It thus combines the important elements of Theseus' adventures on his arrival in Athens with the beginning of the adventure that will result in the ephebic hero becoming the Athenian king.

South Italian vase painting rarely represents Theseus' fight against the Bull of Marathon but does give us two instances of Theseus' recognition by Aegeus, which is not shown on Attic vases. On the krater Adolphseck, Kassel AV 278, the ornate costumes evoke theatrical costumes, which suggests that the scene may have been inspired by a theatrical performance, usually thought to have been that of Euripides' *Aegeus*.[44] On the bell krater Leningrad W 205,[45] the costumes are less ornate and it is not clear whether the ancient viewers would have sensed any evocation of the theater. There are differences between the two scenes: on the first Aegeus is examining a sword, Theseus is pouring a libation on an altar, and Medea has just dropped her jug; in the field there is a *boukranion*. The Leningrad krater represents Aegeus, Theseus, and two women, one of whom is sitting, and there is no altar; instead, a hydria is on the floor between Theseus and Aegeus who are holding one sandal each. There is, then, an important divergence between the two images. On the Adolphseck krater the γνώρισμα (token) through which Aegeus recognized his son is the sword, on the Leningrad krater, the sandals. This may suggest either that one was reflecting the myth presented in a dramatic performance and the other represented a vase painter's version of the myth or that the two were inspired by different dramatic performances, one reflecting

---

[41] Among the vases which are later than 430 and show Medea in Greek dress: cf., e.g., the calyx crater by the Lugano Painter in Agrigento (*ARV* 1347; *Para.* 482 not in Add. [the one included is a different calyx crater]; Griffo and Zirretta 1952:96); in oriental dress: cf., e.g., the calyx crater Adolphseck Kassel AV 462 (*ARV* 1346.2; Add. 368 [which gives the Hesse inv. number]).

[42] Neils 1990:no. 11; Trendall and Cambitoglou 1978:37–38. See n. 38 above (cf. Vojatzi 1982:149 n. 268).

[43] Vojatzi 1982:149 n. 268 attributes this to the influence of free painting.

[44] Trendall and Webster 1971:72–73, III.3.3.

[45] Sourvinou-Inwood 1990a:pl. 7.

Sophocles' *Aegeus*, the other Euripides'. In both images Medea is wearing Greek dress.[46]

The comparison of images created before 430 to later representations pertaining to the same cycles does not show radical changes, only a certain shift in the popularity of certain subjects on Attic vases before and after 430, and some more pronounced differences in preference between Attic and South Italian vases. The most fundamental change is the introduction of the oriental costume, to which I shall return.

New Subjects

Among the new subjects in Medea's imagery, the murder of her children and her escape in the chariot of the Sun are the most important. The events in Corinth, very popular in South Italian vase painting, involve three episodes, sometimes represented together and sometimes separately: the death of Creusa, the infanticide, and Medea's escape in the chariot of the Sun.

On the two scenes where the death of Creusa is represented on its own, Medea is not depicted; these images thus do not affect the present argument.[47] While there is no Attic representation on a surviving classical vase of Medea killing her children, South Italian vases portray the murders, Medea's subsequent escape in the chariot of the Sun, or both.

i. On the early Lucanian hydria (ca. 400) at Policoro, Museo Nazionale della Siritide,[48] Medea is in her chariot, which has already taken off, the corpses are on the ground; and Jason is impotently threatening her with a sword. Aphrodite and Eros flank the chariot. Medea is wearing an oriental headdress, a decorated chiton from under which come long sleeves decorated with the "strokes" pattern, and a himation.

ii. On an early Lucanian bell krater (ca. 400) in the Cleveland Museum of Art (figure 3),[49] Medea is aloft in the chariot, enclosed in a large sun that identifies it as belonging to the Sun; this distances Medea from the other figures even more strongly than on i, creating an even stronger

---

[46] Another representation of the recognition in which Medea is wearing Greek dress is on a series of Roman terra-cotta reliefs that may be reflecting an Attic original of the third quarter of the fifth century. See references and commentary in Sourvinou-Inwood 1979:31.

[47] Lucanian bell krater Louvre CA 2193 (see Trendall and Webster 1971:III.3.35; Berger-Doer 1992:121) and the krater Naples Mus. Naz. SA 526 (Berger-Doer 1992: no. 16).

[48] M. Schmidt 1992:no. 35; Taplin 1993:117 no. 2.103.

[49] M. Schmidt 1992:no. 36; Taplin 1993:116 no. 1.101.

3. Medea in the Chariot of the Sun. Bell krater, Cleveland Museum of Art 91.1 (Leonard D. Hanna Jr. Fund).

supernatural effect. Erinyes flank the chariot. The children's corpses are lying on an altar. Medea wears a tiara, decorated peplos, sleeves decorated with a pattern of lozenges, and a himation.

Taplin remarked that in both i and ii Jason's helplessness below is a "call for acquaintance" with the tragedy.[50] He also notes that both scenes

[50] Taplin 1993:22.

contain elements that are not straight representations of the play, not least the fact that here Medea does not carry away the children's corpses. The differences between the tragedy and the images, he suggests, may be due to iconographic changes, the influence of a local restaging, or a mixture of both. I am inclined to favor the first interpretation. The possibility that local restaging could have altered Medea's treatment of the children's corpses seems to me unlikely; for her burial of the children is an important part of the conclusion of the play, in which Medea, firmly distanced to the divine sphere, announces the institution of a festival, as gods do in tragedy. As the corpses in the chariot are an important element of meaning creation in the tragedy, so are the corpses on the ground in the images: they enhance both the pathos of the scene and the distance between Medea and everyone else.

The two scenes are two iconographical articulations of some South Italian perceptions of important aspects of the tragedy's ending. On vase ii the corpses are lying on an altar. The fact that the boys' corpses are on the altar should be understood in connection with other representations of the murder, such as that on Munich 3296 (iii below), where Medea is preparing to kill one of the boys who is standing on an altar; or on the Campanian neck amphora Paris Louvre K 300 (v), where the murder takes place near an altar; or on the Campanian neck amphora Cabinet des Medailles 876 (iv), where one corpse is on the altar while Medea is about to kill the second child. Accordingly, the viewers would have understood the child on Munich 3296 attempting to take refuge at the altar as a kind of iconographic equivalent to the boys' cries at 1271–2 and 1277–8,[51] an element that increased both the pathos of the representation and Medea's wickedness: she not only killed her sons but did so at the very altar of the gods. If Schmidt is right that the himation gathered around the waist on (our) iv and v would have been seen as a sign of the sacrificer,[52] the combination of this sign and the altar would not, in my view, have created the meaning "the murder is a sacrifice." Read through the ancient assumptions, the horrible deed at the altar would have been contrasted to a proper killing at the altar: it would have been perceived as a perversion of sacrifice.[53]

We can make sense of the artist's choice to diverge from the Euripidean play by not having the boys' corpses in the chariot with Medea:

[51] Cf. also on this question Séchan 1925:411–12 with bibliography.

[52] M. Schmidt 1992:396.

[53] See also McDermott 1989:75–78 for a discussion (with bibliography) of the murder as perverted sacrifice.

such a choice would have cast her in a less negative light. This may have been connected with the choice to represent the Erinyes, which fit this vase painter's perception that Medea will or ought to be punished (the image allows both interpretations). In the eyes of the original Athenian audience, who were all too familiar with Medea's subsequent history, such a representation of Jason's wish was not possible. The South Italian vase painter's addition of the Erinyes suggests that to him the ending of Euripides' *Medea* as it stood was too disturbing. Eros and Aphrodite on vase i are broadly comparable to the Erinyes as an iconographic articulation; they are a partial iconographic correlative to Medea's exclamation at line 330, φεῦ φεῦ, βροτοῖς ἔρωτες ὡς κακὸν μέγα (Alas, how great an evil love is for mankind). But this representation of the forces that brought about the tragic ending here depicted may have deconstructed Medea's wickedness somewhat by evoking her injured status and Jason's culpability.

iii. The Apulian volute krater Munich 3296 (J 810)[54] is decorated with a complex image that combines the main figures and episodes of Medea's Corinthian adventures and even includes her father's ghost. On either side of the naiskos at the center of the two main zones of action are Heracles, Athena, and the Dioscuri. In the upper zone the focus is on Creon and his daughter, who is dying inside the naiskos. In the lower zone the focus is Medea in the process of killing one of her sons, who stands on an altar and whom she has grabbed by the hair, and a torch-bearing Οἶστρος (Frenzy [inscribed]), who drives Medea's waiting chariot. A young man holding spears seems to be trying to remove the other son. Medea is wearing a tiara, a himation around her shoulders, and a decorated double chiton with sleeves of a different material coming out from under it. It has often been assumed that because this image does not accurately reflect Euripides' play, it was inspired by another *Medea*, now lost.[55] But this explanation is far from compelling[56] and depends on the assumption that a vase painter was mechanically dependent on a tragic performance. Our image can be much more satisfactorily explained as a vase painter's creation of a particular articulation of the myth. The representation of the three gods above the action shows that the vase painter was indeed creating his own version and was not simply reproducing tragic incidents. This is an

---

[54] Trendall and Webster 1971:III.5.4; M. Schmidt 1992:no. 29.

[55] Cf. the discussions in Séchan 1925:408–22; Trendall and Webster 1971:110; M. Schmidt 1992:397.

[56] See the discussion in M. Schmidt 1992:397.

IMAGES AND EURIPIDEAN TRAGEDY 273

iconographic version of the myth, partly inspired by Euripides' *Medea*[57] and involving particular choices. One such choice was to elaborate the story through the inclusion of Creon's son and wife; another to evoke the earlier part of Medea's story, her betrayal of her father and murder of her brother, an evocation that was also significantly deployed within the play as part of the construction of Medea's character through its shifting relationships.

iv. On the Campanian neck amphora Cabinet des Medailles 876[58] one corpse is lying on the altar, and Medea is about to kill the second boy, who tries to run away, making a gesture of supplication. She has grabbed him by the hair with her right hand, in which she is also holding the sword, as the παιδαγωγός (boy's attendant) rushes in from afar. Medea wears a tiara, an ornate chiton with no sleeves, and has a himation around her waist.

v. The Campanian neck amphora Paris Louvre K 300[59] shows Medea killing one of her sons, who is making a gesture of supplication toward her. The other boy is not shown. Medea does not have an oriental headdress; she is wearing a chiton and a himation; from under the chiton appear long sleeves of a different material, decorated with the "strokes" pattern. The murder is taking place in a space defined as a sanctuary of Apollo by the representation of two columns, an altar, and a statue of Apollo on a column. If it is correct that Apollo was thought to have participated at the wedding of Jason and Medea,[60] then this image would have called to mind that wedding and all the sorry events that followed afterward, perhaps also evoking Medea's *persona* as a wronged woman and thus setting her act in a more complex perspective.

vi. On the Apulian amphora Naples Museum Nazionale 81954 (H3221),[61] Medea's chariot, though drawn by dragons, is on the ground, pursued by a beardless male on horseback and two figures on foot; one of the murdered children lies on the ground, while parts of the second dead child can be seen on the floor of the chariot. On the other side of the chariot there is a Λύσσα-(Rage-)type demonic figure holding a torch in one hand and a sword in the other; beyond her is Selene, the protector of witches and the antithetical equivalent of the Sun, in whose chariot his granddaughter Medea escapes. The distancing created by

---

[57] See also Séchan 1925:420–22.
[58] M. Schmidt 1992:no. 30.
[59] M. Schmidt 1992:no. 31.
[60] Vojatzi 1982:92.
[61] Neils 1990:73; M. Schmidt 1992:37.

4. Medea and Heroes in the Garden of the Hesperides. Hydria,
London E 224.

the dragon chariot is minimized, as it is shown on the ground operating
like an ordinary chariot, while Medea is apparently about to be attacked
by her pursuer. She wears Greek dress and thus is not iconographically
differentiated from ordinary Greek women. The Λύσσα-figure creates
the notion that Medea was the victim of forces beyond her control. Selene evoked not just Medea's role as a witch but also the notion of divine

5. Detail of Figure 4: Medea with Oriental Headdress, Decorated Chiton, and Himation. Hydria, London E 224.

protection, on which Medea is shown to be dependent. This helped bring her down to the level of other descendants of the gods who had divine help and who, as heroes in narratives—as opposed to recipients of cult—were perceived as the correlatives of ordinary mortals, *mutatis mutandis*.

vii. The fragment of an Apulian vase, Berlin, Staatliche Museen 30916,[62] shows Jason and a piece of Medea's snake chariot; the figure of Medea is not preserved.

Thus, of these scenes, two represent the murder (iv, v), four show the escape in the chariot after the murder (i, ii, vi, vii), and one represents the murder while the chariot is waiting (iii).

Medea's presence is considered problematic in the scene depicted on the hydria London E 224 by the Meidias Painter (figures 4, 5).[63] On the upper zone is depicted the abduction of the Leucippids by the Dioscuri. The lower frieze "separates into three parts, but there is no division and

[62] M. Schmidt 1992:no. 38; Neils 1990:no. 72.

[63] *ARV* 1313.5; Add. 361; M. Schmidt 1992:no. 70; Burn 1987:15–25; Robertson 1992:238–39.

they are probably conceived as merging."[64] On the front there is Heracles in the Garden of the Hesperides, three Hesperides, and Hygieia,
with Iolaus and a youth called Clytius framing the group. A fourth girl
beyond Clytius is another Hesperid, Chryseis, linking the scene on the
front to that on the back. Next to Chryseis are Demophon and Oeneus,
and next to them a group consisting of Clymenus, Antiochus, and Hip-
pothoön, and then Acamas and Philoctetes (the latter youthful like the
others, the former bearded and with a sceptre). Under the handle,
between Iolaus and Philoctetes, there is a group consisting of Medea,
wearing the oriental costume and holding a small casket that represents
her box of poisons, between two female figures named "Elera" and
"Arniope." Elera is walking toward the group of Philoctetes and Acamas but turning back to face Medea. The Medea group is framed by the
two heroes most closely associated with Heracles and who are depicted
in a similar stance; they thus connect the Medea group with both the
Garden of Hesperides proper and with the mostly Attic heroes at the
back. The goddess Hygieia is present in the paradise garden because all
good things are at home there.[65]

Eponymous heroes are popular at this time and fit unproblematically
the context of paradise. But what of Medea? She certainly would have
created a dark note; however, since the heroes in paradise were beyond
her threat, we need to define exactly how she was perceived as a dark
presence here.

A dominant dimension of signification here is heroic status, with a
stress on Attic and especially eponymous heroes. Among those who
are not eponymous, a hero with the *nom parlant*, Clymenus, evokes
generically the notion of heroic fame and at the same time chthonic
cultic connections.[66] Demophon, the son of Theseus, and Philoctetes,
who is shown together with the other son of Theseus, Acamas, would
have evoked the narrative context in which the three belonged: the
Trojan War and in particular the Sack of Troy. Philoctetes was also
intimately connected with Heracles, who is the central figure of the
image. It is context that activates or makes latent a figure's meanings. Here the representation of eponymous heroes and Theseus' sons
would have brought to the fore Medea's own eponymy, which had
resulted from her defeat by Theseus. Thus her *persona* as the enemy's
eponymous heroine would have been highlighted and she would have

---

[64] Robertson 1992:238.
[65] Cf. Robertson 1992:239.
[66] On Clymenus as the name of a form of Hades, see Kearns 1992:82–83.

been perceived as Theseus' enemy, the symbol of the Persians, and a bad woman. She was defeated by Theseus, but here she is again, not far from Theseus' sons. Bad women are a constant menace to men, as is the oriental enemy to Athens. The latter dimension may have gained some additional reinforcement from the presence of Acamas, Demophon, and Philoctetes, an implicit reference to the Sack of Troy; in the fifth-century Troy was, among other things, a symbolic paradigm for Persia.

Medea is represented in the company of Arniope and Elera. *Elera* is the form of the name of one of the Leucippids, Hilaeira, that is inscribed in the Rape of Leucippidai represented on the zone above. Thus, in this context the Athenian viewer would understand Elera to be a Leucippid. But before attempting to reconstruct what a Leucippid in the company of Medea would have suggested to Athenian viewers, we should first consider the other figure, Arniope.

We have no knowledge of a mythological figure by this name.[67] One may well have existed and we do not happen to know about her. If she had been invented by the Meidias Painter she would have been perceived as a companion figure, who would have been seen in terms of her association with Medea. In the proximity of Medea, the name *Arniope* would have evoked the lamb, *arna* (see, e.g., Apollod. 1.9.27; Paus. 8.11.2), to which she had transformed the ram she had rejuvenated in order to persuade the daughters of Pelias to kill their father.[68] The evocation of this episode recalls Medea's *persona* as a bad woman who led good girls to destroy their father. In Spartan cult the Leucippidai were paradigmatic παρθένοι (maidens) in transition to becoming brides and wives.[69] The fact that the marriage of the Leucippidai was illustrated in a painting by Polygnotus in the sanctuary of the Dioscuri in Athens, the Anakeion (Paus. 1.18.1), means that their character as brides was part of the common Athenian assumptions. Their abductors and bridegrooms, the Dioscuri, were Helen's brothers, and the Leucippidai were associated in Spartan cult with Helen in her *persona* as goddess and marriageable παρθένος

---

[67] Cf. Bettini 1984:614.

[68] The name nearest to Arniope known to me is Argiope, the (Thracian) mother of Thamyras (see Nercessian 1984:591). If the name was not unknown to the Athenians (see Nercessian no. 4 for the possibility that a dithyramb may have been involved), it may have carried negative connotations and helped darken the perception of the figure of Arniope; and it also may have facilitated the evocation of *arna* by making the *arn-* element register more strongly precisely because it was not the expected *arg-*.

[69] Cf. Calame 1977:1.323–33.

par excellence.[70]   These perceptions were familiar in Athens at the
time of the production of the vase under consideration; they are reflected in Euripides' *Helen* produced in 412, and Aristophanes' *Lysistrata*, produced in 411.[71]   In our scene, instead of the sometimes
ambivalent, sometimes positive Helen, we have Medea, the totally
negative woman, a destructive force within the family and Theseus'
murderous stepmother.

This association would have created disturbing meanings. It would
have led the audience to perceive the danger that even a good woman
can be corrupted and drift to the bad—a notion that the very ambivalence of Helen's figure also expresses. These negative perceptions are
distanced here, in that they focus on the Spartan "other," and are expressed through Medea in her distanced oriental *persona*. But Medea's
association with Theseus, her implication in the dangers he faced, deconstructs that distance and brings darkness nearer to the Athenian
self. Theseus defeated Medea, but here she is still—with her box of
poisons and near his sons, in paradise. By recalling Medea's role in
the Theseus myth and her symbolic association with the Persians, the
image would also have evoked the perception that her real-life correlatives were like Medea in paradise: though once defeated, the Persians
were then playing an important role in the Peloponnesian War. They
consorted with the Spartan enemy, as Medea consorts with the Spartan Leucippid Elera—and this endangered Athens. Thus the figure of
Medea deconstructs the rosy-colored world of paradise: her connections with darkness bring to the fore the notion of darkness and threat
in real life.

On the Apulian volute krater Princeton University Art Museum
83.13,[72] Medea, inscribed and in Greek dress, and an elderly male of
the παιδαγωγός type are shown inside a building inscribed *ELEUSIS.
TO HIERON*. Under it there is an altar on which are sitting two boys. To
the right of the altar Heracles is in conversation with Iris; above them
are the two Eleusinian goddesses. On the other side of the temple, in
the position corresponding to that of these two goddesses, are Athena
with Nike and the Dioscuri, who are holding Eleusinian torches and
thus shown as *mystai*. M. Schmidt has argued that the boys on the

---

[70] Calame 1977:1.324; 333–46; 355–56; Brelich 1969:162–63; 166; Sommerstein 1990:*ad*
Ar. *Lys*. 1314.
[71] Cf. Eur. *Hel*. 1465ff., 1666–69; Ar. *Lys*. 1314–15; Sommerstein 1990:*ad* 1314; Henderson
1987:221–22 *ad* 1314–15, cf. *ad* 1307–8.
[72] M. Schmidt 1986, and pl. 32.1; M. Schmidt 1992:no. 68.

altar are not Medea's sons but Heracles'; according to one version of his myth, Medea cured him of the madness that made him slaughter them.[73] The narrative location of Heracles, Iris, and the boys on the altar would be Thebes; Medea and the παιδαγωγός are at Eleusis, where the latter would have gone to enlist Medea's help. The image would represent the Eleusinian cult, and Heracles' initiation in it, as crucial for the achievement of his cure. M. Schmidt's interpretation is convincing, and her comparison to the krater Munich 3296 by the Underworld Painter—the main successor of the Darius Painter, who painted the Princeton image—is significant. On the Munich vase, Heracles is a god and Medea in the throes of frenzy kills her son on the altar; on the Princeton vase it is she who is the positive figure, not divine but closely connected with the Eleusinian deities; but Heracles is not shown in the throes of madness and the children are still alive. Athena and the Dioscuri are present in both images, and the Dioscuri evoke an aspect of Heracles' *persona* that they shared: on the Munich vase participation on the Argonaut expedition and divine status, on the Princeton vase their Eleusinian initiation and immortality. Thus one image transforms the other, helping confirm that for these vase painters, Medea and Heracles were in some ways comparable and not simply antithetical.

Commentary

From about 430 Medea appears usually, but not exclusively, in oriental costume. This schema differentiates her from normal women in a new modality, which is combined with the earlier one involving supernatural distancing in representations of the escape in the chariot of the Sun, the supernatural aspect of which recalls that represented on the black figure lekythoi. Among Medea's new subjects in this period, the representation of the murder of her children, which is not represented in any extant Attic images, and its aftermath is the most important. It reflects the influence of the performance of Euripides' *Medea*. One particular aspect of this influence is especially significant.

Medea's appearance in this tragedy is generally thought to have inspired artists to represent her in oriental costume.[74] This reasoning is correct, but not adequate. It does not fully explain why she had not been depicted in oriental costume before, nor does it explain the pattern of selection of oriental and Greek costume in the various images thereafter.

[73] M. Schmidt 1986.

[74] Cf. Page 1938:lxii n. 1; Trendall and Webster 1971:72; see also Brommer 1982:134.

Finally, insofar as it is only through the evidence of the vases that Medea in Euripides' *Medea* has been assumed to have been wearing oriental dress, there is an element of circularity in this argument. I agree that the production of Euripides' *Medea* was crucial; but I believe its involvement was more complex than has been generally thought. The fact that the Athenian artists did not represent Medea in oriental dress before 430 but often do so after 430 needs to be addressed. It is true that oriental costume is found more often on vases in the second half of the fifth century than had been the case before, with figures such as Paris and Orpheus being depicted in oriental dress.[75] Troilus also begins to be represented as a non-Greek around the middle of the fifth century. But this does not absolve us from considering whether there were special reasons in each case, not least because the other figures mentioned appear in oriental dress before Medea, who is shown on the Bologna cup of the late 430s and on the Talus vase of the 430s in Greek costume. If I was right to suggest that Medea as the enemy of Theseus was a symbolic personification of the Persian enemy, it becomes even more puzzling that she had not been represented in oriental costume in the second quarter of the fifth century to make this association explicit. In any case, Medea's intimate association with the Persian enemy is a demonstrable fact:[76] it is found in Herodotus 7.62 and there are good reasons for thinking that it was earlier.[77] Thus the fact that she was not represented in oriental dress before 430 but she was often, but not always, so represented afterward needs to be explained. The ascription of responsibility to Euripides does not explain why he made that choice or why the innovation made such an impact; nor does it explain the pattern of her appearance in oriental dress.

I have argued elsewhere that Medea was not represented in oriental dress before 430 in images of her expulsion from Attica because the Greek dress created a very important nexus of meanings pertaining to her role as bad stepmother and thus bad mother.[78] Why then is she eventually shown in oriental dress, and what does this do for this nexus of meanings pertaining to Medea's *persona* as woman and mother? Let

---

[75] Cf. Raeck 1981:85–87.

[76] On which see Sourvinou-Inwood 1979:49, 1990a:412–13.

[77] Cf. How and Wells 1912:154 *ad loc.*; M. West 1966:429–30 *ad* 1001; see also Sourvinou-Inwood 1990a:413. Cf. below, "Medea at a Shifting Distance."

[78] Sourvinou-Inwood 1990a:439–40.

us set the parameters within which the question must be considered. First, the oriental costume did not replace the Greek one in all scenes. In representations belonging to the Argonauts' cycle Medea is mostly shown wearing oriental dress,[79] but sometimes, though rarely, in Greek dress.[80] In some representations of Theseus' fight against the bull she is wearing oriental dress, in others, Greek. In the two South Italian recognition scenes she is wearing Greek dress, as she is in one infanticide scene and in the Eleusis scene. Second, the oriental costume does not consist of a simple unchanging schema and thus needs to be considered in some detail.

The Oriental Costume

I shall focus on the system of conventions on vases.[81] The exact nature of the different tragic costumes and the relationship between these and costumes on vases are not fully clear, since the reconstruction of the former is based partly on literary evidence and partly on vases thought to reflect dramatic performances in varying degrees of directness.[82] Because we are not sure of the extent to which vases reflected dramatic performances, a specific performance, or a general theatrical influence to represent "stagey-looking" costumes, and because we do not know to what extent such reflections, even when present, were expressed in terms of the painter's own idiom, caution is needed to avoid circular argument. I will try to determine the parameters of differentiation of oriental dress within the iconographic systems of Attic and South Italian vase painting.

A common schema that occurs in different variants in the two centuries of ceramic iconography that concern us consists of an oriental headdress (a soft cap or more often the κίδαρις or tiara); an ensemble involving trousers, usually decorated with zigzag lines, sometimes with

---

[79] E.g., the Attic bell krater fragment in Gela (Neils 1990:no. 11); the Paestan squat lekythos Bochum Univ. S. 1080 (Neils 1990:no. 41); the Apulian bell krater in Turin, private collection (Neils 1990:no. 38); the Apulian volute krater Leningrad Ermitage 1718 (St. 422) (Blatter 1984:no. 21).

[80] See the Apulian volute krater Munich Antikensamml. 3268 (Neils 1990:no. 37).

[81] Real-life oriental costumes (e.g., the description of the Persians' dress in Herodotus 7.61) are irrelevant for our purposes; it is only the ways in which they were deployed conventionally by the vase painters that are pertinent to our investigation (see also Raeck 1981:153–54; cf. 154–56). On references to barbarian costumes in tragedy, see Hall 1989:84 and n. 127, 136–38. On barbarian costumes in Greek art, see Schoppa 1933; cf. 46–48, 63–66 for the representation of Persian costume on Persian monuments.

[82] On tragic costumes, see Pickard-Cambridge 1953:197–204.

a series of strokes or lozenges; and a similarly decorated "top" with long sleeves, which is usually, but not always,[83] worn under a short chiton. In some scenes the costume appears to consist of a jacket and trousers, but in many representations the closely fitting trousers and long sleeves appear to be part of a body stocking type of garment.[84] Various male and female oriental figures in both Attic and South Italian vase painting are shown wearing this costume. Raeck stresses that in the second half of the fifth century one common oriental costume was mostly used for all nationalities.[85] But there are distinctions and differentiations.

First, consider kings.[86] Before and for a short period after the middle of the fifth century, the Persian king is, like other Persians, shown in the jacket and trousers costume. At the turn of the fifth to the fourth century the king wears the common oriental dress, with no differentiation from his subjects; then shortly afterward he is shown in an ankle-length robe. Second, in the 440's women other than Amazons wore the oriental dress described above. This is the costume worn by Andromeda in scenes that are believed to have been inspired by the performance of Sophocles' *Andromeda*.[87] On two vases—one of ca. 440, the other probably a little later—Andromeda wears a form of oriental dress that is a variation on this schema showing only some of its elements. On the calyx krater Basel Antikenmuseum BS 403,[88] she wears an oriental headdress, a sleeved top decorated with zigzags, the long skirt of a normal female chiton, and over it a somewhat shorter skirt with decorated border. In another image,[89] Andromeda's top is decorated with circles and the chiton's skirt only reaches to her shins. This schema is less distanced from the Greek costume than the oriental costume described above. On the Attic calyx krater Berlin Staatliche Museen 3237 of just after 400, thought to reflect Euripides' *Andromeda*,[90] Andromeda wears a different costume: a tiara; chiton; a decorated overgarment, the sleeves of which pick up one of the decorative motifs of the chiton; and a cloak. The tiara

---

[83] E.g., the cup Naples 2613 (*ARV* 1252.50); Raeck 1981:figs. 45–46.

[84] E.g., the skyphos by the Lewis Painter in the Vatican (*ARV* 974.28) (under a short chiton); and, more strikingly, the cup Naples 2613 (*ARV* 1252.50) (not worn under a short chiton). On these variations, see Schoppa 1933:26–27; cf. also 49–50.

[85] See Raeck 1981:153, 292 n. 660.

[86] Raeck 1981:151–57.

[87] Trendall and Webster 1971:63–65, III.2.1–3; white ground calyx krater at Agrigento, Museo Nazionale (*ARV* 1017.53; *Add.* 315), pelike Boston 63.2663 (*Para.* 448; *Add.* 325 [1071]), hydria London BM E 169 (*ARV* 1062; *Add.* 323).

[88] *ARV* 1684.15bis; *Para.* 456; *Add.* 334.

[89] Schauenburg 1981:no. 4.

[90] Trendall and Webster 1971:78, III.3.10.

makes it an oriental costume; but it is an oriental costume less distanced from the Greek tragic costume than those in the oriental schemata seen above. The difference between this costume and that of the oriental king wearing the ankle-length robe is that the king's costume combines the oriental headdress with sleeves of clearly different material, reminiscent of the body stocking—a costume worn, for example, by Darius on the volute krater Naples 3253.[91] The same type of dress is worn by royal women in contexts that appear to be theatrical, as is the case with Europa, who is shown seated on a throne on the Apulian bell krater New York 16.140, her sleeves decorated with lozenges.[92]

In the third quarter of the fifth century, we see an earlier version of this type of costume: on the oinochoe Vatican 16536[93] are represented a Persian king and queen and a third woman, all of whom wear oriental headdress and have long patterned sleeves of different material; the king is wearing an enveloping himation over a close-fitting chiton from under which emerge sleeves decorated with the classically oriental zigzag pattern. The trouser bottoms under the himation have the same decoration. No such trouser bottoms are shown in the case of the women, whose chitons reach to the ground. Under their long chitons are seen long sleeves, decorated with strokes, and a himation. From this time onward women other than Amazons—and certainly royal women—are normally not shown in the common oriental dress involving trousers.

That sleeves decorated with a different pattern from the chiton, especially those decorated with zigzag strokes or lozenges, were perceived to be a significant variation in ancient eyes is shown by the following considerations. Two different types of garments involving such sleeves were part of the oriental costume: the body stocking, which was often shown worn as an undergarment, and a top sometimes worn without a chiton. Thus, these sleeves inevitably evoked both this top and the oriental body stocking; the evocation is strongest when the sleeves are decorated with the zigzag pattern that was perceived as the most characteristically oriental. The strokes and the lozenges, which also appear as body stocking decoration, and (perhaps less strongly) the circles also evoked the oriental and thus distanced this costume from the Greek.

Would it then be true to say that all figures whose sleeves have a different decorative pattern are oriental? It is certainly not the case

[91] Cf. Trendall 1989:fig. 203.
[92] Trendall and Webster 1971:III.1.17.
[93] *ARV* 1065.8; Add. 324.

that all orientals are shown with sleeves with different decoration. The situation is complex. In my view, these sleeves are, first and centrally, worn by oriental figures. Second, they are worn by some figures who can be seen metaphorically as oriental; but in a few cases the possibility of random use cannot be totally excluded.[94]

Sleeves decorated with zigzags (without leggings) are worn by an actor representing a figure without oriental connections in a context likely to reflect actual tragic costume: the actor representing Aegisthus on the Apulian bell krater in New York, Fleischman collection F 93,[95] a comic vase that includes a tragic actor; thus they cannot belong only to the barbarian costume, especially since Aegisthus in this scene is representative of tragedy. But the evocation of an oriental element by these sleeves may pertain to the negative aspect of Aegisthus, a metaphorical orientalism, for transgressive behavior was indeed associated with barbarian behavior, not least in Aeschylus' *Oresteia*.[96] The oriental headdress, which appears to be a stronger marker, may also have been used, albeit rarely, to denote some negative aspect of figures who are not oriental. Thus, if the Lucanian nestoris, London British Museum F 175,[97] does represent Creon and Antigone, Creon's oriental headdress suggests he is metaphorically oriental, a tyrannical king.

This metaphorical use makes it more difficult for us to be certain that we have identified the meanings of the "orientally decorated" sleeves correctly, because we cannot be certain that we are interpreting correctly the images that do not involve a straightforward reading. Despite this problem, the overall pattern of appearance of these sleeves suggests that this is a real pattern of significant usage, and not a cultural construct. But there are difficulties, and it is possible that some versions of the schema may have been used in figures with no oriental connections. Most important, because every element acquires meaning in context,[98] that context cannot be divorced from the attempt to reconstruct its

[94] On the late Paestan volute krater Naples 82126 (H 3248) (Neils 1990:no. 42), the bearded male jabbing at the dragon with a short sword whose sleeves are of a different material decorated with a stroke pattern may not be Jason; a bearded Jason would be unprecedented in this scene, and the wreathed young man with the spear coming at the dragon from the top right better fits the iconography of Jason, who is shown with a spear instead of a sword on the other Paestan representation of this scene known to me, the squat lekythos Bochum, Univ. S 1080 (Neils 1990:no. 41). If the sleeved, bearded man is indeed Jason, clearly the established schemata have changed radically.
[95] Cf. Trendall and Cambitoglou 1991:8; Taplin 1993:55–63.
[96] Hall 1989:202–6.
[97] Trendall and Webster 1971:III.2.4; Taplin 1993:119 no. 21.116.
[98] In complex ways (see Sourvinou-Inwood 1991:11).

meanings. Thus, for the ancient viewer the same element can create different meanings in the same representation.

Let us consider further the image on the Apulian volute krater Munich 3296. Three figures wear sleeves with different decoration and of different material from that of their chiton; two of them, Creon and Medea, wear identical sleeves (dark with white dot decoration). Creon, who in this scene is represented as the victim of Medea's plot, is not wearing a tiara; he is a Greek king, but he is not entirely devoid of negative connections that could be expressed through the metaphor of orientalism. For from Medea's viewpoint his behavior toward her could have been represented as very bad, indeed tyrannical, and his formulation ἥκιστα τοὐμὸν λῆμ' ἔφυ τυραννικόν (my disposition is far from tyrannical, 348) would have evoked precisely that perception in the audience. And, at the very moment of his great disaster, he is shown with sleeves that evoke his guilt through the metaphor of orientalism. Similarly, on the Lucanian bell krater Louvre CA 2193 Creon has a long sleeve of different material, decorated with a zigzag pattern, which would have evoked his guilt. Because he was a Greek king, the viewers would have understood the sleeves not to be denoting a literal origin but to be connoting a metaphorical orientalism. Medea on the other hand is wearing a tiara; thus the sleeves together with the tiara would have enhanced her oriental aspect. The ghost of Medea's father Aeëtes wears the costume that characterizes the oriental king in fourth-century vase painting; his sleeves, when compared to Medea's and Creon's, look more strongly oriental, for they are decorated with lozenges, one of the patterns found on the body stocking of contemporary Amazons and other nonroyal orientals. Thus, elements that may look almost identical to modern eyes help create very different meanings in the same representations as they interact with the other elements and with the semantic frameworks through which viewers made sense of the image.

Medea is never shown wearing trousers or body stocking. The strength of the orientalism of her costume fluctuates. On the Attic skyphos Florence P 80,[99] which represents Theseus and the bull, Medea approaches Aegeus with her box of poisons; she has no headdress but wears a chiton, a short sleeveless overgarment, and sleeves decorated with zigzags. Her sleeves, then, are the only oriental markers and place this image of Medea at the least oriental end of the spectrum. We

[99] Trendall and Webster 1971:III.3.2.

find a comparable example on the Campanian neck amphora in Paris that shows Medea killing one of her sons in a sanctuary. She has no headdress and wears a chiton and himation, but from under the chiton appear long sleeves decorated with a pattern of strokes. Thus, there is not as big a gap as may be thought between representations of Medea in Greek dress, on the one hand, and in oriental costume, on the other.

Most versions of Medea's costume have elements that are more strongly oriental than this, especially in the inclusion of the oriental headdress. On the Talus vase at Ruvo, Medea wears a tiara and a highly decorated peplos and sleeved overgarment. On an Apulian bell krater in a Turin private collection and on the Apulian calyx krater Paris Louvre K 127 she wears a tiara, chiton, and himation.[100] On the Paestan squat lekythos Bochum, Univ. S 1080,[101] she wears a tiara, a decorated chiton with long sleeves, and a himation; the sleeves are of the same material as the chiton up to above the elbow and then they change to a different pattern. On the Paestan volute krater Naples 82126 (H 3248),[102] she wears an oriental headdress with a normal unsleeved chiton and himation. On London E 224 (figure 5) she wears an oriental headdress, a richly decorated chiton with sleeves that are decorated with the same pattern as the rest of the chiton, and a decorated himation. Consequently, there is no simple dichotomy between representations of Medea in Greek or oriental dress, which is another important factor in reconstructing the meanings of oriental dress and the perceptions of Medea articulated in these images.

In addition, if it is correct that oriental dress could be used to represent metaphorical orientalism, it follows that it was selected for reasons more complex than merely ethnicity. This view gains some support when other figures are considered. For example, Cassandra is never shown in oriental dress, while her brother Troilus begins to be represented as a non-Greek around the middle of the fifth century; other Trojans are normally shown in oriental dress on South Italian vases. Thus, a factor other than perceived ethnicity has determined the selection of costume here. Cassandra's dress can probably be explained by the fact that her non-Greek ethnicity was not the most important part of her *persona*, the dominant facets of which were her relationship with Apollo, her identity as a seer, her status as victim of Ajax's sacrilegious rape, and, to a lesser extent perhaps, her status as a joint murder victim with Agamemnon.

[100] Neils 1990:nos. 38, 57.
[101] Neils 1990:no. 41.
[102] Neils 1990:no. 42.

Let us explore this type of choice further by considering the pattern of use of oriental and Greek costume in the case of a female figure whose representations are thought to have been influenced by tragedy, Andromeda. She resembled Medea in that she was an oriental princess whose home was visited by a Greek hero whom she married. But Andromeda was rescued by Perseus, which was a proper womanly role to play; Medea, in contrast, helped Jason defeat her father and eloped with him having betrayed her father and killed her brother, acts that set negatively apart from normal women. Correlatively with that, Andromeda was a good woman and a good wife, while Medea was bad.

An important similarity between the two is their symbolic connection with the contemporary oriental enemy: in one myth Andromeda was the mother of Perses, who was left with her father (who had no male issue) and from whom the Persians took their name (Hdt. 7.61). We considered Andromeda's dress on Attic vases above; the latest was on the calyx krater Berlin 3237 of just after 400, believed to reflect Euripides' *Andromeda*. On the South Italian fourth-century vases she does not wear oriental costume.[103] If this reflects differences in staging we would have to assume that the play(s) did not contain passages that would prevent the shift to Greek dress. But whether this is plausible or whether we must think in terms of purely iconographic shifts, it is clear that fourth-century South Italian perceptions were such that the representation of Andromeda changed from oriental dress to Greek. Since she was a barbarian and so described in Euripides' play,[104] and since the logic of the narrative would dictate that she be shown in oriental costume at that point, we cannot explain the shift as due to narrative factors. What may have allowed for this shift is that the oriental connection of Andromeda, important in fifth-century Athens because of her son's connection with the Persians, would have been perceived to be nonsignificant in fourth-century South Italy and Sicily. Since the other facet of her *persona* was that of good woman, and since when Greek is opposed to oriental the former is positive and the latter negative, it is possible that Greek dress may have been chosen to match her *persona* of good woman. This would confirm the view that oriental dress could be read as carrying negative connotations.

---

[103] Cf. Schauenburg 1981:788. See *passim* on images of Andromeda on Attic and South Italian vases and their relationships to dramatic performances; cf. also Danali-Giole 1982–84:182–86.

[104] In Euripides' *Andromeda*, as in Sophocles' (cf. *TGF* F 126), there were explicit references to Andromeda's native land and people as barbarian (cf. frs. 124, 139 Nauck).

Euripides' Medea and Medea's Oriental Costume

Let us now return to the relationship between the performance of Euripides' *Medea* and the introduction of the oriental costume in Medea's iconography. Because the relationship between images and theatrical performances is very complex, we face severe restrictions in using this evidence. In addition, because we do not have any fifth-century Attic representations of this episode, all our iconographic evidence reflects South Italian productions—though we have no reason to think that costumes and production were different in South Italy.[105] Nonetheless, let us look at this evidence, beginning with the scenes nearest in narrative time to the ending of the tragedy, the four scenes depicting Medea in the chariot after the murder (i, ii, vi, vii).

Vase vii consists of a fragment that does not include Medea and cannot help us. Of the other three, i and ii evoke the performance of Euripides' *Medea*, while vi is an iconographic creation aware of the version of the myth articulated in that tragedy but furthest away from it. It is ii, the Cleveland krater, that conveys most strikingly the distancing between Medea and the rest presented in the play's closing scene. On this vase, Medea is wearing an especially large and prominent oriental headdress, a cloak, and a peplos from under which emerge sleeves decorated with lozenges. On i she is wearing an oriental headdress, a himation, and a peplos from under which emerge sleeves decorated with the strokes pattern. On vi, which least evokes Euripides' *Medea*, Medea is wearing fully Greek dress. Two vases depict scenes representing the murder. On iv she is wearing a tiara and an ornate chiton with no sleeves, and she has a himation around her waist. On v she has no oriental headdress and is wearing only a chiton and a himation; from under the chiton appear long sleeves decorated with the strokes pattern. The fact that the murder was not shown on stage means that an iconographical representation of it did not necessarily reflect the way the audience would have visualized the murder, but more their perceptions of it as they were shaped by the ways in which it was heard and described in the performance. Thus, the boys' proximity to the altar in their last moments or in death may have been one iconographic articulation of their utter helplessness and terror. Medea's dress on v is Greek; the sleeves are an oriental marker, which can function also at the metaphorical level. They evoke Medea's oriental origin, but in

---

[105] See Taplin 1993:95.

connection above all with her barbarous act; their function here is comparable to the way they operate in the figure of Aegisthus. The tiara places Medea's representation on iv within the spectrum of oriental costume, though the absence of sleeves or any other oriental sign from her purely Greek clothes situates her at the least oriental end of that spectrum; on iii, which represents her killing one child while the chariot is waiting, her dress is much further toward the oriental pole, for she is wearing a tiara, a himation around her shoulders, and a decorated double chiton with sleeves of a different material coming out from under it.

Thus, of the representations of Medea in the chariot, the two that otherwise most strongly evoke the Euripidean tragedy show her in oriental dress; the scene that does not evoke the tragedy shows her in Greek dress. The latter choice seems related to her lesser distance from the other human figures in this image, as her chariot is not aloft and she appears vulnerable to her attackers; it also seems connected with the partial deconstruction of her guilt created by the presence of the Λύσσα-like figure. The parameters of selection are different in the case of the murder because the killing was not shown on stage. The two scenes that show only the murder represent Medea at the Greek end of the spectrum: in one she is basically in Greek dress, with one quasi-metaphorical element of orientalism; in the other she is weakly oriental. The scene that combines the murder with the presence of the magical chariot represents her as more oriental. One hypothesis that can explain this pattern is that in Euripides' play Medea was wearing oriental dress when she appeared in the chariot but had been wearing Greek dress until then; representations of the murder thus follow the logic of the narrative. She was wearing Greek dress when she went inside to kill her sons. However, in committing this murder she showed herself to be non-Greek—at least according to the ideology expressed in Jason's (untrue) claim that no Greek woman would have dared do such a thing. To show this, weak—perhaps metaphorical—oriental elements appear in her dress when the murder is shown on its own, without a chariot to make the image more distanced.

Images in other media provide a little additional support for this hypothesis. In a fragmentary Tarentine limestone statuette[106] of the 320s representing Medea in the chariot carrying the corpse of one of her children, she is wearing the oriental headdress. No original

---

[106] M. Schmidt 1992:no. 40.

Greek painting of Medea survives. Roman paintings which may be copies of or at least be inspired by Greek originals,[107] show Medea in Greek costume before and during the murder of her children. A very famous Medea preparing to kill her children, in which Medea is wearing Greek dress, was by Timomachus of Byzantium.[108] Though Timomachus was considerably later than the period that concerns us, he probably adapted earlier paintings; and these earlier representations as well as his own went into the repertory of Roman wall painters.[109]

The hypothesis that Medea was wearing Greek dress throughout the play and oriental dress when she appears in the chariot of the Sun converges with, and would provide a visual correlative for, the reading proposed above in "Euripides' *Medea*": Medea was strongly distanced in the closing scene of the tragedy, having been previously zoomed toward and less radically distanced from normality. The Sun's chariot, Medea's position (equivalent to that of the gods), and her announcement of the institution of a ritual placed her at a physical and symbolic distance, away from normality and toward the supernatural. The oriental costume would have enhanced the effect by distancing her also in another modality, stressing her alien origin and thus her differences from Greek women. This costume therefore would be both a visible expression of and a metaphor for the distance between Medea at her most "other" and female normality, the distance that protects the image of female normality, while allowing this exploration of the negative aspects of the female and the polarized articulation of male fears and systemic faults to take place at a safe symbolic distance. Since the oriental dress is connected with the distanced Medea at the end of the tragedy, while the Greek dress is perceived as neutral, it is the Greek dress that would have made possible both the distancing and the zooming of Medea toward normality and toward the Chorus; the oriental dress, which was charged with otherness, could not have allowed this. Even independently of the argument based on the images,

---

[107] M. Schmidt 1992:nos. 8–14; cf. Zinnerling-Paul 1979:435–36.

[108] Pliny, *HN* 35.136, 145; *AP* 16.135. There was a late-fourth-century Medea by Aristolaus, son of Pausias (Pliny *HN* 35.137); Aristolaus was considered among the most austere painters and his other subjects listed by Pliny, some of which must have been painted for Athens (cf. Robertson 1975:490), are all *polis* subjects (Theseus, Pericles, Epaminondas, Virtue, an image of the Athenian people, a sacrifice of oxen), suggesting that it was this aspect of Medea that came into play here, probably in connection with Theseus.

[109] See Robertson 1975:589–90, 733–34 n. 240.

the logic of the play suggests that Medea was wearing Greek dress until the closing scene, where all facets of her otherness are brought to the fore and visually articulated.

We must now consider whether the text itself signals such a change. Does it suggest that Medea was wearing Greek dress until the closing scene? And does it indicate any change at that time? On the first point, the tragedy presents Medea as a foreigner, but until the end no stress is put on the difference between her and a woman who might have come from another part of Greece.[110] The distinction Medea herself makes after her entrance at 222–23 is between ξένοι (foreigners), a category in which she places herself implicitly, and ἀστοί (citizens). This would be correlative with her wearing Greek costume; if she had been wearing oriental dress, her words would not have matched visual presentation—causing not a conflict adding complexity and richness but a confusion running counter to the grain of the text and the close relationship between Medea and the Chorus at this point. The whole tragedy becomes much flatter if Medea is visually placed at a great distance from her audience from the very beginning. Her barbarian origin is indeed mentioned, but at a later point (256) and as something from which she was taken away (ἐκ γῆς βαρβάρου λελῃσμένη). This origin, and the fact that her barbarian nature has been left behind, is articulated in Jason's boast at 536–40 that she gained more benefits for her help than she had given, because she dwells in Greece instead of in a barbarian land: she knows how to make use of laws so that force may not be gratified, and because all the Greeks know that she is σοφή (clever) she has gained glory. In other words, thanks to him she has become a member of the Greek cultural community. All these things suggest that Medea was wearing Greek dress at this point. The change in her costume is marked by Jason's claim, after Medea has appeared in the chariot of the Sun at 1339–40, that no Greek woman would have dared do the dreadful thing she did. For this would be stressing the modality of her visually articulated distancing constructed in the closing scene by signaling Jason's change of perception. Now he sees her in her true colors: a barbarian.

These are strong arguments in favor of the view that Medea in Euripides' *Medea* had worn Greek dress until the final scene, the moment of her strongest distancing, when she appeared in oriental dress. Euripides, then, created the visual crystallization "Medea in oriental dress"

[110] See also Knox 1983:287.

to represent Medea at her most other, most negative, and most symbolically distanced. Thus, this was a polysemic image, with a multifaceted
distancing from the schema "normal woman."

This crystallization became the preferred, but not universal, schema
for representing Medea. In Attic art this negatively polarized schema is
the preferred choice for Medea, corresponding to the articulation of the
darker side of Medea. But it is the polysemy of this crystallization that
can explain why in the Theseus cycle she is represented through both
schemata after 430. As we saw, Medea is wearing oriental dress in many
but not all of the scenes with the bull painted after ca. 430. In my view,
once the schema "Medea in oriental dress" became established, Medea's
strong symbolic identification with the Persians in the myth of the Bull
of Marathon would have attracted the oriental dress into the myth's
representations. Such a choice also suited the meanings pertaining
to Medea's *persona* as a bad woman: when she is in the process of
endangering Theseus she is shown through the schema that represents
her most negatively and as most distanced "other." An alternative
articulation creates more disturbing meanings: it shows the bad woman
in Greek dress and thus brings her nearer to normal women. Once the
distanced, oriental schema was firmly established, using Greek dress
would no longer have been perceived as neutral: it would have zoomed
Medea somewhat toward normality, making the distinction between
"normal woman" and "bad woman" less stable. Thus such images
became more disturbing.

In South Italian images, we noted the metaphorical orientalism articulated through elements of the costume. If M. Schmidt's interpretation
of the scene at Eleusis is right, Medea is represented in a positive role,
albeit one deconstructed by her general *persona,* and wears Greek dress
in this positively colored representation. But there is not an exact correlation between positive role and Greek dress and negative role and
oriental dress on South Italian vases. For example, in both representations of Theseus' recognition she is wearing Greek dress. This is a scene
that we might have expected to attract oriental dress, once the option
was available; perhaps Medea had worn Greek dress in Sophocles' and
Euripides' *Aegeus,* dress reproduced on the two vases precisely because
that selection was not blocked and because there was no perceived simple equation of Greek with positive, oriental with negative. Two facts
further strengthen the case against the hypothesis that Medea had been
wearing oriental dress in Euripides' *Aegeus*: Medea appears in Greek
dress both in Attic and South Italian representations of Theseus with

the bull,[111] and she is wearing Greek dress in two divergent images of the recognition by Theseus. At the very least, this suggests that the choice to show Medea in Greek dress in the recognition scene fitted the South Italian perceptions of Medea and the episode. For the case of Andromeda showed us that we cannot assume that the South Italian vase painters simply reproduced theatrical costumes. Nevertheless, her Greek dress in the two divergent images of an episode that was dramatized in Euripides' *Aegeus*, the Greek costume in the two South Italian bull scenes and the fact that, unlike Andromeda, she is wearing oriental dress elsewhere on South Italian vases suggest very strongly that in Euripides' *Aegeus* Medea wore Greek, not oriental, dress, which appears to have affected her representation on the vases depicting the relevant subjects.

As for the images of the murder of her children and flight in the chariot, we saw that they have complex relationships with Euripides' *Medea* and that each articulates specific meanings in whose creation the deployment of "oriental costume" or "Greek dress" in various variants plays an important role. The representations of Medea in the chariot that evoke most strongly the Euripidean tragedy and, like the closing scene of that tragedy, distance Medea most strongly from "normality" show her in oriental dress. The representation of her flight that is furthest from its depiction in the tragedy, which shows Medea less distanced from the other figures in the image—her chariot is not aloft and she appears physically vulnerable to her attackers—depicts her in Greek dress. The image is thus more disturbing, in that the murderous mother is represented as almost—though not quite—like a normal woman. Images of the murder represent Medea at the Greek but not fully Greek end of her iconographic spectrum: on one vase she is basically in Greek dress, with one metaphorical element of orientalism; on the other she is shown as weakly oriental. These disturbing images are shaped by the

---

[111] E.g., the Apulian volute krater Milan 377 (*CVA* Italy 49, pl.5); context and iconographic schema ensure that the ancient viewers would have identified the seated woman wearing chiton and himation and pulling at her veil, in front of whom the servant girl is holding an open box, as Medea—not, as has been thought by some, Aphrodite.

The figure on the bell krater Naples 2413 (Trendall and Cambitoglou 1961:23, pl. 6 figs. 25–26) has been identified as either Theseus or Jason (see, e.g., Neils 1990:no. 16) struggling with the bull; in either case the woman in Greek dress is Medea. This krater is thought to have been influenced by the performance of a tragedy, perhaps Euripides' *Aegeus* (pl. 6). Medea's presence in these images was the expression of her role in the affair in an emblematic mode, whether or not it was also taken to indicate her physical presence during the fight—which is less likely; these images represent a scene that in tragedy could only have been included in a messenger speech.

interaction of the perceptions articulated in the tragedy, the audience's visualizations (she was wearing Greek dress when she went inside to kill her children and this is how the audience would have imagined her in the act), the alleged alienness of her action and consequent pressure to stress her non-Greek origin, the desire to distance this threatening figure from female normality, and the iconographic modality of metaphorical orientalism.

The Munich scene that combines the murder with the presence of the magical chariot represents her as more oriental. As we saw, here Creon's guilt, his tyrannical behavior toward Medea, is evoked at the moment of his disaster through the metaphor of orientalism articulated by his sleeves. The (partial) deconstruction of Medea's wickedness entailed by the evocation of Creon's guilt and his exercise of power against a wronged woman is correlative to the representation of Οἶστρος (Frenzy) as Medea's charioteer, for she is thus shown as being at the mercy of an undefeatable power, in that respect no less a victim than Heracles under the sway of Λύσσα.[112] On the other hand, the ghost of Medea's father evokes her betrayal of him and murder of her brother. If this analysis is right, this vase articulates more complex and ambivalent perceptions of the drama than has been hitherto assumed. That Creon's tragedy is not diminished by this evocation of his guilt and that the horror of the child's death on the very altar is made no less poignant and horrible by Medea's domination by Οἶστρος is surely an articulation of the complexity of human actions, human character, and the human condition, in which if one exercises power unjustly one may suffer unforeseen consequences, and the wronged victim can become a monster in seeking revenge— especially since the weapons of the weak are inevitably violent.

Medea at a Shifting Distance

Medea was, among other things, a negative polarization of "bad woman," itself a negative polarization of the notion "normal woman," in which male fears concerning women and men's vulnerability to women within the family were crystallized.[113] Euripides' *Medea* created a new version of this negative polarization, placed at a safe symbolic distance through the activation and articulation of Medea's supernatural facet and through a stress on her alienness and barbarism. However,

---

[112] On the figure of Οἶστρος and its relationship to Λύσσα, see Séchan 1926:415–16, 422.
[113] See Sourvinou-Inwood 1990a:409–12.

this distanced negative polarization depends on—indeed it is the climax of—a complex and dynamic articulation in which, through a series of shifts in the symbolic distances at which Medea and the other women were presented, Medea has been shown as also like "normal" Greek women. Moreover, what may be crudely called the "normal women's point of view" has been articulated, and the possibility that the disadvantages of women's position may be causally connected to women's "badness," lightly sketched. In the tragedy, the oppositional relationship "male self:good :: female other:(potentially) bad" is partly deconstructed.

Images are static crystallizations and thus cannot represent shifting relationships and shifting symbolic distances. But different images reflect different choices, as each represents Medea at different distances from "normal woman"; to create the equivalent of the Euripidean shifting distances would require a series of images, together presenting a spectrum of distances. The correlation is far from exact; for the images articulate alternatives, offering a range of distances between Medea and normality in the same central scenes. It is as though the dynamic shifts and developing perceptions of the Euripidean tragedy were frozen on film and made into stills that were translated into synchronic alternatives deployed in the images representing one of the story's crucial moments or condensing several, alternative placings of Medea at a nearer or further distance—her dress crucial to the construction of these distances.

Some South Italian vase painters presented Medea as in some ways comparable to Heracles, correlatively with the presentation of her crime as the result of frenzy and her representation in a positive role. Because this deconstruction of the fundamental opposition between the supreme male hero and the monstrous woman appears to take place in the context of a fourth-century South Italian mystery ideology,[114] such representations are outside the mainstream. But even so, that the figure of Medea was amenable to such development indicates its complexity and ambivalence. The zooming of Medea toward the normal articulates the notion that there is not a radical distance between this monster-woman and ordinary women, therefore allowing the exploration of male fears about women's negative potential and threat. The distanced articulations of Medea seem less disturbing. At the same time, however, they, together with the alternation between Medea in oriental dress

---

[114] See M. Schmidt 1986:171–72.

and Medea in Greek dress, articulate the notion that there is less of a distance than there seems between the barbarian other and the self. More precisely, since the culture's central self is male, the barbarian is brought closer to that self's nearest other, the citizen woman, daughter, wife, mother, sister—a distinction that is active in Medea's myth, which explores the woman as other.

Seen in opposition to barbarians, Greek woman is the self of the culture; therefore the diminishing distance between Medea and Greek women partly deconstructs the opposition between Greek (superior) and barbarian (inferior). But then this opposition is less stable than is often assumed. The perception of the barbarian as the radically constructed other, a construction that allows the exploration of the self, is one—the dominant and explicit—strand in the Greek collective representations; another, more complex perception, is that the barbarian is not so different from the self.

12

MEDEA AS POLITICIAN AND DIVA

RIDING THE DRAGÓN INTO THE FUTURE

Marianne McDonald

Medea as a Special "Other"

EDEA HAUNTS the imagination. Made famous in antiquity by Euripides, Apollonius of Rhodes, Seneca, Ovid, and others, she has wended her way into the modern psyche. She is the philanderer's nightmare: the ex-wife who drives a dragon-drawn chariot. Medea is the wife who kills her husband's lover, the mother who murders her own children. She is the Betty Broderick who gets acquitted, the Susan Smith who escapes punishment. She is the local bitch and folk archetype (cf. in this volume Johnston's "reproductive demon"). We read about her in the news, we see her in plays and on the screen, and we hear her sing. We would like to think these performances could effect some sort of permanent *katharsis*, but Medea always seems to return. She, and her pain, and her all-too-successful vengeance come back again and again.

Pierre Corneille, Luigi Cherubini, Richard Glover, Franz Grillparzer, Giannis Xenakis, and many others offer variations.[1] The twentieth century is especially rich in reworkings of this myth. Hans Henny Jahnn featured a black Medea in his biracial version, which prefigured much of

First I thank both Brendan Kennelly and Mikis Theodorakis not only for their extraordinary creations but also for making material available and offering invaluable suggestions. Thanks are also due to Karen Elaine for her superb musical exegesis of Theodorakis' opera. Special thanks also to James Diggle, Alastair Hannay, Tony Harrison, Bernard Knox, Albert Liu, Thomas MacCary, Bridget McDonald, and Thomas Rosenmeyer for their editorial comments. Many thanks also to James Clauss and the readers at Princeton University Press, who have helped not only with the details but with the clarification of issues. The faults remain mine. A version of a section of this paper on Brendan Kennelly's work appeared in McDonald 1993, and some of the section on Theodorakis' *Medea* appeared in McDonald 1994.

[1] See a discussion of some of these versions by Friedrich 1968; see also Schondorff 1963.

Brecht and Müller in its critique of society (1926). Carl Theodor Dreyer, who filmed *La Passion de Jeanne d'Arc* (1928), recognized Medea's similar heroism and wrote a screenplay about her. In 1933 Agnes Straub, who had played the first black Medea in Jahnn's production, as a director of her own company revived Grillparzer's *Medea* and played her as black—an indictment of Nazi racist policies; this play was also revived in the 1960s.

In 1946 Martha Graham created her *Cave of the Heart*, with music by Samuel Barber, a ballet based on *Medea*. Jean Anouilh's *Médée* was also done in 1946; in his version Medea, after killing the princess and the king, kills herself with the children, a grim indictment of Jason's search for a mediocre "happiness" without her. She throws herself into the fire, using again the image of her externalized passion, which destroys her. In the next year, Robinson Jeffers translated the ancient poetry into a modern *Medea* created for Judith Anderson.

In 1954 the director and playwright Félix Morisseau-Leroy presented Anouilh's *Médée* in Haitian costume at the Théâtre d'Haiti. The dictator Paul Magloire attended the production, surrounded by his police guard. Pier Paolo Pasolini's film *Medea* (1970), starring Maria Callas, celebrates Medea as an earth mother who contrasts with the rootless Jason; she is a life principle whose imperatives must be fulfilled.[2] Robert Wilson has produced various versions of *Medea* in plays and film, including *Deafman Glance* in 1970, a prologue (1980), and an overture (1982). In each case the murder of a child is enacted in slow pantomime. In *Overture to the Fourth Act of Deafman Glance*, a mother silently brings milk to her child, then leaves to return with a knife to kill him. The mother who feeds is the mother who can kill.

Peter Sellars directed Charpentier's opera *Médée* (originally pro-duced in 1693) and his own opera *Medea* (1984), based on Euripides and written in collaboration with Gavin Bryars. Andrei Serban created *Fragments of a Greek Trilogy: Medea, The Trojan Women*, and *Elektra* for the LaMama theater in 1974, a work shown again in 1992 at the Edinburgh festival as *An Ancient Trilogy*. This *Medea* combines characteristics Eu-ripides and Seneca gave her, and the Senecan witch wins out: the theater becomes a site for ritualistic incantations of ancient Greek, and a huge snake is charmed before our eyes. Jules Dassin particularizes our hero-ine in *Dream of Passion* (1978); she is a religious housewife fanatically inflicting a deadly penalty on her Jason.[3] Heiner Müller's *Medeaspiel*

[2] See McDonald 1983:3–50.
[3] See McDonald 1983:51–87.

(1974) and *Medeamaterial* (1982) show the abused Medea exploited by Jason just as colonizer exploits the colonized and the earth is abused by man.[4] Each victim turns the tables on the aggressor; it is now earth's turn to kill man, who has raped her body for years. Tony Harrison wrote a libretto for *Medea: A Sex War Opera* (1985), commissioned by the Metropolitan Opera, but it has not yet been performed because Jacob Druckman did not complete the score.[5] This text was merged with Valerie Salonas' *SCUM (Society for Cutting Up Men) Manifesto* and performed in the 1991 Edinburgh festival. In 1988, Dublin saw Brendan Kennelly's *Medea* raging against the abuses of men, and Desmond Egan gave us a new translation of Euripides in 1991. In 1990, *Demea* was done in South Africa, with Demea (Medea) as a black princess abandoned by the Dutch trekker Jason. In 1992, Diana Rigg starred in a *Medea* newly translated by Alistair Elliot. The chorus, dressed in black costumes, suggests victimized and mourning women, perhaps imprisoned, and Medea is a form of liberator for women in general. Amy Greenfield, who made the film *Antigone* (1990), is working on a *Medea* in which the heroine is a Mexican woman abandoned by her American lover. A new version was played in Athens this year, Μήδεια, by Bost (Costas Bostantzoglou). In this comedy Medea's story is used to threaten children: if they do not study hard, their mothers will kill them. Medea even lends her names to novels, such as Kate Braverman's *Lithium for Medea*, and poetic fantasies, such as *Medea the Sorceress* by Diane Wakoski.

What can we abstract from these various versions? Medea, as a character, refutes what Simone Weil said of the *Iliad*: "To the same degree, though in different fashion, those who use force and those who endure it are turned to stone." Euripides' Medea is one who both suffered and inflicted suffering, and her wrath earns her immortality in a union with Achilles as her husband in Elysium.[6] She becomes a living myth (as Seneca's Medea says at line 171, *fiam Medea*: "I shall become Medea"). She gained the κλέος ἄφθιτον (undying fame) so prized by the Homeric hero; Medea's name is on people's lips and she haunts their dreams.

Euripides may have been the first to have Medea kill her own children, although many scholars make convincing arguments that he

---

[4] See McDonald 1992:147–58.
[5] See McDonald 1992:115–25.
[6] Ibycus fr. 289 (Campbell); Simonides fr. 558 (Campbell); Ap. Rhod. 4.805ff.

borrowed from a preexistent tradition.[7] After Euripides, Medea is synonymous with child murderer. She is neither a madwoman nor a witch;
both conceptions undercut the heroic greatness Euripides bestowed on
her.[8] As Newlands shows in this volume, Ovid struggled with the dual
image of Medea as woman in the *Heroides* and witch in the *Metamorphoses*, perhaps reconciling the two in his lost tragedy. Be that as it may,
the Roman poet showed how women are maligned (by male authors)
for entering the male spheres of either violence or expressive intelligence. When we turn to the present, we find Brendan Kennelly's *Medea*
(discussed below) addressing a modern variation of such concerns.

A variation on interpreting Medea as witch is the theory that makes
her into a goddess or a priestess whose ritual somehow sanctifies her
act.[9] Several contributors to this volume have given us some idea of the
wide range of superhuman associations that Medea possesses: assimilation with Hera and Aphrodite (Graf, Johnston); Muse (O'Higgins);
foundation heroine (Krevans); Satanic helper-maiden (Clauss). Seneca
was another who gave Medea the characteristics of a witch/daemon;
but although Medea in myth is the niece of Circe and has supernatural
powers, Euripides, with his usual psychological acuity, concentrates on
her human characteristics (nicely elucidated by Sourvinou-Inwood).

Helene Foley divides Medea into male and female, claiming that
Medea performs characteristically male actions while indicting the
heroic code.[10] Medea, indeed, turns the male weapons against the males
but fundamentally remains female: I see her as relying on rather than
indicting the old code. Foley claims Medea is dissembling in her first
speech to the women of Corinth, because in fact she herself did not
pay a dowry, nor indeed was she ever the passive housewife described.

[7] See Graf and Johnston in this volume; Michelini 1987, 1989, with their helpful
bibliographies.

[8] For Medea as witch, see Page 1938:xiv. The witch image emerges in the versions of
Apollonius, Ovid, and Seneca, as Graf, Johnston, Clauss, Newlands, and Nussbaum have
noted in this volume. For the heroic view of Medea, see, among others, Knox 1977:297;
Bongie 1977:27; McDonald 1991:127; Albini 1990:xiv.

[9] The ritual aspect of Medea is stressed by Girard 1977:9. Pucci 1980:159, 165, also
claims that Medea has "mythical and divine attributes." I think Euripides creates such
a feeling of horror in the audience at the acts depicted that the "triumph" becomes highly
ambivalent.

[10] Foley 1989. Rehm 1989 offers a variation of this view. He claims that Medea struggles
against the heroic code, as expressed by the λόγος of heroic epic, and would rather identify
with feminine lyric, but she finally falls into the trap of the masculine and destructive
λόγος. See also Barlow 1989, who sees Medea as reversing the stereotype of the passive
female, although because she is female, her destruction of the children entails her own
destruction.

I think instead that Medea paid a very costly dowry in killing her brother and helping to steal the Golden Fleece. She also gave birth and was the model housewife until she was crossed in love and honor; then she becomes, as she says, "truly a woman," expanding her claim with misogynist terms, "impotent for good, but most clever weaver of evil" (*Med.* 407–9). She uses not only typically male weapons but also male language.

Medea is a woman of consuming passion; perhaps she even personifies θυμός, which Euripides will externalize in Dionysus in his *Bacchae*. At the same time, however, she can use her reason to plan her vengeance. Neither Jason nor Creon can govern her, nor is she a simple slave of passion. She gains her victory, and her enemies do not laugh at her, but she pays the most terrible price. Her victory is in fact a defeat, because it costs the lives of those dearest to her. Medea takes the lives she gave. But we remember Apollo's defense of Orestes in Aeschylus' *Eumenides*: the woman is the mere incubator or soil for the man who sows the seed. She is the conduit, whereas the only parent is he who mounts. Aristotle's biology also supports this claim, so according to this logic, Medea in killing her children is predominantly sacrificing Jason's seed. The children thus can be seen as the product of one who violated her: her body was not her own just as the colonized land does not belong to the colonized but to the colonizer. Medea's heroism then is a protest against her self-alienation.

Medea was first performed in 431 B.C. at the outbreak of the Peloponnesian War, and one can interpret it as ominously foretelling the price paid when the drive for power violates human needs. Previous scholarship has noted that Euripides, particularly in his *Hecuba*, shows that brutalizing brutalizes.[11] Suffering in Aeschylus led to learning; suffering in Euripides leads to arming: it teaches the victim to imitate the victimizer.

I shall try to broaden this claim to include Medea, showing that she can be adopted as a revolutionary symbol. I shall also show her as an operatic heroine whose suffering is emphasized more than her triumph. Both interpretations show the wide range of Medea as a modern signifier: Bernadette Devlin or Tosca.

Just as Antigone has become an inspiring symbol of civil disobedience, Medea, as the exploited barbarian, can be the symbol of the

---

[11] One of the earliest to note that Medea is a product of her sufferings was Masqueray 1908:309. On Hecuba, see Rosenmeyer 1985:269; Michelini 1987:170–71; Segal 1990. On Procne in the lost *Tereus*, see Segal 1994:277.

freedom fighter, particularly in modern representations. In Africa, Haiti, and Ireland, as in other colonized countries, performances of *Medea* are staged as an affirmation of liberty. The play of the oppressor (since *Medea* is from the colonizer's literary tradition) is co-opted as a weapon directed at the oppressor's heart. The performances elate the oppressed. The words and mimes of today may become the acts and reality of tomorrow. The Medea myth often supplies the vocabulary for expressing modern political concerns; she is the exploited "other" who fights back.

Medea illustrates what happens in every revolution: when the oppressed come to power, they often perpetuate the abuses they have suffered. Frantz Fanon expressed this well in a chapter called "The Pitfalls of National Consciousness"; he warns, "nationalization quite simply means the transfer into native hands of those unfair advantages which are a legacy of the colonial period."[12] We remember the excesses of Robespierre, who ultimately fell a victim to the bloodbath of the French Revolution and the killing he himself had fostered.

Medea is also a warning against the tyrant, both as one who takes vengeance on the tyrant who abuses her and as one who becomes a tyrant herself: she finally gets power and imperiously and impulsively uses it. As a barbarian princess, she is used to getting what she wants. She will help her friends and harm her enemies (*Med.* 807–10).[13] The Nurse speaks of her violent passion as that of tyrants, those who are ruled with difficulty and have power (*Med.* 119–20).

Aristotle, in discussing the overthrow of tyrants, poses the dilemma of emotion versus rationality and uses the same terms that Medea does in debating whether she shall kill her children, ending with the claim that her θυμός (passion) is stronger than her βουλεύματα (reasoning, *Med.* 1079–80).[14] She is driven by θυμός: the θυμός of love is transformed

[12] Fanon 1963:152. For a brilliant discussion of this phenomenon of the abused turning abuser, see E. Said 1993, esp. the chapter "Resistance and Opposition." Medea exerted her imperial will over her victims.

[13] "Helping friends and harming enemies" articulates an old heroic code that can be traced to Homer (cf. *Od.* 6.182–85, although this is in the context of marriage with the couple being a delight to their friends and a bane to their enemies, and *passim*) and appears frequently in later Greek literature, e.g., Plato *Meno* 71e.

M. Blundell 1989:27 expands on the ethical implications of not only rejoicing in the success of friends but being "pained by our enemies' success and taking pleasure in their downfall." The German word *Schadenfreude* (joy at another's misfortune) expresses this idea. Medea was true to the heroic code and delighted in the downfall of her enemies. This code of not letting your enemies laugh at you is pure Greek, thus contributing to the irony that Medea, a barbarian, out-Greeks the Greek.

[14] Many scholars, ancient and modern (see Dillon in this volume), have dealt with the interpretation of this passage, but the power of θυμός is unquestioned, and Knox 1977:225

into the θυμός of hate, via the θυμός of anger. Aristotle says that anger is more effective than hatred because it is devoid of reasoning (*Pol.* 5.1312b28–29). Medea cedes to her θυμός, to irrational anger, but allows it to harness hatred and rationality so it is most effective. Aristotle also gives insult, or an insolent act (ὕβρις), as one of the main reasons for overthrowing a tyrant (*Pol.* 5.1311a25); Medea's anger burns all the brighter for her sense of having been insulted.

Medea is also a heroine for women who refuse to be confined to the role of "producer of legitimate offspring." By killing her children to gain her vengeance, she thus asserts herself as independent of husband and patriarchy generally. She still inhabits a patriarchal world and needs a refuge, which Aegeus, king of Athens, fortuitously provides. Then she goes full speed ahead and indulges her θυμός with every weapon she has: guile, magic/poison, and her own children. Her vengeance, like Dionysus' in *Bacchae*, goes too far and thus gains a dubious admiration. She can aptly be called δεινή (awful), with all the ambiguity of the term, as Sophocles used it in his ode to man in the *Antigone* (332ff.).

Medea is a complex being. Following the model of the soul that Plato gives us in the *Phaedrus*, with the λογιστικόν element (reason) as a charioteer driving the horses ἐπιθυμητικόν (desire) and θυμοειδές (passion, 246a; cf. *Rep.* 4.440e for these labels), some see Medea with runaway horses, others as clearly in command.[15] I tend toward the latter interpretation but realize that the horses Medea drives are powerful. She will in Hamlet's words, "greatly . . . find quarrel in a straw when honor's at the stake." She is also a woman and this adds to her power. She is in touch with herself and the elements, harnessing both in single-minded purpose.

As we have seen, Medea has been viewed in many ways, as either articulating the heroic code or criticizing it (see nn. 8, 10). One interpretation emphasizes Medea's glory, and the other her suffering. She can be a witch, or priestess, or a passionate woman.[16] She is not simple, and neither are her interpretations. She overflows constricting categories.

---

sees Medea at the end of the play as deified θυμός. The question of whether lines 1056–80 are genuine has also been raised, and Diggle 1984:138–39 has eliminated them from his recent edition. Arguments for their acceptance are made by Seidensticker 1991. Diggle now admits that 1078–80 may be by Euripides, but in that case other adjustments must be made, such as deleting lines 1044–48 and 1053–66.

[15] On which, see Dillon and Nussbaum in this volume.

[16] On Medea as a witch, see n. 8 above with text; as goddess or priestess, see n. 9 with text and Pucci 1980; as passionate woman, see Barlow 1989 and Nussbaum in this volume.

Medea shows the heroism of a Sophoclean hero, but she is not a Sophoclean Electra. She cannot murder with emotional impunity; this is a woman conscious of the suffering she will inflict, and the suffering that she will feel, *before* she commits the act. I see Medea's act as heroic, and all the more so because she is a woman and must suffer as a woman: no one suffers the loss of a child more than that child's mother. Medea co-opts male arms to bring about her moment of triumph, and in the final scene she relishes her victory. As a woman she also has chosen the means that will effect the most deadly punishment: her family rights were violated and she will use the family to effect the punishment. This is frequently the case of modern women who murder.[17] As an archetypal passionate Mediterranean, Medea glories in her vengeance. In the final scene Jason says that Medea will also suffer, but she spits out her response—using Jason's materialistic language—that suffering will pay off (λύει δ'ἄλγος, 1362) as long as he will not laugh (returning to the heroic code in which the laughter of enemies is a great offense). The dragon chariot endorses her triumph, as does her later myth.[18] She knew the price, but she reaped the reward.

Medea's anger turns to violent action, which can make her into a symbol of freedom, an emblem for the colonized turning the tables on the colonizer. Euripides, more than all other tragedians, has predicted many of the horrors that occur in the modern world, showing both the glory and the monstrosity of the oppressed turned oppressor.

Just as scholars interpret, so do modern renditions. Two works bring Medea into modern times: a play by Brendan Kennelly and an opera by Mikis Theodorakis.[19] The first *Medea* deals with the exploitation of women by men, Ireland by England, and the vengeance lurking in the rear of exploitation. This is an overtly political interpretation.

[17] Danto 1982:6, 10–11, gives some interesting statistics: "A quarter of all murderers today are women; their victims are usually someone close. In order of greatest frequency, the victims are a husband, a lover, or an older child of the woman," and "there are twice as many mothers who killed [their children] as fathers." He cites D. J. West's category of "spouse revenge filicide" in which "the child was killed to deprive the spouse and cause suffering through the loss of a favorite child." In his chapter on Euripides' *Medea*, B. Simon 1988:70 pointed out how "in Euripides there is much greater consciousness about children; . . . fifteen of about nineteen extant plays . . . are quite explicitly involved with stories about the death, murder, or sacrifice of children."

[18] See Worthington 1990, who shows that Medea's exit in a dragon-drawn chariot is a logical development from the plot and Medea's characterization. See also Nussbaum's brilliant interpretation of this symbol.

[19] References to Kennelly 1991 will be parenthesized in the text. The references to Theodorakis' score and text are from unpublished handwritten copies.

Women realize that their suffering is political in origin, so t.
political solutions. Theodorakis, by contrast, shows us that w.
ten have political purposes that are incompatible with their personal
lives. He has tamed Medea and is more sympathetic to Jason: he
makes the theme express universal suffering, and it is hard to disas-
sociate it from Greece's own experience. Theodorakis expands the text
into an opera, and the music offers another medium for interpreting
the text.

Brendan Kennelly's *Medea:* The Colonized Fight Back

Kennelly, who had done an *Antigone* in 1985, here turns his attention to
another type of heroine. His preface quotes a woman saying of *Medea,*
"Many people say the play is about jealousy. It's not, it's about rage"
(p. 6). Medea's rage, we have seen, is love turned to hate through
dishonor. Kennelly has written a paean to rage, specifically to woman's
rage. He deals not only with specific contemporary issues, such as
"the Irish question," but also with universal themes, such as those that
surround love between man and woman.

There are 2242 lines in Kennelly's play versus Euripides' 1419; the
length is thus increased by a little more than half. The discussion of
various issues adds to the prolixity, but the charm of the words makes
the additions attractive.

The translation is far from literal, but the major ideas are there. For
instance, the Nurse's opening speech contains a violent image in the
Greek: "now all is hostile and that which was beloved is sick" (νῦν δ'
ἐχθρὰ πάντα, καὶ νοσεῖ τὰ φίλτατα, 16). Kennelly renders this, "Medea's
love is hatred now." This gains succinctness but loses the harsh image
of disease. Then images are used that Euripides does not even suggest:
"Betrayal is the ripest crop in this land. / The more it is slashed, the
stronger it grows" (13). The love/hate of Jason and Medea hereby can
be extended to an image of modern politics. One thinks of betrayal not
only on the personal level but on the political: for instance, in modern
Ireland, "supergrasses" are informers suborned by the English, who
turn in their brothers.

And further,

> Her soul is hurt. She will not listen
> to the words of friends, as if these words

were the stupid croaking of crows
in the sky that is more meaningless than dust.

(13)

Not only does this describe the gossip of Dublin, the endless meaningless words from and about friends, savored like choice delicacies
served up daily in the bars—it accurately conveys Euripidean despair
over the breakdown in the meaning of words at this time in Athens,
so well described by Thucydides (3.81–82).

Kennelly's lines have varied rhythms and an occasional rhyme, sometimes when least expected.

> Among women, Medea has the most cunning mind of all.
> She is fox and badger, ferret and stoat, eagle and hawk.
> She can master seven kinds of talk,
> using the same words.

(15)

The imagery is Semonidean; the rhyme of "talk" and "hawk" titillates
the ear.

The images pile up:

> She is the clouds the sun cannot penetrate,
> she is the sun the clouds cannot resist,
> she is the voices of the rain,
> she is the silence of an unread book,
> she has a tongue to flay anyone who
> bandies words with her. Those who
> feel the lash of that tongue take
> a long time to heal. A few have
> never found the cure.

(15)

Kennelly's Medea proceeds from animal, to force of nature, to master
of language; she uses words as weapons. Euripides' Nurse, on the
contrary, focuses more on her sufferings.

The tutor speaks the language of the Dublin barfly, answering the
nurse with a monologue that resembles a parabasis: he addresses the
audience on a philosophical issue. What Euripides' Tutor says in four
lines about each man loving himself more than his neighbor is here
expanded to thirty-seven:

> Do you not realize that people love themselves
> more than anyone else in the world?...

Consider one such man. In a gesture of defiance
against himself and what he stands for,
he becomes, one summer evening, a little tipsy.
There grows in him a strange compulsion
to spill his little, hidden agonies
into the ear of a twitching stranger
who has left his wife and children
for reasons that he tries to drown in a glass,
seeing himself risking a thrilling freedom
in some hallucinating city of the future.
But come, I am frogleaping the centuries.
Still that is a teacher's privilege—
the one inspiring madness his profession allows—
the knowledge that all things happen at the same time,
to the same people (though they all die)
as the centuries flow by, smiles upon their lips
at the spectacle of honest, helpless repetition.
It is a simple tale. People love themselves
as they sense they should.
Failing in this, they invent a successful god
and plague him with their failures.

(17–18)

The myth itself frogleaps the centuries, and the similarities are seen with a Dublin accent. God and alcohol enter as definers of self.

There are many other alterations; Euripides' original now has sexual explicitness. Medea is said possibly to

steal into the palace
where Jason lies, drive a sword
into his heart, his belly, chop
his penis and his testicles for the pure pleasure of revenge.

(14; Medea as Lorena Bobbitt)

Medea's speech to the "women of Corinth," called simply here "chorus" and played by one woman, is a feminist tract. The language might have come from Aristophanes:

Men, the horny despots of our bodies,
sucking, fucking, licking, chewing, farting into our skin,
sitting on our faces, fingering our arses,
exploring our cunts, widening our thighs,
drawing the milk that gave the bastards life.

(25)

These are not words, as they were in Euripides, to win over the average citizen.[20] The graphic obscenities are weapons for Medea. Her anger is verbal, until she formulates her plan of action. Medea's statement that she would rather face an army three times than give birth once (*Med.* 250–51) becomes

It is often said that
we women have a comfortable life
in the safety of our homes, while
men go out to sweat at work,
or risk their lives in the terrible
dangers of war. Nonsense.
I'd rather sweat it out
in some stinking hellhole, or
fight a war in a foreign land
than give birth to a brat
who will add to the pollution
of this befouled earth
where even the seas are thick with poison.

(26)

Our "politically correct" Medea's concerns extend to the environment and modern problems. Nevertheless, seeing a child as pollution, however valid the idea is, tends to dehumanize Medea.

Kennelly alters the chorus in Euripides (41ff.) that tells of new songs to be written about women commemorating their wisdom and skills, rather than repeating the old lies told about them by men:

The time is coming when honour
will be paid to women, when
their feelings will not be made
by men, when slavery will not
masquerade as love, when
a man's tone of voice will not
create a tremor in a woman's
reply, when a woman will
not live to please
an inferior man, when a woman
will not sit in silence while
her master broods in sullen

---

[20] Sourvinou-Inwood in this volume elucidates well how the Euripidean original appeals to the sympathy of the audience.

> superiority, when decisions
> are her agreement to his
> suggestions, when her hate
> can show itself, articulate
> and pure. Then, too, the
> shadow of justice may be
> thrown across the earth,
> like a warm coat across
> the shoulders of a shivering beggar.

(33–34)

Here rhetoric and conviction come together powerfully, so that no one—militant feminist or reactionary male—can complain.

Medea returns to her attack in her meeting with Jason. Jason says platitudinously to Medea, "The best prayer is the prayer / that helps us to cope / with the folly and evil of this world" (42). This materialistic Jason hides his words behind the mask of prayer. Medea answers:

> Your prayer for sense—
> the commonest of common sense—
> is an insult.
>   Prayer is not
> a way of coping with fools.
> Prayer is for dealing
> with the injustice *caused* by fools,
> rhetorical idiots
> and blind, ambitious,
> power-hungry cretins.
> Prayer, my plausible friend, is
> anger at what is, and a longing
> for what should be.
> Prayer is a bomb at the door of your house.

(42)

The Catholic church and a sense of justice mingle in this response. It is also the response of Ireland to England. In a brilliant maneuver Kennelly has Jason speak like Cromwell.[21] Jason/Cromwell preaches Protestant virtue and discipline to the barbarian. Medea/Ireland should be grateful for the lessons, although she has been raped in the process.

---

[21] Brendan Kennelly had a book of poems called *Cromwell* (rpt. 1987); a stage version of it was performed in Dublin's Damer Hall in 1986 and 1987.

Medea secures her refuge with Aegeus in modern terms of diplomacy:

> I have powerful enemies
>
> . . . .
>
> if you were bound
> by oath, you could never hand me
> over to my enemies, if they tried
> to extradite me.
>
> (52)

We think of those Irish political prisoners who have fled to America. Many, having escaped from, e.g., the British Maze prison, claim they were beaten to confess to crimes they never committed. They create new lives in America, but they are discovered years later and extradited. They lack Medea's resources: Medea wins her sanctuary from Creon. She can fight back and secure a safe haven.

Medea succeeds in convincing Jason to bring deadly gifts to the princess; the last lines of her monologue are altered. Instead of describing passion overcoming reason, Kennelly's Medea says, "Passion strangles all my love" (66). An Irish Medea seems hardly bothered by rationality.

The Greek Chorus sings of the dangers in having children and then the threat of their dying; Kennelly speaks instead of aged parents abandoned by their grown children:

> And finally,
> suppose the children have grown up properly,
> how can the father know
> if the child is good or bad,
> ready to help the father in his old age
> or ditch him like a toothless old dog?
> Many a father knows what it means
> to be driven into exile
> in the land that helped him rear his family.
> I know many a father in this city,
> not far from where his son begets
> more sons. It is ludicrous succession.
>
> (66–67)

As if in afterthought, women are mentioned (not mothers): "Many women are aware of this, / but keep their silence" (67). The messenger

MEDEA AS POLITICIAN AND DIVA **311**

speech is replete with the gore of the Euripidean original. The victim could well have died in a bomb explosion: "We were all afraid to touch the corpse, / appalled by poison and by fire, / by the black ruin that was once a fair princess" (69). Medea understood what would torture Jason. She sentenced him to life, adding "Sorrow, / when deep enough, castrates a man" (73). In Euripides' play, Medea's victory was ambiguous; in Kennelly's play she wins. His play extends Euripides' ending: "What was expected has not been / accomplished. What was unexpected has come / to happen. That is the end of the story" (75). This was an almost formulaic ending that Euripides used in five plays: *Andromache, Helen, Alcestis,* and *Bacchae* in addition to *Medea*. It fits these plays, but its reversals of fortune also would fit most of Greek tragedy. In Euripides there is a special change because it is the underdog—and in all but *Bacchae*, the woman—who triumphs. Given Dionysus' sexual ambiguity, perhaps we can say a woman triumphs there also. To have a woman triumph does make the unexpected come to pass, given most representations of women in antiquity. Kennelly adds, "And yet I wonder, and will always wonder— / Is Medea's crime Medea's glory?" (75). If we have listened well, we know the answer is "yes."

Kennelly has a poem entitled "Hope":

> Time has triumphed, the wind has scattered all,
> Alexander, Caesar, empires, cities are lost.
> Tara and Troy flourished a while and fell
> And even England itself, maybe, will bite the dust.[22]

Greece informs Ireland; England may learn from Medea, even as Jason did. Kennelly has brought Medea up to date. He shows that her power is still impressive. His particular version has tapped into the universal "force that through the green fuse drives the flower."

Kennelly's Medea differs from Euripides' in several ways. She engages feminist, environmental, and political issues, in addition to the original issues in the earlier play. Her hostility blazes forth and makes her somewhat weaker than the woman whom Euripides gave us: that Medea was more adept at playing the game of deception, and using her femininity as another weapon. Kennelly's Medea is as much Hillary Clinton as Betty Broderick. She is no longer quite as Homeric or Sophoclean as her Euripidean predecessor. She is more angry in a political

---

[22] Kennelly 1989:43.

way, with specific ends in mind rather than her honor per se. Medea now is a lightning rod for political questions, and a suitable heiress to the dragon chariot.

These are controversial themes, but one of the functions of Greek tragedy is to say the unsayable and ask the forbidden question. Television and newspapers are for the most part vehicles for deception or pacification. Greek tragedy is one of the last remaining repositories of truth.

Tragedy into Opera

If a modern performance of Greek tragedy is not just a translation of the original Greek text presented in spoken form by actors on a stage, but rather an operatic adaptation with music and dance supplementing the text, then our experience is again enriched and elevated. Ancient Greek tragedy was originally presented in alternating passages of spoken and sung verbal exchanges. Generally, the action moves forward in the dialogue sections spoken by the actors; the chorus then provide commentary and meditation in their lyrics, which were accompanied by the αὐλός (flute), and perhaps by the κιθάρα (lyre), and choreographed.

We see in operas by Mozart the obvious analogy with ancient tragedy, since he divides his libretto between arias and recitatives: the action moves forward in the recitatives, and we learn from the characters in their arias how they feel about these developments. A verbal text set to music is by nature more abstract and more philosophical—indeed, more idealized—than a simple spoken utterance. It is further from our own everyday experience and we perceive it differently. A musical setting simultaneously invites us into the character's own peculiar emotional range and universalizes these emotions.

These two dimensions—the profound response of the modern audience to the seemingly alien matter of ancient Greek tragedy and the elevating and universalizing effect of music—make the experience of a modern opera based on Greek tragedy an extraordinarily demanding and rewarding one. Friedrich Nietzsche claimed that music reveals the essence of the truth, not an image of the phenomenon.[23] Along

---

[23] Nietzsche 1956:100 refers to Schopenhauer and says that music "is not a copy of the phenomenon, but an immediate copy of the will itself, and therefore complements everything physical in the world and every phenomenon by representing

with a few other masterpieces of that genre, the *Medea* of Theodorakis involves us in an almost religious ritual: we worship not some god, or even some philosophical concept, but rather the rarefied and clarified essence of human emotion. We hear ourselves in elevated song and see ourselves on stage.

Aristotle lists the primary components of tragedy as plot, character, words, thought, spectacle, and music (*Poet.* 1450a). Many performances I have seen of Greek tragedy slight one or another of these elements. I claim, along with the seventeenth-century Italian theorists, that opera approximates most closely the total experience that Aristotle says is characteristic of tragedy.[24] Both Wagner and Nietzsche drew parallels between Greek tragedy and the *Gesamtkunstwerk* that was opera, with its alliances between Apollonian and Dionysian. The appeal to the intellect has to be joined with an emotional component, and this has obvious correlations with Aristotelian κάθαρσις (cleansing) and ἀναγνώρισις (recognition). I would interpret κάθαρσις, however, as not so much a "purging" as an "entering into," a type of κατάβασις (descent) analogous to what ancient heroes endured in epic when they descended into the Underworld, so that they could emerge renewed and enlightened. I see emotions being felt and confronted, as ghosts are in the Underworld, and thus acknowledged (ἀναγνώρισις) if not mastered. Those undergoing this experience (κάθαρσις and ἀναγνώρισις) attain a type of freedom, akin to that enjoyed by patients at the end of psychoanalysis: they will no longer be subject to the return of the repressed in disguised forms but will have integrated the traumatic experience behind it by confronting it. Perhaps one uses the shield of Perseus to see the head of Medusa so as not to be turned to stone: the agency of art or therapy is required for facing oneself. Unlike the tragic hero, we survive the play; in fact, we are more alive, because we admit that Medusa is inside us, and we have learned to harness the energy of her snakes.

---

what is metaphysical, the thing in itself." This expresses Aristotle's correction of Plato: art is not an imitation of an imitation (and therefore a further distance from the Form, which is "real") but rather the revelation of an actual pattern in human experience.

[24] See the theory put out by the Camerata, Italian theorists credited with the "invention" of opera around 1600. As Sadie 1989:3 claims, "It was their understanding of the powerful role exercised by music in Greek tragedy that spurred the Florentine intellectuals of the late 16th century to take steps toward the establishment of what we call 'opera.'"

Mikis Theodorakis' *Medea:*
An Opera of Passion and Loss

Ancient tragedy was made to be performed and viewed.[25] Opera can be used as an interpretative tool, and I have chosen Mikis Theodorakis' opera based on Euripides' *Medea* as another splendid example of how a modern work can elucidate this ancient text. The physicality of the performances in 1991 at the Arriga Theater of Bilbao, Spain, and in 1993 at the Herodes Atticus theater in Athens, which incorporated song and dance, invited a physical response from the audience. This physical response is part of what Aristotle meant by κάθαρσις.

While Theodorakis' opera may not resolve all the controversies, its perspective lets us see the complexities of this powerful heroine. His opera also allows us to appreciate Jason's tragedy even more than Euripides' or Kennelly's versions. Music functions as an additional chorus and provides a commentary of its own. There are certain areas of human intellectual and emotional activity that one could claim are only accessible through music. These are like those moments in which, as T. S. Eliot said, "We touch the border of those feelings which only music can express."[26] Music is best for expressing Medea's persona as passion incarnate, θυμός made flesh. The music lifts and abstracts the emotional, manifesting the ineffable.

Theodorakis' biography, with its account of the intermittent persecutions and celebrations of his work, reads like a history of Greece.[27] He was one of the leaders of the resistance to the Greek Junta, the military dictatorship that held power from 1967 to 1974. He was imprisoned and tortured for his beliefs, but he never gave up his struggle for freedom. He has been composing works based on ancient drama since

[25] As this volume went to press, I read that Rolf Liebermann had just had his fifth opera performed, *Freispruch für Medea.* In an interview published in *Der Speigel* 34 (1995) 171, he says he sees the war between the sexes as a form of colonization: "Ich variiere den antiken Mythos. Es geht um die Einbruch der Männer in eine friedliche Frauenwelt— der Geschlecterkampf als eine Form von Kolonialisierung. Deshalb ist es natürlich auch ein Stück über Gewalt. Musikalisch habe ich das so gelöst: die harmonische Frauengemeinschaft der Medea wird durch ein asiatisches Gamelan-Orchester untermalt. Erst wenn der Eindringling Jason, der moderne Macho, mit seiner Männerhorde das Matriarchat zerstört und die Frauen brutal vergewaltigt, setzt mit schrillen Missklägen das traditionalle Orchester ein."

[26] "Poetry and Drama," quoted by Kerman 1956:5.

[27] Two useful books in English that give us background are Giannaris 1972 and Holst-Warhaft 1980. There is hardly a mention of Theodorakis that does not involve social context.

1960, when he wrote the music for Euripides' *Phoenissae*. In 1987, his Symphony no. 4 was performed, consisting of two parts: Aeschylus' *Eumenides* and Euripides' *Phoenissae*. In the same year, his ballet based on *Zorba* was performed in Verona's opera house, along with Verdi's *Aida* and Puccini's *Turandot*. In a letter he said that he felt inspired to compose a *Medea* in honor of Verdi, an *Electra* in honor of Puccini, and a *Hecuba* in honor of Bellini. His first opera, *Kostas Kariotakis* or the *Metamorphoses of Dionysos*, actually was in honor of the brave poet who died tragically; it was performed at the Lyriki Skene in 1987. He has now finished an *Electra*.

From 1940 to 1960 Theodorakis wrote symphonic works and a ballet called *Antigone*, which was performed at Covent Garden in London in 1959. From 1960 to 1980 he composed melodies to accompany both Greek and foreign poetry, including many productions of ancient classics such as Minotis' production of the *Phoenissae* (Euripides), Mouzenidis' *Ajax* and *Troades* (Sophocles and Euripides), Evangelatos' *Suppliants* and *Trilogy* (Aeschylus), Koun's *Knights* (Aristophanes), and Solomos' *Hecuba* (Euripides), among others. He mastered melody and felt he was able to meet Euripides on his own terms and as an equal. He made the λόγος (word) lyrical as he translated Euripides himself—from ancient into modern Greek—and set his own words to music. He effected the marriage that Strauss' poet and composer in *Capriccio* tried to accomplish: words and music are in glorious harmony and equal masterworks.

Theodorakis has given a number of reasons for his choice of Euripides.[28] He believes this poet saw man as more autonomous and responsible for his own choices than did Aeschylus, who saw man more as a plaything of the gods. Modern man faces the existential question of his own identity and has to come to terms with Sartre's insight: "L'Enfer, c'est les Autres" (*Huis Clos*). Tragedy helps with the ultimate confrontation—self-knowledge. Perhaps this is also a κάθαρσις that contributes to freedom; otherwise, we are like the princess trapped in her robes: the more she tries to free herself, the more she becomes entangled—so we are trapped in our prejudices and blindness. The suffering tragedy forces us to undergo is, perhaps, the suffering that leads to knowledge. Κάθαρσις then gives us the clarity to see; we participate in the tragic heroes' ἀναγνώρισις. Theodorakis couples music with words

---

[28] I am quoting and translating the Greek from a letter Theodorakis wrote to me in April 1992.

to make our experience of the modern opera as unified, and as intellectually and emotively cathartic, as the experience of ancient tragedy.

When experiencing opera one must learn to read a second text. The music can agree or disagree with the written text, or simply serve as background. One is impressed by the musical neutrality toward text in works like Arnold Schönberg's *Pierrot Lunaire*, Alban Berg's *Wozzeck*, and John Adams' *Nixon in China*, although they have some programmatic moments. There are other operas that are quite programmatic; works of Richard Wagner and Richard Strauss spring immediately to mind.

Theodorakis had the palette of minimalism at his disposal, but he chose instead to keep many of the traditional elements that we have come to appreciate in Italian opera of the nineteenth and early twentieth centuries. Like the Italian masters, he is highly original in using and combining traditional European symphonic music with folk music; *Rembetika*, the augmented intervals of the pentatonic scale and the ancient modes, suggest the "oriental" and even at times orthodox liturgical music. His *melos* also has elements from the music of Crete, demotic and laical melodies, Arabic and Turkish themes, jazz, symphonic music, and the general classical heritage of Europe. His simplified approach to vocal counterpoint asserts the primacy of the verbal text. At times the orchestration adds a colorful dance motif, often derived from the Greek and Arabic dances with which he is familiar. Theodorakis calls his music "metasymphonic," because it consists of a synthesis of Western music with these Eastern elements.[29]

Many of the choruses are also delivered by the choral leader. The scoring often shows an antiphonal and responsorial vocal setting which allows for greater understanding of the text. At the same time the use of beautifully lush nineteenth-century harmonies and polyphonic textures in the orchestra vividly contrast with the plainsong or Gregorian chant recitatives that contribute toward the composer's material for the singers.

The triple meter and triplet ornamentation add graceful dancelike rhythms to the text. These rhythms are also most often associated with Medea, whereas marchlike rhythms characterize both Creon and Jason. The 2/4 or 4/8 rhythm of the *Chassipiko*, the more masculine "butcher's dance" in the folk tradition, is suitable for Jason, the butcher of Medea's

---

[29] See Giannaris 1972:x. Holst-Warhaft 1980:62–63 further classifies Theodorakis' music into "seven categories, all based on song," and the music from the score to *Elektra* is classified as "metasymphonic."

dreams. The *Rembetika* free rhythms and the triplets of *Zembekiko* remind one of the music that the exiles used as their own κάθαρσις, following the catastrophe in 1921–23, when Greeks were forced out of Asia Minor. These Ionian Greeks resettled in Greece proper and were thus foreigners in their own land; their plight resembles Medea's exile to a new homeland where she is treated as a stranger even when things are going well. Greece itself is culturally and geographically located between East and West; thus Medea can become a metaphor for Greek history.

The final plainchant lamentation by Jason has nothing dancelike in it. Dance rhythms are associated with Medea's final victory. Hers are the triple-metered arias, which suggest a type of freedom, whereas Jason is trapped by the foursquare double meters: the tools he uses for domination, force, and power end up dominating and destroying him. Gail Holst-Warhaft claims of the *Axion Esti*, the great composition by Theodorakis based on the poem of the Nobel Prize–winner Odysseus Elytis, "It was closely guided by the structure of the poem in which the sacred and pagan symbolism of the number three plays an important part."[30] The number three, associated with the trinity, may symbolize an additional divine endorsement of Medea, since most of her music is in triple rhythm, including her main aria before she kills her children: it is a waltz, in triple time. She herself certainly shows the characteristics of a goddess, but Euripides' genius shows that she is equally human. Theodorakis evokes Euripides' interpretive genius through the symbolic associations of the music.

Medea has for accompaniment long and soaring melodies in the strings, the woodwinds, and gentle chimes, while Jason and Creon are backed by aggressive marches in the lower brass, with crashing percussion. This reverses at the end: Medea has aggressive music in the brass and percussion, but Jason's final lament incorporates chimes and is a true dirge, resembling μοιρολόγια, the laments that women sing at funerals.

What is gained and what is lost by the musical interpretation? First of all, by contrast with the Kennelly version, this text is a close translation done by Theodorakis himself. Nevertheless, with the addition of music and various repetitions, the performance time of the opera is longer than that of Kennelly's play. As a result, various sections are omitted in actual performance, although Theodorakis would prefer that the entire

[30] Holst-Warhaft 1980:84.

work be performed. At Bilbao the performance was about three hours, compared to less than two hours for the play.

There are also leitmotivs. The opera begins with a theme for the clarinet that suggests Medea, her vengeance, death, and fate. It is quite similar to the theme that Theodorakis used years before in his prologue to Cacoyannis' *Elektra*, only in the earlier work it was accompanied by other woodwinds in addition to the clarinet, with percussion and a more obviously Middle Eastern rhythm. The theme in *Medea* will recur just before she goes off to kill her children. There are also themes associated with the children, one a lullaby and another that suggests their carefree play, which signal the arrival of the children. The children's theme also appears in Medea's speech to the women of Corinth, proleptically suggesting her means for vengeance.

We find the music also gives characterization, such as an "Eastern" theme for Medea. The nurse, a mezzo-soprano, gives us the celebrated prologue that begins Euripides' play. A modal "Byzantine" theme accompanies the words that tell of Medea's flight from Colchis after helping Jason steal the Golden Fleece, when she murders her own brother to aid Jason's escape. Medea is the foreigner, the other, and this is conveyed by the music. A marchlike theme illuminates the nurse's comment that Medea will not stop until someone is hurt, whether friend or enemy (see *Med.* 94–95). The march tells us that Medea is as powerful as any soldier.

Theodorakis' martial theme shows Medea not only as a Sophoclean hero but as a Homeric hero, a claim already discussed in some general terms. We have considered the revealing assertion that recurs various times throughout the play: Medea does not want her enemies to laugh at her (e.g., *Med.* 383, 404). Her honor is all important, and this is the primary concern of the Greek hero in Homer.[31] Even when Medea makes the famous claim that she would rather stand in the front of the battle line three times than to bear a child once (*Med.* 251), she illustrates by her actions that she does not fear standing in battle. It is this that the music emphasizes also. There are other programmatic touches as the music reproduces what it describes, such as imitating the rolling of waves when Medea's voyage is mentioned.

There is an interesting use of two choruses, and this emphasizes the confrontations of the sexes. A male chorus accompanies Creon, Jason

---

[31] See Snell 1961:73. Medea seems to be motivated by her own honor as much as by Jason's guilt. There is thus the suggestion of an archaic, even primitive, cast to her character.

and Aegeus. This leads to many uses of the mixed choir, as men and women confront each other with their conflicting claims. The opposition of Jason and Medea is extended to the opposition of men and women. Moreover, Jason is a tenor and Creon and Aegeus are basses. This reinforces the authority of the latter two and the love interest of the former (most romantic leads in opera are tenors). Medea is a *soprano dramatico*.

There is also an interesting use of modern religious music, blending with the mention of the Greek gods. The swearing of oaths that ends the meeting between Aegeus and Medea takes place before a statue of Zeus. The music is quite reminiscent of Greek Orthodox services, and the religious quality is obvious. There is a formality in this use of the chorus: one is aware of collective will and prayer, rather than an individual's desire. Theodorakis has endorsed Medea's plea with the sanction of modern gods in addition to the ancient ones. The ending of the play also shows this link. Religion adds its touch and changes Euripides' close into a prayer for peace and a plea to the gods to bring light and scatter the shadows. Medea joins in. The words of Euripides' formulaic ending are transformed into an effective prayer.

The culmination of Medea's decision is enhanced by the music. Just before her aria that tells of her decision to kill the children, we hear the fate/death/Medea theme that opened the opera; now in the minor key, it is followed by the ominous tam-tam, or gong, symbolizing (among other things) death, time, and the inexorable. The key goes abruptly from minor to major, and Medea sings an emotive aria in 3/4 rhythm. This aria shows Medea as resigned, yet passionately glorying in her tragic decision. She says that she will kill her children, and now she must go forward. The major key and the waltzlike rhythm are at odds with the tragic text, as Medea tells herself to take arms and forget her children for this one day (*Med.* 1242–50). The music conveys the ambiguity of a woman's triumph shot with sorrow. The final lines of this climactic aria show the children will always be beloved and that her mourning will be forever. Aristotle's famous statement that Euripides was the most tragic of the tragedians is illustrated by Medea calling herself the unhappiest of women. This display of bravura adds another dimension to the text and brilliantly colors Medea's tragic heroism. She is driven to the limit of human emotion and defines herself by her act.

Her lament differs from Jason's in that the music conveys the joy of victory at the same time as the sorrow of loss. Theodorakis has set Medea's lament in a soaring major key; he used this same jarring juxtaposition once before when he wrote songs to commemorate Antonio Torres Heredia's arrest and death. As Gail Holst-Warhaft observes, "The actual murder is described in a deceptively gay passage which slows to a climax in a cadence mirroring the opening phrase. It is a heroic death."[32] Theodorakis brilliantly conveys the tragic dilemma of Medea's decision: she will kill her beloved children to achieve her heroic vengeance.

More drama is conveyed by the music, which also acts like the messenger in adding its own commentary during the scene when Medea kills her children. In the Spanish production, following Medea's tragically decisive aria, the fate/death/Medea theme is heard against the appearance of Death/Time, who is dressed in black and circles the stage carrying a scythe, which turns from silver to red. The theme builds to a climax and we hear the children's cries. There is a crash in the orchestra and a rhythmic atonality that could have come from the *Rite of Spring*.

The final confrontation between Medea and Jason is vividly conveyed by the music, which includes an addition that makes us understand Euripides' text in a new way. There is a touching lament for Jason, which beyond what the words convey allows us to appreciate his loss. Jason sings a lament that has a theme resembling *The Ballad of Mauthausen*, Theodorakis' song cycle of 1965. The text of this cycle was written by Iakovos Campanellis to commemorate the suffering of the Jews during the Holocaust. This theme is now applied to Jason, who is hardly as innocent as the victims of the Holocaust, but the music shows us his suffering in a new light. Has Medea taken over the methods of Hitler? Is she imitating the occupying Turks, as conveyed by the "orientalism" of her costume and musical themes (see discussion below)?

This interpretation, which emphasizes the suffering of both Medea and Jason, can derive from the historical experience of the Greeks as witnessed by Theodorakis. Both sides saw killings during a civil war, and Theodorakis is sensitive to this struggle. He has politically been on both sides, opting finally for a role as an artist more than a politician. He understands human suffering, and his opera is a commemoration of this suffering. His position differs from Kennelly's as more universal but still informed by a national experience.

At the end of the play Euripides shows us a Medea who goes too far. By killing the children there is a shift in our sympathy; this is comparable to what we experience in *Bacchae*, when Dionysus goes too

---

[32] Holst-Warhaft 1980:125.

far in his vengeance. Here, the power of music shifts our sympathy. The brutal militaristic themes with the assertive brass now move to Medea, whereas Jason has become a lyric tenor, poignant in his lament.

A descending arpeggio by the tuba ends the opera as Medea arises in her dragon-drawn chariot carrying the bodies of the children. In the 1993 performance in Athens, Medea appears in a long black robe wearing a golden tiara, and the robe extends as an elevator carries her upward: she elongates like Maleficent at the end of Walt Disney's *Sleeping Beauty*. The pervasive use of the tuba has implied power when it appeared before, and now it becomes Medea's power theme in the brass, and it is with difficulty that the dissonance is harmonized at the end. Only the chorale of the gods ended in a major key. Whatever Jason and Medea may ultimately signify as a couple, dissonances will remain in our mind every bit as much as their harmony.

By showing the power shift through the use for Medea of the brass that earlier had characterized Jason and Creon, Theodorakis musically illustrates Medea's adoption of Jason's methods to destroy him (as Boedeker points out in this volume). Girard's "mimetic desire" is here expressed by mimetic instrumentation. Not only does Medea take over Jason's dominant role, but Jason takes over Medea's role of lamentation. The music shows the reversal: what characterized one at the beginning now characterizes the other at the end. As Nussbaum observed (in this volume) of Seneca's modification of Euripides, Theodorakis' music gives Jason "a new humanity and dignity."

Jason's lament—intermingled with a noble chorale—undercuts the bitter exchange between Jason and Medea that Euripides used to end his play, though we might say the final discord conveys this bitterness. Euripides employed a vigorous *Verfremdungseffekt* not only in Medea's killing the children, which alienates her from the audience's sympathy, but then in the screaming debate between her and Jason: the exchanged insults serve to alienate the audience from both of them. Euripides' culminating agon might validate some of Nietzsche's criticisms: poetry is lost when debate takes over.

Theodorakis' version lacks the screaming foul-mouthed feminism of Kennelly's play, as well as a clear-cut paradigm for imperialism. Medea sings a lyrical feminine complaint. The emphasis now is on loss, both by the male and the female. Medea triumphs but the price she has paid is dear, and Jason's anguish is translated into heartrending song. The suffering of Medea and Jason can stand for the suffering of the Greek nation, with its history of occupation by the Turks and briefly by

...ɔ, and of civil wars. This is a nation that has long understood
...ɪentation, from the early times when women conducted rituals of
cries and tears for the departed (μοιρολόγια). Theodorakis shows us
conflict and its aftermath, with an emphasis on tears. In Theodorakis'
music we hear the price of passion in the notes of sorrow wrenched out
of the heart.

Aristotle and Nietzsche would be pleased with Theodorakis' render-
ing, because he successfully incorporates some of the Aeschylean and
Sophoclean genius into the Euripidean text. In the opera we find the reli-
giosity and mystery of Aeschylus coupled with the nobility that Sophocles gave to his heroes and heroines. In *Medea*, Euripides questioned
both religion and heroism by undermining their ethical basis. Through
Theodorakis' musical transformations, κάθαρσις and ἀναγνώρισις are
better effected, since both seem augmented by the audience's identification with the characters. Villainy tends to destroy the will to identify.
Aristotle claimed that unnecessary villainy is an additional flaw, using
Menelaus in *Orestes* to illustrate his point (*Poet*.1454a).

This merging of modern with ancient genius, Theodorakis with
Euripides, tempers Euripidean irony but emphasizes the tragic. It is
significant that the music owes nearly as much to the nineteenth century
as to the twentieth. The emphasis now is on feeling and suffering
rather than heroics. The opera is profoundly moving; by stressing the
femininity of Medea, Theodorakis is being true to Euripides.

Dramatic κάθαρσις is complete: besides clarifying our emotions, it focuses our attention on the Dionysian universal. The historical resonance
of modern times enhances the ancient message. Theodorakis himself
understood suffering, and Jason and Medea reflect his own experience
besides that of Greece. Thus we see that Aristotle's idea of κάθαρσις
and ἀναγνώρισις, types of particular inner experience each spectator
undergoes, is merged in Theodorakis' opera with Nietzsche's idea of
the emotional universal which underlies reality. Theodorakis' *Medea* is
a new Hermes, leading us into the inner world, from which we emerge
with new insights. We perceive the universal and, through this art, we
learn "all we shall know for truth, / Before we grow old and die."[33]

Brendan Kennelly and Mikis Theodorakis have focused their presen-
tations in different ways. Kennelly deals with the question of imperialism and shows us Medea as the victim who fights back. Theodorakis

---

[33] William Butler Yeats, "A Drinking Song" (1910), in Yeats 1966:34.

universalizes the issues into a symphony of suffering joined with Euripides' sung text; he also links this suffering with the Greek historical experience. In Kennelly's and Theodorakis' works, respectively, one can see the two aspects of the victim: (a) the victim becomes the victor, one who triumphs; and (b) the victim as victim, one who suffers. Both modern artists, in contrast to Euripides, emphasize the emotional elements in Medea over the rational.

The god in these works is often Christian instead of pagan. We see two different aspects of Medea: Kennelly shows us a Medea as an icon of blazing hate, and Theodorakis shows us the tragedies of both a woman and a man with an irrevocable loss. He humanizes Jason so that we sympathize with his agony as well as Medea's. Both Kennelly and Theodorakis broaden the definition of Medea, but reproduce what is essential to her. Both works bring Euripides into modern times and into modern nations. In their own ways, they are true to Euripides and aim at the heart.

BIBLIOGRAPHY

Ahl 1985. F. Ahl, *Metaformations: Soundplay and Wordplay in Ovid and Other Classical Poets* (Ithaca 1985). [Newlands]

Ahl 1986. F. Ahl, *Medea* (Ithaca 1986). [Nussbaum]

al-Isfahânî 1870. Al-Râghib al-Isfahânî, *Muhâdarât al-udabâ'*, vol. 1 (Bûlâq 1870). [Bremmer]

Albini 1990. U. Albini, *Medea, Ippolito* (Garzanti 1990). [McDonald]

Alexiou 1974. M. Alexiou, *The Ritual Lament in Greek Tradition* (Cambridge 1974). [O'Higgins]

Allatius 1645. L. Allatius, *De Graecorum hodie quorundam opiniationibus in de templis Graecorum* (Cologne 1645). [Johnston]

Allen and Italie 1954. J. T. Allen and G. Italie, *A Concordance to Euripides* (Berkeley 1954). [Boedeker]

Anderson 1963. W. S. Anderson, "Multiple Change in the *Metamorphoses*," *TAPA* 94 (1963) 1–27. [Newlands]

Anderson 1972. W. S. Anderson, *Ovid's Metamorphoses Books 6–10* (Norman, Okla., 1972). [Newlands]

Anderson 1988. W. S. Anderson (ed.), *P. Ovidi Nasonis Metamorphoses* (Leipzig 1988). [Newlands]

Anderson 1990. W. S. Anderson, "The Example of Procris in the *Ars Amatoria*," in *The Cabinet of the Muses: Essays on Classical and Comparative Literature in Honor of Thomas G. Rosenmeyer*, M. Griffith and D. J. Mastronarde (eds.) (Atlanta 1990) 131–45. [Newlands]

Annas 1992. J. Annas, *Hellenistic Philosophy of Mind* (Berkeley 1992). [Dillon]

Arcellaschi 1990. A. Arcellaschi, *Médée dans le théâtre latin d'Ennius à Sénèque* (Rome 1990). [Graf]

Ardizzoni 1976. A. Ardizzoni, "Il pianto di Medea e la similitudine della giovane vedova (Apollonio Rodio 3.656–673)," *GIF* 28 (1976) 233–40. [Clauss]

Arthur 1973. M. Arthur, "Early Greece: The Origins of the Western Attitude towards Women," *Arethusa* 6 (1973) 7–58. [O'Higgins]

Bachofen 1966. J. J. Bachofen, *Gesammelte Werke*, vol. 7 (Basel 1966). [Bremmer]

Barkhuizen 1979. J. H. Barkhuizen, "The Psychological Characterization of Medea in Apollonius of Rhodes, *Argonautica* 3.744–824," *AClass* 22 (1979) 33–48. [Clauss]

Barlow 1971. S. A. Barlow, *The Imagery of Euripides: A Study in the Dramatic Use of Pictorial Language* (London 1971; rpt. Bristol 1986). [Boedeker]

Barlow 1989. S. A. Barlow, "Stereotype and Reversal in Euripides' *Medea*," *G&R* 36 (1989) 158–171. [Boedeker, McDonald]

Barrera 1989. J. C. B. Barrera, "Zeus, Hera y el Matrimonio Sagrado" *Quaderni di Storia* 15 (1989) no. 30 133–56. [Johnston]

Barron 1980. J. P. Barron, "Bakchylides, Theseus and a Woolly Cloak," *BICS* 27 (1980) 1–8. [Sourvinou-Inwood]

Beekes 1986. R. S. P. Beekes, " 'You Can Get New Children . . .': Turkish and Other Parallels to Ancient Ideas in Herodotus, Thucydides, Sophocles, and Euripides," *Mnemosyne* 39 (1986) 225–39. [Bremmer]

Belloni 1981. L. Belloni, "Medea πολυφάρμαχος" *CCC* 2 (1981) 117–33. [Clauss]

Benveniste 1969. E. Benveniste, *Le vocabulaire des institutions indo-européennes* vol. 1 (Paris 1969). [Bremmer]

Berger-Doer 1992. G. Berger-Doer, "Kreousa II," *LIMC* 6 (1992) 120–27. [Sourvinou-Inwood]

Bergk 1884. T. Bergk, *Griechische Literaturgeschichte*, 4 vols. (Berlin 1872–87). [Dillon]

Bergren 1983. A. L. T. Bergren, "Language and the Female in Early Greek Thought," *Arethusa* 16 (1983) 69–95. [O'Higgins]

Bergson 1971. L. Bergson, *Die Relativität der Werte im Frühwerk des Euripides* (Stockholm 1971). [Boedeker]

Berthiaume 1982. G. Berthiaume, *Les rôles du mágeiros: Études sur la boucherie, la cuisine et le sacrifice dans la Grèce ancienne* (Leiden/Montréal 1982). [Bremmer]

Bettini 1984. A. Bettini, "Arniope," *LIMC* 2 (1984) 614. [Sourvinou-Inwood]

Beye 1969. C. R. Beye, "Jason as Love-hero in Apollonius' *Argonautica*," *GRBS* 10 (1969) 31–55. [Clauss]

Beye 1982. C. R. Beye, *Epic and Romance in the Argonautica of Apollonius: Literary Structures* (Carbondale, Ill., 1982). [Clauss]

Blatter 1984. R. Blatter, "Argonautai," *LIMC* 2 (1984) 591–99. [Sourvinou-Inwood]

Blome 1983. P. Blome, "Der Tod des Apsyrtos auf einem römischen Sarkophagdeckel," *Römische Mitteilungen* 90 (1983) 201–9. [Bremmer]

M. Blundell 1989. M. W. Blundell, *Helping Friends and Harming Enemies: A Study in Sophocles and Greek Ethics* (Cambridge 1989). [McDonald]

S. Blundell 1986. S. Blundell, *The Origins of Civilization in Greek and Roman Thought* (London 1986). [Nussbaum]

Boardman 1976. J. Boardman, "The Kleophrades Painter at Troy," *Antike Kunst* 19 (1976) 3–18. [Sourvinou-Inwood]

Boardman 1980. J. Boardman, *The Greeks Overseas: Their Early Colonies and Trade*, 3rd ed. (New York 1980). [Graf]

Boedeker 1991. D. Boedeker, "Euripides' Medea and the Vanity of ΛΟΓΟΙ," *CP* 86 (1991) 95–112. [Boedeker]

Bol 1989. P. C. Bol, *Argivische Schilde*, Olympische Forschungen 17 (Berlin 1989). [Sourvinou-Inwood]

Bömer 1976–77. F. Bömer, *P. Ovidius Naso: Metamorphosen*, vols. 3–4 (books 6–7, 8–9) (Heidelberg 1976–77). [Newlands]

Bongie 1977. E. B. Bongie, "Heroic Elements in the *Medea* of Euripides." *TAPA* 107 (1977) 27–56. [Boedeker, McDonald]

Bourdieu 1977. P. Bourdieu, *Outline of a Theory of Practice* (Cambridge 1977). [Bremmer]

Brashear 1990. W. Brashear, "Zauberformular," *Archiv für Papyrusforschung und verwandte Gebiete* 36 (1990) 49–74. [Johnston]

Braswell 1988. B. K. Braswell, *A Commentary on the Fourth Pythian Ode of Pindar* (Berlin 1988). [Boedeker, Graf, Johnston, Krevans, O'Higgins]

Braverman 1989. K. Braverman, *Lithium for Medea* (New York 1979; 1989). [McDonald]

Brelich 1955–57. A. Brelich, "Les monosandales," *La Nouvelle Clio* 7–10 (1955–57) 469–84. [Graf]

Brelich 1959. A. Brelich, "I figli di Medea," *SMSR* 30 (1959) 213–54. [Graf, Johnston]

Brelich 1969. A. Brelich, *Paides e parthenoi* (Rome 1969). [Sourvinou-Inwood]

Bremer 1987. J. M. Bremer et al., *Some Recently Found Greek Poems: Text and Commentary* (Leiden 1987). [Bremmer]

Bremmer 1978. J. Bremmer, "Heroes, Rituals, and the Trojan War," *SSR* 2 (1978) 5–38. [Bremmer]

Bremmer 1983a. J. Bremmer, *The Early Greek Concept of the Soul* (Princeton 1983). [Johnston]

Bremmer 1983b. J. Bremmer, "The Importance of the Maternal Uncle and Grandfather in Archaic and Classical Greece and Early Byzantium," *ZPE* 50 (1983) 173–86. [Bremmer]

Bremmer 1987a. J. Bremmer (ed.) *Interpretations of Greek Mythology* (London 1987). [Bremmer]

Bremmer 1987b. J. Bremmer, "Romulus, Remus, and the Foundation of Rome." In *Roman Myth and Mythography*, J. Bremmer and N. M. Horsfall (eds.), *BICS*, Supplement 52 (London 1987) 25–48. [Krevans]

Bremmer 1988. J. Bremmer, "La plasticité du mythe: Méléagre dans la poésie homérique," in *Métamorphoses du mythe en Grèce antique*, C. Calame (ed.) (Lausanne 1988) 37–56. [Bremmer, Graf]

Bremmer 1991. J. Bremmer, "Walking, Standing, and Sitting in Ancient Greek Culture," in *A Cultural History of Gesture from Antiquity to the Present Day*, J. Bremmer and H. Roodenburg (eds.) (Cambridge 1991) 15–35. [Bremmer]

Bremmer 1992. J. Bremmer, "Dionysos travesti," in *L'initiation: Les rites d'ado-lesence et les mystères* vol. 1, A. Moreau (ed.) (Montpellier 1992) 189–98. [Bremmer]

Bremmer and Horsfall 1987. J. Bremmer and N. M. Horsfall, *Roman Myth and Mythography* (London 1987). [Bremmer, Graf]

Brinkmann 1878. F. V. Brinkmann, *Die Metaphern* (Bonn 1878). [Boedeker]

Brommer 1982. F. Brommer, *Theseus: Die Taten des griechischen Helden in der antiken Kunst und Literatur* (Darmstadt 1982). [Sourvinou-Inwood]

Bron and Kassapoglou 1992. C. Bron and E. Kassapoglou (eds.), *L'image en jeu de l'Antiquité à Paul Klee* (Lausanne, 1992). [Bremmer]

Brulè 1987. P. Brulè, *La fille d'Athènes: La religion des filles à Athènes à l'époque classique—mythes, cultes, et société* (Paris 1957). [Graf]

Brundage 1979. B. C. Brundage, *The Fifth Sun: Aztec Gods, Aztec World* (Austin 1979). [Johnston]

Buck 1979. R. J. Buck, *A History of Boeotia* (Edmonton 1979). [Krevans]

Buresch 1889. K. Buresch, *Klaros: Untersuchungen zum Orakelwesen des späteren Altertums* (Leipzig 1889). [Johnston]

Burkert 1966. W. Burkert, "Greek Tragedy and Sacrifical Ritual," *GRBS* 7 (1966) 87–121. [Johnston]

Burkert 1979. W. Burkert, *Structure and History in Greek Mythology and Ritual* (Berkeley 1979). [Graf, Krevans]

Burkert 1983. W. Burkert, *Homo Necans: The Anthropology of Ancient Greek Sacrificial Ritual and Myth*, Peter Bing (trans.) (Berkeley 1983). [Bremmer, Graf, Johnston]

Burkert 1985. W. Burkert, *Greek Religion: Archaic and Classical*, John Raffan (trans.) (Oxford 1985). [Johnston, Sourvinou-Inwood]

Burkert 1992. W. Burkert, *The Orientalizing Revolution: Near Eastern Influence on Greek Culture in the Early Archaic Age*, Margaret E. Pinder and W. Burkert (trans.) (Cambridge, Mass., 1992). [Bremmer, Johnston]

Burn 1987. L. Burn, *The Meidias Painter* (Oxford 1987). [Sourvinou-Inwood]

Burnett 1973. A. P. Burnett, "*Medea* and the Tragedy of Revenge," *CP* 68 (1973) 1–24. [Boedeker]

Busa and Zampolli 1975. R. Busa and A. Zampolli, *Concordantiae Senecanae*, 2 vols. (Hildesheim 1975). [Nussbaum]

Buschor 1944. E. Buschor, *Die Musen des Jenseits* (Munich 1944). [O'Higgins]

Buxton 1994. R. G. A. Buxton, *Imaginary Greece: The Contents of Mythology* (Cambridge 1994). [Bremmer]

Calame 1977. C. Calame, *Les choeurs de jeunes filles en Grèce archaïque*, 2 vols. (Rome 1977). [O'Higgins, Sourvinou-Inwood]

Calame 1988. C. Calame (ed.), *Métamorphoses du mythe en Grèce antique* (Geneva 1988). [Bremmer]

Calame 1990. C. Calame, *Thésée et l'imaginaire athénien: Légende et culte en Grèce antique* (Lausanne 1990). [Graf]

J. Campbell 1964. J. K. Campbell, *Honour, Family, and Patronage: A Study of Institutions and Moral Values in a Greek Mountain Community* (Oxford 1964). [Bremmer]

M. Campbell 1983. M. Campbell, *Studies in the Third Book of Apollonius Rhodius' Argonautica* (Hildesheim 1983). [Clauss]

M. Campbell 1994. M. Campbell, *A Commentary on Apollonius Rhodius Argonautica III 1–471* (Leiden 1994). [Clauss]

Carrière 1959. J. Carrière, "En relisant le chant III des Argonautiques," *Euphrosyne* 2 (1959) 41–63. [Clauss]

Carson 1990. A. Carson, "Putting Her in Her Place: Woman Dirt and Desire," in *Before Sexuality: The Construction of Erotic Experience in the Ancient Greek World*, D. M. Halperin, J. J. Winkler, and F. I. Zeitlin (eds.) (Princeton 1990) 135–169. [O'Higgins]

Chamoux 1953. *Cyrène sur la Monarchie des Battiades* (Paris 1953). [O'Higgins]

Charachidzé 1986. G. Charachidzé, *Prométhée ou le Caucase: Essai de mythologie contrastive* (Paris 1986). [Bremmer]

Clark 1968. R. J. Clark, "A Note on Medea's Plant and the Mandrake," *Folklore* 79 (1968) 227–31. [Clauss]

Clauss 1990. J. J. Clauss, "Hellenistic Imitations of Hesiod, *Catalogue of Women*, fr. 1.6–7 M&W," *QUCC* 36 (1990) 129–40. [Clauss]

Clauss 1993. J. J. Clauss, *The Best of the Argonauts: The Redefinition of the Epic Hero in Book 1 of Apollonius's Argonautica* (Berkeley 1993). [Clauss, Krevans]

Collard 1975. C. Collard, "Medea and Dido," *Prometheus* 1 (1975) 131–51. [Clauss]

Collinge 1962. N. E. Collinge, "Medea *ex machina*," *CP* 57 (1962) 170–72. [Boedeker]

Conacher 1967. D. J. Conacher, *Euripidean Drama: Myth, Theme and Structure* (Toronto 1967). [Boedeker]

Costa 1973. C. D. N. Costa, *Seneca: Medea* (Oxford 1973). [Nussbaum]

Cowell 1895. E. B. Cowell (ed.), *The Jakata; or, Stories of the Buddha's Former Births translated from the Pali by Various Hands*, vol. 1 (Cambridge 1895). [Bremmer]

Cox 1988. C. A. Cox, "Sibling Relationships in Classical Athens: Brother-Sister Ties," *Journal of Family History* 13 (1988) 377–95. [Bremmer]

Crane 1988. G. Crane, *Calypso: Backgrounds and Conventions of the Odyssey* (Frankfurt 1988). [Bremmer]

Cumont 1922. F. Cumont, *Afterlife in Roman Paganism* (New Haven 1922). [Johnston]

Cumont 1949. F. Cumont, *Lux Perpetua* (Paris 1949). [Johnston]

Cunningham 1954. M. P. Cunningham, "Medea ἀπὸ μηχανῆς," *CP* 49 (1954) 151–160. [Boedeker]

Curley 1986. T. F. Curley, *The Nature of Senecan Drama* (Rome 1986). [Boedeker]

Danali-Giole 1982–84. K. Danali-Giole, "Ο ΕΥΡΙΠΙΔΗΣ ΣΤΗΝ ΑΘΗΝΑ ΚΑΙ ΣΤΗΝ Κ. ΙΤΑΛΙΑ: Εἰκονογραφικές παρατηρήσεις," *Archaiognosia* 3 (1982–4) 163–94. [Sourvinou-Inwood]

Daniel 1975. R. Daniel, "Two Love Charms," *ZPE* 19 (1975) 249–64. [Johnston]

Danto 1982. B. L. Danto, J. Bruhns, and A. H. Kutscher (eds.), *The Human Side of Homicide* (New York 1982). [McDonald]

Davidoff 1992. L. Davidoff, "Quello que e straniero: Inizia nel rapporto 'fratello-sorella,' " *Quaderni Storici* 28 (1992) 555–65. [Bremmer]

De Forest 1994. M. M. De Forest, *Apollonius' Argonautica: A Callimachean Epic* (Leiden 1994). [Clauss]

de Jong 1991. I. J. F. de Jong, *Narrative in Drama: The Art of the Euripidean Messenger-Speech* (Leiden 1991). [Boedeker, Sourvinou-Inwood]

De Lacy 1958. P. H. De Lacy, "*Ou Mallon* and the Antecedents of Ancient Scepticism," *Phronesis* 3 (1958) 59–71. [Nussbaum]

Delcourt 1938. M. Delcourt, *Stérilités mystérieuses et naissances maléfiques dans l'antiquité classique* (Liege 1938). [Johnston]

de Romilly 1961. J. de Romilly, *L'evolution du pathétique d'Eschyle à Euripide.* (Paris 1961). [Boedeker]

Detienne and Vernant 1978. M. Detienne and J.-P. Vernant, *Cunning Intelligence in Greek Culture and Society*, Janet Lloyd (trans.) (Hassocks [Eng.]/Atlantic Highlands, N.J., 1978). [O'Higgins]

Devoto 1967. G. Devoto, "Il Panteone di Agnone," *SE* 35 (1967) 179–97. [Graf]

Dickie 1990. M. Dickie, "Talos Bewitched: Magic, Atomic Theory, and Paradoxography in Apollonius *Argonautica* 4.1638–88," *PLLS* 6 (1990) 267–296. [Clauss]

Diggle 1984. J. Diggle (ed.), *Euripidis Fabulae*, vol. 1 (Oxford 1984). [McDonald, Sourvinou-Inwood]

Dihle 1977. A. Dihle, *Euripides' Medea*, Sitz. der Heidelberger Akad. der Wiss., Phil.-Hist. Klasse, 5 (Heidelberg 1977). [Boedeker]

Dingel 1974. J. Dingel, *Seneca und die Dichtung* (Heidelberg 1974). [Nussbaum]

Dodds 1951. E. R. Dodds, *The Greeks and the Irrational* (Berkeley 1951). [Dillon, Introduction]

Dombrowski 1984. B. W. W. Dombrowski, *Der Name Europa auf seinem griechischen und altsyrischen Hintergrund* (Amsterdam 1984). [Krevans]

Doniger 1973. W. Doniger, *Asceticism and Eroticism in the Mythology of Siva* (Chicago 1973). [Nussbaum]

Dorson 1964. R. M. Dorson, *Buying the Wind: Regional Folklore in the United States* (Chicago 1964). [Johnston]

Dougherty 1993. C. Dougherty, *The Poetics of Colonization: From City to Text in Archaic Greece* (Oxford 1993). [Krevans]

Dougherty-Glenn 1988. C. Dougherty-Glenn, "Apollo, Ktisis, and Pindar: Literary Representations of Archaic City Foundations" (Ph.D. diss. Princeton 1988). [Krevans]

Dover 1974. K. J. Dover, *Greek Popular Morality in the Time of Plato and Aristotle* (Berkeley 1974). [Bremmer]

Dowden 1989. K. Dowden, *Death and the Maiden: Girls' Initiation Rites in Greek Mythology* (London 1989). [Graf]

Dräger 1993. P. Dräger, *Argo Pasimelousa: Der Argonautenmythos in der griechischen und römischen Literatur* (Stuttgart 1993). [Graf]

duBois 1988. P. duBois, *Sowing the Body: Psychoanalysis and Ancient Representations of Women* (Chicago 1988). [Krevans]

Du Boulay 1974. J. Du Boulay, *Portrait of a Greek Mountain Village* (Oxford 1974). [Bremmer]

Dufner 1988. C. M. Dufner, "The *Odyssey* in the *Argonautica*: Reminiscence, Revision, Reconstruction" (Diss., Princeton 1988). [Clauss]

Dumézil 1947. G. Dumézil, *Tarpeia: essais de philologie comparative indo-européenne* (Paris 1947). [Graf]

Dunn 1994. F. M. Dunn, "Euripides and the Rites of Hera Akraia," *GRBS* 35 (1994) 103–15. [Johnston]

Dyck 1989. A. R. Dyck, "On the Way from Colchis to Corinth: Medea in Book 4 of the 'Argonautica,'" *Hermes* 117 (1989) 455–70. [Clauss]

Easterling 1990. P. E. Easterling, "Constructing Character in Greek Tragedy," in *Characterization and Individuality in Greek Literature*, C. Pelling (ed.) (Oxford 1990) 83–99. [Sourvinou-Inwood]

Egan 1991. D. Egan (trans.), *Medea / Euripides*. (Laurinburg, N.C./Newbridge, Co. Kildare, 1991). [McDonald]

Egermann 1940. F. Egermann, "Seneca als Dichterphilosoph," *Neue Jahrbücher für Antike und deutsche Bildung* 3 (1940) 18–36. [Nussbaum]

Eisner 1979. R. Eisner, "Euripides' Use of Myth," *Arethusa* 12 (1979) 153–74. [Boedeker]

Eliot 1950. T. S. Eliot, "Seneca in Elizabethan Translation," and "Shakespeare and the Stoicism of Seneca," in *Selected Essays* (New York 1950) 51–90, 107–20. [Nussbaum]

Elliot 1994. A. Elliot (trans.), *Euripides' Medea* (London 1994). [McDonald]

Faerber 1932. H. Faerber, *Zur dichterischen Kunst in Apollonios Rhodios' Argonautica* (Diss., Berlin 1932). [Clauss]

Fanon 1963. F. Fanon, *The Wretched of the Earth: A Handbook for the Black Revolution That Is Changing the Shape of the World*, Constance Farrington (trans.) (New York 1963). [McDonald]

Fantham 1982. E. Fantham, *Seneca's Troades: A Literary Introduction with Text, Translation, and Commentary* (Princeton 1982). [Nussbaum]

Faraone 1991. "Binding and Burying the Forces of Evil: The Defensive Use of 'Voodoo Dolls' in Ancient Greece," *ClAnt* 10 (1991) 165–205. [Johnston]

Faraone 1992. C. A. Faraone, *Talismans and Trojan Horses: Guardian Statues in Ancient Greek Myth and Ritual* (New York 1992). [Johnston]

Faraone 1993. C. A. Faraone, "The Wheel, the Whip, and Other Implements of Torture: Erotic Magic in Pindar *Pythian* 4.213–19," *CJ* 89 (1993) 1–19. [O'Higgins]

Farenga 1977. V. Farenga, "Pindaric Craft and the Writing of *Pythia IV*," *Helios* 2 (1977) 3–37. [O'Higgins]

Farnell 1896–1909. L. R. Farnell, *The Cults of the Greek States*, 5 vols. (Oxford 1896–1909). [Johnston]

Fausbøll 1877. V. Fausbøll, *The Jataka together with Its Commentary Being Tales of the Anterior Births of Gotama Buddha*, vol. 1 (London 1877; rpt. 1962). [Bremmer]

Feeney 1987. D. C. Feeney, "Following after Hercules, in Virgil and Apollonius," *PVS* 18 (1987) 47–85. [Clauss]

Feeney 1991. D. C. Feeney, *The Gods in Epic: Poets and Critics of the Classical Tradition* (Oxford 1991). [Clauss]

Foley 1989. H. Foley, "Medea's Divided Self," *ClAnt* 8 (1989) 61–85. [Boedeker, Krevans, McDonald]

Fontenrose 1978. J. Fontenrose, *The Delphic Oracle: Its Responses and Operations, with a Catalogue of Responses* (Berkeley 1978). [Krevans]

Foucault 1984. M. Foucault, *Histoire de la sexualité*, vol. 3, *Le souci de soi* (Paris 1984). [Nussbaum]

Fox 1985. R. L. Fox, "Aspects of inheritance in the Greek world," in *Crux: Essays Present to G. E. M. de Ste. Croix*, P. Cartledge and F.D. Harvey (eds.) (London 1985) 208–32. [Bremmer]

Francis 1990. E. D. Francis, *Image and Idea in Fifth-Century Greece: Art and Literature after the Persian Wars* (London 1990). [Sourvinou-Inwood]

Fränkel 1950. H. Fränkel, "Problems of Text and Interpretation in Apollonius' *Argonautica*," *AJPh* 71 (1950) 113–33. [Clauss]

Frazer 1921. J. G. Frazer, *Apollodorus, The Library*, 2 vols. (London 1921). [Krevans]

Frécaut 1989. J. M. Frécaut, "Une double antithèse oxymorique, clèf d'un épisode des Métamorphoses d'Ovide: Le meurtre de Pélias par Médée," *RPh* 63 (1989) 67–74. [Newlands]

Freud 1955. S. Freud, *The Interpretation of Dreams*, J. Strachey (trans.) (New York 1955). [Nussbaum]

Fridh-Haneson 1988. B. M. Fridh-Haneson, "Hera's Wedding on Samos: A Change of Paradigms," in *Early Greek Cult Practice: Proceedings of the Fifth*

International Symposium at the Swedish Institute at Athens, 26–29 June 1986 (Stockholm 1988) 205–13. [Johnston]

Friedl 1962. E. Friedl, *Vasilika: A Village in Modern Greece* (New York 1962). [Bremmer]

Friedländer 1914. P. Friedländer, "Kritische Untersuchungen zur Geschichte der Heldensage" *RhM* 69 (1914) 299–341; rpt. in *Studien zur antiken Literatur und Kunst* (Berlin 1969) 19–53. [Graf]

Friedrich 1966. W.-H. Friedrich, "Medea in Kolchis," *A&A* 12 (1966) 3–28. [Graf]

Friedrich 1968. W.-H. Friedrich, "Medeas Rache," in *Euripides*, E.-R. Schwinge (ed.) (Darmstadt 1968) 177–237. [McDonald]

Friedrich 1990 (unpubl.). R. Friedrich, "Medea Apolis: On Euripides' Dramatization of the Crisis of the Polis," a paper presented at the conference "Tragedy, Comedy, and the Polis," held at the University of Nottingham, 18–20 July 1990. [Boedeker]

Fusillo 1985. M. Fusillo, *Il tempo delle Argonautiche: Un' analisi del racconto in Apollonio Rodio* (Rome 1985). [Clauss]

Fyfe 1983. H. Fyfe, "An Analysis of Seneca's *Medea*," *Ramus* 12 (1983) 77–93. [Nussbaum]

García-Ramón 1988–90. J. L. García-Ramón, "Homérico κέκασμαι: vedico sasad-, protoario *scand, IE *(s)kend-, 'aparecer, hacserse visible,' " *Die Sprache* 34 (1988–90) 27–134. [Bremmer]

Garland 1985. R. Garland, *The Greek Way of Death* (London 1985). [Johnston]

M. Gaster 1900. M. Gaster, "Two Thousand Years of a Charm against the Child-Stealing Witch," *Folklore* 11 (1900) 129–62; rpt. in *Studies and Texts in Folklore, Magic, Mediaeval Romance, Hebrew Apocrypha, and Samaritan Archaeology*, M. Gaster (ed.), vol. 2 (New York 1971) 1005–38. [Johnston]

T. Gaster 1942. T. H. Gaster, "A Canaanite Magical Text," *Orientalia* 11 (1942) 41–79. [Johnston]

Giannaris 1972. G. Giannaris, *Mikis Theodorakis: Music and Social Change* (New York 1972). [McDonald]

Giannini 1980. P. Giannini, "Metis e Themis nella *Pitica* 4 di Pindaro," *Annali della Facoltà di Lettere di Lecce* 8–10 (1980) 133–44. [Boedeker]

Gill 1983. C. Gill, "Did Chrysippus Understand Medea?" *Phronesis* 28 (1983) 136–49. [Dillon, Nussbaum]

Gillies 1928. M. M. Gillies, *The Argonautica of Apollonius Rhodius, Book III* (Cambridge 1928; rpt. New York 1979). [Clauss]

Ginzburg 1990. C. Ginzburg, *Ecstasies: Deciphering the Witches' Sabbath* (London 1990). [Bremmer]

Girard 1977. R. Girard, *Violence and the Sacred*, P. Gregory (trans.) (Baltimore 1977). [McDonald]

Golden 1990. M. Golden, *Children and Childhood in Classical Athens* (Baltimore 1990). [Bremmer]

Golden 1992. M. Golden, "The Uses of Cross-Cultural Comparison in Ancient Social History," *EMC* 36 (1992) 7–18. [Bremmer]

Goldhill 1986. S. Goldhill, *Reading Greek Tragedy* (Cambridge 1986). [O'Higgins]

Goldhill 1991. S. Goldhill, *The Poet's Voice: Essays on Poetics and Greek Literature* (Cambridge 1991). [Clauss]

Goldman 1980. R. P. Goldman, "Ramah Sahalaksmanah: Psychological and Literary Aspects of the Composite Hero of Valmaki's *Ramayana*," *Journal of Indian Philosophy* 8 (1980) 149–89. [Bremmer]

Gordon 1987a. R. Gordon, "Aelian's Peony: The Location of Magic in the Graeco-Roman Tradition," *Comparative Criticism* 9 (1987) 59–95. [Graf, Johnston]

Gordon 1987b. R. Gordon, "Lucan's Erictho," in *Homo Viator: Classical Essays for John Bramble*, P. Hardie and M. Whitby (eds.) (Bristol 1987) 231–41. [Johnston]

Graf 1978. F. Graf, "Die lokrischen Mädchen," *Studi Storico-Religiosi* 2 (1978) 61–79. [Graf]

Graf 1979a. F. Graf, "Apollon Delphinos," *MH* 36 (1979) 2–22. [Graf]

Graf 1979b. F. Graf, "Das Götterbild aus dem Taurerland," *AW* 10.4 (1979) 33–41. [Graf]

Graf 1980. F. Graf, "Milch, Honig und Wein: Zum Verständnis der Libation im griechischen Ritual," in *Perennitas: Studi in onore di Angelo Brelich* (Rome 1980) 209–21. [Graf]

Graf 1985. F. Graf, *Nordionische Kulte: Religionsgeschichtliche und epigraphische Untersuchungen zu den Kulten von Chios, Erythrai, Klazomenai und Phoikaia* (Rome 1985). [Bremmer, Graf]

Graf 1987. F. Graf, "Orpheus, a Poet among Men," in Bremmer 1987a:80–106. [Bremmer]

Graf 1991. F. Graf, "Religion und Mythologie im Zusammenhang mit Homer; Forschung und Ausblick," in *Zweihundert Jahre Homer-Forschung: Rückblick und Ausblick* J. Latacz (ed.) (Stuttgart 1991) 331–62. [Bremmer]

Graf 1993. F. Graf, *Greek Mythology: An Introduction*, T. Marier (trans.) (Baltimore 1993; German version Munich/Zurich 1985). [Graf]

Graf 1994. F. Graf, *La Magie dans L'antiquité gréco-romaine: Idéologie et pratique* (Paris 1994). [Graf]

Griffin 1976. M. Griffin, *Seneca: A Philosopher in Politics* (Oxford 1976). [Nussbaum]

Griffo and Zirretta 1952. P. Griffo and G. Zirretta, *Il Museo civico di Agrigento: Cenni sulla sua storia e sulle sue collezione* (Agrigento 1952). [Sourvinou-Inwood]

Grillo 1988. A. Grillo, *Tra filologia e narratologia: Dai poemi omerici ad Apollonio Rodio, Ilias Latina, Ditti Settimio, Darete Frigio, Draconizio* (Rome 1988). [Clauss]

Grube 1941. G. M. A. Grube, *The Drama of Euripides* (London 1941). [Boedeker]

Gruppe 1906. O. Gruppe, *Griechische Mythologie und Religionsgeschichte* (Munich 1906). [Johnston]

Haase 1893–95. F. Hasse (ed.), *L. Annaei Senecae Opera Quae Supersunt*, 3 vols. (Leipzig 1893–95). [Nussbaum]

Hadot 1969. I. Hadot, *Seneca und die griechische-römische Tradition der Seelenleitung* (Berlin 1969). [Nussbaum]

Hall 1989. E. Hall, *Inventing the Barbarian: Greek Self-Definition through Tragedy* (Oxford 1989). [Sourvinou-Inwood]

Halm-Tisserant 1989. M. Halm-Tisserant, "Folklore et Superstition en Grèce Classique: Lamia Torturée?" *Kernos* 2 (1989) 67–82. [Johnston]

Halm-Tisserant 1993. M. Halm-Tisserant, *Cannibalisme et immortalité: L'enfant dans le chaudron en Grèce ancienne* (Paris 1993). [Graf, Sourvinou-Inwood]

Händel 1954. P. Händel, *Beobachtungen zur epischen Technik des Apollonios Rhodios*, Zetemata 7 (Munich 1954). [Clauss]

Hansen 1983. P. A. Hansen, *Carmina Epigraphica Graeca Saeculorum VII–V a.Chr.N.* (Berlin 1983). [Bremmer]

Harder 1985. A. Harder, *Euripides' Kresphontes and Archelaos: Introduction, Text, and Commentary* (Leiden 1985). [Bremmer]

Harrison 1968. A. R. W. Harrison, *The Law of Athens*, vol. 1 (Oxford 1968). [Bremmer]

Hartog 1980. F. Hartog, *Le miroir d'Hérodote: Essai sur la représentation de l'autre* (Paris 1980). [Graf]

Henderson 1987. J. Henderson (ed.), *Aristophanes: Lysistrata* (Oxford 1987). [Sourvinou-Inwood]

Henrichs 1991. A. Henrichs, "Namenlosigkeit und Euphemismus: Zur Ambivalenz der chthonischen Mächte im attischen Drama," in *Fragmenta Dramatica: Beiträge zur Interpretation der griechischen Tragikerfragmente und ihrer Wirkungsgeschichte* A. Harder and H. Hofmann (eds.) (Göttingen 1991) 161–201. [Johnston]

Henry and Henry 1985. D. Henry and E. Henry, *The Mask of Power: Seneca's Tragedies and Imperial Rome* (Warminster 1985). [Nussbaum]

Hense 1905. O. Hense (ed.), *C. Musonii Rufi Reliquiae* (Leipzig 1905). [Nussbaum]

Herington 1966. C. J. Herington, "Senecan Tragedy," *Arion* 5 (1966) 422–71. [Nussbaum]

Herter 1950. H. Herter, "Böse Dämonen im frühgreichischen Volksglauben" *Rhein. Jb. für Volkskunde* 1 (1950) 112–43. [Johnston]

Heubeck 1988. A. Heubeck et al., *A Commentary on Homer's Odyssey*, vol. 1 (Oxford 1988). [Bremmer]

Hinds 1993. S. E. Hinds, "Medea in Ovid: Scenes from the Life of an Intertextual Heroine," *MD* 30 (1993) 9–47. [Newlands]

Hofkes-Brukker 1967. C. Hofkes-Brukker, "Vermutete Werke des Paionios," *BABesch* 42 (1967) 10–71. [Sourvinou-Inwood]

Hölscher 1990. U. Hölscher, *Die Odyssee: Epos zwischen Märchen und Roman* (Munich 1990). [Boedeker]

Holst-Warhaft 1980. G. Holst-Warhaft, *Theodorakis: Myth and Politics in Modern Greek Music* (Amsterdam 1980). [McDonald]

Holst-Warhaft 1992. G. Holst-Warhaft, *Dangerous Voices: Women's Laments and Greek Literature* (London 1992). [Bremmer]

Hopfner 1921. T. Hopfner, *Griechische-aegyptischer Offenbarungszauber* (Leipzig 1921). [Johnston]

How and Wells 1912. W. W. How and J. Wells, *A Commentary on Herodotus* (Oxford 1912; rpt. 1957). [Sourvinou-Inwood]

Huber 1926. G. Huber, *Lebensschilderung und Kleinmalerei im Hellenistischen Epos* (Diss., Basel 1926). [Clauss]

Hughes 1991. D. D. Hughes, *Human Sacrifice in Ancient Greece* (London 1991). [Graf]

Humphreys 1983. S. C. Humphreys, *The Family, Women and Death: Comparative Studies* (London 1983). [Bremmer, O'Higgins]

Humphreys 1986. S. C. Humphreys, "Kinship Patterns in the Athenian Courts," *GRBS* 27 (1986) 57–91. [Bremmer]

Hunter 1987. R. L. Hunter, "Medea's Flight: The Fourth Book of the *Argonautica*," *CQ* 37 (1987) 129–39. [Clauss]

Hunter 1989. R. L. Hunter, *Apollonius of Rhodes, Argonautica Book III* (Cambridge 1989). [Clauss]

Hunter 1993. R. L. Hunter, *The Argonautica of Apollonius: Literary Studies* (Cambridge 1993). [Bremmer, Clauss]

Immerwahr 1985. H. R. Immerwahr, "Herodotus," in *Cambridge History of Classical Literature*, P. A. Easterling and B. M. W. Knox (eds.) (Cambridge 1985) 426–41. [O'Higgins]

Inwood 1985. B. Inwood, *Ethics and Human Action in Early Stoicism* (Oxford 1985). [Nussbaum]

Jackson 1987. S. Jackson, "Apollonius' *Argonautica*: Euphemus, a Clod, and a Tripod," *ICS* 12 (1987) 23–30. [Krevans]

G. Jacobsen 1984. G. A. Jacobsen, "Apollo and Tereus: Parallel Motifs in Ovid's *Metamorphoses*," *CJ* 80 (1984) 45–52. [Newlands]

H. Jacobson 1974. H. Jacobson, *Ovid's Heroides* (Princeton 1974). [Newlands]

Jahn 1855. O. Jahn, *Über den Aberglauben den bösen Blicks bei den Alten* (Leipzig 1855) 28–110 = Berichte über die Verhandlungen der königlich sächsischen Gesellschaft der Wissenschaften zu Leipzig 7. [Johnston]

Janko 1992. R. Janko, *The Iliad: A Commentary*, vol. 4, G. S. Kirk (ed.) (Cambridge 1992). [Bremmer]

Jeanmaire 1939. H. Jeanmaire, *Couroi et Courétes* (Lille 1939; rpt. New York 1975). [Graf, Johnston]

Johnston 1990. S. I. Johnston, *Hekate Soteira: A Study of Hekate's Role in the Chaldean Oracles and Related Literature* (Atlanta 1990). [Graf, O'Higgins]

Johnston 1994. S. I. Johnston, "Penelope and the Erinyes: *Od.* XX.61–82," *Helios* 21 (1994) 137–60. [Johnston]

Johnston 1995a. S. I. Johnston, "Defining the Dreadful: Remarks on the Greek Child-Killing Demon," in *Ancient Magic and Ritual Power*, M. Meyer and P. Mirecki, (eds.) (Leiden 1995) 361–87. [Johnston]

Johnston 1995b. S. I. Johnston, "The Song of the *Iynx*: Magic and Rhetoric in *Pythian* 4," *TAPA* 125 (1995) 177–206. [Graf, Johnston, O'Higgins]

Joplin 1984. P. K. Joplin, "The Voice of the Shuttle Is Ours," *Stanford Literature Review* 1 (1984) 25–53. [Newlands]

Jouan 1990. F. Jouan, "La figure de Médée chez Euripide, Sénèque et Corneille," *Attualità dell' antico* 2 (1990) 181–200. [McDonald]

Kannicht 1969. R. Kannicht, *Helena: Einleitung und Text*, vol. 1 (Heidelberg 1969). [Graf]

Kassel and Austin 1983–. R. Kassel and C. Austin (eds), *Poeta Comici Graeci* (Berlin 1983-). [Bremmer]

Kearns 1992. E. Kearns, "Between God and Man: Status and Function of Heroes and Their Sanctuaries," in *Le sanctuaire grec*, O. Reverdin and B. Grange (eds.) Entretiens sur l' antiquite classique, vol. 37), (Geneva 1992) 65–99. [Sourvinou-Inwood]

Keith 1992. A. Keith, *A Play of Fictions: Studies in Ovid's Metamorphoses Book 2* (Ann Arbor 1992). [Newlands]

Kennedy 1986. R. Kennedy, "Women's Friendships on Crete: A Psychological Prespective," in *Gender and Power in Rural Greece*, J. Dubisch (ed.) (Princeton 1986) 121–38. [Bremmer]

Kennelly 1989. B. Kennelly, collector, *Love of Ireland: Poems from the Irish* (Dublin 1989). [McDonald]

Kennelly 1991. B. Kennelly (comp.), *Euripides' Medea: A New Version* (Newcastle upon Tyne 1991). [McDonald]

Kennelly 1992. B. Kennelly, *Cromwell* (Dublin 1983; rpt. Newcastle upon Tyne 1992). [McDonald]

Kerman 1956. J. Kerman, *Opera as Drama* (New York 1956; rpt. Berkeley 1988). [McDonald]

Kirkwood 1982. G. M. Kirkwood, *Selections from Pindar* (Chico, Calif., 1982). [O'Higgins]

L. Klein 1931. L. Klein, "Die Göttertechnik in den Argonautika des Apollonios Rhodios," *Philologus* 40 (1931) 18–51, 215–57. [Clauss]

T. Klein 1980–81. T. M. Klein, "Apollonius Rhodius, Vates Ludens: Eros' Golden Ball (*Arg.* 3.113–50)," *CW* 74 (1980–81) 225–27. [Clauss]

Knight 1991. V. Knight, "Apollonius Rhodius, *Argonautica* 4.167–70 and Euripides' *Medea*," *CQ* 41 (1991) 248–50. [Clauss]

Knox 1950. B. M. W. Knox, "The Serpent and the Flame," *AJPh* 71 (1950) 379–400. [Nussbaum]

Knox 1977. B. M. W. Knox, "The *Medea* of Euripides," *YClS* 25 (1977) 193–225; rpt. in *Word and Action. Essays on the Ancient Theatre* (Baltimore 1979) 259–322. [Boedeker, Graf, Johnston, McDonald, Nussbaum]

Knox 1983. B. M. W. Knox, "The *Medea* of Euripides," in *Oxford Readings in Greek Tragedy*, E. Segal (ed.) (Oxford 1983) 272–93. [Sourvinou-Inwood]

Konstan 1977. D. Konstan, *Catullus' Indictment of Rome: The Meaning of Catullus 64* (Amsterdam 1977). [Nussbaum]

Kovacs 1986. D. Kovacs, "On Medea's Great Monologue (E. *Med.* 1021–8," *CQ* 36 (1986) 343–52. [Dillon, Sourvinou-Inwood]

Kovacs 1993. D. Kovacs, "Zeus in Euripides' *Medea*," *AJPh* 114 (1993) 45–70. [Sourvinou-Inwood]

Krappe 1929. A. H. Krappe, "Die Sage von Tarpeia," *RhM* 78 (1929) 249–67. [Graf]

Kraus 1960. T. Kraus, *Hekate: Studien zu Wesen und Bild der Gottin in Kleinasien und Griechenland* (Heidelberg 1960). [Graf]

Krevans 1993. N. Krevans, "Ilia's Dream: Ennius, Virgil, and the Mythology of Seduction," *HSCP* 95 (1993) 257–71. [Krevans]

Kron 1981. U. Kron, "Aigeus," *LIMC* 1 (1981) 359–67. [Sourvinou-Inwood]

Krullmann 1991. W. Krullmann, "Ergebnisse der motivgeschichtlichen Forschung zu Homer (Neoanalyse)" in *Zweihundert Jahre Homer-Forschung: Rückblick und Ausblick*, J. Latacz (ed.) (Stuttgart 1991) 425–55. [Bremmer]

Kurtz 1985. E. Kurtz, *Die bildliche Ausdrucksweise in den Tragödien des Euripides* (Amsterdam 1985). [Boedeker]

Kwapong 1969. A. A. Kwapong, "Citizenship and Democracy in Fourth Century Cyrene," in *Africa in Classical Antiquity: Nine Studies*, L. A. Thompson and J. Ferguson (eds.) (Ibadan 1969). [O'Higgins]

Kyrieleis 1988. H. Kyrieleis, "Offerings of 'the Common Man' in the Heraion at Samos," in *Early Greek Cult Practice: Proceedings of the Fifth International Symposium at the Swedish Institute at Athens, 26–29 July 1986* (Stockholm 1988) 215–21. [Johnston]

Larmour 1990. D. H. J. Larmour, "Tragic *Contaminatio* in Ovid's *Metamorphoses*: Procne and Medea; Philomela and Iphigeneia (6.424–674); Scylla and Phaedra (8.19–151)," *ICS* 15 (1990) 131–41. [Newlands]

Lavelle 1986. B. M. Lavelle, "The Nature of Hiapparchos' Insult to Harmodios," *AJPh* 107 (1986) 318–31. [Bremmer]

Lawall 1979. G. Lawall, "Seneca's *Medea*: The Elusive Triumph of Civilization," in *Arktouros: Hellenic Studies Presented to B. M. W. Knox*, G. Bowersock (ed.) (Berlin 1979) 419–26. [Nussbaum]

Lawson 1910. J. C. Lawson, *Modern Greek Folklore and Ancient Greek Religion: A Study in Survivals* (Cambridge 1910; rpt. New York 1964). [Johnston]

Leitao 1993. D. D. Leitao, "The 'Measure of Youth': Body and Gender in Boys' Transitions in Ancient Greece" (Phd. diss., University of Michigan 1993). [Johnston]

Leitao 1995. D. D. Leitao, "The Perils of Leukippos: Initiatory Transvestism and Male Gender Ideology in the Ekdusia at Phaistos," *ClAnt* 14 (1995) 130–63. [Johnston]

Lendle 1979. O. Lendle, "Die Spielkugel des Zeus (Apoll. Rhod., Arg. 3.137–140)," *Hermes* 107 (1979) 493–95. [Clauss]

Lennox 1980. P. G. Lennox, "Apollonius, *Argonautica* 3.1ff. and Homer," *Hermes* 108 (1980) 45–73. [Clauss]

Lenz 1964. F. W. Lenz, *Aristeidesstudien* (Berlin 1964). [Johnston]

Lesky 1931. A. Lesky, "Medeia," *RE* 15 (1931) 29–65. [Graf, Johnston]

Lesky 1948. A. Lesky, "Aia," *WS* 63 (1948) 22–68; rpt. in *Gesammelte Schriften: Aufsätze und Reden zu antiker und deutscher Dichtung und Kultur,* Walther Kraus (ed.) (Bern 1966) 22–62. [Graf]

Lesky 1972. A. Lesky, *Die Tragische Dichtung der Hellenen* (Göttingen 1956; rpt. 1972). [Graf]

Levy 1959. R. Levy, *The Tales of Marzuban* (Bloomington, Ind., 1959). [Bremmer]

Lloyd-Jones 1980. H. Lloyd-Jones, "Euripides, *Medea* 1056–80," *Würzbürger Jahrbücher für die Altertumswissenschaft* 6 (1980) 51–59. [Dillon]

Lloyd-Jones and Wilson 1990. H. Lloyd-Jones and N. G. Wilson, *Sophoclea: Studies on the Text of Sophocles* (Oxford/New York 1990). [Bremmer]

Lobeck 1829. C. Lobeck, *Aglaophamus, sive de Theologiae Mysticae Graecorum Causis Libri Tres*, 2 vols. (Königsberg 1829). [Johnston]

Lobeck 1837. C. Lobeck, *Paralipomena* (Leipzig 1837). [Johnston]

Loraux 1978. N. Loraux, "Sur la race des femmes et quelques-unes de ses tribus," *Arethusa* 11 (1978) 43–87. [O'Higgins]

Losfeld 1991. G. Losfeld, *Essai sur le costume grec* (Paris 1991). [Sourvinou-Inwood]

Lovejoy and Boas 1935. A. Lovejoy and G. Boas, *Primitivism and Related Ideas in Antiquity* (Baltimore 1935). [Nussbaum]

Maddalena 1963. A. Maddalena, "La Medea di Euripide," *Rivista di Filologia* 91 (1963) 129–52. [Boedeker]

Mair 1969. L. Mair, *Witchcraft* (New York 1969). [Johnston]

Mandilaras 1992. B. Mandilaras, "A New Papyrus Fragment of the Certamen Homeri et Hesiodi," in *Papiri letterari greci e latini*, M. Capasso (ed.) (Galatina 1992) 55–62. [Bremmer]

Manfrini 1992. I. Manfrini, "Femmes à la fontaine: Réalité et imaginaire," in Bron and Kassapoglou 1992:127–48. [Bremmer]

Manuwald 1983. B. Manuwald, "Der Mord an den Kindern: Bemerkungen zu den Medea-Tragödien des Euripides und des Neophron," *WS* n.s., 17 (1983) 27–61. [Boedeker, Graf, Johnston, O'Higgins]

Marti 1945. B. Marti, "Seneca's Tragedies: A New Interpretation," *TAPA* 76 (1945) 216–45. [Nussbaum]

Marti 1947. B. Marti, "The Prototypes of Seneca's Tragedies," *CP* 42 (1947) 1–16. [Nussbaum]

Masqueray 1908. P. Masqueray, *Euripide et ses idées* (Paris 1908). [McDonald]

Mattingly 1971. H. Mattingly, *University of Leeds Review* 14 (1971) 285–87. [Bremmer]

Maurach 1966. G. Maurach, "Jason und Medea bei Seneca," *A&A* 12 (1966) 125–40. [Nussbaum]

McDermott 1989. E. A. McDermott, *Euripides' Medea: The Incarnation of Disorder* (University Park, Pa., 1989). [Boedeker, Graf, Johnston, McDonald, Sourvinou-Inwood]

McDonald 1978. M. McDonald, *Terms for Happiness in Euripides*, Hypomnemata 54 (Gottingen 1978). [McDonald]

McDonald 1983. M. McDonald, *Euripides in Cinema: The Heart Made Visible* (Philadelphia 1983; rpt. Boston 1991). [McDonald]

McDonald 1991. M. McDonald, "Cacoyannis' and Euripides' Iphigenia: The Dialectic of Power," in *Classics and Cinema*, M. M. Winkler (ed.), (Lewisburg, Pa./London 1991) 127–41. [McDonald]

McDonald 1992. M. McDonald, *Ancient Sun, Modern Light: Greek Drama on the Modern Stage* (New York 1992). [McDonald]

McDonald 1993. M. McDonald, "A Bomb at the Door: Kennelly's Medea, 1988," *Éire-Ireland* 28.2 (1993) 129–37. [McDonald]

McDonald 1994. M. McDonald, "Ancient Katharsis into Modern Opera: Theodorakis' Medea," *Journal of Modern Greek Arts* 1 (Spring 1994) 37–44. [McDonald]

Meuli 1921. K. Meuli, *Odyssee und Argonautika: Untersuchungen zur griechischen Sagengeschichte und zum Epos* (Berlin 1921). [Clauss, Graf]

Meuli 1975. K. Meuli, "Die Baumbestattung und die Ursprünge der Göttin Artemis," in *Gesammelte Schriften*, T. Gelzer (ed.) (Basel 1975) 1083–118. [Graf]

Meyer 1980. H. Meyer, *Medeia und die Peliaden: Eine attische Novelle und ihre Entstehung. Ein Versuch zur Sagenforschung auf archäologischer Grundlage* (Rome 1980). [Graf, Sourvinou-Inwood]

Michelini 1987. A. N. Michelini, *Euripides and the Tragic Tradition* (Madison, Wisc., 1987). [Johnston, McDonald]

Michelini 1989. A. Michelini, "Neophron and Euripides' *Medea* 1056–80," *TAPA* 119 (1989) 115–35. [Boedeker, Dillon, Graf, Johnston, McDonald, O'Higgins]

Miller 1917. F. J. Miller (ed. and trans.), *Seneca's Tragedies*, 2 vols. (London/New York 1917; rpt. Cambridge, Mass., 1929). [Nussbaum]

Mills 1980. S. P. Mills, "The Sorrows of Medea," *CP* 75 (1980) 289–96. [Boedeker]

Mimoso-Ruiz 1982. D. Mimoso-Ruiz, *Médée antique et moderne: Aspects rituels et socio-politiques d'un mythe* (Paris 1982). [Graf]

Mitchell 1991. R. Mitchell, "Miasma, Mimesis, and Scapegoating in Euripides' *Hippolytus*," *ClAnt* 10 (1991) 97–122. [Boedeker]

Mokhtar 1981. G. Mokhtar (ed.), *General History of Africa*, vol. 2 (London/Berkeley 1981). [O'Higgins]

Moreau 1985–87. A. Moreau, "Introduction à la mythologie X–XIX: Les mille et une facettes de Médée," *Connaissance hellénique* 30 (1985–87) 69–80. [Graf]

Moreau 1988. A. Moreau, "Polynice le querelleur," *BAGB* (1988) 224–31. [Bremmer]

Moreau 1994. A. Moreau, *Le mythe de Jason et Médée* (Paris 1994). [Bremmer, Graf, Introduction]

Moret 1991. J.-M. Moret, "Circé tisseuse sur les vases du Cabirion," *RA* 2 (1991) 227–66. [Bremmer]

Motto 1970. A. L. Motto, *Seneca Sourcebook; Guide to the Thought of Lucius Annaeus Seneca, in the Extant Prose Works* (Amsterdam 1970). [Nussbaum]

Muccioli 1994. F. Muccioli, "Considerazioni generali sull' epitheto *Philadelphos* nelle dinastie ellenistiche e sulla sua applicazione nella titolatura degli ultimi Seleucidi," *Historia* 43 (1994) 402–22. [Bremmer]

Nagy 1979. G. Nagy, *The Best of the Achaeans: Concepts of the Hero in Archaic Greek Poetry* (Baltimore 1979). [O'Higgins]

Nagy 1990a. G. Nagy, *Greek Mythology and Poetics* (Ithaca 1990). [O'Higgins]

Nagy 1990b. G. Nagy, *Pindar's Homer: The Lyric Possession of an Epic Past* (Baltimore 1990). [O'Higgins]

Neils 1987. J. Neils, *The Youthful Deeds of Theseus* (Rome 1987). [Sourvinou-Inwood]

Neils 1990. J. Neils, "Iason," *LIMC* 5 (1990) 629–38. [Graf, Sourvinou-Inwood]

Nercessian 1984. A. Nercessian, "Argiope," *LIMC* 2 (1984) 591. [Sourvinou-Inwood]

Newton 1985. R. M. Newton, "Ino in Euripides' *Medea*," *AJPh* 106 (1985) 496–502. [Boedeker]

Nietzsche 1956. F. Nietzsche, *The Birth of Tragedy and the Genealogy of Morals*, F. Golffing (trans.) (Garden City, N.Y., 1956). [McDonald]

Nikolaidis 1985. A. G. Nikolaidis, "Some Observations on Ovid's Lost *Medea*," *Latomus* 44 (1985) 383–87. [Newlands]

Nilsson 1906. M. P. Nilsson, *Griechische Feste von religiöser Bedeutung: Mit Ausschluss des attischen* (Berlin 1906; rpt. Stuttgart 1957). [Graf, Johnston]

Nilsson 1967. M. P. Nilsson, *Geschichte der griechische Religion*, 3rd ed., vol. 1 (Munich 1967). [Johnston]

Nock 1950. A. D. Nock, "Tertullian and the Ahori," *VChr* 4 (1950) 129–41. [Johnston]

Nöldeke 1894. T. Nöldeke, "Zu Herodot 3,119 (Sophokles Antigone 903–913)," *Hermes* 29 (1894) 155–56. [Bremmer]

Nussbaum 1986. M. Nussbaum, *The Fragility of Goodness: Luck and Ethics in Greek Tragedy and Philosophy* (Cambridge 1986). [Nussbaum]

Nussbaum 1993. M. Nussbaum, "Equity and Mercy," *Philosophy and Public Affairs* 22 (1993) 83–125. [Nussbaum]

Nussbaum 1994. M. Nussbaum, *The Therapy of Desire: Theory and Practice in Hellenistic Ethics* (Princeton 1994). [Nussbaum]

Oldfather 1926–28. W. A. Oldfather (trans.), *Epictetus: The Discourses as reported by Arrian, the Manual, and Fragments*, 2 vols. (London/New York 1926–28)

Otis 1964. B. Otis, *Virgil: A Study in Civilized Poetry* (Oxford 1964). [Clauss]

Otis 1966. B. Otis, *Ovid as an Epic Poet* (Cambridge 1966; rpt. 1970). [Newlands]

Oudemans and Lardinois 1987. T. C. W. Oudemans and A. P. M. H. Lardinois, *Tragic Ambiguity: Anthropology, Philosophy, and Sophocles' Antigone* (Leiden 1987). [Bremmer]

Padel 1992. R. Padel, *In and Out of the Mind: Greek Images of the Tragic Self* (Princeton 1992). [Introduction]

Padel 1994. R. Padel, *Whom the Gods Destroy: Elements of Greek and Tragic Madness* (Princeton 1994). [Introduction]

Paduano 1970–71. G. Paduano, "L' episodio di Talos: Osservazioni sull' esperienza magica nelle Argonautiche di Apollonio Rodio," *SCO* 19–20 (1970–71) 46–67. [Clauss]

Paduano 1972. G. Paduano, *Studi su Apollonio Rodio* (Rome 1972). [Clauss]

Paduano and Fusillo 1986. G. Paduano and M. Fusillo, *Apollonio Rodio: Le Argonautiche* (Milan 1986). [Clauss]

Page 1938. D. L. Page, *Euripides: Medea.* (Oxford 1938). [Boedeker, Graf, McDonald, O'Higgins, Sourvinou-Inwood]

Parke 1985. H. W. Parke, *The Oracles of Apollo in Asia Minor* (London 1985). [Johnston]

Parker 1983. R. Parker, *Miasma: Pollution and Purification in Early Greek Religion* (Oxford 1983). [Bremmer]

Parker 1984. R. Parker, "A Note on φόνος, θυσία, and μασχαλισμός," *LCM* 9 (1984) 138. [Bremmer]

Pathmanathan 1965. R. S. Pathmanathan, "Death in Greek Tragedy," *G&R* 12 (1965) 2–14. [Boedeker]

Paulme 1976. D. Paulme, *La mère dévorante: Essai sur la morphologie des contes africaines* (Paris 1976). [Bremmer]

Pavlock 1990. B. Pavlock, *Eros, Imitation, and the Epic Tradition* (Ithaca 1990). [Clauss]

Payne 1940. H. Payne, *Perachora, the Sanctuaries of Hera Akraia and Limenia* (London 1940). [Johnston]

Payne and Dunbabin 1962. H. Payne and T. J. Dunbabin, *Perachora, the Sanctuaries of Hera Akraia and Limenia*, vol. 2 (London 1962). [Johnston]

Pechillo 1990. M. Pechillo, "Ovid's Framing Technique: The Aeacus and Cephalus Epyllion (*Met.* 7.490–8.5)," *CJ* 86 (1990) 35–44. [Newlands]

Pelling 1990. C. Pelling, conclusion to *Characterization and Individuality in Greek Literature*, C. Pelling (ed.) (Oxford 1990) 245–62. [Sourvinou-Inwood]

Pembroke 1965. S. Pembroke, "The Last of the Matriarchs: A Study in the Inscriptions of Lycia," *JESHO* 8 (1965) 217–47. [Sourvinou-Inwood]

Pembroke 1967. S. Pembroke, "Women in Charge: The Function of Alternatives in Early Greek Tradition and the Ancient Ideas of Matriarchy," *JWI* 30 (1967) 1–35. [Sourvinou-Inwood]

Pendergraft 1991. M. L. Pendergraft, "Eros ludens: Apollonius' *Argonautica* 3.132–41," *MD* 26 (1991) 95–102. [Clauss]

Perdrizet 1922. P. Perdrizet, *Negotium Perambulans in Tenebris* (Strasbourg 1922). [Johnston]

Pfeiffer 1949–53. R. Pfeiffer, *Callimachus*, 2 vols. (Oxford 1949–53). [Krevans]

Phinney 1967. E. Phinney, "Narrative Unity in the *Argonautica*, the Medea-Jason Romance," *TAPA* 98 (1967) 327–41. [Clauss]

Picard 1932. C. Picard, "L'Héraeon de Pérachora et les Enfants de Médée," *RA* 35 (1932) 218–29. [Johnston]

Picard 1933. C. Picard, "Le cénotaph de Midéa et les 'colosses' des Ménélaus," *RPh* 7 (1933) 341–54. [Johnston]

Picard 1946. C. Picard, "La Triade Zeus-Héra-Dionysos dans L'Orient Hellénique d'Après les Nouveaux Fragments d'Alcée," *BCH* 70 (1946) 455–73. [Johnston]

Pickard-Cambridge 1953. A. Pickard-Cambridge, *The Dramatic Festivals of Athens* (Oxford 1953; rpt. 1968). [Sourvinou-Inwood]

Pingiatoglou 1981. S. Pingiatoglou, *Eileithyia* (Wurzburg 1981). [Johnston]

Pirenne-Delforge 1994. V. Pirenne-Delforge, *L'Aphrodite grecque* (Athens 1994). [Graf]

Pischel 1893. R. Pischel, "Zu Sophokles Antigone 909–12," *Hermes* 28 (1893) 465–68. [Bremmer]

Pollitt 1990. J. J. Pollitt, *The Art of Ancient Greece: Sources and Documents* (Cambridge 1990). [Sourvinou-Inwood]

Pomari 1992. A. Pomari, "Le massacre des innocents," in Bron and Kassapoglou 1992:103–25. [Bremmer]

Pöschl 1959. V. Pöschl, "Kephalos und Prokris in Ovids *Metamorphosen*," *Hermes* 87 (1959) 328–43. [Newlands]

Pratt 1948. N. T. Pratt, "The Stoic Base of Senecan Drama," *TAPA* 79 (1948) 1–11. [Nussbaum]

Pratt 1983. N. T. Pratt, *Seneca's Drama* (Chapel Hill 1983). [Nussbaum]

A. Price 1989. A. W. Price, *Love and Friendship in Plato and Aristotle* (Oxford/New York 1989). [Nussbaum]

T. Price 1978. T. Hadzisteliou Price, *Kourotrophos: Cults and Representations of the Greek Nursing Deities* (Leiden 1978). [Johnston]

Prinz 1979. F. Prinz, *Gründungsmythen und Sagenchronologie*; Zetemata 72 (Munich 1979). [Krevans]

Propp 1946. V. Propp, *Istoriceski korni volsebnoj skazki* (Leningrad 1946). [Graf]

Propp 1968. V. Propp, *Morphology of the Folk-tale*, 2nd ed., L. Scott (trans.) (Austin 1968). [Bremmer, Graf]

Propp 1972. V. Propp, *Le radici storiche dei racconti di fate* (Turin 1972; trans. of Propp 1946). [Bremmer]

Pucci 1977. P. Pucci, *Hesiod and the Language of Poetry*, (Baltimore 1977). [O'Higgins]

Pucci 1979. P. Pucci, "The Song of the Sirens," *Arethusa* 12 (1979) 121–32. [O'Higgins]

Pucci 1980. P. Pucci, *The Violence of Pity in Euripides' "Medea"* (Ithaca 1980). [Boedeker, McDonald]

Putnam 1985. M. C. J. Putnam, "Possessiveness, Sexuality, and Heroism in the *Aeneid*," *Vergilius* 31 (1985) 1–21. [Nussbaum]

Putnam 1987. M. C. J. Putnam, "Daedalus, Virgil, and the End of Art," *AJPh* 108 (1987) 173–98. [Nussbaum]

Putnam 1990. M. C. J. Putnam, "Anger and Blindness in Virgil's *Aeneid*," *Apeiron* 23 (1990) 7–40. [Nussbaum]

Rabbow 1954. P. Rabbow, *Seelenführung: Methodik der Exerzitien in der Antike* (Munich 1954). [Nussbaum]

Radermacher 1943. L. Radermacher, *Mythos und Sage bei den Griechen* (Vienna 1943; rpt. Darmstadt 1968). [Graf]

Raeck 1981. W. Raeck, *Zum Barbarenbild in der Kunst Athens im 6. und 5. Jahrhundert v.Chr.* (Bonn 1981). [Sourvinou-Inwood]

Reeve 1972. M. D. Reeve, "Euripides, *Medea* 1021–1080," *CQ* 22 (1972) 51–61. [Dillon]

Regenbogen 1927–28. O. Regenbogen, "Schmerz und Tod in den Tragodien Senecas," *Vortrage der Bibliothek Warburg, 1927–28*, F. Saxi (ed.) (Leipzig 1927–28) 167–218; rpt. in *Kleine Schriften* (Munich 1961) 411–64. [Nussbaum]

Rehm 1989. R. Rehm, "*Medea* and the λόγος of the Heroic," *Eranos* 87 (1989) 97–115. [Boedeker, McDonald]

Reid 1993. J. D. Reid (ed.), *The Oxford Guide to Classical Mythology in the Arts, 1300–1990s*, 2 vols. (Oxford 1993). [Introduction]

Reinach 1906. S. Reinach, "Aoroi biaiothanatoi," *Archiv für Religionssissenschaft* 9 (1906) 312–20. [Johnston]

Rengakos 1993. A. Rengakos, *Der Homertext und die hellenistischen Dichter* (Stuttgart 1993). [Clauss]

Rist 1969. J. M. Rist, *Stoic Philosophy* (London 1969). [Dillon]

Rivier 1960. A. Rivier, "L'élément démonique chez Euripide jusqu'en 428," in *Euripide*, Entretiens sur l'antiquité classique 6 (Vandœuvres-Genève 1960) 43–86. [Boedeker]

Robertson 1975. M. Robertson, *A History of Greek Art* (London 1975). [Sourvinou-Inwood]

Robertson 1977. M. Robertson, "The Death of Talos," *JHS* 97 (1977) 158–60. [Sourvinou-Inwood]

Robertson 1992. M. Robertson, *The Art of Vase Painting in Classical Athens* (Cambridge 1992). [Sourvinou-Inwood]

Rohde 1925. Rohde, *Psyche: The Cult of Souls and Belief in Immortality among the Greeks*, W. P. Hillis (trans.) (London 1925; trans. of the 8th German ed.). [Johnston]

Rohdich 1968. H. Rohdich, *Die euripideische Tragödie: Untersuchungen zu ihrer Tragik* (Heidelberg 1968). [Boedeker]

Rose 1958. H. J. Rose, *A Handbook of Greek Mythology Including Its Extension to Rome*, 6th ed. (London 1958). [Graf, Krevans]

Rosenmeyer 1985. T. G. Rosenmeyer, "Euripides' *Hecuba*: Horror Story or Tragedy," *Proceedings of the First International Meeting of Ancient Greek Drama at Delphi* (1985) 269. [McDonald]

Rosenmeyer 1989. T. G. Rosenmeyer, *Senecan Drama and Stoic Cosmology* (Berkeley 1989). [Nussbaum]

Rosenmeyer 1992. T. G. Rosenmeyer, "Apollonius Lyricus," *SIFC* 10 (1992) 177–98. [Clauss]

Rosner-Siegel 1982. A. Rosner-Siegel, "Amor, Metamorphosis, and Magic: Ovid's Medea (*Met.* 7.1–424)," *CJ* 77 (1982) 231–43. [Newlands]

Roussel 1920. P. Roussel, "Médée et le meurtre de ses enfants" *REA* 22 (1920) 157–71. [Graf, Johnston]

Roux 1963. G. Roux, "Commentaires sur Théocrite, Apollonios et quelques épigrammes de l'Anthologie," *RPh* 37 (1963) 76–92. [Clauss]

Rusten 1982. J. S. Rusten, *Dionysius Scytobrachion* (Opladen 1982). [Graf]

Sadie 1989. S. Sadie (ed.), *History of Opera* (Basingstoke 1989). [McDonald]

E. Said 1993. E. Said, *Culture and Imperialism* (New York 1993). [McDonald]

S. Saïd 1993. S. Saïd, "Couples fraternels chex Sophocle," in *Sophocle: Le text, les personnages*, A. Machin and L. Pernée (eds.) (Aix-en-Provence 1993) 299–327. [Bremmer]

Salemme 1991. C. Salemme, *Medea: Un antico mito in Valerio Flacco* (Naples 1991). [Graf]

Salmon 1972. J. Salmon, "The Heraeum at Perachora, and the Early History of Corinth and Megara," *ABSA* 67 (1972) 159–204. [Johnston]

Schauenburg 1981. K. Schauenburg, "Andromeda," *LIMC* 1 (1981) 774–90. [Sourvinou-Inwood]

Schefold 1966. K. Schefold, *Myth and Legend in Early Greek Art*, A. Hicks (trans.) (New York 1966). [Sourvinou-Inwood]

Schefold 1978. K. Schefold, "Die Basler Peliadenschale," *Antike Kunst* 21 (1978) 100–106. [Sourvinou-Inwood]

Schefold 1992. K. Schefold, *Gods and Heroes in Late Archaic Greek Art*, Alan Griffiths (trans.) (Cambridge 1992). [Sourvinou-Inwood]

Schlesinger 1966. E. Schlesinger, "Zu Euripides' Medea," *Hermes* 94 (1966) 26–53. [Boedeker]

Schlesinger 1968. E. Schlesinger, "On Euripides' *Medea*," in *Euripides: A Collection of Critical Essays*, E. Segal (ed.) (Englewood Cliffs, N.J., 1968) 70–89. [McDonald]

Schmid 1947. P. B. Schmid, *Studien zu griechischen Ktisissagen* (Diss., Freiburg 1947). [Krevans]

B. Schmidt 1871. B. Schmidt, *Das Volksleben der Neugriechen und das hellenische Altertum* (Leipzig 1871). [Johnston]

M. Schmidt 1979. M. Schmidt, "Eine unteritalische Vasendarstellung des Laokoon-mythos," in *Antike Kunstwerke aus der Sammlung Ludwig*, vol. 1, *Katalog und Einzeldarstellungen*, E. Berger and R. Lullies (eds.) (Basel 1979), 239–48. [Bremmer]

M. Schmidt 1986. M. Schmidt, "Medea und Herakles, zwei tragische Kindermörder," in *Studien zur Mythologie und Vasenmalerei*, E. Böhr and W. Martini (eds.) (Mainz am Rhein 1986) 169–74. [Sourvinou-Inwood]

Schmidt 1990. M. Schmidt, *Eumousia: Ceramic and Iconographic Studies in Honour of Alexander Cambitoglou*, J.-P. Descoeudres (ed.) (Sydney 1990) 221–26. [Bremmer]

M. Schmidt 1992. M. Schmidt, "Medeia," *LIMC* 6 (1992) 386–98; 6 (1992) 194–202. [Bremmer, Introduction, Sourvinou-Inwood]

Schoffeleers 1991. J. M. Schoffeleers, "Twins and Unilateral Figures in Central and Southern Africa: Symmetry and Assymetry in the Symbolization of the Sacred," *Journal of Religion in Africa* 21 (1991) 345–72. [Bremmer]

Scholem 1972. G. Scholem, "Lilith," *Encyclopedia Judaica*, vol. 2 (Jerusalem 1972) 245–49. [Johnston]

Schondorff 1963. J. Schondorff (ed.), *Medea: Euripides, Seneca, Corneille, Cherubini, Grillparzer, Jahnn, Anouilh, Jeffers, Braun* (Munich 1963). [McDonald]

Schoppa 1933. H. Schoppa, *Die Darstellung der Perser in der griechischen Kunst bis zum Beginn des Hellenismus* (Coburg 1933). [Sourvinou-Inwood]

Schubert 1989. W. Schubert, "Medeas Flucht aus Iolcos (Ovid, *Met.* 7, 350–93)," *WJA* 15 (1989) 175–81. [Newlands]

Scranton 1941. R. L. Scranton, "Temple C and the Sanctuary of Hera Akraia," in *Corinth*, R. Stillwell, R. L. Scranton, and S. E. Freeman (eds.), vol. 1.2 (Cambridge, Mass., 1941) 131–65. [Johnston]

Scurlock 1991. J. A. Scurlock, "Baby-Snatching Demons, Restless Souls and the Dangers of Childbirth: Medico-Magical Means of Dealing with Some of the Perils of Motherhood in Ancient Mesopotamia," *Incognita* 2 (1991) 1–112. [Johnston]

Seaford 1989. R. Seaford, "Homeric and Tragic Sacrifice," *TAPA* 119 (1989) 87–95. [Boedeker]

Seaford 1990. R. Seaford, "The Structural Problems of Marriage in Euripides," in *Euripides, Women and Sexuality*, A. Powell (ed.) (London 1990) 151–76. [Bremmer]

Sealey 1990. R. Sealey, *Women and Law in Classical Greece* (Chapel Hill 1990). [O'Higgins]

Séchan 1925. L. Séchan, *Études sur la tragédie greque dans ses rapports avec la céramique* (Paris 1925; rpt. 1967). [Graf, Johnston, Sourvinou-Inwood]

Séchan 1927. L. Séchan, "La Légende de Médée," *REG* 40 (1927) 234–310. [Boedeker, Graf, Johnston]

Segal 1973. C. P. Segal, "Simaetha and the Iynx (Theocritus, *Idyll* II)," *QUCC* 15 (1973) 32–43. [O'Higgins]

Segal 1982. C. P. Segal, "*Nomen sacrum*: Medea and Other Names in Senecan Tragedy," *Maia*, n.s., 3 (1982) 241–46. [Boedeker]

Segal 1983a. C. P. Segal, "Boundary Violation and the Landscape of the Self in Senecan Tragedy," *Antike und Abendland* 29 (1983) 172–87. [Nussbaum]

Segal 1983b. C. P. Segal, "Dissonant Sympathy: Song, Orpheus, and the Golden Age in Seneca's Tragedies," *Ramus* 12 (1983) 229–251. [Nussbaum]

Segal 1986. C. P. Segal, *Pindar's Mythmaking: The Fourth Pythian Ode* (Princeton 1986). [Boedeker, Graf, Krevans, O'Higgins]

Segal 1990. C. P. Segal, "Violence and the Other: Greek, Female, and Barbarian in Euripides' *Hecuba,* " *TAPA* 120 (1990) 109–31. [McDonald, Sourvinou-Inwood]

Segal 1994. C. P. Segal, "Philomela's Web and the Pleasures of the Text: Reader and Violence in the *Metamorphoses* of Ovid," in *Modern Critical Theory and Classical Literature*, I. J. F. de Jong and J. P. Sullivan (eds.) (Leiden 1994) 257–280. [McDonald]

Seidensticker 1991. B. Seidensticker, "Euripides, *Medea* 1056–1080, an Interpolation?" in *Cabinet of the Muses: Essays on Classical and Comparative Literature in Honor of Thomas G. Rosenmeyer*, M. Griffith and D. Mastronarde (eds.) (Atlanta 1991) 89–102. [McDonald]

Shapiro 1993. H. A. Shapiro, *Personifications in Greek Art: The Representation of Abstract Concepts, 600–400 BC* (Zurich 1993). [Graf]

Shaw 1975. M. Shaw, "The Female Intruder: Women in Fifth-Century Drama," *CP* 70 (1975) 255–66. [Boedeker]

Shefton 1956. B. Shefton, "Medea at Marathon," *AJA* 60 (1956) 159–63. [Sourvinou-Inwood]

Silk 1974. M. S. Silk, *Interaction in Poetic Imagery with Special Reference to Early Greek Poetry* (London 1974). [Boedeker]

B. Simon 1988. B. Simon, *Tragic Drama and the Family: Psychoanalytic Studies from Aeschylus to Beckett* (New Haven 1988). [McDonald]

E. Simon 1954. E. Simon, "Die Typen der Medeadarstellung in der antiken Kunst," *Gymnasium* 61 (1954) 203–27. [Sourvinou-Inwood]

E. Simon 1961. E. Simon, "Medea," *Enciclopedia dell'Arte Antica Classica e Orientale*, vol. 4 (Rome 1961) 950–57. [Sourvinou-Inwood]

Simon 1987. E. Simon, "Griechische Muttergottheiten," in *Matronen und verwandte Gottheiten*, H. Jankuhn (ed.) (Köln 1987) 157–69. [Johnston]

Skinner 1983. M. Skinner, "Clodia Metelli," *TAPA* 113 (1983) 273–287. [Graf]

Slezák 1981. T. A. Slezák, "Bemerkungen zur Diskussion um Sophocles, *Antigone* 904–920," *RhM* 124 (1981) 108–42. [Bremmer]

Snell 1948. B. Snell, "Das frühste Zeugnis über Sokrates," *Philologus* 97 (1948) 125–34. [Dillon]

Snell 1961. B. Snell, *Poetry and Society: The Role of Poetry in Ancient Greece* (Bloomington, Ind., 1961; rpt. 1971). [McDonald]

Snowden 1970. F. Snowden, *Blacks in Antiquity: Ethiopians in the Greco-Roman Experience* (Cambridge, Mass., 1970). [O'Higgins]

Sommerstein 1990. A. H. Sommerstein (ed.), *The Comedies of Aristophanes: "Lysistrata"* (Warminster 1990). [Sourvinou-Inwood]

Sourvinou-Inwood 1979. C. Sourvinou-Inwood, *Theseus as Son and Stepson: A Tentative Illustration of the Greek Mythological Mentality* (London 1979). [Graf, Sourvinou-Inwood]

Sourvinou-Inwood 1987–88. C. Sourvinou-Inwood, "Sophocles' *Antigone* 904–20: A Reading," *AION* 9–10 (1987–88) 19–35. [Bremmer]

Sourvinou-Inwood 1989. C. Sourvinou-Inwood, "Assumptions and the Creation of Meaning: Reading Sophocles' *Antigone*," *JHS* 109 (1989) 134–48. [Sourvinou-Inwood]

Sourvinou-Inwood 1990a. C. Sourvinou-Inwood, "Myths in Images: Theseus and Medea as a Case Study," in *Approaches to Greek Myth*, L. Edmunds (ed.) (Baltimore 1990) 395–445. [Sourvinou-Inwood]

Sourvinou-Inwood 1990b. C. Sourvinou-Inwood, "Sophocles' Antigone as a 'Bad Woman,'" in *Writing Women into History* F. Dieteren and E. Kloek (eds.) (Amsterdam 1990) 11–38. [Bremmer]

Sourvinou-Inwood 1991. C. Sourvinou-Inwood, *"Reading" Greek Culture: Texts and Images, Rituals and Myths* (Oxford 1991). [Bremmer, Sourvinou-Inwood]

Sourvinou-Inwood 1992. C. Sourvinou-Inwood, "The Cup Bologna PU 273: A Reading," *Metis* 5 (1990) 137–53. [Sourvinou-Inwood]

Stanford 1936. W. B. Stanford, *Greek Metaphor: Studies in Theory and Practice* (Oxford 1936; rpt. New York 1972). [Boedeker]

Stewart 1991. C. Stewart, *Demons and the Devil: Moral Imagination in Modern Greek Culture* (Princeton 1991). [Johnston]

Strohm 1957. H. Strohm, *Euripides: Interpretationen zur dramatischen Form*, Zetemata 15 (Munich 1957). [Boedeker]

Stroud 1976. R. Stroud, "Perachora," in *The Princeton Encyclopedia of Classical Sites*, R. Stillwell (ed.) (Princeton 1976) 687–88. [Johnston]

Sutton 1987. D. Sutton, *Two Lost Plays of Euripides* (New York 1987). [Krevans]

Taplin 1993. O. Taplin, *Comic Angels and Other Approaches to Greek Drama through Vase-paintings* (Oxford/New York 1993). [Sourvinou-Inwood]

Tawney 1881. C. H. Tawney, "A Folk-Lore Parallel," *Indian Antiquary* 10 (1881) 370–71. [Bremmer]

ter Vrugt-Lenz 1960. J. ter Vrugt-Lenz, *Mors Immatura* (Groningen 1960). [Johnston]

Teufel 1939. M. Teufel, *Brauch und Ritus bei Apollonius Rhodius* (Diss., Tübingen 1939). [Bremmer]

Theodoridis 1975. C. Theodoridis, "*Appharion*: Ein neues Wort fur Menander," *Philologus* 119 (1975) 259–61. [Bremmer]

Thiel 1993. K. Thiel, *Erzählung und Beschreibung in den Argonautika des Apollonios Rhodios* (Stuttgart 1993). [Clauss]

Thompson 1944. E. A. Thompson "Neophron and Euripides' *Medea*," *CQ* 38 (1944) 10–14. [Graf, Johnston]

Thompson 1955. S. Thompson, *Motif Index of Folk Literature: A Classification of Narrative Elements in Folktales, Ballads, Myths, Fables, Mediaeval Romances, Exempla, Fabliaux, Jest-Books, and Local Legends*, rev. and enlarged ed. (Bloomington, Ind., 1955–58; original ed. 1932). [Clauss]

Tomlinson 1977. R. A. Tomlinson, "The Upper Terraces at Perachora," *ABSA* 72 (1977) 197–202. [Johnston]

Traina 1979. A. Traina, "Due note a Seneca tragico," *Maia* 31 (1979) 273–76. [Boedeker]

Trendall 1989. A. D. Trendall, *Red Figure Vases of South Italy and Sicily: A Handbook* (London 1989). [Sourvinou-Inwood]

Trendall and Cambitoglou 1961. A. D. Trendall and A. Cambitoglou, *Apulian Red figure Vase-painters of the Plain Style* (Rutland, Vt., 1961). [Sourvinou-Inwood]

Trendall and Cambitoglou 1978. A. D. Trendall and A. Cambitoglou, *The Red Figure Vases of Apulia*, vol. 1, *Early and Middle Apulian* (Oxford/New York 1978). [Sourvinou-Inwood]

Trendall and Cambitoglou 1982. A. D. Trendall and A. Cambitoglou, *The Red Figure Vases of Apulia*, vol. 2, *Late Apulian* (Oxford/New York 1982). [Sourvinou-Inwood]

Trendall and Cambitoglou 1991. A. D. Trendall and A. Cambitoglou, *Second Supplement to the Red Figure Vases of Apulia*, BICS suppl. 60 (London 1991). [Sourvinou-Inwood]

Trendall and Webster 1971. A. D. Trendall and T. B. L. Webster, *Illustrations of Greek Drama* (London 1973). [Sourvinou-Inwood]

Uhsadel-Gülke 1972. C. Uhsadel-Gülke, *Knochen und Kessel* (Meisenheim am Glan 1972). [Graf]

Valgiglio 1970. E. Valgiglio, "Motivi arcaici ed euripidei nelle figure di Giasone e Medea nelle *Argonautice* di Apollonio Rodio," *RSC* 18 (1970) 325–31. [Clauss]

Varavini 1909. Sa'd al-Din Varavini, *The Marzuban-nama*, Mirza Muhammad of Qazvin (ed.) (London 1909). [Bremmer]

Verducci 1985. F. Verducci, *Ovid's Toyshop of the Heart: Epistulae Heroidum* (Princeton 1985). [Newlands]

Vermeule 1977. E. Vermeule, "Herakles Brings a Tribute," in *Festschrift für Frank Brommer*, U. Höckmann and A. Krug eds.) (Mainz am Rhein 1977) 295–301. [Johnston]

Vernant 1979. J.-P. Vernant, *Religions, histoires, raisons* (Paris 1979). [Johnston]

Vernant 1983. J.-P. Vernant, *Myth and Thought among the Greeks* (London 1983). [O'Higgins]

Versnel 1973. H. S. Versnel, "A Note on the *Maschalismos* of Apsyrtos," *Mnemosyne*, 426 (1973) 62–63. [Bremmer]

Versnel 1993. H. S. Versnel, *Transition and Reversal in Myth and Ritual* (Leiden 1993). [Bremmer]

Vian 1963. F. Vian, "Apollonios de Rhodes et le renouveau de la poésie épique," *IL* 15 (1963) 25–30. [Clauss]

Vian 1978. F. Vian, "ΙΗΣΩΝ ΑΜΗΧΑΝΕΩΝ," in *Studi in onore di Anthos Ardizzoni*, E. Livrea and G. A. Privitera (eds.) (Rome 1978) 1025–41. [Clauss]

Vian and Delage 1974. F. Vian and E. Delage, *Apollonios de Rhodes Argonautiques*, vol. 1, Chant I–II (Paris 1974). [Clauss]

Vian and Delage 1980. F. Vian and E. Delage, *Apollonios de Rhodes Argonautiques*, vol. 2, Chant III (Paris 1980). [Clauss]

Vian and Delage 1981. F. Vian and E. Delage, *Apollonius de Rhodes. Argonautiques*, vol. 3, Chant IV (Paris 1981). [Clauss, Krevans]

Visser 1982. M. Visser, "Worship Your Enemy: Aspects of the Cult of Heroes in Ancient Greece," *HThR* 75 (1982) 403–28. [Johnston]

Visser 1986. M. Visser, "Medea: Daughter, Sister, Wife, and Mother—Natal Family *versus* Conjugal Family in Greek and Roman Myths about Women," in *Greek Tragedy and its Legacy. Essays Presented to D. J. Conacher*, M. J. Cropp et al. (eds.) (Calgary 1986) 149–65. [Bremmer]

Vojatzi 1982. M. Vojatzi, *Frühe Argonautenbilder* (Würzburg 1982). [Graf, Sourvinou-Inwood]

von Fritz 1959. K. von Fritz, "Die Entwicklung der Iason-Medea-Sage und die Medea des Euripides," *A&A* 8 (1959) 33–106, rpt. in von Fritz 1962, 322–429. [Graf]

von Fritz 1962. K. von Fritz, *Antike und moderne Tragödie: Neun Abhandlungen* (Berlin 1962). [Boedeker]

Wackernagel 1955. J. Wackernagel, *Kleine Schriften*, vol. 1 (Göttingen, 1955). [Bremmer]

Walsh 1979. G. B. Walsh, "Public and Private in Three Plays of Euripides," *CP* 74 (1979) 294–309. [Boedeker]

Walsh 1984. G. B. Walsh, *The Varieties of Enchantment: Early Greek Views of the Nature and Function of Poetry* (Chapel Hill 1984). [O'Higgins]

Waszink 1954. J. H. Waszink, "Biothanati," in *Reallexicon für Antike und Christentum*, vol. 2, I. Klauser (ed.) (Stuttgart 1954) 391–94. [Johnston]

Weinreich 1913. O. Weinreich "Heros Propylaios und Apollo Propylaios," *MDAI(A)* 38 (1913) 62–72. [Johnston]

D. West 1991. D. R. West, "Gello and Lamia: Two Hellenic Daemons of Semitic Origin," *Ugarit-Forschungen* 23 (1991) 361–68. [Johnston]

M. West 1966. M. L. West, *Hesiod: Theogony* (Oxford 1966). [Graf, Krevans, Sourvinou-Inwood]

M. West 1967. M. L. West, "Oracles of Apollo Kareios: A Revised Text," *ZPE* 1 (1967) 183–87. [Johnston]

Westermann 1974. C. Westermann, *Genesis I* (Neukirchen-Vluyn 1974). [Bremmer]

Whittaker 1990. J. Whittaker, *Alcinoos: Enseignement des Doctrines de Platon* (Paris 1990). [Dillon]

Wilamowitz 1880. U. von Wilamowitz-Moellendorff, "Excurse zu Euripides' *Medeia*," *Hermes* 15 (1880) 481–523. [Graf, Johnston]

Wilamowitz 1906. U. von Wilamowitz-Moellendorff, *Griechische Tragödien*, 4 vols. (Berlin 1906). [Johnston]

Wilamowitz 1924. U. von Wilamowitz Moellendorff, *Hellenistische Dichtung in der Zeit des Kallimachos*, 2 vols. (Berlin 1924, rpt. Dublin 1973). [Bremmer, Clauss, Graf, Johnston]

Wilamowitz 1931–32. U. von Wilamowitz-Moellendorff, *Der Glaube der Hellenen*, 2 vols. (Berlin 1931–32). [Johnston]

Will 1955. É. Will, *Korinthiaka* (Paris 1955). [Johnston]

Williams and Zervos 1984. C. K. Williams II and O. Zervos, "Corinth 1983: The Road to Sikyon" *Hesperia* 53 (1984) 83–108. [Johnston]

Williamson 1990. M. Williamson, "A Woman's Place in Euripides' *Medea*," in *Euripides, Women, and Sexuality*, Anton Powell (ed.) (London 1990). [McDonald]

Wise 1982. V. Wise, "Ovid's Medea and the Magic of Language," *Ramus* 11 (1982) 16–25. [Newlands]

Worthington 1990. I. Worthington, "The Ending of Euripides' *Medea*," *Hermes* 118 (1990) 502–5. [Graf, McDonald]

Wright 1974. J. R. G. Wright, "Form and Content in the *Moral Essays,*" in *Seneca,* C. D. N. Costa (ed.) (London 1974). [Nussbaum]

Yeats 1966. W. B. Yeats, *Selected Poems and Two Plays of William Butler Yeats,* M. L. Rosenthal (ed.) (New York 1966). [McDonald]

Zanker 1979. G. Zanker, "The Love Theme in Apollonius Rhodius' *Argonautica,*" *WS* 13 (1979) 52–75. [Clauss]

Zanker 1987. G. Zanker, *Realism in Alexandrian Poetry: A Literature and Its Audience* (London 1987). [Clauss]

Zeitlin 1978: F. I. Zeitlin, "The Dynamics of Misogyny: Myth and Mythmaking in the *Oresteia,*" *Arethusa* 11 (1978) 149–84. [Sourvinou-Inwood]

Zeitlin 1985. F. I. Zeitlin, "The Power of Aphrodite: Eros and the Boundaries of the Self in the *Hippolytus,*" in *Directions in Euripidean Criticism: A Collection of Essays,* P. Burian (ed.) (Durham 1985) 52–111. [Boedeker]

Zeitlin 1990. F. Zeitlin, "Playing the Other: Theater, Theatricality, and the Feminine in Greek Drama," in *Nothing to Do with Dionysos?* J. J. Winkler and F. Zeitlin (eds.) (Princeton 1990) 63–96. [Sourvinou-Inwood]

Zinnerling-Paul 1979. V. Zinnerling-Paul, "Zum Bild der Medea in der antiken Kunst," *Klio* 61 (1979) 407–36. [Sourvinou-Inwood]

Zwierlein 1986a. O. Zwierlein, *Kritischer Kommentar zu den Tragodien Senecas* (Mainz/Weisbaden 1986). [Nussbaum]

Zwierlein 1986b. O. Zwierlein, *Seneca, Tragoediae* (Oxford 1986). [Nussbaum]

CONTRIBUTORS

JAN N. BREMMER is professor of history of religion at the Rijksuniversiteit Groningen. He is the author of *The Early Greek Concept of the Soul* (1983), *Greek Religion* (1994), and articles on religion, myth and literature. He is the coauthor of *Roman Myth and Mythography* (1987), editor of *Interpretations of Greek Mythology* (1987) and *From Sappho to De Sade: Moments in the History of Sexuality* (1989), and co-editor of *A Cultural History of Gesture* (1991) and *Between Poverty and the Pyre: Moments in the History of Widowhood* (1994).

DEBORAH BOEDEKER is co-director of the Center for Hellenic Studies. Her publications include *Aphrodite's Entry into Greek Epic* (1974), *Descent from Heaven: Images of Dew in Greek Poetry and Religion* (1984), and articles on Homer, Hesiod, Sappho, Greek Religion, Euripides, and Herodotus; she is the editor of *Herodotus and the Invention of History* (1987).

JAMES J. CLAUSS, co-editor of this volume, is associate professor of classics at the University of Washington. He is the author of *The Best of the Argonauts: The Redefinition of the Epic Hero in Book 1 of Apollonius's Argonautica* (1993) and articles and reviews on topics pertaining to Hellenistic and Roman poetry and Roman history and historiography.

JOHN M. DILLON is Regius Professor of Greek at Trinity College, Dublin. His books include *Iamblichi Chalcidensis in Platonis Dialogos Commentariorum Fragmenta* (1973), *The Middle Platonists, 80 B.C. to A.D. 220* (1977), and *Alcinous: The Handbook of Platonism* (1993); he is the coauthor of *A Classical Lexicon for Finnegans Wake* (1977) and co-editor of *The Question of "Eclecticism": Studies in Later Greek Philosophy* (1988), He has produced by himself or jointly several annotated translations and commentaries, including *Two Treatises of Philo of Alexandria* (1983), *Proclus' Commentary on Plato's Parmenides* (1987), *On Aristotle's Categories* (1990), and *The Handbook of Platonism* (1993).

FRITZ GRAF is professor of classical philology at the University of Basel, Switzerland. His publications include *La Magie dans L'antiquité gréco-romaine* (1994; soon to be published in English), *Griechische Mythologie* (1985; available in English as *Greek Mythology* [1993]), *Nordionische Kulte* (1985), *Eleusis und die orphische Dichtung Athens in vorhellenistischer Zeit* (1974), and articles on Greek and Roman religion, myth, and literature.

SARAH ILES JOHNSTON, co-editor of this volume, is associate professor of classics at The Ohio State University. Her publications include *Hekate Soteira* (1990) and articles on Greek religion, myth, and literature. She is the editor of a special issue of *Helios* that examines ancient attitudes toward magic and superstition (1994).

NITA KREVANS is associate professor of classical studies at the University of Minnesota. She is the author of a forthcoming book on poetry collections, *The Poet as Editor,* and of various articles on Hellenistic and Latin poetry.

MARIANNE McDONALD is adjunct professor of Greek drama at the University of California, San Diego. She is the founder of the *Thesaurus Linguae Graecae* project and the author of *Terms for Happiness in Euripides* (1978), *Euripides in Cinema: The Heart Made Visible* (1983), *Ancient Sun, Modern Light* (1992), and articles on ancient Greek drama, particularly in modern productions.

CAROLE E. NEWLANDS is associate professor of classics at the University of California, Los Angeles. She is the author of *Playing with Time: Ovid's Fasti* (1995) and articles on classical and medieval Latin literature.

MARTHA C. NUSSBAUM is professor of law and divinity at the University of Chicago. She is the author of *Aristotle's De Motu Animalium* (1978), *The Fragility of Goodness: Luck and Ethics in Greek Tragedy and Philosophy* (1986), *Love's Knowledge: Essays on Philosophy and Literature* (1990), *The Therapy of Desire: Theory and Practice in Hellenistic Ethics* (1994), and *Upheavals of Thought: A Theory of the Emotions* (forthcoming). She is also the editor of *The Poetics of Therapy: Hellenistic Ethics in Its Rhetorical and Literary Context* and co-editor of *Essays on Aristotle's De Anima* (1992) and *The Quality of Life* (1993).

DOLORES M. O'HIGGINS is associate professor of classics at Bates College, Maine. She has written articles on Greek lyric and tragedy and Roman epic. In 1991 she co-edited a special edition of *Ramus,* entitled *The Enigmatic Text: Approaches to Greek Tragedy.*

CHRISTIANE SOURVINOU-INWOOD is reader in classics at the University of Reading. She is the author of *Theseus as Son and Stepson: A Tentative Illustration of Greek Mythological Mentality* (1979), *Studies in Girl's Transitions: Aspects of the Arkteia and Age Representation in Attic Iconography* (1988), *"Reading" Greek Culture: Texts and Images, Rituals and Myths* (1991), *"Reading" Greek Death: To the End of the Classical Period* (1995), and articles on Greek literature, archaeology, religion, mythology, and iconography.

INDEX LOCORUM

Procopius
De Bello Gothico
  2.11ff.: 86
  2.14: 86

Propertius
  4.4: 24

Pseudo-Diogenianus
  apud Choerob. Cramer 2.293:
  59 n.49

Sappho
  16 Campbell: 111 n.26

Seneca
Agamemnon
  506: 239 n.23
De Beneficiis
  6.16.7: 243
De Clementia
  1.17.1: 235 n.19
  1.25.4: 235 n.19
De Ira
  1.1.5–6: 235 n.19
  1.16.5: 235 n.19
  1.17.6: 235 n.19
  3.24.2: 243
Epistulae
  24.6: 222 n.4
  59.16: 240
  66.16: 243
  74.30: 243
Hercules Furens
  125ff.: 242 n.28
  159: 245
  159–60: 243
  162–63: 243
  175: 244
  186: 244
  192–201: 244
Hercules Oetaeus
  677: 239 n.23
  686: 239 n.23
  854: 239 n.23
Medea
  1–2: 223
  5: 238 n.21
  9–10: 223
  12: 223
  13ff.: 234
  13–18: 223

28ff.: 235
28–36: 219 n.1
41–42: 230–31
47–48: 234
98: 238 n.21
102–4: 230
103–4: 219
123–24: 231
135–36: 234
140–41: 230
155: 233
155–56: 226
166–67: 147 n.66
171: 127, 225, 299
176: 225
200–201: 239 n.24
203–4: 233
203–6: 148 n.66
207–10: 219 n.1
301–8: 240
329–34: 241
335: 241
337: 241
363: 241
364: 230
365–79: 241
372: 238 n.21
378: 238 n.21
385: 227
387–92: 228–29
392: 231, 233
397–98: 233
408–10: 132 n.18
414: 148 n.66
424–5: 148 n.66
431ff.: 230
445–6: 228
504: 230
510–12: 219 n.1
518: 230
527–28: 148 n.66
537: 230
547–49: 226
550: 220, 226, 232
558–59: 230
570ff.: 219 n.1
579ff.: 230, 233, 234
591–92: 233
599: 239 n.23
653: 235
671–2: 233

GENERAL INDEX

THIS IS A selective index. Due to the nature of this collection, which touches on a large variety of topics, we chose not to index every occurrence of each word listed below. Generally, only those occurrences that arise in the context of a substantive discussion are listed; passing mentions of a word or name that have little relevance to the larger discussion usually were omitted. We have tried to include, however, the names of all postclassical authors and artists who have interpreted Medea's myth, however briefly they are mentioned in the essays, and of all contemporary figures to whom the essayists compare her. Some words that occur very frequently in this volume but have little to do with Medea herself, such as "Argonaut" and "fleece," are not indexed at all.

Printed in the United Kingdom
by Lightning Source UK Ltd.
101642UKS00001B/154-174

9 780691 043760